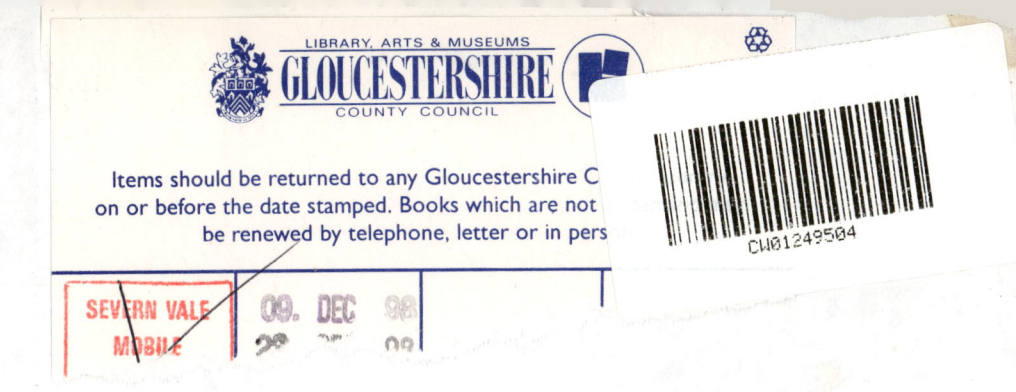

Breaking into Windows
— for Windows 95 and Office 95

Breaking into Windows

— for Windows 95 and Office 95

Bill Stott

Mark Brearley

BUTTERWORTH HEINEMANN

Butterworth–Heinemann Ltd
Linacre House, Jordan Hill, Oxford, OX2 8DP

A member of the Reed Elsevier group

OXFORD   LONDON   BOSTON
MUNICH   NEW DELHI   SINGAPORE   SYDNEY
TOKYO   TORONTO   WELLINGTON

First published 1995

© Bill Stott, Mark Brearley 1995

All rights reserved. No part of this publication may be reproduced in any material form (including photocopying or storing in any medium by electronic means and whether or not transiently or incidentally to some other use of this publication) without the written permission of the copyright holder except in accordance with the provisions of the Copyright, Designs and Patents Act 1988 or under the terms of a license issued by the Copyrights Licensing Agency Ltd, 90 Tottenham Court Road, London, England W1P 9HE. Applications for the copyright holder's written permission to reproduce any part of this publication should be addressed to the publishers

NOTICE

The author and the publisher have used their best efforts to prepare the book, including the computer examples contained in it. The computer examples have all been tested. The author and the publisher make no warranty, implicit or explicit, about the documentation. The author and the publisher will not be liable under any circumstances for any direct or indirect damages arising from any use, direct or indirect, of the documentation or computer examples contained in this book

TRADEMARKS/REGISTERED TRADEMARKS

Computer hardware and software brand names mentioned in this book are protected by their respective trademarks and are acknowledged

British Library Cataloguing in Publication Data
A catalogue record for this book is available from the British Library

ISBN 0 7506 2085 4

Typeset by Co-publications, Loughborough

Cartoon illustrations © Joe Shepherd 1995

— all part of the Sylvester Press

Printed in Great Britain by Scotprint Ltd., Musselburgh

Contents

Contents

Preface
The origin and features of Windows 95 1

Part A — Introduction to Windows

1	Start here! — the first steps	13
2	What's a window, how it is used?	29
3	Writing a letter in a window — menus	51
4	Printing a letter — dialog boxes	73
5	Mouse and keyboard skills	91
6	Storing your work in files and folders	113
7	Transferring information between documents	139

Part B — Microsoft Office 95

8	Working with Office 95	159
9	Word processing — Word	167
10	Spreadsheets — Excel	201
11	Lists and calculations — Excel	233
12	Presentations — PowerPoint	255

Part C — Working with Windows 95

13	The Windows 95 Desktop	275
14	Exploring files and folders	299
15	Working with an office network — LAN	321
16	Using your modem to work at home	341
17	Microsoft Exchange — fax and mail	369
18	Taskbar settings — Control Panel	391

Appendices

A	Help	403
B	Windows 95 controls	411
C	Keyboard shortcuts	419
D	Modem troubleshooting	423
E	Microsoft Office Binder and Briefcase	433

Glossaries 440
Index 459

Detailed contents

The origin and features of Windows 95   1

Why people don't like computers. How Windows 95 makes using computers easy. Microsoft's vision for the future. How does Windows 95 help you?

PART A — Introduction to Windows

1   Start here! — the first steps   13
Switching your PC on — logging on. Using the mouse. Starting your first program. Shutting down Windows 95 before switching your PC off.

2   What's a Window, how is it used?   29
Why a window is better than a screen. How a window is constructed. Manipulating windows on your Desktop. How to find a *lost* window. Tidying-up your Desktop before shutting down.

3   Writing a letter in a window — menus   51
How to create a window for a document. Setting your document's typeface and style from a template. The difference between a pointer and a cursor. Scroll bars — returning back to the top of your letter. Finding your way around the menu bar. What is a toolbar? How to use your program's **Help** menu.

4   Printing a letter — dialog boxes   73
What is a dialog box and how is it used? Obtaining help when completing a dialog box — Help pointer. Changing your printer's settings — printing on both sides of the paper and using different paper sizes. How to select a printer and connect it to your PC. What happens when you print your document — progress indicators. Handling print problems — running out of paper! How to preview your document before printing it.

5   Mouse and keyboard skills   91
The way Windows works — select and apply an action. Dragging and dropping things on Desktop objects. How to double-click with your mouse. Using your right mouse button. How your mouse pointer shape reflects its function — the Help pointer. Why tabs are better than spaces for aligning columns of text. How to apply menu actions from your keyboard — shortcuts. Pressing [Alt]+[Tab] to switch between programs.

6   Storing your work in files and folders   113
How documents are filed in Windows 95, What are files, folders and drives? How to format a floppy disk. Rules for naming your files and folders. How to create your own filing system. Storing a document in a file — the **Save As** dialog box. Restoring a document from a file – the **Open** dialog box. Matching names in a list — wildcard characters. How to protect your documents — read only files. Recovering documents after a power-cut.

7   Transferring information between documents   139
Dragging information between documents. The Windows clipboard — **Edit↪Cut** and **Edit↪Paste**. Importing different types of files into Office 95. How to embed and link Excel files to a Word document. Inserting pictures into a your documents. Adding sound to your documents — object packaging.

PART B — Microsoft Office 95

8   Working with Office 95   159
What are the differences between your old and new application programs? Learning to use a program. Introducing Office 95 and the Office Bar. How to open and create documents from the Office 95 toolbar. Creating a folder for your own document templates. Customizing the Office Bar to provide easy access to your documents and programs.

9   Word processing — Word   167
How to create a document template for your own headed note paper. Features of Word's windows. Adding headers and footers to your pages. How to create a bulleted list. Inserting symbols and footnotes into your document — **Insert** menu. How to insert the current date — fields. Why you should use a frame to contain and manipulate a picture. Using the **Table** menu to insert a table into your document. Altering your **Page Setup** — margins, paper size and orientation. How to use the **Format** menu — box and shade text; apply a different typeface or style; alter a paragraph's

margins, alignment or line spacing. Reviewing and revising documents — using Word's spell checker, how to mark the changes you have made to a document, searching (and replacing) words, phrases or punctuation marks.

10 Spreadsheets — Excel   201

What is a spreadsheet? Creating your own Excel template. Features of Excel's windows. How to enter a set of figures, format them as currency, and then totalize them with **AutoSum**. Filling a group of cells with a series of values. How to select and move a group of cells in a worksheet using your mouse. Inserting a **Name** for a group of cells — why a name is better than a reference. How to print your worksheet — setting the print area; removing gridlines; adding your own page headers and footers. Altering your **Page Setup** — margins, paper size and orientation. Using the **Format** menu to improve the presentation of your data — applying a **Style**, **AutoFormat**. How to change a cell's alignment, typeface, border style or shading. Changing the way negative numbers are displayed — numeric format codes.

11 Lists and calculations — Excel   233

How to design an efficient list and avoid common pitfalls. Looking-up information contained in other worksheets — Function Wizard and **vlookup**. How to design an invoice, address list and stock list. What is better, a spreadsheet or database? Importing text into a worksheet. Maintaining your lists with data entry forms. How to sort and filter a list to find the information you need. Using the Formula bar to write formulas for your own calculations. Why the accuracy of an Excel calculation might create a rounding error in your worksheet. Protecting your data and formulas from alteration or theft. How to handle worksheet errors — Excel's error codes explained.

12 Presentations — PowerPoint   255

Creating presentations from a standard template — training, reporting good news and so forth. Features of PowerPoint's windows. Different views of the same presentation — outline, slides, slide sorter, lecture notes and slide show. How to plan a presentation. Producing your speaker's notes and re-arranging the order of your slides — slide sorter. How to insert illustrations into a slide — ClipArt Gallery. Applying a house style to your slides by copying master slide information from another presentation. How to give a slide show on your PC screen — keyboard commands. How to print the various components of your presentation.

PART C — Working with Windows 95

13   The Windows 95 Desktop   275

Components of your Desktop — **Welcome** window. How your Taskbar allows you to do several things at the same time — multitasking. Changing the Taskbar's position and size and behaviour on your screen. Using the **Start** button to access your programs, documents and PC settings. How to **Find** the files, folders and computers that are available from your Desktop. How to **Run** a program from your floppy disk. Explaining **Shut down** options — logging-off, switching to MS-DOS mode (and back). Windows 95 Desktop — a new way of working for people upgrading from Windows 3.1.

14   Exploring files and folders   299

How to display the contents of a folder in a View window. Using the View window's menu bar to operate on its contents — creating a new folder, displaying the free space on your hard disk, selecting items in the window, displaying a list rather than a collection of icons. How the Windows Explorer displays the contents of your entire system — folders, files, drives and devices. Use your View and Explorer windows in the same way as they share a similar purpose. Folders with special functions — how to recover your files from the **Recycle Bin**, how to delete your print jobs from the queue in your **Printer** folder.

15   Working with an office network — LAN   321

What is a network of computers? Why you need a user name and password. How to change your password. Exploring your **Network Neighborhood** — files, folders and printers that are located on other computers. What is a network server and a domain? How to share the contents of your folder with other people who are connected to the network. Sharing someone else's files — mapping a network folder to a drive name on your PC. How to install a printer on your Desktop.

16   Using your modem to work at home   341

How do modems and Fax machines work? The different ways in which Windows 95 makes it easier for you to use a modem. How to setup a PC to work in different places — defining **Dialing properties** for pulse or tone dialing, setting different country and area codes. Using **HyperTerminal** to gain dial-up access to a BBS. How to link your home PC to the office network — **Remote Access**. Gaining access to public computer networks — how to install TCP/IP and a dial-up connection to an Internet service provider; how to join MSN (the Microsoft Network); how to install WinCim so you can access CompuServe.

17 Microsoft Exchange — Fax and mail   369

How Exchange provides a uniform way of accessing different types of message services — MS Mail, CompuServe, MSN and Fax. Installing a Fax message service — **Exchange Setup** Wizard. Storing information about a message recipient in your Personal Address Book. How to send a message from Microsoft Exchange — read and delivery receipts. Composing a message in Exchange's document window and attaching a file. Accessing your Personal Information Store — a collection of folders for arranging your messages. How to read the messages delivered to your **Inbox** — retrieving a file attached to a message. Use the Fax Wizard to help you whenever you send a Fax message from Windows 95. Generating messages from Office 95 programs — how you can **Add Routing Slip** to distribute your documents or **Send** them to an Exchange folder for group working.

18 Taskbar settings — Control Panel   391

How to add or remove items from your **Start** menu. The contents of the **Control Panel** folder. Installing a new font and viewing the typefaces available to your programs — **Font** folder. How to change your computer's date and time settings. Tuning your mouse and keyboard response. How to store passwords securely on your PC and restore your user profile whenever you log on. Installing a screen saver to secure the Desktop display when you are away from your PC.

Appendices

A Help   403

How to obtain help when using Windows 95 or your application programs. Finding help topics — contents, index, find and Answer Wizard. Using a help window to display the information you need — using hypertext; keeping the Help window on top of your Desktop.

B Windows 95 controls   411

How to use standard controls; push-buttons, check boxes, edit boxes, scroll bars, list boxes, drop-down and combination controls, column headers, spin boxes, slide controls, split handles.

C Keyboard shortcuts   419

Use your keyboard to manipulate windows, operate dialog boxes, qualify mouse operations (extended selection), manipulate text, operate the menu bar and so forth.

D	Modem troubleshooting		423

The steps required to establish a connection, how protocols allow programs to communicate, modem properties, fixing some common problems.

E	Microsoft Office Binder and Briefcase		433

How to bind a collection of documents together, creating a set of documents for a new project, synchronizing different copies of the same document, controlling different versions of your documents.

Glossary of terms   440

Icon gossary   456

Index   459

Preface

You may feel apprehensive about computers and wonder just how much of this book you will understand. Don't worry, for you can get by with just a few essentials at first and even if you initially fail to understand something, take comfort, as often enlightenment only comes with practice. This book does not attempt to cover everything but it does try to deal with what is important. It has one overriding aim — enabling you to master Windows 95 and Microsoft Office 95 without requiring a master's degree in Rocket Science!

Note

> There are no assumptions made about your previous knowledge of computers, beyond knowing what a keyboard looks like and where to find your computer's on/off switch!

Breaking into Windows is for people who want to make their personal computer work for them. The book is organized as a series of exercises designed to remove the mystery of computers while instilling practical skills. From switching-on your PC to producing your own business reports, your confidence and ability will grow as each task is completed. This book contains all you need to discover the potential of Microsoft Office and Windows within your home or organisation.

Using computers can be fun!

What you will need...

While reading *Breaking into Windows* you should have access to an IBM-compatible PC (with a mouse) on which the software described in the next paragraph has been freshly installed. This computer may be connected to a network of PCs or may stand alone, but in either case, you will also need access to a printer and modem if you are to make best use of all the exercises.

To complete the majority of this book you will need no other software apart from Windows 95 and Microsoft Word. However, to complete all of the exercises you will require version 7.0 of Microsoft Word, Excel and PowerPoint — the main components of Microsoft Office 95.

A language of its own

You might be forgiven for thinking that computers have a language of their own — they do! Many innocent sounding English words have very particular meanings in the computer industry and — unfortunately — until you have gained some familiarity with this computer-speak, much of the material that can help you remains inaccessible. To help you learn this language we have tried to define in the text those expressions that have unconventional meanings, as well as providing a glossary of terms at the back of the book.

Printing conventions

Considerable care has been taken with the layout and structure of the book to make it consistent and fun to read. A number of symbols have been devised to help you find your way around, but don't worry if you don't understand them at present as they are fully explained before they are first used:

- **File↪Open** — The symbol ↪ indicates that this is the **Open** choice from the **File** menu.
- ⟦Shift⟧+⟦F1⟧ — This indicates two keys on the keyboard that must be pressed together. The + symbol indicates two things that must be done at the same time.

Parts of the text are also highlighted or printed in a special way so that you can identify tips, notes and defined terms such as...

Definition

window . . . . rectangular area displayed on your PC monitor, which forms a small screen for a particular program; arrange them so you can use several programs at the same time

How the book is structured

Breaking into Windows is divided into three parts with a comprehensive set of appendices, glossary, and full index. There is also an introductory chapter about the origin and nature of Windows 95 to explain why it represents such an important advance in our use of the computer.

Part A: Introduction to Windows

An introduction for people new to computers or Windows 95 style programs which provides you with a general understanding of the Windows environment so you can work more efficiently. Learn how to compose a letter, send it to your printer and then store this document in a file.

Part B: Microsoft Office 95

Understand how to use three of the programs you are most likely to need in a modern office — a word processor (Word) to write your documents, a spreadsheet (Excel) to create and manipulate lists of information, and a graphics package (PowerPoint) to generate stunning presentations.

Part C: Working with Windows 95

An explanation of how to use the new features of Windows 95. It builds on previous chapters to present a fully integrated working environment in which you can organize and share information as well as manage your PC. Part C is a good place to start if you are upgrading from earlier versions of Windows.

WPQS, MNB — London, August, 1995

http://www.demon.co.uk/billstott

Acknowledgements

The authors wish to acknowledge the encouragement, helpful advice and occasional criticism received from everyone involved with this project. The following people are owed particular acknowledgement for their help with our previous book on Windows 3.1:

Rod Bunn, Robert Bowmer, David Colver, Kate Ford, Robert Hurst, Delyth Thomas.

Recognition is due to the following people for their practical assistance in producing this finished book:

Mike Cash, Keith Brindley, Keith Cowlam.

A special thank you is also owed to Christopher Pearson and Belinda Stott whose total lack of knowledge about computers made them ideal guinea-pigs for testing the exercises and editing the text — they have assured us that they are now computer experts!

Introduction

The origin and features of Windows 95

Objectives

This introduction explains how Windows 95 makes the power of computers available to everyone. In particular, it covers:

- the dual roles of Windows 95 — controlling the way you interact with your computer as well as unleashing its power

- why people don't like computers — without interactive control early computers had a language barrier

- how Windows 95 makes using computers easy — control your PC from a graphical Desktop (just like a video game)

- Windows 95 past & future — Microsoft provides a consistent way of using all types of computers

- how does Windows 95 help me? — how both beginner and expert can expect to benefit from this product.

After reading this introduction you will understand why Windows 95 provides such an important advance in the way we use computers.

The dual roles of Windows 95

Windows 95 has two roles; one visible and the other hidden. The visible side of Windows 95 is represented by the things you can see on your screen and the way it responds to your mouse and keyboard — the user interface. The hidden side of Windows 95 is concerned with providing the power of the PC's hardware to the software programs running on it — the operating system.

While programmers and rocket scientists might be interested in Windows 95 as an operating system, most people are only interested in how it makes their computers easier to use — its user interface. This book is about the Windows 95 user interface.

Why people don't like computers

People don't like things that they find difficult to use. If you have used an early PC you may find the following scenario familiar:

> *The knowledgeable friend who helped set-up your PC has now gone, leaving you alone with the machine. You switch the computer on and watch its screen light-up with obscure messages; they disappear even before you have had time to read them. Lights on the front panel flash, internal mechanisms whirr but eventually all is quiet; you are faced with a screen on which there are a few cryptic messages ending with a character that flashes at you unremittingly — your friend called it the MS-DOS prompt. Now it's your move.*
>
> *You type* Hello *on your keyboard then press the key labelled* Enter *to initiate some form of dialogue. However the computer responds to your greeting with the message* **Bad command or file name**. *You try a few more likely phrases but it soon becomes apparent that further attempts at communicating with the computer are pointless; you must learn its language.*

Definition

DOS prompt . . . .(`C:\>_`) provides the means to converse by typed commands with the MS-DOS operating system, an ancestor of Windows 95

Anyone who operates a PC from the MS-DOS prompt has to acquire some knowledge of the nouns, verbs and syntax that form its command language — a language far removed from a natural language like English, but just as difficult to learn.

Figure 0.1
Meaningless interaction with a computer

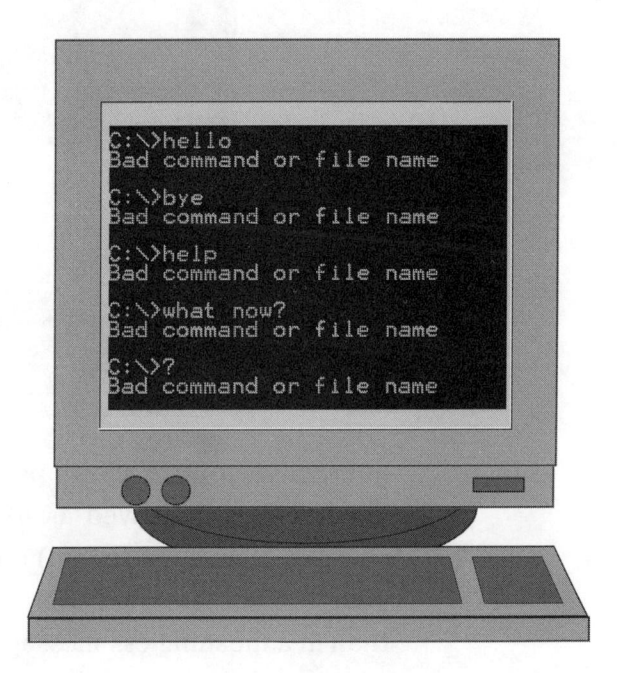

```
C:\>hello
Bad command or file name
C:\>bye
Bad command or file name
C:\>help
Bad command or file name
C:\>what now?
Bad command or file name
C:\>?
Bad command or file name
```

Command language may help the rocket scientist operate a computer, but for most people it provides a clumsy and awkward way of operating a machine. Learning the computer's language is only part of the problem, for even when its commands and messages are understood the interaction lacks any direct response to your actions. The result is that you are left without any sense of control, you can't see what's going on — language is simply not an effective way of driving a machine.

Early PCs would never have caught-on if they had relied only on language for their interaction with users. Fortunately software developers listened to their customers and developed programs that had an interactive feel, like a computer game, therefore putting you in control.

Figure 0.2
Interactive programs give better control

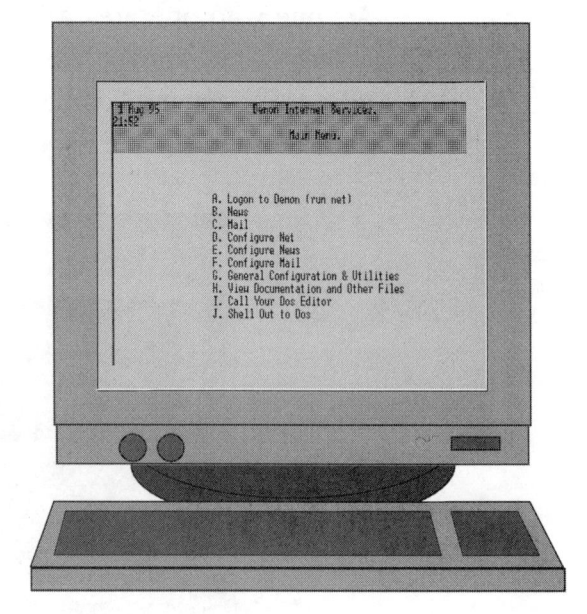

Interactive control allows people to see what is going on; the document is displayed as it will be printed, commands are selected from a list (menu) on your screen, and the results of your actions are reflected directly in the document rather than in a meaningless message at a command prompt. Easy to use programs brought PCs into the mass market but there were still some serious shortcomings in the way people used computers:

- programs started and finished at the DOS prompt, a language interface that many users hated
- each program developer had a particular way of doing things. Skills learnt with one program couldn't be transferred to another
- programs couldn't be used in conjunction with each other. It was difficult to share information between them
- commands often had to be memorized and applied in a specific order from the keyboard. This didn't reflect

the natural way that people work and so made learning difficult

▷ new programs with superior features failed, simply because people couldn't be bothered to learn the new set of commands required to operate them. Innovation then became choked by a resistance to change from familiar, albeit awkward and inefficient, programs.

The computer industry needed to develop a new way for people to use computers; a way that would make computers more accessible.

How Windows 95 makes using computers easy!

Over the last twenty years millions of dollars have been poured into research about the basic problem of how people best relate to computers.

The most significant result of this work is the graphical user interface or GUI (pronounced *gooey*) which is an attempt to replicate the sort of natural interaction that occurs when you use the things on an office desk. This Desktop is illustrated by Figure 0.3 and forms the backdrop to your interaction with the PC.

Figure 0.3
The Desktop metaphor: your screen represents a desktop

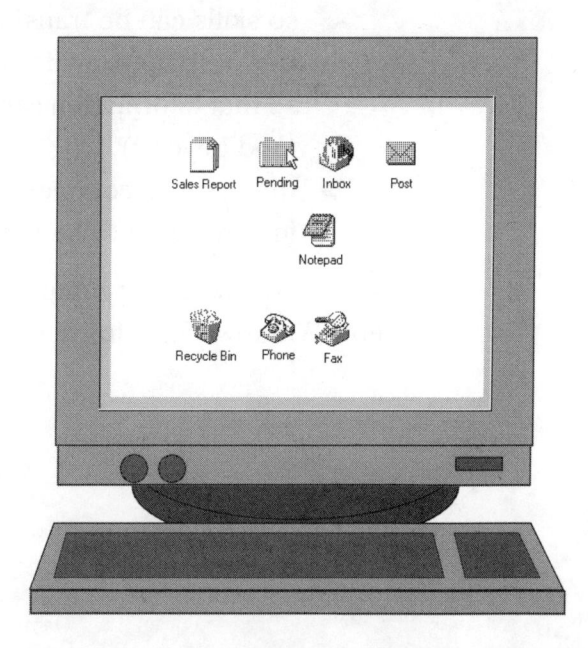

Definition

desktop . . . . .when a graphical user interface like Windows 95 is installed on your PC, the computer screen is termed a Desktop in deference to the real life desktop that it attempts to replicate.

Therefore the original promise of the GUI, to provide a completely natural and intuitive way to use your computer, was not realized in some of the earlier products developed for mass market computers. Windows 95 evolved during a gradual process of trial and error that attempted to improve on what was provided by Windows 3.1, but without requiring you to relearn everything or throw out your existing programs.

Windows 95 solves many of the problems that have made computers difficult to use:

- programs start, operate and finish on the Desktop which appears after you switch-on your PC, and remains until you switch-off
- Windows 95 style programs work in a consistent way so skills can be transferred from program to program
- the Desktop provides a tightly integrated environment so that information can be moved anywhere on your PC (and beyond)
- there are no complex commands to learn or fixed order for programs to be used.

Your enthusiasm for computers will grow as you discover just how Windows 95 helps make your life easier.

Windows 95 — past & future

Microsoft, has sold Windows software for more than ten years. Windows 95's most immediate ancestor, Windows 3.1, was the most successful operating system of all time and has sold over 90 million copies world-wide. Windows 95 replaces both Windows 3.1 and the version used on networks of computers, Windows for Workgroups 3.11.

Figure 0.4
Consistent platform across all PCs

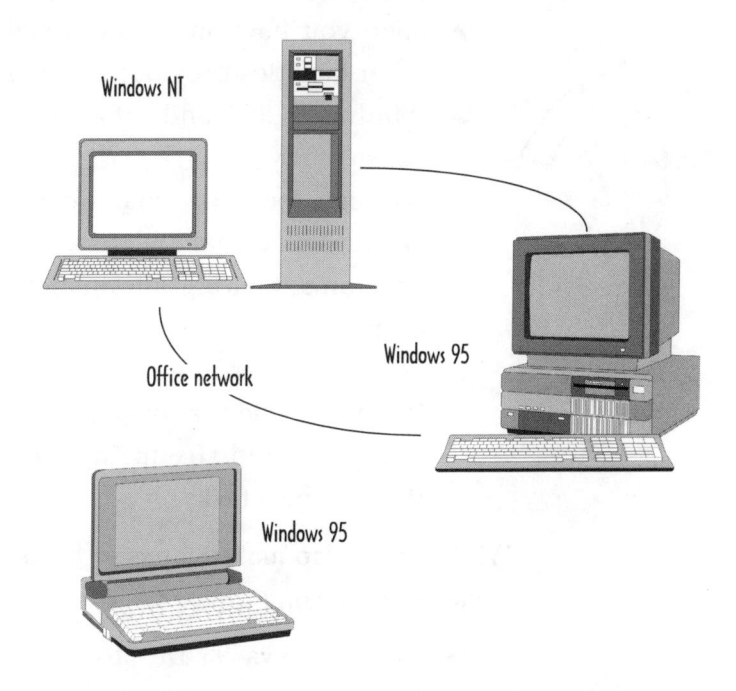

Note

> Microsoft is committed to standardising the way you use its future products on the foundation provided by Windows 95

Windows 95 comes from a long evolutionary pedigree. The way that we use Windows 95 forms a central part of the Microsoft vision for a PC serving as a universal appliance that can be used by anyone, anywhere.

Introduction — The origin and features of Windows 95

How does Windows 95 help me?

To the users of programs, such as Word and Excel, it provides a better working environment:

- programs are seamlessly started and finished from the Windows 95 Desktop — you don't see the MS-DOS prompt even when switching the computer on or off
- once you have mastered a skill it can be applied to other facilities provided on your Desktop
- Windows 95 and its programs behave more consistently
- you can focus on your documents and the Desktop facilities that manipulate them rather than individual programs. Sharing information across the Desktop is easier
- commands are more intuitive and the system is more forgiving when a mistake it made. Help is always available and frequently takes you step-by-step through new tasks.

Windows 95 also makes it easier for people simply wanting an easier way of using their PC:

- the Windows 95 Desktop has a simple, uncluttered, look — an inviting environment in which to start work
- most of the things you want to do (starting programs, opening documents, changing settings, finding things) can be instigated from a single control that stays at the bottom of your screen — the Taskbar
- documents can be identified by natural names that reflect their content, such as **Budget summary 12th June** rather than **BUD12-6.DOC**
- documents can be organized on your Desktop into folders, with folders placed within other folders to reflect the way your office filing system works. This idea extends beyond documents to all the resources available to your computer.

Windows 95 comes with numerous programs and features for people who use their PC in a more powerful way, including:

- several programs can be started from the Desktop at the same time. Time-consuming operations can be left running while you do something else
- the Windows Explorer provides a single window from which you can access all the resources and information available to your computer
- the contents of documents can be quickly previewed using the Quick View — there is no need to open the program that created the document
- support is provided for multimedia including a video playback program.

Definition

multimedia . . . . the addition of sound, video and other technologies to the facilities of a standard computer in order to provide a platform for educational programs and so forth

> *The success of previous versions of Windows spawned an entire industry to produce programs, known as applications, that can be operated from your Desktop. There are thousands of applications available from companies around the world — not to mention programs such as Word, Excel and PowerPoint that are sold by Microsoft itself.*

For people wanting to maintain their investment in existing systems Windows 95 provides compatibility with Windows 3.1 and MS-DOS:

- it runs your existing Windows 3.1 and MS-DOS programs without modification
- many games programs can now be run directly from the Desktop without a significant reduction in performance
- support for MS-DOS is better than that provided by previous versions of Windows

- support is provided for your existing peripheral devices (scanners, fax cards, and so forth) as well as many new ones
- popular programs like Program Manager and File Manager that were supplied with previous versions of Windows are also supplied with Windows 95 to provide a gradual, phased upgrade path.

Windows 95 helps people who use a portable PC between the office and home — computing on the move:

- a special Briefcase folder on your Desktop holds the documents you are working on and keeps the most recent versions when you are moving between two machines
- facilities are provided to give your portable PC remote access to the office machine via a modem and telephone line
- peripherals, such as CD-ROMs and so forth, can be connected and disconnected without expert help — just plug-in and play!

Definition

modem .... a device for converting data into tones that can be transmitted via the telephone system to a matching device that converts the tones back into data

For people who need to communicate and have a PC equipped with a modem:

- high speed communication that can continue even when your attention is elsewhere on the Desktop. Windows 95 is much better adapted to communication than earlier versions of Windows
- the Windows 95 Exchange provides facilities such as fax and e-mail in addition to support for Internet

▷ it is much easier to configure communications devices as programs called Wizards take you step-by-step through the process.

Windows 95 benefits people using a PC in a network of computers within their organisation:

▷ a special folder on your Desktop called Network Neighbourhood, permits you to browse through all the information and resources available to you on other computers
▷ resources and information that are distributed on other computers in the network can be accessed as if they are found on your PC
▷ improved set-up and system management reduces the time taken for support staff to help you.

For all users, expert and beginner, Windows 95 provides a more robust operating environment which is capable of unleashing the true power of new-generation computers and peripherals.

Summary

▷ Computers have come a long way from machines that only scientists could use — Windows 95 makes them available to everyone.

▷ You communicate with your computer via the Windows 95 Desktop which is formed by your PC's screen.

▷ Windows 95 benefits all types of people from beginners to experts using PCs in their homes, their offices and while on the move.

Chapter 1

Start here! — the first steps

Objectives

This chapter should be read by anyone who hasn't used a mouse before or is slightly apprehensive about using Windows 95 on their PC. It covers:

- ▷ switching your PC on — how to start Windows 95 and open its Desktop

- ▷ using the mouse — control your Desktop by pointing, clicking, and dragging things with your mouse

- ▷ starting your first program — how menus contained in the Taskbar's **Start** button allow you to start your programs

- ▷ shut down Windows 95 — prepare your PC so that you can safely switch-off.

After reading this chapter you will understand how to use your mouse to start a program. You will also know how to start and properly shut down Windows 95 on your PC.

> **Caution:** Always follow the shut down procedure before switching-off your personal computer

Switching your PC on — starting Windows 95

A supplier (or support staff) should prepare your PC so that Windows 95 will start when it is switched-on.

> **Note:** Installing or upgrading Windows 95 (or Microsoft Office) on your PC is beyond the scope of this book — excellent instructions are given in the appropriate Microsoft manuals

1 *Remove any disks from your PC's floppy drives then switch-on your computer — you may also have to switch-on the monitor (refer to your manuals for specific details).*

The starting of Windows 95 from this point onward is automatic so just watch and wait for the following steps to complete.

- When your PC is switched-on lights might flash and machinery whirr, but eventually something will appear on the computer screen — check the power-socket, cabling and then call the service department if this does not happen.
- The first thing your computer does after power-up is to test and initialize itself. The time taken varies from machine to machine but is unlikely to be more than three minutes. Watch for any error messages or other indications of problems, but otherwise don't worry about the information that appears on your screen at this time.

▷ Once the computer has finished initialising, the screen will clear and the following message will briefly appear at the top of your screen:

Starting Windows 95...

Any problems hereafter should be reported to Microsoft rather than your computer supplier.

▷ The screen will clear again (it might also flicker) and the Windows 95 screen will appear. This indicates that Windows 95 is being loaded from your computer's internal hard-disk. The load process continues for a minute or so, depending on the performance of your computer — contact Microsoft if after five minutes nothing else happens.

If your PC is connected to a network of other computers you must first supply a user name and password in order to unlock the Desktop — see page 16.

When Windows 95 has successfully started your screen will look something like Figure 1.1. Your computer screen is called the Desktop. This Desktop forms the backdrop for your interaction with the PC.

Figure 1.1
How Windows 95 appears on your screen.

Chapter 1 Start here! — the first steps   15

Chapter 1

Connecting to your network

When you switch on a PC that has been setup to operate Windows 95 in conjunction with a network of other computers the Desktop is initially secured by the **Enter Network Password** box. To unlock the Desktop you must identify yourself by typing a user name and password into the appropriate areas of the box — you may also be prompted for a domain name (see Chapter 15). You can create your own identity by inventing a unique user name and password but often someone in your organization will supply these details to you.

Figure 1.2
The **Enter Network Password** dialog box

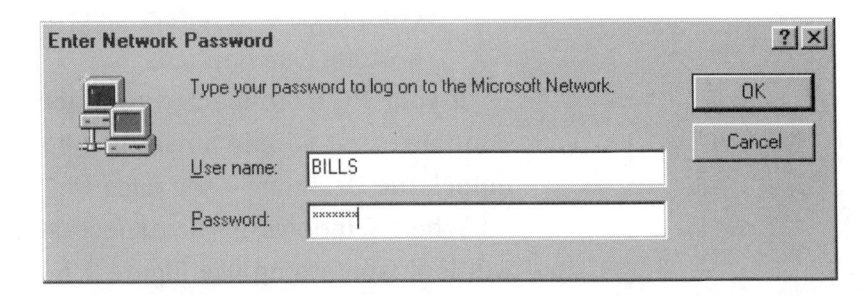

> The flashing prompt indicates where your keystrokes will be entered. Switch between user name and password areas by pressing the [Tab] key on your keyboard.

Tip

Press [Enter] when you have completed the box to remove it from your screen. Whenever you create a new user name you will be asked to confirm this action (press [Enter] again) and be prompted to confirm your new password's spelling but otherwise the Windows 95 Desktop will open as shown in Figure 1.1.

Welcome to Windows 95

A dialog box called **Welcome to Windows 95** appears on your Desktop immediately after it has started (but this feature can be disabled). You may wish to explore this box when you have gained more experience using the mouse and Windows 95.

Using the mouse

Windows 95 is designed for computers with some form of pointing device or mouse. While the same operation can be performed from your keyboard, the mouse remains an essential part of the system. It is important therefore that you should master the use of your mouse — fortunately this is very easy.

What type of mouse?

Mice come in all shapes and colours, though mostly they belong to one of the varieties shown in Figure 1.3. The tabletop or Microsoft mouse is by far the commonest variety and was used to produce this book. Other mouse varieties provide the same basic operations as described here, though they may work in a slightly different way — consult your mouse or computer manual for details. The mouse allows you to move a pointer on your Desktop and perform the following operations:

> ▷ pointing — place the mouse's pointer over something on your Desktop
> ▷ clicking — select (or pick) whatever is beneath the pointer on your Desktop
> ▷ dragging — move something from one place on the Desktop to another
> ▷ double-clicking — make the object beneath your pointer perform an operation.

Figure 1.3
Varieties of mouse

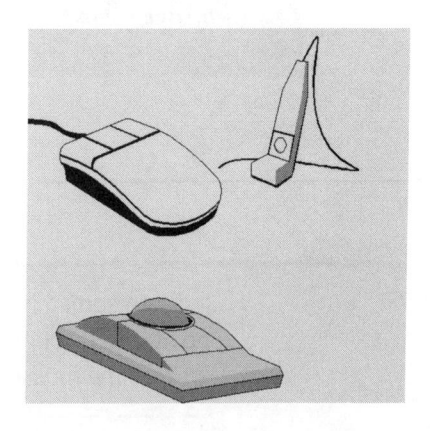

Chapter 1

> **Note**
>
> Your mouse skills are developed more fully in Chapter 5 *Mouse and keyboard skills* — this is where double-clicking is described

Getting comfortable

The Microsoft mouse works best when moved on a smooth hard surface, such as a tabletop or a specially designed mouse mat.

2 *Place the mouse on the mat, flat side down, with the cable away from you. Cup the palm of your hand snugly around its sculptured body and position your index finger over the left-hand button.*

Left-handed people (like one of the authors) should try using the mouse with their right hand while using its left and right buttons as described, so as to retain compatibility with the right-handed world.

It is important to feel comfortable with your mouse. Hold the mouse firmly, don't grip it too tightly or too loosely.

> **Tip**
>
> Learning to use the mouse with your non-writing hand allows you to take notes and operate your computer at the same time — a surprisingly common requirement

Pointing

Definition

point . . . . .indicate something on your Desktop with the tip of your mouse pointer (e.g. *point to* **My Computer** means *move your mouse so that the mouse pointer is placed over this object*)

18 Chapter 1 Start here! — the first steps

Moving the mouse moves a small pointer on your screen. This mouse pointer is used to direct your action on the Desktop.

3 *Keeping the mouse firmly pressed against the mat, move the mouse to the left and watch the desktop's mouse pointer move to the left in synchronism. Use your mouse to move the pointer around the screen — don't press the mouse buttons yet!*

It is the movement of the mouse and not its position that determines how the mouse pointer moves. Once the rubber ball on the underside of the mouse stops moving the pointer stays still.

Figure 1.4
Pointing with the mouse

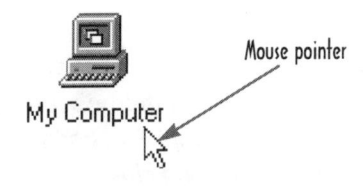

My Computer   Mouse pointer

> **Tip**
>
> When you reach the edge of the mat simply lift up the mouse and replace it nearer the centre

Your brain needs time to learn the co-ordination required to operate a mouse — much like it did when learning to walk! Spend some time training your hand and eye for this movement and after a few minutes, you will be able to move the mouse pointer with some accuracy to any spot in the screen (Desktop) without even thinking about it. You cannot move the pointer completely off your screen — at least the tip of its nose is always visible.

> **Note**
>
> The shape of the pointer changes when it is moved (slowly) over certain objects on your Desktop. The pointer's shape reflects the effect of various mouse operations on the object beneath it

Chapter 1 Start here! — the first steps

Chapter 1

Clicking (or pressing)

Definition — *click* (or *press*) . . . . . . select or activate something by placing your mouse pointer over it and momentarily pressing the left-hand mouse button; a single click

You click something on your Desktop by positioning the mouse pointer over it then briefly pressing the left mouse button.

4 *Point at the button labelled* **Close** *in the bottom right corner of the* **Welcome to Windows** *dialog box, the window in the middle of your Desktop. Press and release the left mouse button to press this button and close the window — nothings happens if your the mouse pointer is positioned over a blank area of the screen.*

Different things behave in different ways when clicked. Some of the things on your Desktop will simply do something when clicked, for example, start a program — other things are highlighted to show that they have been selected and are now responsive to any further action that you might wish to apply.

Figure 1.5
Clicking with your mouse

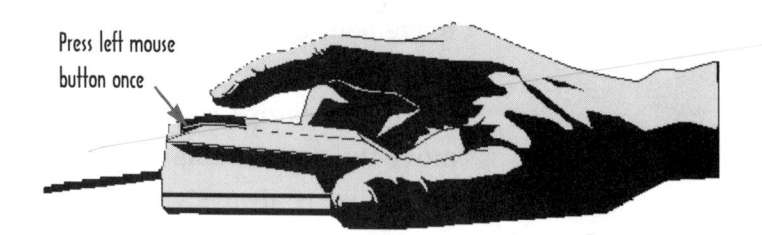

Press left mouse button once

5 *Move the mouse pointer to the object on your Desktop labelled* **My Computer** *then momentarily press the left mouse button — it becomes highlighted. Click the object on your Desktop labelled* **Recycle Bin** *— it becomes highlighted.*

Note — If you click something by mistake (this happens frequently until you have learnt to control your mouse) you can easily recover the situation simply by clicking something else

You will learn as you become more familiar with Windows 95 how the various objects on your Desktop behave when clicked. This is made easier because similar objects behave in similar ways.

Dragging

Definition — *drag* . . . . .move an object by positioning the mouse pointer over it, holding down a mouse button, then repositioning the pointer before releasing the button

Dragging involves moving things with your mouse pointer. To drag something you must first pick it up by positioning the mouse pointer over the object then holding the left mouse button down. This attaches the object to your pointer. Once attached, the object moves with the mouse pointer until you drop it in a new location by releasing the left mouse button.

6 *Point to the object on your Desktop labelled* **My Computer** *then hold down the left mouse button while moving the pointer across your Desktop. Release the button to move* **My Computer** *to a new location on the Desktop.*

You can arrange the things on your Desktop in any way you choose. Organize your Desktop to suit the way you work. Although there are several different types of dragging operations that can be performed with your mouse, the basic mechanism remains the same. The dragging operation you have just completed is called *drag and drop*.

Figure 1.6
Dragging an object with your mouse

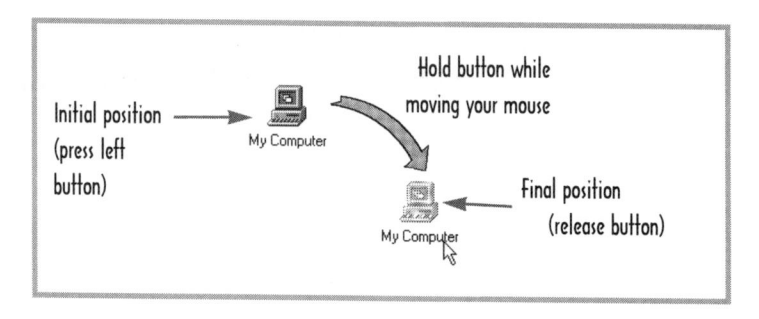

```
Initial position ———→  [My Computer]   Hold button while
(press left                              moving your mouse
button)
                            ↘
                          [My Computer] ←——— Final position
                                              (release button)
```

We can now use the mouse to point, click and drag objects on the Desktop. Let's discover how these techniques can be used to orchestrate an action on your Desktop.

Note

> Always use your left mouse button to drag unless explicitly told to use your right mouse button. Dragging with your right mouse button is described in **Chapter 5**

Menus

Definition

menu . . . . a short list of options from which you make a selection to perform the operation of your choice

Anyone who has used a vending machine knows how to use a menu; a list of items from which you make a selection in order to perform a particular action. Pressing our vending machine's third button produces a cup of black coffee with no sugar.

Menus appear on your Desktop when you click various objects with your mouse. These menus each contain a list of options from which you can make a choice by pointing at the item and then clicking your left mouse button. Menus provide an easy way for you to control the Desktop (or a program) without the need to memorize commands or keystrokes.

The Taskbar — starting your first program

The Taskbar is the grey bar at the bottom of your screen — it helps you to orchestrate the action on your Desktop.

Figure 1.7
The Taskbar and its primary menu

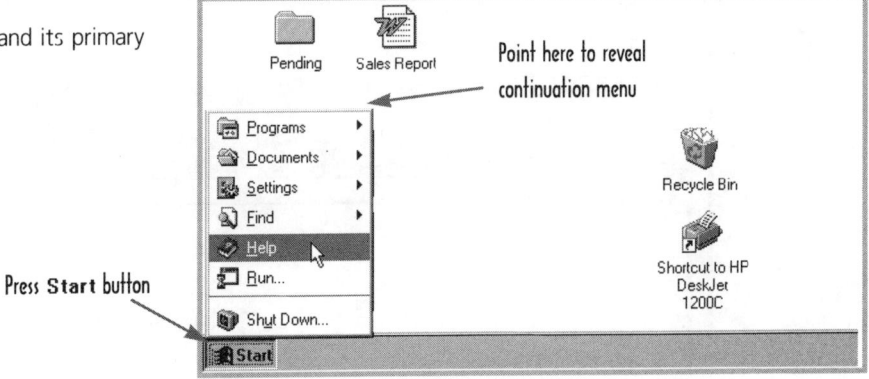

Point here to reveal continuation menu

Press Start button

The Taskbar's **Start** button provides an entrance into Windows 95.

7   Click the **Start** button to reveal its menu. Point to the menu choice **Programs** and wait for a further menu (called a continuation menu) to appear — there is no need to press a mouse button.

Definition

continuation menu . . .an additional menu revealed when you point to a menu choice with an arrowhead. They categorize related items and so reduce the size of individual menus

---

8   Point to the menu choice **Accessories** in the **Program** continuation menu and wait for a further continuation menu to appear. Click on the name **WordPad** to open this program's window on your Desktop. This whole process is shown in this book as **Start**↪**Programs**↪**Accessories**↪**WordPad**.

Note

> When your computer is busy your mouse pointer changes into an hourglass to indicate that its use has been temporarily suspended — see page 100

Chapter 1 Start here! — the first steps   23

Figure 1.8
Starting WordPad

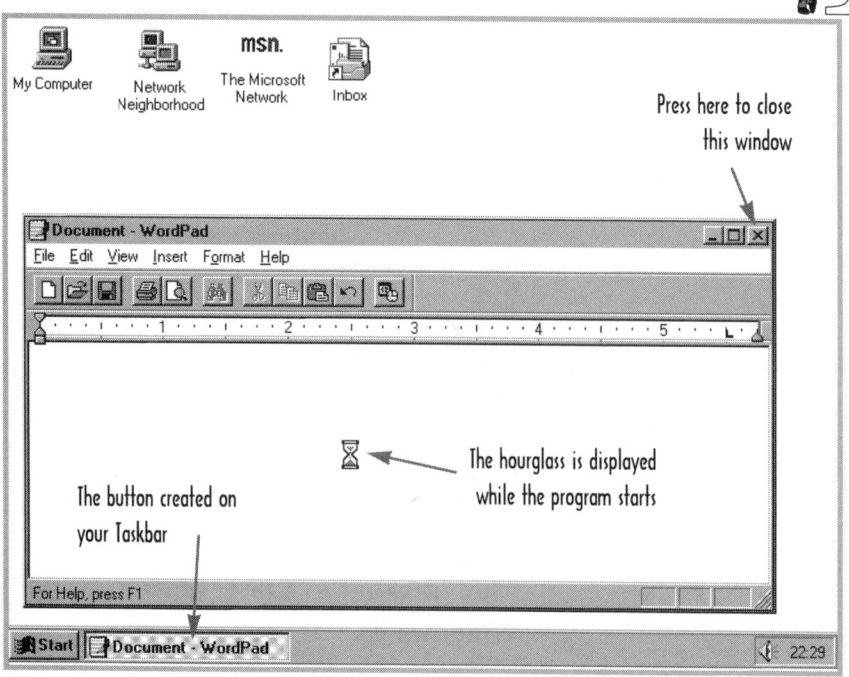

You have now started WordPad, an application (like Word) that processes text. It has created an area for itself on the Desktop called a window. The next two chapters describe windows and how they are used — for now just take a quick look.

Definition

window . . . . rectangular area displayed on your PC monitor, which forms a small screen for a particular program; arrange them so you can use several programs at the same time

9   Click on the small cross at the top right of the WordPad window to stop the program and close the window (also do this to any other windows you might have accidentally opened while completing the previous steps). You are now ready to start the final part of this exercise — shutting down.

24   Chapter 1 Start here! — the first steps

Definition   application . . . . .a program developed specifically for operation on your Desktop (e.g. Word, Excel and so forth)

Congratulations! You have just started, used and then stopped the WordPad application program, which is a basic word-processor. Using the same techniques you can now open and close any Windows 95 application that has been installed on your PC.

Shut down Windows 95

The Taskbar has other uses besides starting programs, one of which is shutting down Windows 95 prior to switching off your PC.

10 *Click the Taskbar's* **Start** *button and click on the menu choice* **Shut Down** *(that is, choose* **Start↪Shut Down***) This brings-up the* **Shut Down Windows** *dialog box (Figure 1.9) prompting you to confirm this action — the Desktop also darkens to reflect the potential result of the action.*

Tip

> **Move your mouse pointer to each edge of the screen in turn if you can't see the Taskbar (see Chapter 13)**

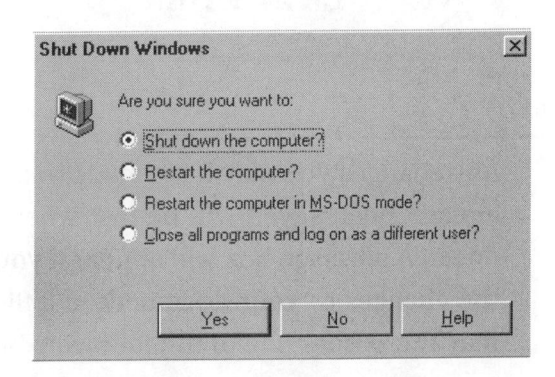

Figure 1.9
The **Shut Down Windows** dialog box

11 *Select the type of shut down you require by clicking the circle next to the appropriate label in the* **Shut Down Windows** *dialog box. Finally press the* **OK** *button in this box to prepare your PC for shut down but do not switch-off yet!*

There's a number of ways in which you may shut down Windows 95:

- shut down the computer — (normally selected) prepare Windows 95 for switching off the PC as you have finished for the day
- restart the computer — prepare to restart Windows 95 without switching-off your PC. This option is sometimes required after installing new software or devices
- close all programs and log on as a different user — this option is only available if your computer is connected to a network (see Chapter 15)
- restart the computer in MS-DOS mode — see page 290.

Programs that have not already been terminated may become involved with the shut down process to prevent the accidental loss of information from your Desktop — see *Save your changes*.

Note

> You may abort the shut down by pressing the No button in the Shut Down Windows dialog box — this restores your Desktop to its previous state

Save your changes

Any changes you may have made to a document that have not already been saved will be lost when you complete the shut down. A message box will appear if you have forgotten to save the changes to your document in a file (see Figure 1.10). You may then press one of the following buttons:

> **Yes** — save your work and cancel the shut down
> **No** — continue with the shut down so that the changes to your documents are lost
> **Cancel** — cancel the shut down.

Failing to save changes in a document will not damage the file or your system.

Figure 1.10
The message that appears if you forget to save your work

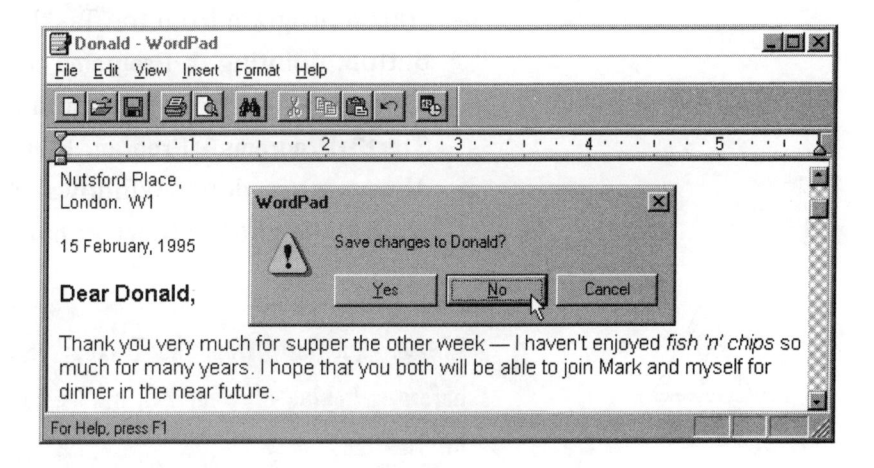

12 *Press the **No** button in any **Save Changes** dialog box that might appear during the shut down process and wait for the Desktop to clear.*

Definition

save . . . . your documents are saved (stored) in a file on a hard or floppy disk so that when you turn-off your computer the information is not lost (see Chapter 6)

Switch-off the power

13 *Switch-off your computer when the Windows 95 screen reappears with a message informing you that it is safe to do so. This completes the exercise!*

Any problems experienced during the Windows 95 shut down procedure should be reported to your support staff or Microsoft customer support.

Chapter 1

Summary

- Switch-on your PC to start Windows 95.
- Negotiate your way round the Desktop using your mouse to point, click (press) and drag.
- Start a program from the Taskbar by pressing the **Start** button, pointing to **Programs** then clicking on its name within one of the continuation menus (that is, choose: Start↪Programs↪**Program Name**).
- Always shut down Windows 95 before switching off your PC — choose Start↪**Shut Down**.

Caution

> Always shut down from the Taskbar (Start↪Shut Down) before switching off your PC, otherwise Windows 95 may lose information

Chapter 2

What's a window, how is it used?

Objectives

This chapter introduces a window — the basic component of your Desktop. It explains what windows do and how they are used in the Windows 95 environment. We see:

- why a window is better than a screen — you can open a window on your Desktop to create a new screen for your program

- standard window construction — how to recognize the standard parts of a window

- different kinds of windows — dialog boxes, document windows, message boxes

- how to use windows — discover the way windows are opened, closed, and positioned on your Desktop

- how to manage windows on your Desktop — how to arrange a collection of windows so you can find the one you need.

After reading this chapter you will be able to recognize and use a window. Subsequent chapters build on this foundation, so it is important to persevere until the concepts are firmly established in your own mind — re-read the chapter several times if necessary.

Take heart for there is nothing difficult in this chapter and once you have mastered these skills they will never be forgotten!

Chapter 2

Why a window is better than a screen

In the previous chapter when you started a program it opened its own window on the Desktop. This window acted like a small computer screen in which you could interact with the program.

Figure 2.1
Mark Brearley's desk!

Windows allows your single PC screen to be shared by a number of programs so that you can use them all simultaneously. You can, for example, edit a letter using Word, look up some figures and perform a few calculations with Excel, then copy a quote from the PowerPoint slide used in the presentation you gave last week.

Using Windows 95 is like having a dozen or more computer monitors on your desk, each running a different program — but much better, for on your Windows 95 Desktop:

- there are no cumbersome monitors to hump about your desk; windows can be moved, positioned or hidden with just your fingertips (and the mouse)
- you have no difficulty working out which screen you are addressing; the active window is always on the top of the Desktop and displayed differently to the others

30   Chapter 2   What's a window, how is it used?

▷ moving information between screens is easy; each window forms part of the whole Desktop and has in-built mechanisms for transferring data — Chapter 7 gives details.

Definition

monitor ....the display unit connected to a computer that looks like a small television set. When your PC is switched-on, the Windows 95 Desktop is displayed on the monitor's screen

Note

> You should only ever need one monitor on your desk if you are running Windows 95

Once you understand how to use Windows 95 you will often find yourself working with several programs at the same time, each with its own window on your Desktop. However before you learn how to use a Windows program (Chapter 3) you must understand how to operate a window — the subject of *this* chapter. Let's take a closer look at the construction of a standard window.

Standard window construction

Most of the windows associated with a program look something like the one in Figure 2.2. They occupy a rectangular area on the screen and will respond to your mouse and keyboard as well as displaying material from the program to which they belong. You might want to put a bookmark in the following page so that you can easily refer back to the window components it illustrates.

Figure 2.2
A typical window — WordPad

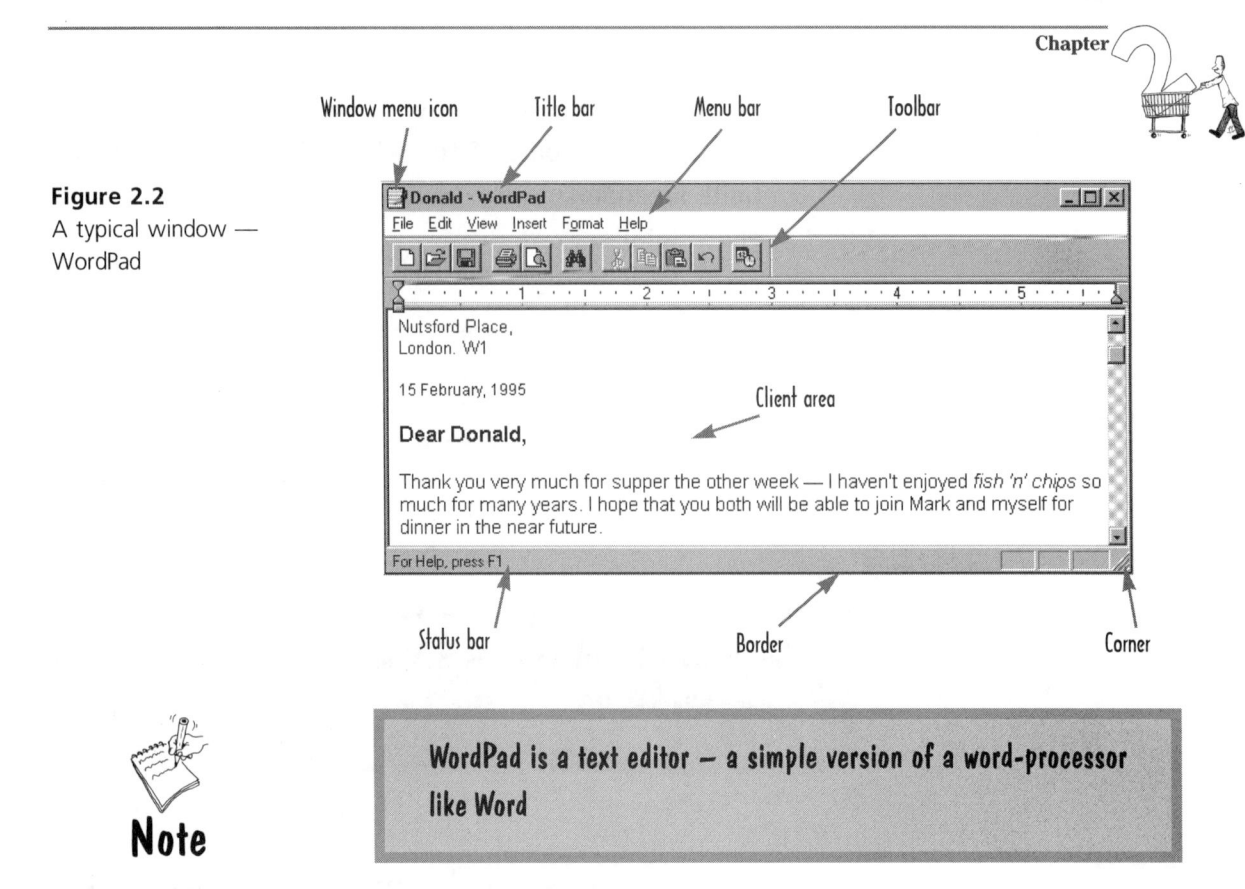

[Figure shows a WordPad window with labels: Window menu icon, Title bar, Menu bar, Toolbar, Client area, Status bar, Border, Corner. Window contains text: "Donald - WordPad", "Nutsford Place, London. W1", "15 February, 1995", "Dear Donald,", "Thank you very much for supper the other week — I haven't enjoyed fish 'n' chips so much for many years. I hope that you both will be able to join Mark and myself for dinner in the near future.", "For Help, press F1"]

> **Note:** WordPad is a text editor — a simple version of a word-processor like Word

Different kinds of windows

The window in Figure 2.2 is WordPad's main window and is created when you start the program from your Taskbar or open a document from your Desktop. However this is not the only type of window that can appear on your Desktop, for programs like WordPad or Word often display subsidiary or *child* windows to perform particular tasks or serve certain functions.

> **Note:** Learning Windows 95 is made much easier because each kind of window works in a similar way

Figure 2.3 shows several different kinds of window created by Word. Each window belongs to the program and shares several of the features identified in its main window. One of the more important windows created by Word is its document

Figure 2.3
Some different kinds of windows created by Word

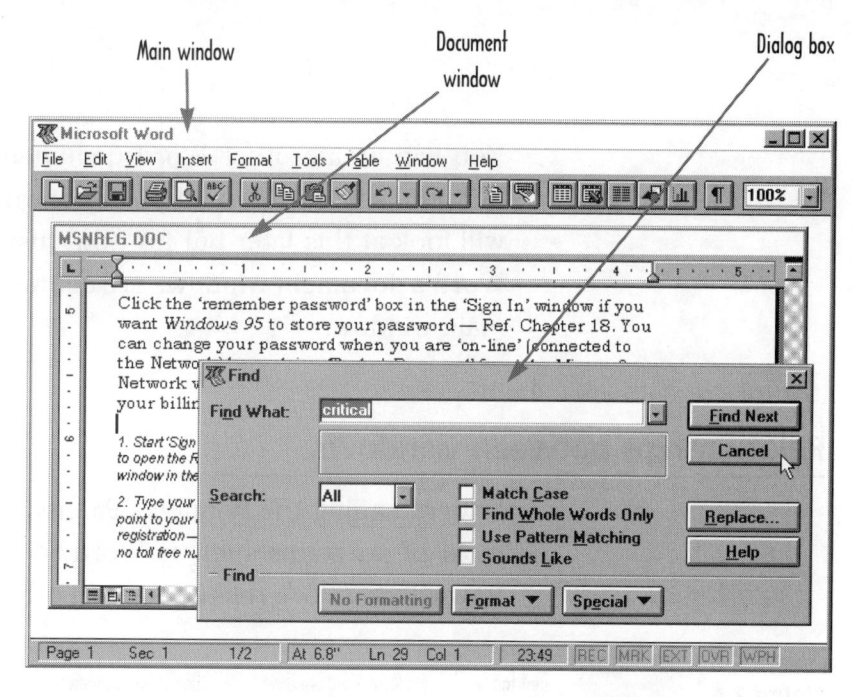

[Figure 2.3: Screenshot of Microsoft Word showing the Main window, Document window (MSNREG.DOC), and a Find Dialog box with "critical" in the Find What field.]

window; this window more than any other defines the nature of a program because it contains the information a program operates upon.

Definition

document ....the information a program operates upon, i.e. the report, drawing or other item of work displayed in a window on your Desktop

Document windows

When Word is started it automatically creates a document window so that you can begin writing. This window is difficult to differentiate from the program's main window because it initially fills the whole client area (the working area of the window). You can however change the size of a document window (like Figure 2.3) so that the distinction is clear.

Note

Some programs, like WordPad, do not have separate document windows but instead display a document within their main window's client area

Chapter 2   What's a window, how is it used?   33

You can create other Word document windows so that you may edit several different pieces of work at the same time. We will look at this later but for now, just grasp the concept that Word's document windows are contained in, and belong to, its main window.

Relationships between windows

Understanding the Windows 95 environment and making the most of programs such as Word requires an appreciation of how windows are related to each other.

Figure 2.4
Windows coupled together forming a hierarchy

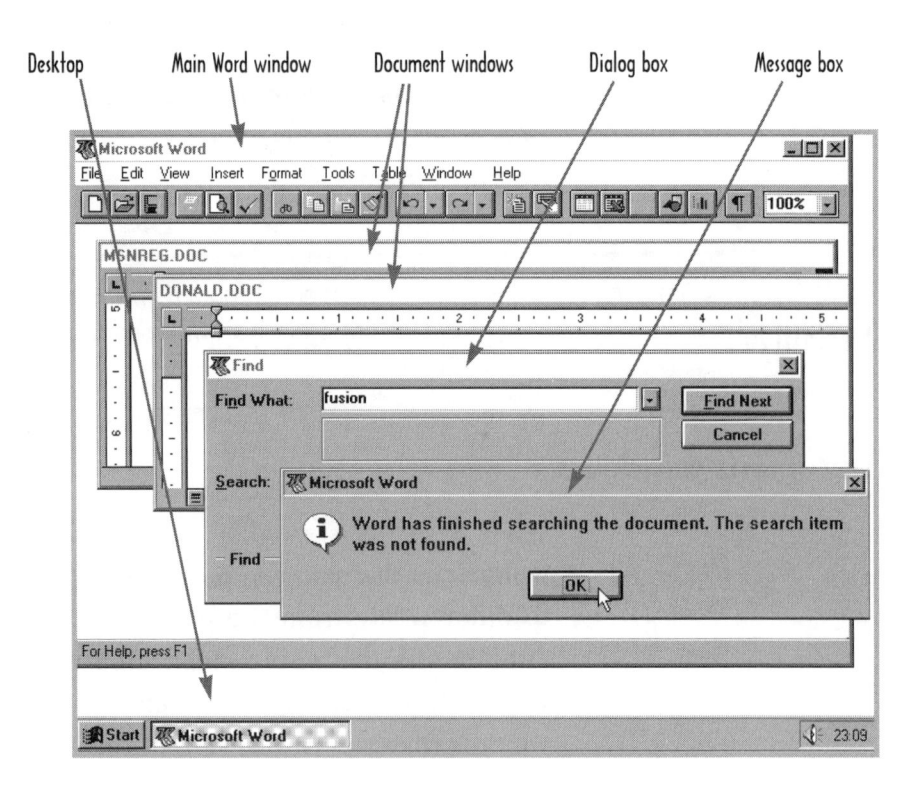

Figure 2.4 shows a number of different windows forming a hierarchy from your Desktop to the final message box. These windows have specific properties and responsibilities in addition to the common behaviour explored in the following section.

> **Note** — On its own the message box is meaningless. It only makes sense when read in context with the other windows on your Desktop

Doing things with windows

There's a number of general operations that you can perform on a window. You can:

- open and close a window
- switch between the three basic forms of a window
- adjust a window's size and position
- use a window menu.

These operations can be performed in a variety of different ways, however we will concentrate on the more straightforward and obvious methods.

> **Note** — This book uses the short-hand Programs↪Accessories in order to refer to the continuation menu Accessories accessed from the Start button's Programs menu

Opening and closing a window

Word's main window is opened on your Desktop when you start the program — a button is also created in your Taskbar. Other types of windows are opened as you use programs to perform various tasks.

> **Note** — Some windows are opened as a result of actions that were not initiated by you, for example, receipt of an e-mail message from another computer

When a window is closed it is removed from your Desktop. Closing a program's main window closes all the windows it contains as well as stopping the program — its button is removed from the Taskbar. However you may close a window that belongs to another window without closing its parent window (i.e. closing a document window does not close the main window).

1   *Start Word from the Taskbar (***Start➔Programs➔ Microsoft Office➔Microsoft Word***). Observe the button that now appears on your Taskbar.*

2   *Close the Word window (and stop the program) by pressing the close button* ☒ *in its main window — its button disappears from the Taskbar. This completes the exercise!*

> **Note**
>
> Windows 95 often provides several ways to perform the same action — see *Using a window menu* later to discover another method for closing a window

You can start and stop any of the programs that have been installed on your PC, in the same way that you have just started and stopped Word.

You should associate starting a program with opening its main window on your Desktop, and stopping the program with closing this window.

Switching between basic window forms

There are three basic forms of window and you can change between them at the touch of a button:

▷ maximized windows occupy the largest area, typically the entire Desktop. It is often easier to write letters and so forth in a maximized window

- resizeable windows have a border that allows them to be dragged to almost any size. It is possible to work with several windows on your Desktop at the same time if they are resizeable and arranged to fit your screen
- minimized windows are represented solely by buttons on your Taskbar (or within the working area of their main window) — they are hidden. A collection of buttons is often easier to manipulate than a set of windows.

> **Note**
>
> Resizeable windows are the normal form of a window on your Desktop. We have used the term *resizeable* because it best describes the functionality displayed by this form of window

Maximizing a window

Word's main window usually occupies the entire Desktop (apart from the Taskbar) — it is maximized. Maximized windows do not necessarily fill the Desktop but they do occupy as much space as their program allows. The initial document window is maximized to occupy the entire area of Word's main window. You can maximize a window simply by pressing its maximize button ▢ in the title bar.

1 *Start the program Word from your Taskbar (***Start**↪ **Programs**↪**Microsoft Office**↪**Microsoft Word***) — its main and document windows usually appear in their maximized form.*

When a window is maximized this button may be disabled (greyed) or replaced by a different button — you can't maximize what is already maximized!

Chapter 2 What's a window, how is it used? 37

Minimizing a window

When you press a window's minimize button ▬, the window disappears from your Desktop and is represented only by a button containing an icon and a label which serve to identify it.

Definition

icon . . . . an icon is a small graphic picture that symbolizes a window, file, folder and so forth. Icons can also represent physical devices like printers and modems

Each application program has its own specific icon while the label is formed from text contained in the window's title bar — see Figure 2.2. Minimizing a window does not stop the program (its button remains on the Taskbar), but simply removes the window from the Desktop.

The way that a window behaves when minimized depends on the type of window:

- pressing the minimize button ▬ in Word's *main* window removes it from your Desktop, together with any document windows that it contains
- pressing the minimize button ▬ in a *document* window replaces it with a button that is located within the program's main window, in place of the window.

Figure 2.5
Word's main window represented as a button on your Taskbar

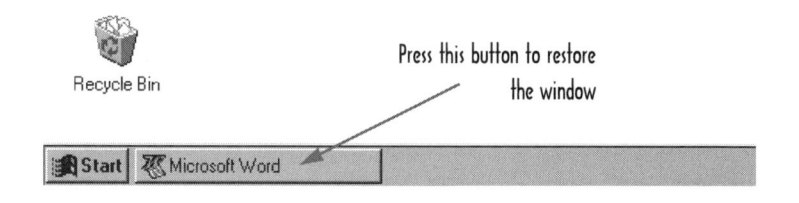

Press this button to restore the window

2 *Press the minimize button ▬ in Word's title bar (see Figure 2.6) to remove its main window from your Desktop. It remains only as the button created in the Desktop's Taskbar when the program was started. Press this Taskbar button to restore the window.*

Resizable windows

Resizeable windows provide the most flexibility, as windows in this form can be displayed side by side on your Desktop. When you press a window's restore button you change it to a resizeable window on your Desktop (Figure 2.2).

Note

> Some windows must be made resizeable before they display the button that is needed to minimize them

3 Now that Word's main window is maximized again press its restore button to make it change into a smaller bordered window on your Desktop. Repeat this operation with the document window — its restore button is immediately below the main window's maximize button.

You can recognize a resizeable window because of its thick border, which provides the means to alter the window's height or width. Moving over a window's border changes the mouse pointer into a double-headed arrow — this indicates you can drag the border to a new location.

4 Press the minimize button in the document's window (now resizeable) to reduce it to a button. Click on the button to reveal a menu then choose **Restore** to transform the icon back into a resizeable window.

Figure 2.6
Word's main and document window buttons

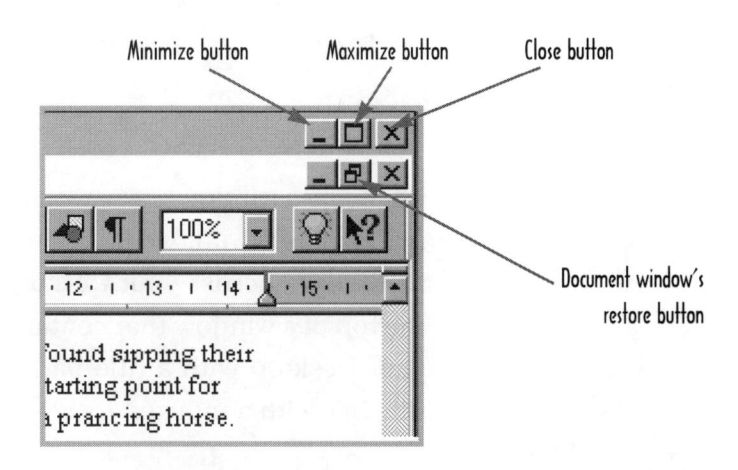

Minimize button — Maximize button — Close button

Document window's restore button

Chapter 2 What's a window, how is it used? 39

The advantage of a resizeable window is that it can be adjusted in terms of its size and location. You can arrange such windows so that you can simultaneously view several different pieces of information.

Note

> When a window is made resizeable its restore button is replaced by a maximize button

Adjusting a window's size and position

The size of a window with a thick border can be adjusted simply by dragging the border to a new height or width: dragging the horizontal border changes its height, dragging the vertical border changes its width, dragging the border's corner changes both height and width at the same time.

5   *Use your mouse to drag the window's border to change its size — the mouse pointer must change shape into a double-headed arrow ↔. Drag the window's corners to change both the window's height and width.*

Note

> Some windows have a thin border that serves only to mark its boundary — such windows cannot be resized

Changing a window's size would have limited value if you were not also able to move it around your Desktop. A window can be dragged across your Desktop by its *title bar* — the area at the top of a window that contains its name. All the windows on your Desktop with a title bar can be moved by dragging the title bar with a mouse.

Definition

handle . . . . .the part used to move something. A window's title bar forms the handle that permits it to be dragged across your Desktop

There are some restrictions on moving windows. Word's main window can be moved anywhere *on* the Desktop but it cannot be moved *beyond*. Similarly, some of the other windows created by Word (e.g. document windows) cannot be moved beyond the boundaries of their main window.

Figure 2.7
Moving a window

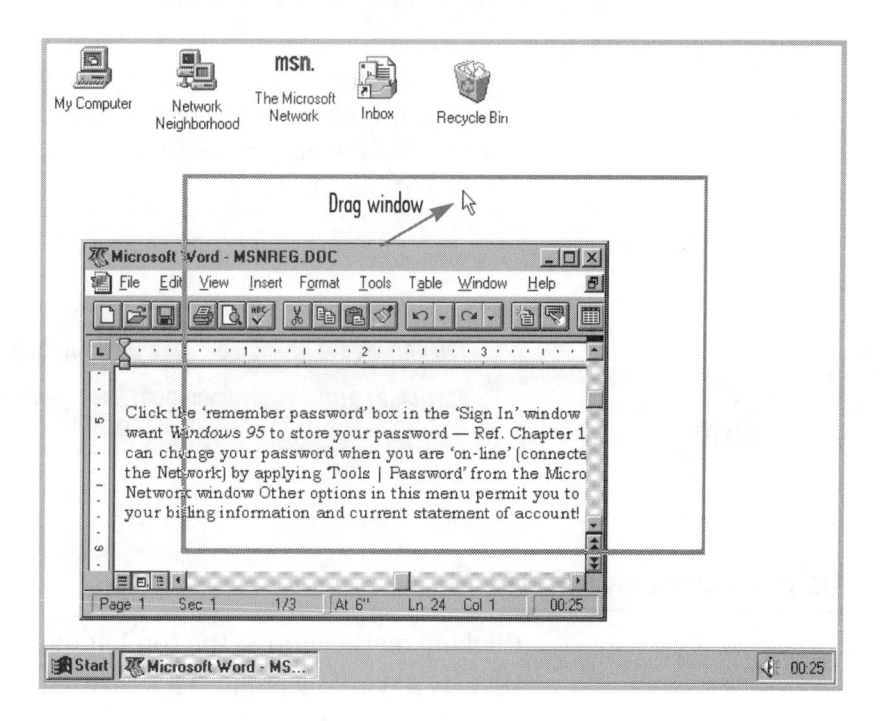

6   *Use your mouse to point to the title bar in Word's main window. Hold down your left mouse button to drag the window across the Desktop, release the left mouse button to leave the window in its new location. Minimize the windows you have opened.*

Note

Some windows do not have a title bar and this indicates that they cannot be moved

Chapter 2   **What's a window, how is it used?**   41

Chapter 2

My Computer

Your Desktop contains a number of icons, such as **My Computer**, that belong to Windows 95 rather than a particular application program. These icons each open into a window just like the window opened when you start a program from your Taskbar.

Icons of this type can be moved and arranged like the windows they portray; either their graphic representation or label can be used as a handle.

7   *Use your mouse to point to the icon on your Desktop labelled* **My Computer**. *Hold down your left mouse button and drag the icon across the Desktop, release the left mouse button to leave the icon in its new location.*

Note

> You can create an icon on your Desktop to provide a short-cut to a particular program or document (see page 293 for details)

Using a window menu

Clicking on the icon at the top left of a window (see Figure 2.8) reveals a Window menu. This menu permits you to control the arrangement of the window on your Desktop. It can also be used to adjust the size of the window as well as permitting it to be moved or closed.

The window menu belonging to a document window is also revealed when you press the icon in the top left of its window — when the document window is maximized this icon is immediately below the main window's icon.

Figure 2.8
Window menu

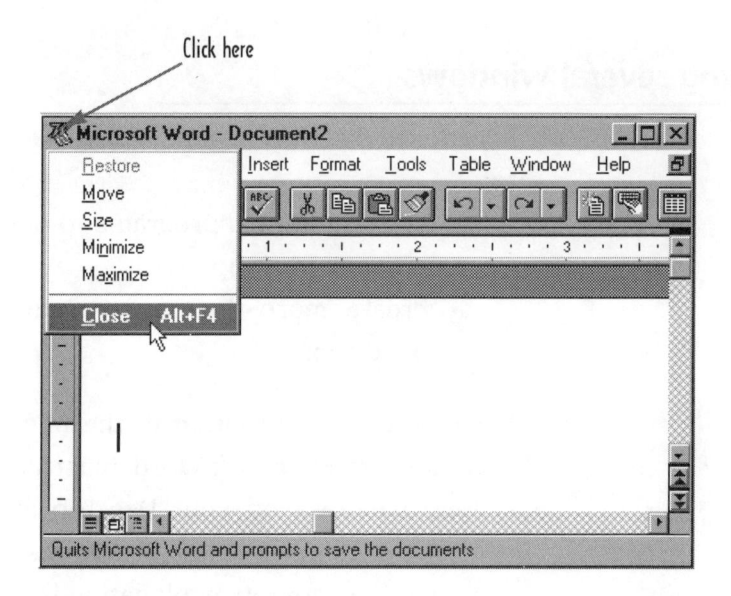

Click here

> **Note**
>
> The Window menu choices, like the window's buttons, reflect the current style of the window so the 'maximize' choice is disabled (greyed) when the window is already maximized

Managing windows on your Desktop

The benefits of permitting windows to be resized and moved becomes evident when you are managing more than one window, and include:

- arranging several windows
- activating a window
- finding lost windows on the Desktop
- tidying up your Desktop.

> **Note**
>
> Windows 95 is termed a *multi-tasking* operating system because you can use a number of windows belonging to different programs at the same time

Arranging several windows

In order to discover how to arrange several windows you need to:

- ▷ start additional programs to open more main windows on your Desktop.
- ▷ create more document windows within these main windows.

Excel is another program in the Microsoft Office suite and, together with Microsoft Word, illustrates how you can manage several windows on your Desktop at the same time. Excel windows are operated in a similar fashion as those belonging to Word — a separate explanation is unnecessary.

8 *Use the Taskbar to start Microsoft Excel (**Start↪Programs↪Microsoft Office↪Microsoft Excel**). This creates another main window on your Desktop. Press both restore buttons* 🗗 *so the main windows of both Excel and Word can be seen on your Desktop. Spend some time resizing and moving these windows.*

Tip

> You can use another program, say WordPad, (**Start↪Programs↪Accessories↪WordPad**) in place of Excel if you wish

Arranging document windows

Document windows are manipulated within their main window in the same way as the Excel and Word main windows are manipulated on your Desktop.

9 *Click the word **File** on Word's menu bar to reveal a menu. Click on the choice **New** (that is, choose **File↪New**) to open a special type of window called a property sheet. Press the **OK** button in this dialog box to create a further document window — it is maximized.*

44   Chapter 2   What's a window, how is it used?

> **Note**
>
> The process of choosing a menu entry from a menu in any application is described from now on in the form:
> Menu→Menu Entry

10 *Press the document window's restore button so both document windows are visible inside Word's main window. Spend some time resizing and moving these document windows.*

Figure 2.9
Manipulating several windows

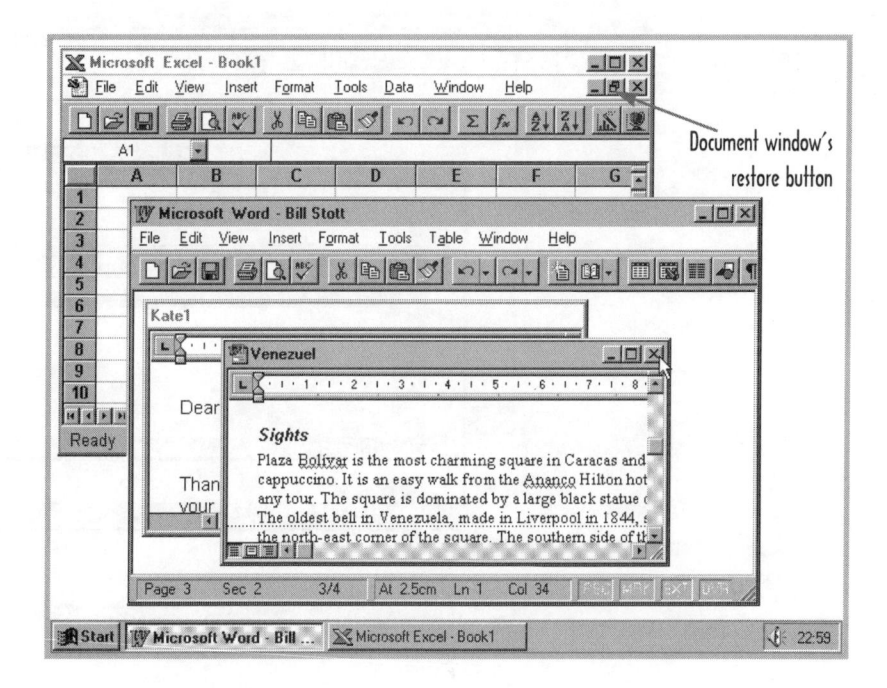

Activating a window

You may have already noticed that using a different window on your Desktop changes its look: its title bar takes on a more striking colour and if partly hidden by another window, it moves to the top of your Desktop. Clicking anywhere within the border of a window makes it active — ready for action!

> **Definition**
>
> *focus* . . . . applies to the part of the Desktop that responds to the actions of your mouse and keyboard. Your actions are always directed to whatever has obtained the focus of your Desktop

Chapter 2 What's a window, how is it used? 45

An active window has the focus of the Desktop and responds to your mouse or keyboard. Pointing with your mouse does not normally change the Desktop's focus, *clicking* does.

Figure 2.10
Activating a window

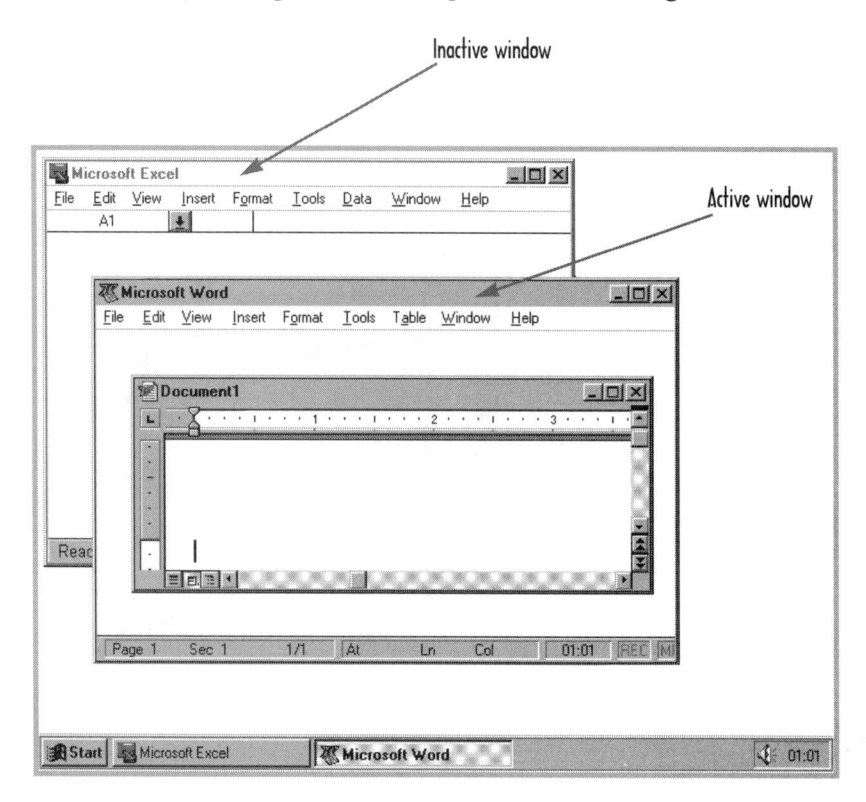

There are also ways to change the Desktop's focus with your keyboard (see Chapter 5), but first practice using the mouse to direct the action on your Desktop.

11 *Click in the Excel (or WordPad) main window. Click in the Word main window. Watch the windows change state. Repeat this exercise with the two Word document windows, typing something into each. Minimize one of the document windows and notice the change of focus that occurs when you click its icon after clicking in the other (resizeable) document window.*

It is not hard to manipulate a *few* windows on your Desktop but as the number of windows increases it becomes more and more difficult.

12. Use the Taskbar's **Start** button to open a few more windows on your Desktop (start programs like Paint and Phone Dialer from the **Start➔Programs➔Accessories** menu). Can you find all these windows? What happens if you maximize one of the windows?

One of the major problems faced by people learning earlier versions of Windows, such as Windows 3.1, was the sudden disappearance of a window from view. This problem becomes more acute when there are several maximized windows on your Desktop.

Finding lost windows on the Desktop

The easiest way to find a missing window is to look on your Taskbar. When you start a program a button is created on the Taskbar — press the button and up pops the window! Document windows lost within a program's main window can be found in a similar way using its menu bar (see Chapter 3).

Figure 2.11
Taskbar's window buttons

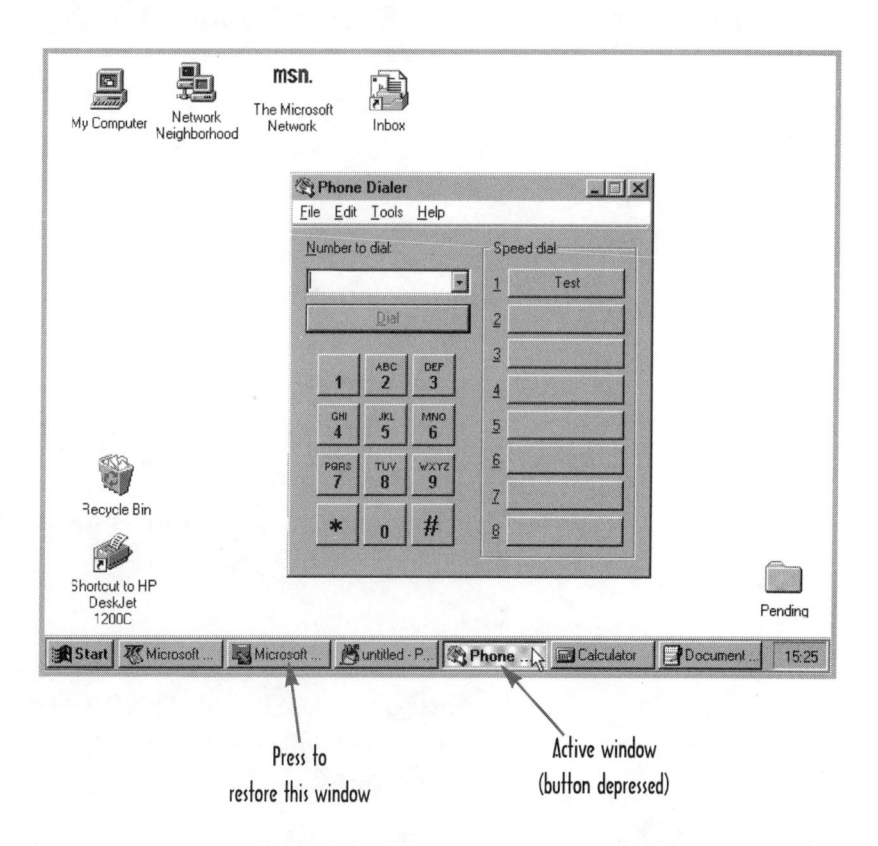

Press to restore this window

Active window (button depressed)

Chapter 2 **What's a window, how is it used?** 47

> **Tip**
>
> The Taskbar acts like the channel selector on your television — press the button to display the window. They work like restore buttons for the windows they represent

Tidying up your Desktop

Keeping your Desktop tidy makes it much more difficult to lose things — much like your real desk! You should also tidy your Desktop before shutting down Windows 95 for the day.

The steps required to clear your Desktop are as follows:

13 *Click on a Taskbar button to restore the window to your Desktop.*

14 *If there is a restore button ▣ beneath the window's maximize button ▢, press it to make all the program's document windows resizeable.*

15 *Click on a document window and close it by pressing the close button ☒ on its title bar. If prompted to save changes, press the **No** button unless you wish to save your work (see Chapter 6). Repeat for all document windows until the program's main window is empty.*

> **Note**
>
> Until you understand how to store the changes you have made to a document by saving it in a file (see Chapter 6), press the **No** button when prompted Save Changes

16 *Close the program's (main) window and stop the program by pressing the close button ☒ on its title bar. If prompted to save changes, press the **No** button unless you wish to save your work (see Chapter 6).*

17 *Click on the next program's button in your Taskbar to bring its main window to the top of your Desktop. Repeat steps 15 and 16 until there are no more buttons on your Taskbar.*

When your Desktop is clear the Taskbar will contain only the **Start** button — see Figure 2.12 — all the programs you have started have now been stopped (or terminated).

Definition

terminate . . . . .to stop or halt a program that has been started on your computer. Closing a program's main window terminates the program to which it belongs

18 *Shut down your Desktop using the Taskbar's* **Start↪Shut Down** *command as described in Chapter 1 — this exercise is complete!*

Note

When you switch-on your PC its Desktop is usually restored to the same state as you left it last time you shutdown Windows 95

Figure 2.12
A tidy Desktop clear of any programs

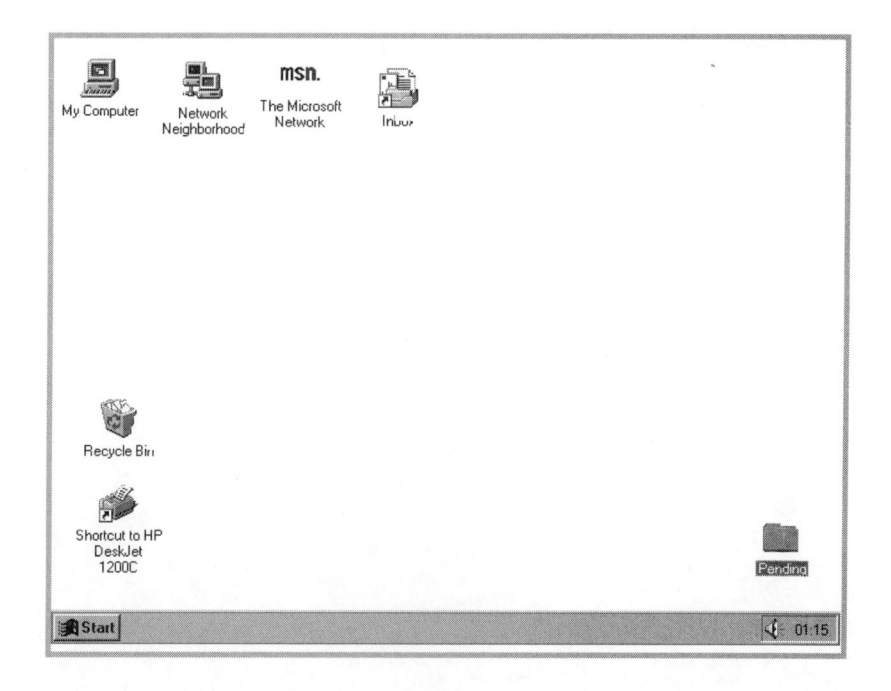

Chapter 2 What's a window, how is it used? 49

Summary

- A number of windows can be open on your Desktop at the same time, each representing a screen from a different program.
- Move a window with its title bar and change its size with its buttons or border — make the window fill the whole screen or occupy only a small part of it.
- Open and arrange a number of windows on your Desktop so you can simultaneously view a number of different documents on your PC's screen.
- Reveal a program's window by pressing its button on your Taskbar. Keep your Desktop tidy by closing windows when you have finished with them.

Note

Your understanding of Windows 95 will improve as you learn to identify in different contexts the various parts of the system and the job that they each perform

Chapter 3

Writing a letter in a window — menus

Objectives

This chapter extends your knowledge by operating various windows and doing something useful with them.

Following topics are included:

- creating a new document window — make a window into which you can type your letter

- composing a letter in Word's document window — moving your cursor, typing a letter, using scroll bars and split windows, editing and correcting mistakes

- finding your way around the menu bar — the standard contents of the **File**, **Edit**, **Window** and **Help** menus

- different types of menus entries — use menus to initiate an action, change a setting, or open a dialog box

- toolbars — shortcut to a menu selection, changing the toolbars displayed in your window

- contents of the program's **Window** and **Help** menus.

After reading this chapter you will have mastered the basic operation of a Windows program.

Chapter 3

Creating a new document window

Your letter will be composed in a document window contained within Word's main window. This document window will be associated exclusively with your letter and holds various settings that determine how the letter will appear; its typeface, the page size and so forth.

Definition

template . . . . the stencil from which a document's initial style and content are copied. The normal template creates a blank document with a conventional typeface (see Chapter 9)

The document window created when you start Word copies its initial settings from the *normal* template — a file stored on your computer's hard-disk. However when subsequent document windows are created a list appears containing a selection of templates — any of these templates can be selected as the source for your new document's initial style and content. Writing a letter with a different style is simply a matter of using a document window created from a different template.

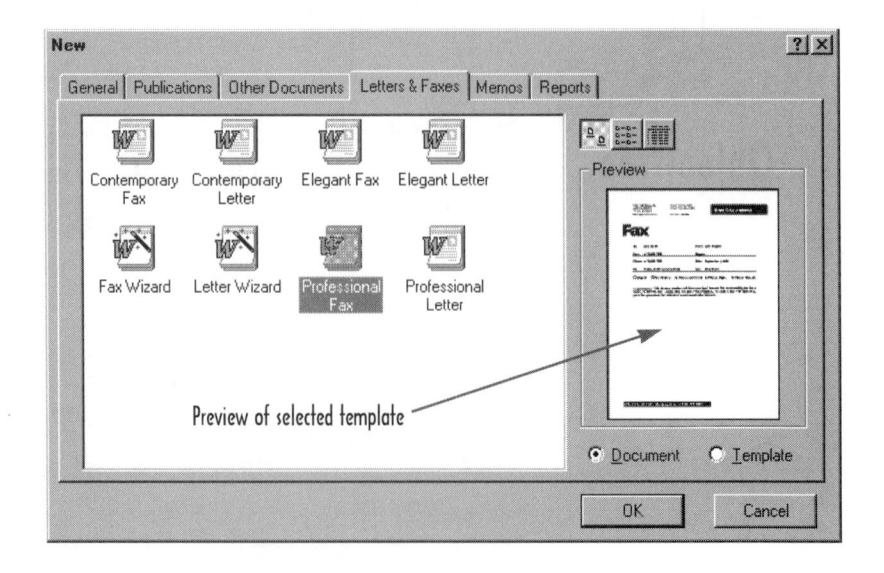

Figure 3.1
Word's **New** property sheet

52 Chapter 3 Writing a letter in a window — menus

Definition

property sheet — a collection of pages within a dialog box that contain settings, options and so forth. You can bring a page to the forefront by clicking its label (tab) so that it opens-up like a section of a ring-binder.

1 *Start Word from your Taskbar (***Start**↪**Programs**↪**Microsoft Office**↪**Microsoft Word***). Click on the word* **File** *in the menu bar to reveal Word's* **File** *menu. Click on the menu choice* **New** *to open a property sheet containing a collection of document templates (the action of choosing a menu entry in this way will be written as* **File**↪**New** *from now on).*

2 *Click the tab at the top of the property sheet labelled* **Letters & Faxes** *to bring this page to the front. Select the* **Elegant Letter** *template (click the icon) to display its layout in the property sheet's preview area — don't worry, you will use a much simpler template to create your first letter!*

3 *Return to the page where the* **Normal** *template is displayed (click the* **General** *tab). Select the* **Normal** *template (click its icon) then press* **OK** *to close the property sheet and create a new document window. This window will be maximized within Word's main window and have a style suitable for writing a simple letter.*

Note

Chapter 9 contains a more complete description of how Word's templates can be used to create different styles of documents

Tip

It may help you to think of a document window as a *container* for a document that is *itself* contained within your program's main window. A program's main window can contain several document windows so you can view several different documents at the same time.

> **Note**
>
> **NOTE:** Programs like WordPad are limited to displaying only a single document because their main window displays the document rather than acting as a container for further windows

Composing a letter in Word

Word's document windows are particularly adapted for entering and manipulating text. Typing text into a document window is not very different to typing on a sheet of paper within a typewriter carriage.

The general techniques of text entry are similar throughout the Windows 95 environment. Press a key on your keyboard and the corresponding letter (or symbol) is inserted into the document window at the cursor. The cursor then moves one space forward ready for the next letter.

4   *Type a sentence into your document window. Press the* [Shift] *key while typing to enter uppercase letters (or the top symbol on the keyface).*

Definition   *cursor* . . . . the flashing bar that marks where a character typed at the keyboard will be inserted into your document; this is your document's insertion point

---

Cursor and mouse pointer

When you initially typed text into your document window, the cursor was kept at the end of the document — this is where the characters were inserted. However by moving the cursor back into the middle of your text, further characters typed at the keyboard will be inserted *there* rather than appended to the end of the document.

The cursor can be moved by the arrow keys ←, →, ↓, and ↑ on your keyboard. The cursor is also moved by the mouse — it jumps to the mouse pointer when you click on any character in your document.

5   *Use the mouse to point to any letter in the sentence you have typed. Click the mouse (left button) and the cursor jumps to that character.*

People who have just started learning Word often confuse the cursor and the mouse pointer. Although they look similar they have very different jobs.

▷ the cursor marks your document's current insertion point and can be moved only within the document text
▷ the mouse pointer is used to point, select, drag and apply actions to your text. It can be moved anywhere on your Desktop.

Tip

> **The cursor is always represented by a flashing bar whereas the mouse pointer can assume a number of shapes but does not flash**

Paragraphs and carriage returns

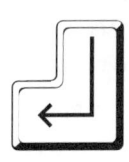

Mechanical typewriters have a lever that moves the carriage holding the paper to the left hand margin of the next line. Your keyboard has a carriage return ↵ or enter [Enter] key that performs the same purpose for the cursor on your screen, however unlike a typewriter this key must be pressed only when you reach the end of a paragraph.

Tip

> **Do not press the carriage return key ↵ (or enter key [Enter]) at the end of each line as this task is handled automatically by the program**

Chapter 3   Writing a letter in a window — menus   55

6   Type a long sentence and watch the word at the end of a line *automatically* wrap-around to the start of the next line when the line becomes full.

Paragraphs are formed when you press the carriage return key ⏎ or the enter key [Enter] — these insert a *hard* carriage return into your text, as opposed to the *soft* returns automatically inserted at the end of each line.

> **Tip**
> Press the ¶ button at the top of Word's window (below its title bar) to display all the hard returns in your document. Press it again to hide them once more (see Figure 3.2)

Typing a letter

Now you know how to type into a document window you are ready to start your letter and learn a bit more about using the type of programs found on your Desktop.

Definition

character . . . . the individual letters typed into a document window. Your keyboard and the Windows 95 *regional* settings (see Control Panel — page 394) determine the set of available characters

7   Click just before the first letter at the beginning of your letter to move the cursor (insertion point) to the start of your document then press the carriage return key ⏎ (or enter [Enter]) twice to create space for the addressee information.

8   Move the cursor back to the top line of your letter and type the addressee's name — don't worry about mistakes as you will discover how to correct those later.

9 Press [Enter] to start the next line of the address, then type the street name. Repeat this operation for each line of the address, the date and your standard letter opening (e.g. Dear Sir).

10 Click just after the last character in the text you typed in step 6 to move the cursor to the end of the letter and type a few more sentences. Start a new paragraph by pressing [Enter] but otherwise let Word decide where to insert line breaks.

Definition

scroll . . . . .changing the part of a document (or list) displayed in a window when the document (or list) is larger than the window itself

When you reach the bottom of your document window the top few lines scroll off the top of the window leaving you space to continue typing. You will never run out of space!

Figure 3.2
Typing the addressee information in a Word document

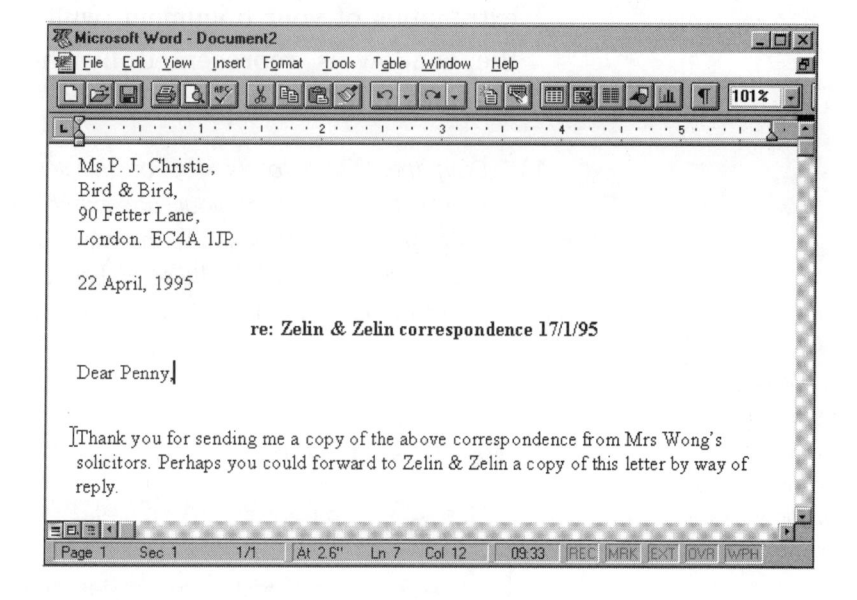

11 Continue typing until you have reached the last line of the window. Watch the document scroll as you type further text.

12 Repeatedly press the [↑] key on your keyboard to move the cursor back to the top of your document — the document will scroll back in its window. Press the [↓] key repeatedly to move the cursor forward to the bottom of your document — it will scroll forward in its window.

Chapter 3 Writing a letter in a window — menus   57

Chapter 3

> **Note:** Scroll bars are standard Windows 95 controls (see Appendix B) and are also found in dialog boxes

Scroll bars

Document windows are equipped with both vertical and horizontal scroll bars that allow you to move through any document even when it is too long, or too wide, to be wholly displayed within its window. These scroll bars move the location of the window with respect to the document — like a moveable spy-hole over a microfiche!

The top and bottom of the scroll bar represents the extremities of your document, while the current position of the window is represented by the moveable button (or 'thumb') in the scroll bar.

13 *Drag the thumb to the top of the scroll bar and the window moves to the top of your document. Drag the thumb to the bottom of the scroll bar and the window moves to the bottom of your document. Click in the scroll bar above and below the thumb to move up and down the document by the height of the window.*

Figure 3.3
Scroll bars moving a window over a document

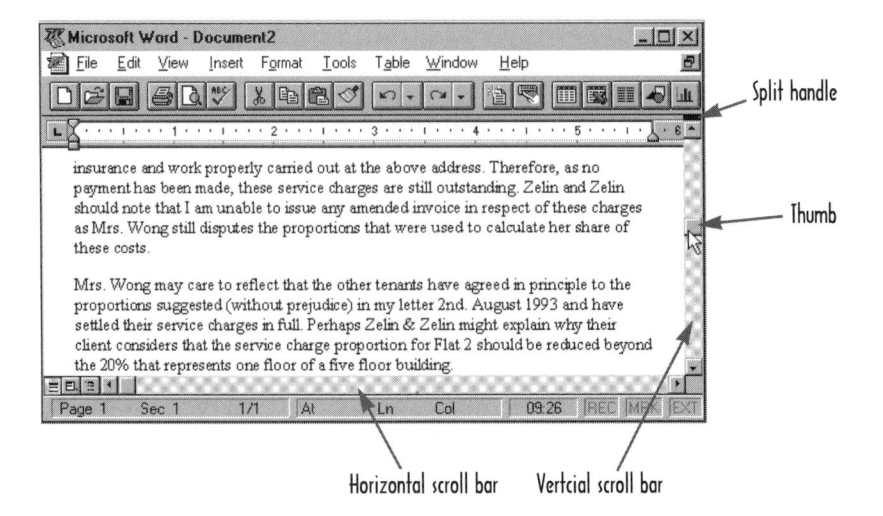

58 Chapter 3 Writing a letter in a window — menus

> **Note**
> The scroll bar's thumb often changes size to represent the proportion of the document displayed in the window

Splitting document windows

At the top of the vertical scroll bar is a small handle (see Figure 3.3) that can be used to drag the window into two separate halves — this can be useful if you need to view two areas of a long document at the same time.

14 *Drag your document window into two halves by pointing to the split handle (the mouse changes shape) then dragging it down the scroll bar. Release your mouse button to split the window — the scroll bars in each half of the window can be used to view different parts of the same document.*

15 *Reunite the two halves of the window by dragging the split handle to the top (or bottom) of the window.*

Figure 3.4
Entering text into a document window

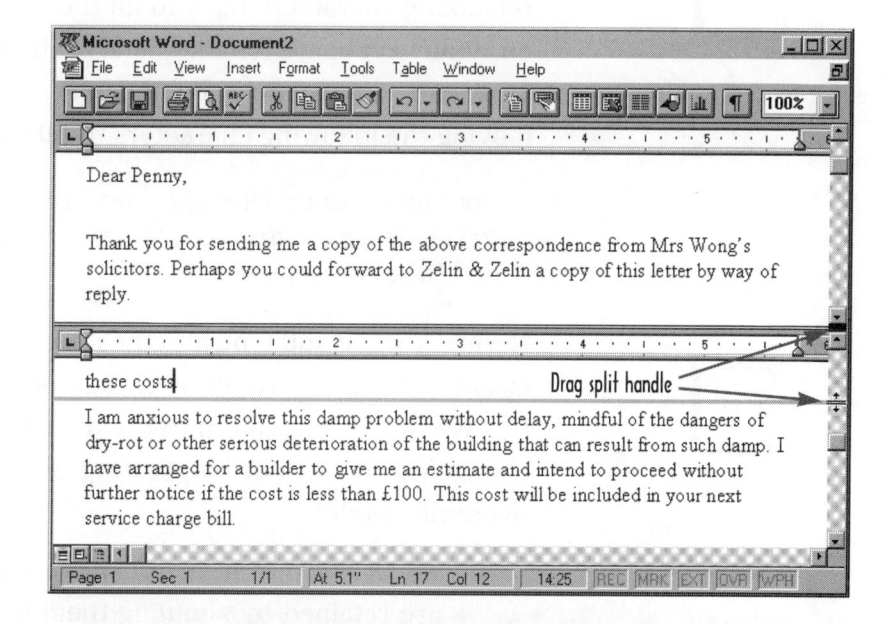

> **Note**
> Word only permits its document windows to be split horizontally whereas other application programs such as Excel have windows that can be split both horizontally and vertically

Chapter 3   Writing a letter in a window — menus

16   *Finish your letter by typing* `Yours faithfully` *on a new line then adding your name on the last line of the document.*

Well done — you can now use Word to type your letters. However it is rare that the first draft of a letter is perfect and therefore you must also learn how to edit and correct any mistakes.

Editing and correcting mistakes

Moving the cursor to any character in your document is easy — just click the character with your mouse or use the arrow keys on your keyboard. You can then remove or insert characters at this point by pressing special keys on your keyboard, two of which are described below.

Pressing ⌫ on your keyboard removes the character immediately in front of the cursor position moving the remaining characters back to fill the gap. Pressing backspace on your keyboard (immediately above ⏎) removes the character immediately behind the cursor position, again moving the following characters to fill the gap.

17   *Move the cursor until it is just in front of a character in your text. Press* ⌫ *to remove this character then press backspace to remove the character that preceded it.*

Normally when you type into the middle of your document the existing characters (right of the cursor) are moved forward — the new text is inserted into the document. However you can change this behaviour by pressing ⌫ to switch from insert to overwrite mode:

> When Word is in insert mode the existing characters are retained by shuffling them forward and expanding the size of the document

> When Word is in overwrite mode the existing characters are overwritten by the new character you have entered. The document remains the same length (unless you have reached the end of the document).

Each time you press ⌑ Word switches modes. The current mode is indicated by the letters OVR on the status bar at the bottom of the main Word window (see Figure 3.4). Word is in overwrite mode when these letters are black and in insert mode when they are grey.

18   *Use your cursor keys (or mouse) to move the cursor into the middle of your letter then press ⌑ on your keyboard (right of the backspace key) — watch the letters OVR light-up in Word's status bar. Enter some characters into your document and watch them overwrite the existing text.*

19   *Press ⌑ again to return Word to insert mode and type some more characters into your letter — they shuffle the existing text forward to make room.*

> **Note**
>
> Your skills at editing and correcting mistakes in your documents will be improved by reading Chapter 5

When you have finished the letter you will want to print a copy on the printer attached to your PC — the subject of the next chapter. However printing is only one of the many actions that you can apply to a Word document and to make best use of a program you must know where to find its actions and how to use them.

Finding your way around the menu bar

Word's menu bar (see Figure 3.6) contains more than one hundred different types of actions that can be applied to your documents. However finding the actions you need is not difficult because they are classified, like books in a library, under appropriate menu headings.

Definition

action . . . . .a choice within a menu that makes the program do something; create a document window for your letter, search for a given word, and so forth

Figure 3.5
Standard menu headings

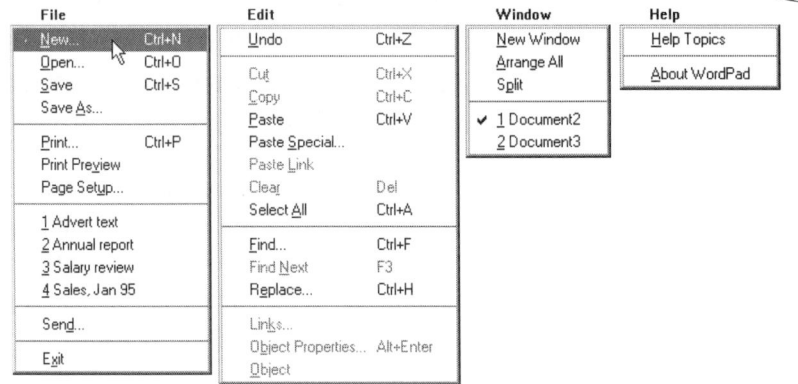

File		Edit		Window	Help
New...	Ctrl+N	Undo	Ctrl+Z	New Window	Help Topics
Open...	Ctrl+O			Arrange All	About WordPad
Save	Ctrl+S	Cut	Ctrl+X	Split	
Save As...		Copy	Ctrl+C		
		Paste	Ctrl+V	✓ 1 Document2	
Print...	Ctrl+P	Paste Special...		2 Document3	
Print Preview		Paste Link			
Page Setup...		Clear	Del		
		Select All	Ctrl+A		
1 Advert text					
2 Annual report		Find...	Ctrl+F		
3 Salary review		Find Next	F3		
4 Sales, Jan 95		Replace...	Ctrl+H		
Send...		Links...			
		Object Properties...	Alt+Enter		
Exit		Object			

The standard menu headings are:

- **File** — actions related to documents and the files in which they are stored (see Chapter 6)
- **Edit** — operations that are applied to the contents of a document window; remove, copy, find (see Chapter 7)
- Actions specific to the program appear in menu headings located between **Edit** and **Window**
- **Window** — list of document windows and actions you can perform on them (described later in this chapter)
- **Help** — assistance about the program and how it is used (see Appendix A)

> **Note**
> Programs are used consistently on your Desktop because they have menu bars that behave in the same way, with similar menu headings and containing many common actions

Operating the menu bar with your mouse — File↪New

It is easier, though not necessarily quicker, to operate the menu bar with your mouse rather than the keyboard (see Chapter 5). Three simple steps are required to choose an action from the menu bar with your mouse:

- click on a menu heading (e.g. **File**) to activate the menu bar and reveal a list of the items it contains

▷ point to an item in the menu to highlight your choice — there is no need to click once the menu bar is activated
▷ click an item to initiate the action (e.g. **New**) and close the menu. When the action has been completed your focus returns back to the window from which you started.

> File↪New is a shorthand way of saying "point to the heading File in the menu bar and click to activate its menu, then click on the choice New within this menu to perform the action"

Note

You can return the Desktop's focus back to your document without making a selection from a menu by pressing ⎋ key (top left of the keyboard) a few times — alternatively click elsewhere on the Desktop (see Chapter 2, Activating a window).

Figure 3.6
Menu bars, toolbars and status bars

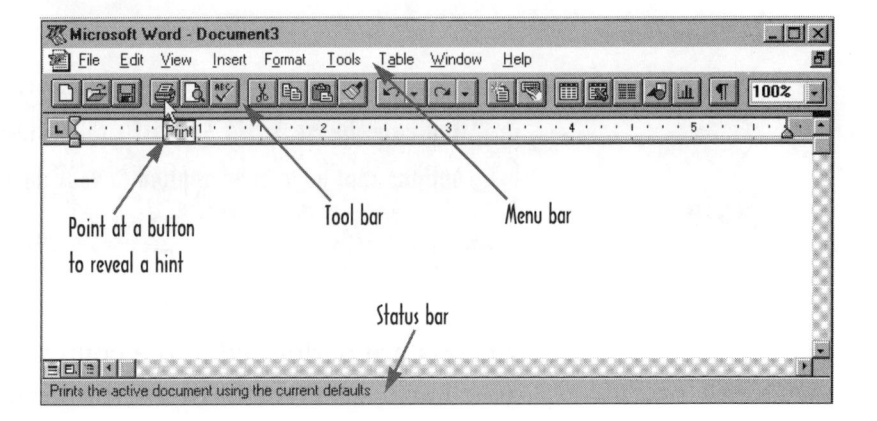

Point at a button to reveal a hint — Tool bar — Menu bar — Status bar

Different types of menu entries

Three different forms of entries can be found in the menus that appear on your Desktop:
▷ entries that initiate an action without further qualification (e.g. **Edit↪Undo**)
▷ entries that directly change a setting (e.g. **View↪Normal**)

▷ entries that bring-up a dialog box so that you can supply the necessary values or settings to complete an action (e.g. **File↪New**).

Definition — *toolbar* . . . . .some items in the menu belonging to a window are duplicated as single buttons beneath the menu bar. The picture on the button reflects its function (see Figure 3.6)

Performing an action without further qualification

Some actions require no further qualification and can be initiated directly from the menu.

20 *Choose* **Edit↪Undo** *from Word's menu bar to remove the piece of text that you typed into your letter at step 19.*

Note — You can choose **Edit↪Undo** repetitively to undo a series of actions that have been applied to your document

Actions are performed in the context of the thing (or things) you have selected. Most of the actions performed in this chapter apply to your active (selected) document window. However in subsequent chapters you will learn to direct actions at specific (selected) words or letters within a document.

Changing settings — menu check marks

Certain actions do not act on the contents of a document window but change its state or mode to modify its subsequent behaviour.

Definition

check-mark . . . . .a tick, cross or dot next to an item in a menu that indicates it is selected. Check marks also appear next to items in a list or within dialog boxes (see Appendix B)

Word can display your letter in a number of different ways within the document window. 'Normal' view displays the letter as if it was on a continuous roll of paper, whereas 'Page Layout' displays the letter superimposed on a sheet of paper — most evident when you have scrolled your document to the break between two pages. The current display mode of your document window is shown by a check mark against a particular entry in the **View** menu. Clicking against a different choice changes the document viewing mode.

21 Click the **View** heading in the menu bar to reveal its menu. The current view is indicated with a check mark — **Normal**. Click **Page Layout** to change the display mode of your document. Choose **View**↪**Normal** to restore the original view.

Note

> When Windows 95 programs enter a special mode there is usually a visible clue. Word changes the state of the buttons to the left of the horizontal scroll bar when the view mode changes

Actions that require further qualification

You can qualify certain actions by completing a dialog box. It allows you to specify the settings to be used with your action — see Figure 3.7. Dislog boxes are described in the next chapter.

Definition

default . . . . .the settings or options that apply when no alternatives are specified by you. These values are normally stored within the program itself

You could print your letter simply by pressing the print button that appears in Word's toolbar. However, this is a direct action and gives you no control over how the document is printed — default settings are used for the number of copies that will be made, the quality of the print job and even the printer that will be used.

Figure 3.7
A dialog box

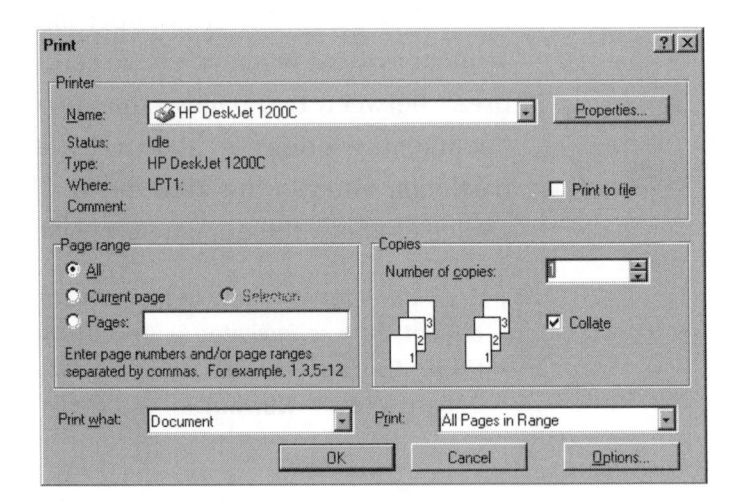

> **Note**
>
> Choices in menu bars that relate to actions whose settings are defined by a dialog box are marked by a set of three dots – known as an ellipsis (...). A dialog box will appear when this choice is selected

Toolbars — shortcut to a menu selection

Programs often provide toolbars (see Figure 3.6) that have buttons to represent many of the actions found in the menu bar. This provides, with a single click of your mouse, a shortcut to the action.

22   Press the new file button 🗋 on Word's toolbar to open a new document just as if you had chosen **File→New** from the menu bar — the **Normal** template is used by default.

Figure 3.8
Word's **Toolbars** dialog box and its standard toolbars

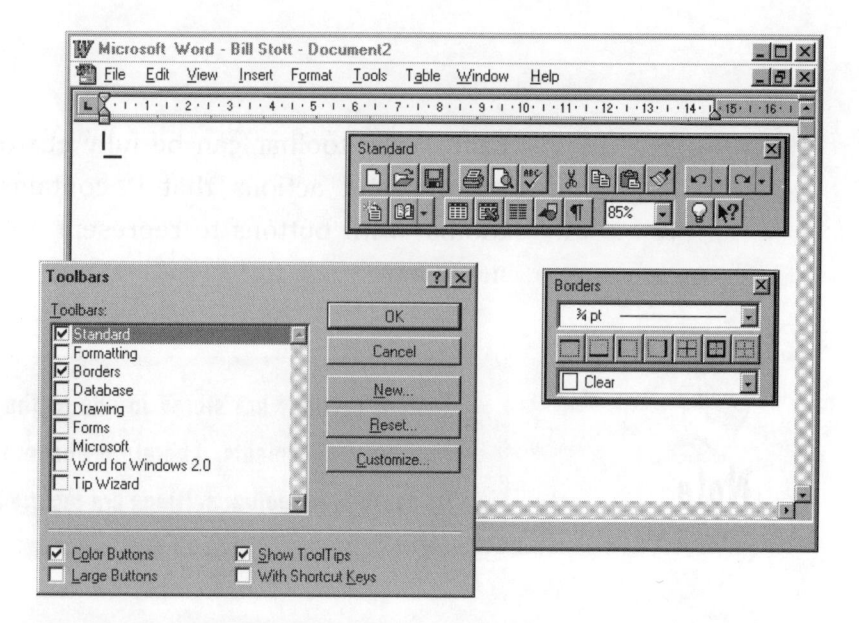

> **Note**
>
> A toolbar button performs an action directly using a set of default values to qualify the action — dialog boxes give you better control over how an action is performed

23 Open Word's **Toolbars** dialog box by choosing **View↪Toolbars** from its menu bar. Click one of the unticked boxes (e.g. **Borders**) then click the **OK** push-button to close this dialog box and display a further toolbar in Word's main window.

Word's toolbars may be attached to the top of its main window or may be contained within their own window so they can be dragged across your Desktop — a facility shared by toolbars belonging to other programs.

24 Position your mouse pointer over a blank area at the left side of a toolbar then drag the toolbar away from the menu bar — drop it in the middle of your document window.

25 Re-attach the toolbar to the menu bar by dragging it to the top of the main window. Close the **Borders** toolbar by opening the **Toolbars** dialog box (**View↪Toolbars**) and clicking the **Borders** check box to remove its check mark before pressing **OK** to close both the dialog box and **Borders** toolbar.

Each Word toolbar can be fully customized in terms of the buttons and actions that it contains — create your own toolbar with buttons to represent any of the choices in the menu bar.

> **Note**
>
> Toolbar settings are stored in one of the templates attached to your Word documents. Therefore whenever you open a document its associated toolbar settings are restored

The contents of the program's Window menu

Programs, like Word, that allow you to create more than one document window provide a menu to help manipulate them. The exact content of such menus varies from program to program but generally contain two sections:

- actions that initiate change to the arrangement of the document windows with the program's main window
- a list of the document windows with a check mark that sets the currently active window (on top of your Desktop)

Word's **Window** menu is shown left — you can activate any of the document windows that have been opened by the program simply by clicking against their name in the list.

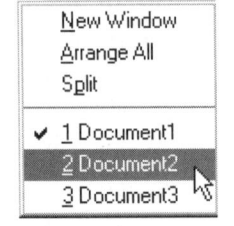

23 Click on the **Window** menu heading to reveal the list of document windows contained within Word's main window — the original document window (**Document1**), your letter (**Document2**) and the new document you created in step 22 (**Document3**). Click on the document name without the check mark to switch between the document windows.

The other part of Word's window menu contains a number of actions that can rearrange the document windows:

- **Arrange All** — makes all the document windows resizeable then arranges them so they don't overlap each other
- **Split** — the mouse pointer is replaced by line in the active document window. Position the line with your mouse then click to divide the document window so you can view two different parts of the same document (see *Splitting document windows*) . When the window is split in this way its **Window** menu contains **Remove Split** which can be applied to remove this split
- **New Window** — create a duplicate document window so that you can view different parts of the same document, like a split window but more flexible.

> **Note**
>
> Actions apply to the active document window — the one on top of your Desktop with the coloured or highlighted title bar

The contents of the Help menu

The Word Help menu provides you with assistance about the program. This menu is often divided into the following general categories:
- access to help topics — Windows 95 provides a special program that can read the help information provided by the program's manufacturer and present it in a window as a series of topics. Appendix A gives further details about the Windows 95 help program
- tutorials and demonstrations — some programs are supplied with utilities that present its features within an interactive tutorial program
- **About the program** — this menu option displays a dialog box containing information about the program and your PC

▷ **Answer Wizard** — finds a help topic from the description you have given of the problem

▷ **Microsoft Network** — starts MSN and takes you directly to the forum where the program is supported so you can have your questions answered by technical staff.

Figure 3.9
Word's **About** dialog box

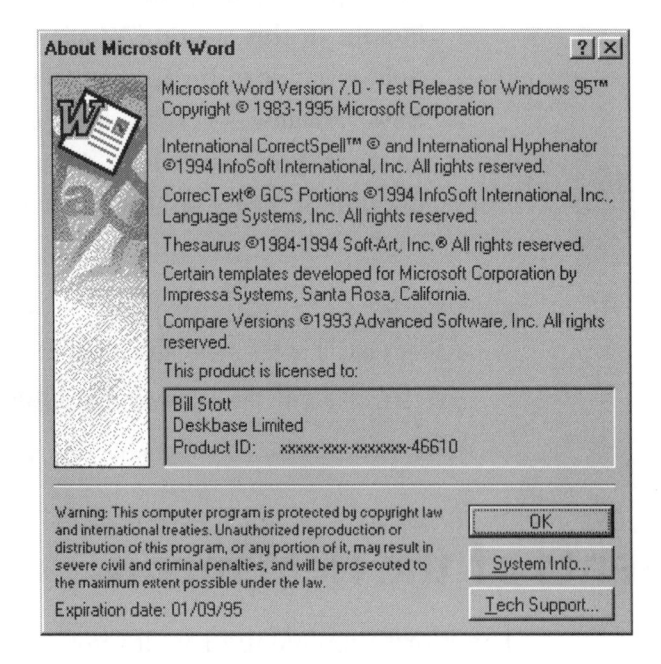

24 *Choose* **Help**⇥**About Microsoft Word** *to display the dialog box shown in Figure 3.9. Use your mouse to press the* OK *button and close the dialog box.*

25 *Close Word's main window, (don't save changes) tidy up your Desktop (described at the end of Chapter 2) then choose* **Start**⇥**Shut Down** *to shut down Windows 95 — this completes the exercise!*

> **Note**
>
> Most application programs contain an About dialog box to acknowledge the program's copyright, licence and version information

Summary

- Write a letter using Word by creating a document window (**File→New**) into which you can type your text. Start each new paragraph by pressing [Enter] but leave Word to automatically insert new lines.
- The actions and operations you can apply to your document are contained in the menu bar belonging to the program's main window.
- Many programs contain the same actions in their menu bars so that common operations (e.g. **File**, **Edit**, **Window**, **Help**) are applied by different programs in the same way.
- Many menu bar choices perform an action directly while others bring-up a dialog box so that you can qualify the action by changing its default settings.
- Toolbars provide a way to perform an action with single click of your mouse — a shortcut to the menu bar.

Chapter 4

Printing a letter from a dialog box

Objectives

Many tasks done with Windows 95 are qualified by settings in a dialog box. This chapter looks at the way dialog boxes are used:

> ▷ operating dialog boxes — how settings in a dialog box change the way an action is performed

> ▷ changing a document's print settings — how to print several copies of your document, print documents on a network printer, alter your printer's internal settings

> ▷ sending your letter to the printer — create a print job then get your printer ready to receive it

> ▷ responding to message boxes — how to handle problems that might arise while printing, e.g. running out of paper!

> ▷ previewing your letter before it is printed — open a window that displays your document as it will appear when printed.

After you have completed this chapter you will have printed the letter composed in the previous chapter and know how to use any dialog box that might appear on your Desktop.

Chapter 4

Operating dialog boxes

You make a program do something by applying an action from its menu bar. However many actions require further qualification so that you can specify precisely what you mean to do; for example print the whole document or just the first page. This qualification is provided by adjusting settings in a dialog box.

1   *Start Word from your Taskbar (***Start⤷Programs⤷Microsoft Office⤷Microsoft Word***) and compose another letter as you did in Chapter 3.*

> Print your document simply by pressing the **Print** button in Word's toolbar. Use the **Print** dialog box only if you need to change the way your document is printed

The initial settings of the dialog box are supplied by the program and indicate how the action would be performed without any further qualification — the default settings. In order to change these settings you need to understand how to operate a dialog box; the subject of this chapter.

2   *Choose* **File⤷Print** *to open the* **Print** *dialog box (Figure 4.1).*

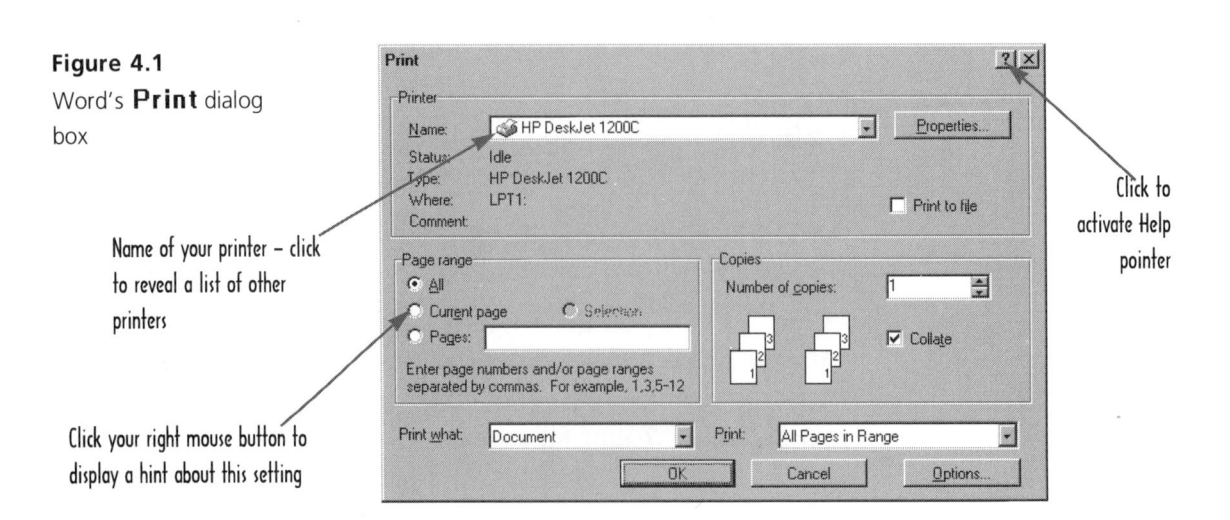

Figure 4.1
Word's **Print** dialog box

Name of your printer – click to reveal a list of other printers

Click your right mouse button to display a hint about this setting

Click to activate Help pointer

74   Chapter 4 — Printing a letter from a dialog box

Definition *control* . . . . .the elements of a dialog box that contain settings or values are termed controls (see Appendix B)

The dialog box of Figure 4.1 (and others) contains controls used to change settings. These controls work in the same way irrespective of the dialog box they are found in. Thus, like windows, they add to the consistency of the Windows 95 environment.

Dialog boxes — a special form of window

A dialog box is special form of window. The name of the dialog box is contained in its title bar which also can be used to drag the box across your Desktop — just like the other windows you have encountered. However unlike normal windows most dialog boxes cannot be resized and must be closed before you can continue working in your document window.

3   *Click in the document window behind the* **Print** *dialog box. Your PC will beep to tell you that this action is not permitted.*

You cannot work in any other window belonging to Word while the **Print** dialog box is still open on your Desktop — it is modal.

Most dialog boxes are *modal* — they must be completed (and closed) before you can return to your work; the **Print** dialog box is modal. However other dialog boxes are *modeless* so that you can continue working on your document while keeping the dialog box open on your Desktop ready to perform its action; the **Find** dialog box (**Edit**↪**Find**) is modeless.

System modal dialog boxes are different from *application* modal dialog boxes in that they must be completed before you can perform any other action with Windows 95. The **Shutdown** dialog box is a system modal dialog box, because you cannot operate the Taskbar or any other program until it has been closed. However the **Print** dialog box is modal only in terms of

Chapter 4

the program to which it belongs; you can still operate the Taskbar or other programs on your Desktop while it remains open.

There are usually two ways in which a dialog box can be closed (you will do this later as part of the exercise):

▷ **OK** push-button — closes the dialog box and performs the action as qualified by your settings and options

▷ **Cancel** push-button — closes the dialog box without performing any part of the action; any changes that you might have made to the settings in the box are lost — just as if you hadn't brought up the dialog box in the first place.

Other push-buttons may open further dialog boxes containing additional settings (e.g. **Options** button).

Obtaining help with actions — help topics

Many dialog boxes contain a **Help** button in their top right corner. Pressing this button changes the mouse pointer's shape and function — it becomes the help pointer. You can click any of the controls in the dialog box with your help pointer to display a hint about what they do (shown in Figure 4.2).

You can also obtain help when using some dialog boxes by pressing a special **Help** push-button (or by pressing F1 on your keyboard). This starts the Windows 95 Help program with a help topic appropriate to the action you are attempting to perform. A help topic is contained within its own window which can be operated like any of the other windows on your Desktop but with its own specific properties.

Note

> The Windows 95 help program is described in Appendix A and provides a consistent way to locate and view help topics from a variety of programs

76 Chapter 4 — Printing a letter from a dialog box

Figure 4.2
Hints about a dialog box control

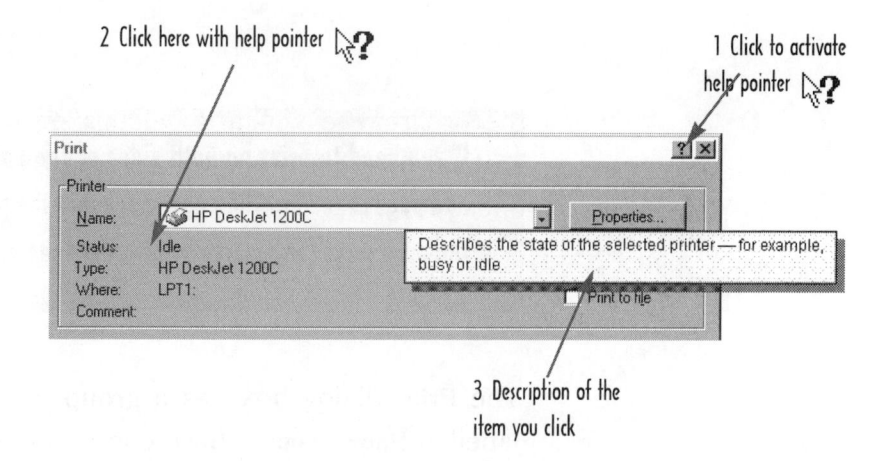

2 Click here with help pointer

1 Click to activate help pointer

```
Print                                                    ? X
┌─Printer─────────────────────────────────────────────┐
│  Name:    HP DeskJet 1200C              ▼  Properties..│
│  Status:  Idle          Describes the state of the selected printer—for example,
│  Type:    HP DeskJet 1200C    busy or idle.
│  Where:   LPT1:                              ☐ Print to file
│  Comment:
```

3 Description of the item you click

> **Tip**
> Click a setting with your right mouse button to display a hint related to the task you are performing – context-sensitive help

Changing your document's print settings

You can use the controls in Word's print dialog box to change its settings so that you can:

- print more than one copy of your document
- print only the odd or even pages of a document
- print only part of a document.

There is no defined order for altering the controls in a dialog box.

4   *Press the uppermost of the two small (spin) buttons at the right side of the box labeled* **Number of Copies** *to print more than one copy of your document. Press the lower of the two button to restore the number of copies to one.*

5   *Press the button at the right side of the box labeled* **Print** *(immediately above the* **Options** *button) and select (click)* **Odd Pages** *from the list that appears.*

Tip

> If you need to print on both sides of the paper you can print the odd pages then put the paper back into the printer before printing the even pages in reverse print order (see page 79)

The **Print** dialog box has a group of controls within a box labelled **Page range**. These controls determine how much of the document will be printed — all pages, a selection of pages, or just the page currently containing the cursor.

6   Click the circular button labelled **Pages** to select this option (the dot appears in the circle) then type a list of the pages in your letter that you wish to print (see Figure 4.1).

Tip

> If you first select a part of your document (see Chapter 9) then open the Print dialog box, you may choose the Selection option to print only the part of your document you have selected

The **Print** dialog box also contains two specific push-buttons that when pressed display further dialog boxes to further modify the way your document is printed:

- ▷ **Options** — your program's options for printing its documents
- ▷ **Properties** — set the options for the way the selected printer prints your document (i.e. the paper tray to use, the print quality required and so forth).

Changing Word's print options

Word's option settings are contained in a property sheet that is displayed when you press the **Options** button in its **Print** dialog box, or choose **Tools↪Options** from its menu bar.

7   Press the **Options** button from Word's **Print** dialog box to bring up the **Options** property sheet — open at the **Print** page.

8   Click the box labelled **Reverse Print Order** then close the property sheet by pressing its **OK** button — you return to the **Print** dialog box.

Figure 4.3
Word's **Options** property sheet

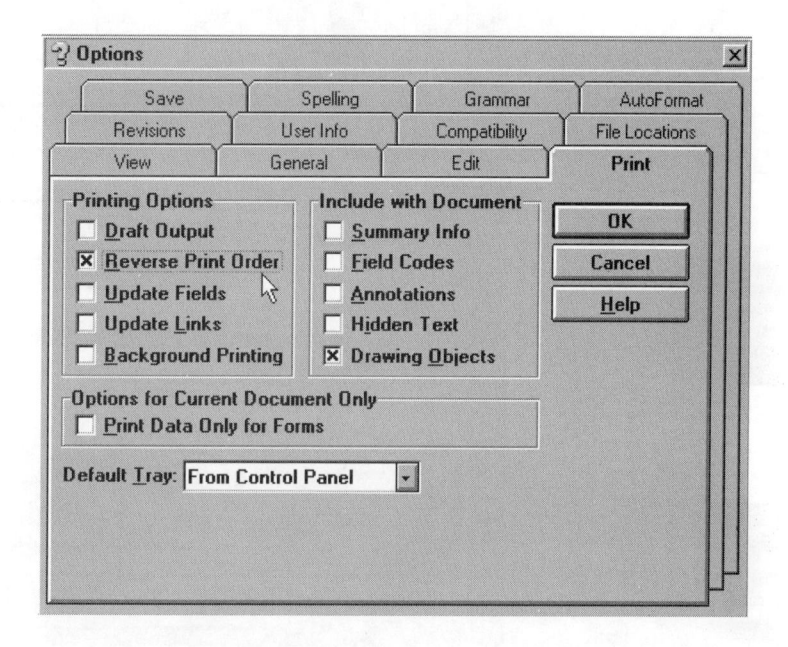

> **Note**
>
> Reversing the print order means that the first page of your document will be printed last and therefore the page order of your document will be correct when collected from the printer

Changing printer properties

Changing your printer's properties allows you to alter the way it will process your documents. Each printer has its own individual options that determine the way it prints. Figure 4.4 shows the options for an HP-DeskJet 1200C but *your* printer may have different options.

Chapter

Figure 4.4
HP DeskJet 1200C printer properties

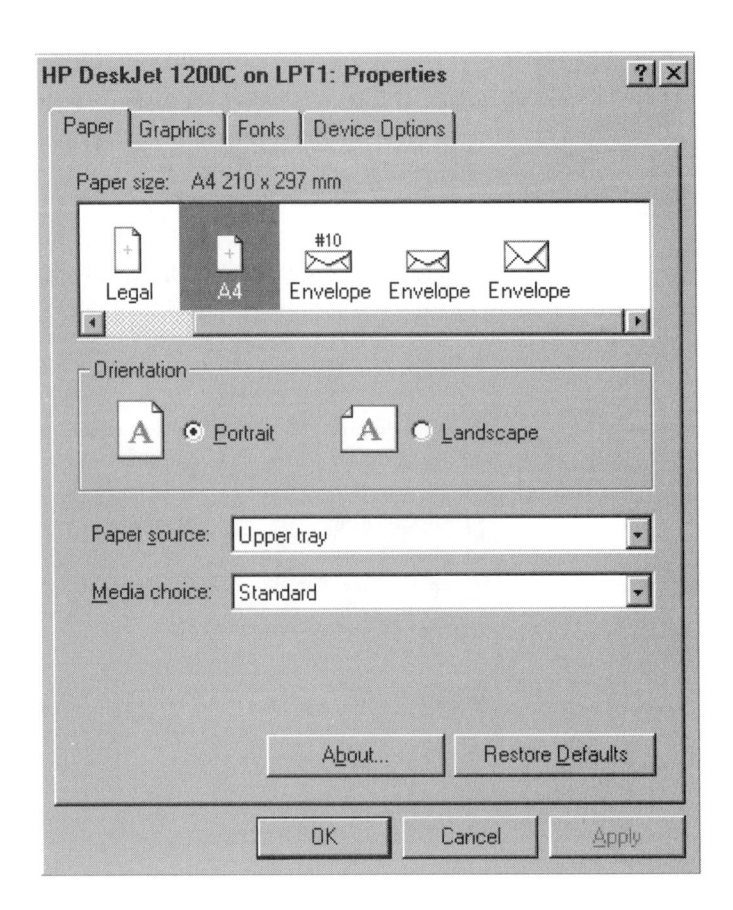

> **Note**
>
> Changes made to settings in your printer's property sheet only affect the document you are printing. They change the way the print job is generated (see page 314) rather than permanently altering any of the printer's internal settings

9   Press the **Properties** button from Word's **Print** dialog box to open the property sheet for the selected printer. Click the tab for each page of the property sheet in order to review the various printer settings that you may alter.

10 Click the tab labeled **Paper** to bring this page to the front of the property sheet. Select (click) the icon that correctly reflects the

80   Chapter 4 — Printing a letter from a dialog box

size of paper (i.e. A4) in the printer's paper tray. If you printer has more than one paper tray (or a manual feed facility) then check that the **Paper source** is also set correctly.

> **Note**
>
> Some printers have an upper and lower paper tray so that you may put blank paper in one tray and headed notepaper in the other tray. In this case you should adjust the printer properties before printing so that the correct tray is specified as the paper source for your document

11 Press the button labeled **About** at the bottom of the property sheet to display information about the printer driver associated with the selected printer. Press **OK** to close this message box then press **OK** to close the property sheet — you are now ready to send your letter to the printer!

Figure 4.5
About message box

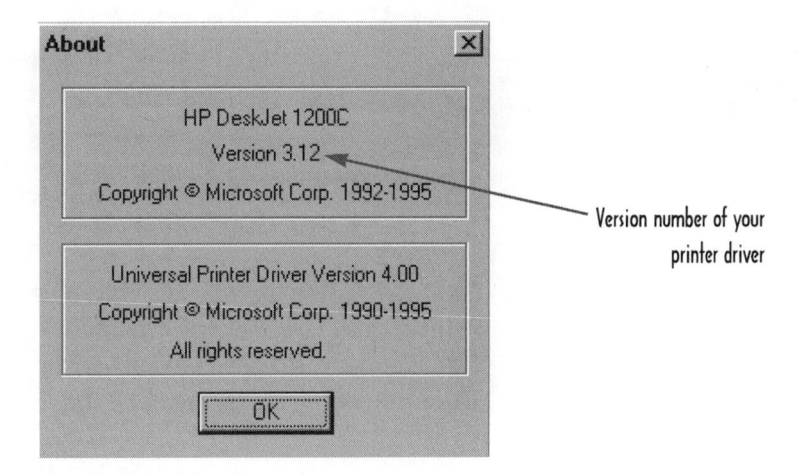

Printer manufacturers have developed special programs, called printer drivers, to provide tight integration of individual printers into the Windows 95 environment. You automatically set up the appropriate printer driver whenever you install a printer on your Desktop (see page 337). It is this printer driver which is responsible for managing the printer's property sheet and therefore the above exercise may not exactly correspond to the way your particular driver behaves.

Selecting a different printer

Your Desktop may have access to several printers or just one, depending on the number of printers installed on your Desktop. The names of printers currently available to print your documents are listed in the control at the top of the **Print** dialog box. You can reveal this list by clicking the button located to the right of the control. Printers are usually named in such a way that they can be readily identified (e.g. **Bill's personal printer**).

Figure 4.6
Print dialog box showing **Printer** name box

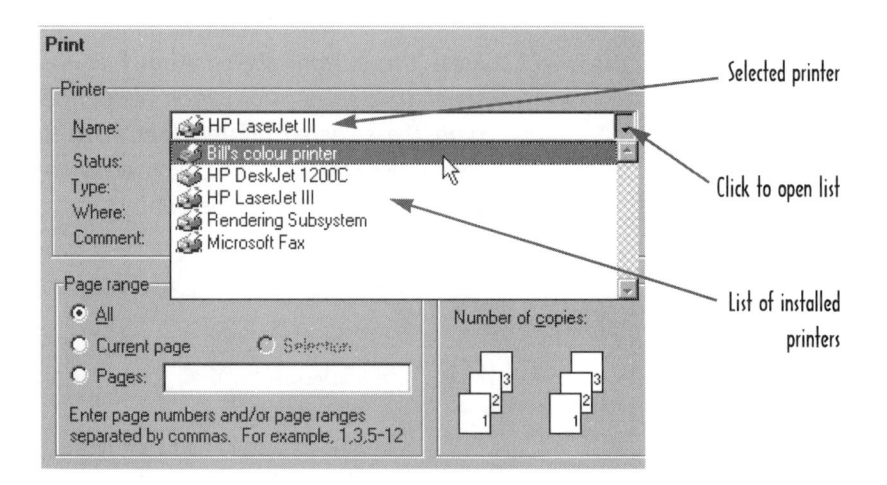

12 Click the button at the far right side of the control labeled **Printer** to reveal the list of printers installed on your Desktop. Click the name that corresponds to the printer you have already set up to print your document — the list disappears.

> **Note**
>
> The Print dialog box also describes the type (i.e. HP DeskJet 1200C), the status, and the location of the printer which is currently selected to print your document

A printer may be located next to your PC and connected by a simple cable in which case it is a *local* printer. However in large organizations it is more common for a printer to be located elsewhere in the building and connected to your Desktop through a computer network — this is a *network* printer. Both types of printers are selected and used in much the same way; the only real difference is the need to move from your desk in order to collect the print-outs from a network printer!

Connecting a printer to your PC

To connect a local printer to your PC you will need a special printer cable which plugs into one of the sockets at the rear of your computer (see the instruction manuals for specific details). These sockets have pre-assigned communication port names, such as LPT1, which you will need to remember if it becomes necessary to install the printer (and its driver) on your Desktop. However in most cases your supplier (or technical staff) will have already installed the printer and so once you have plugged in the cable you are ready to print.

Note

> There is a special program (Wizard) that takes you step-by-step through the process of installing a printer on your Desktop – see page 337

Your connections to network printers are usually established automatically whenever you *logon* to the computer network (see page 16) — there are no cables to attach beyond your network connection. Again, you can expect your supplier (or technical staff) to have installed the appropriate printers on your Desktop so that they appear in the list of printers within the **Print** dialog box.

Table 4.1 contains a list of the printers that have been installed on the authors' Desktop. It illustrates the diversity of printing facilities provided by Windows 95 which may be utilized simply by selecting the name of a printer from your **Print** dialog box.

Table 4.1
Examples of printers

Name	Where	Type	Comment
Bill's colour printer	LPT1	HP-1200C	colour ink jet printer locally connected to the PC's LPT1 socket
Visitor's printer	LPT2	generic/text only	works for any printer that might be connected to the PC's LPT2 socket (no graphics)
Bill's laser	COM1	WinWriter600	laser printer locally connected to the PC's COM1 socket
Microsoft fax	fax	Microsoft fax driver	supports the fax-modem (Chapter 17)
Office colour printer	\\TOWER\hp-1200	HP-1200C	colour network printer shared by office

Note

Chapter 14 describes how a printer can receive documents sent from many different programs and then arrange for each one to be printed in turn – print jobs and print queues. Chapter 15 explains how a number of people can share a single network printer

Sending your letter to the printer

You should check that the printer is switched-on and ready to print before sending it a document; refer to your printer manual for specific details, but at least refer to Figure 4.7 and check that:

- ▷ cables are connected
- ▷ enough suitable paper is in the appropriate tray
- ▷ lamps show that printer is ready to receive a print job.

Figure 4.7
Printer ready to print

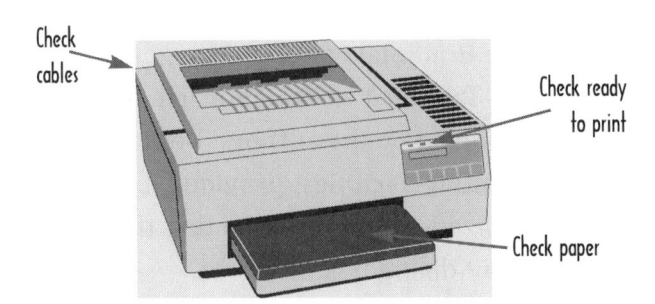

84   Chapter 4 — Printing a letter from a dialog box

Once you are satisfied the printer is ready you can complete the print action.

13 Press **OK** in the **Print** dialog box to close the box and send the print job to your printer.

Definition

print job . . . . .the collection of information that must be sent to a printer to reproduce your document exactly the way you have specified — it includes any instructions necessary to configure the printer

---

While a print job is being prepared an icon appears in Word's status bar indicating the number of pages that have been processed. The print job, when complete, is automatically submitted to the printer by Windows 95 (see page 314) and a further icon appears in your Taskbar to indicate the printer is occupied. Although your computer is busy from the moment you close the **Print** dialog box you may continue to work on the document (and your Desktop) while processing the print job because Windows 95 is a multi-tasking operating system — it can do more than one task at once.

Figure 4.8
Word's status bar and Windows 95's Taskbar while printing

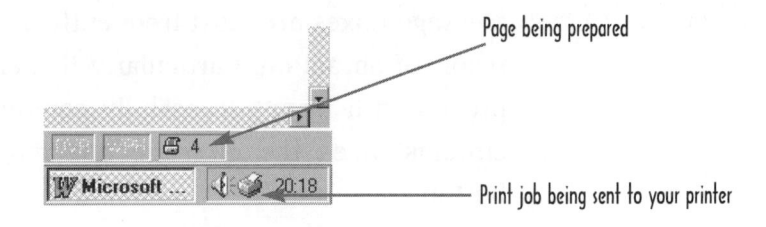

Page being prepared

Print job being sent to your printer

Note

> Earlier versions of Word displayed a modal message box while preparing a print job so that you had to wait until the print job was complete before continuing work on your document

Office 95 programs only display a message box while printing a document if a problem arises, for example if the printer runs out of paper.

Chapter 4

Responding to message boxes

A message box arises from the inception of an action (or event) and serves to:

> display the result of an action or problem that has arisen during its execution (Figure 4.9)

> confirm your intent to execute a non-reversible or hazardous action before it is performed (Figure 4.10)

> inform you of the action's progress as it is being performed.

Figure 4.9
Printer out of paper

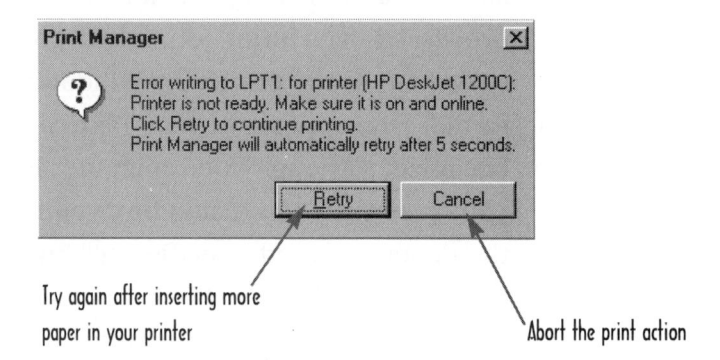

> **Print Manager**
> Error writing to LPT1: for printer (HP DeskJet 1200C): Printer is not ready. Make sure it is on and online. Click Retry to continue printing.
> Print Manager will automatically retry after 5 seconds.
> [Retry] [Cancel]

Try again after inserting more paper in your printer — Retry

Abort the print action — Cancel

Message boxes are most frequently used to inform you of the result of an action, particularly if there was a problem that prevented it from successfully completing the task. In such circumstances the message box may contain three push-buttons:

> **Accept** — continue with the action, accepting any limitations that the problem might have imposed

> **Retry** — try the action again now you have had the opportunity to fix the problem, i.e. add more paper

> **Cancel** — abort the action and restore everything to its state before the action.

Another example of the type of message box that prompts you to confirm an action before it is performed can be seen when you attempt to close the document window without first saving your work into a file (se Figure 4.10).

Note

Windows 95 tries to make most actions reversible so that once applied they can be easily undone. However some actions are irreversible by their nature (i.e. formatting a floppy disk)

Figure 4.10
Confirm close action without saving changes

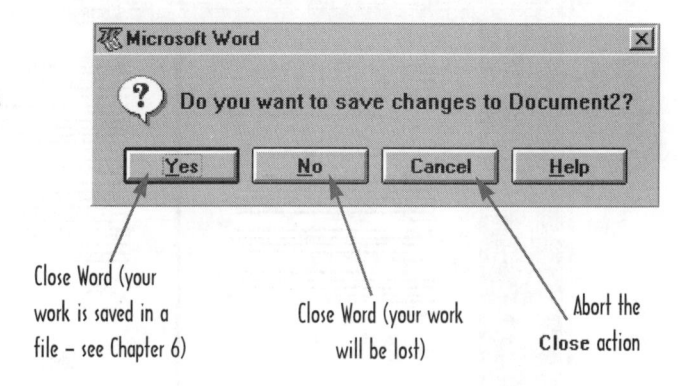

Close Word (your work is saved in a file – see Chapter 6)

Close Word (your work will be lost)

Abort the Close action

Viewing your letter as it will print

You may notice that your letter has a slightly different appearance in its document window than it does when printed on paper. For example, the words on your screen are bigger than the words on paper because it is difficult to read small characters displayed on a monitor. However you can view your letter on screen exactly as it will appear when printed by choosing File↪Print Preview from Word's menu bar.

Tip

Save paper by using File↪Print Preview before printing your document to check that it appears as you expect

Choose File↪Print Preview from Word's menu bar to view your letter on screen exactly as it will appear when printed. The mouse pointer changes into a magnifying glass shape and will zoom-in on part of a page when you click. Press **Close** to return to your document window.

Figure 4.11
Print Preview
window

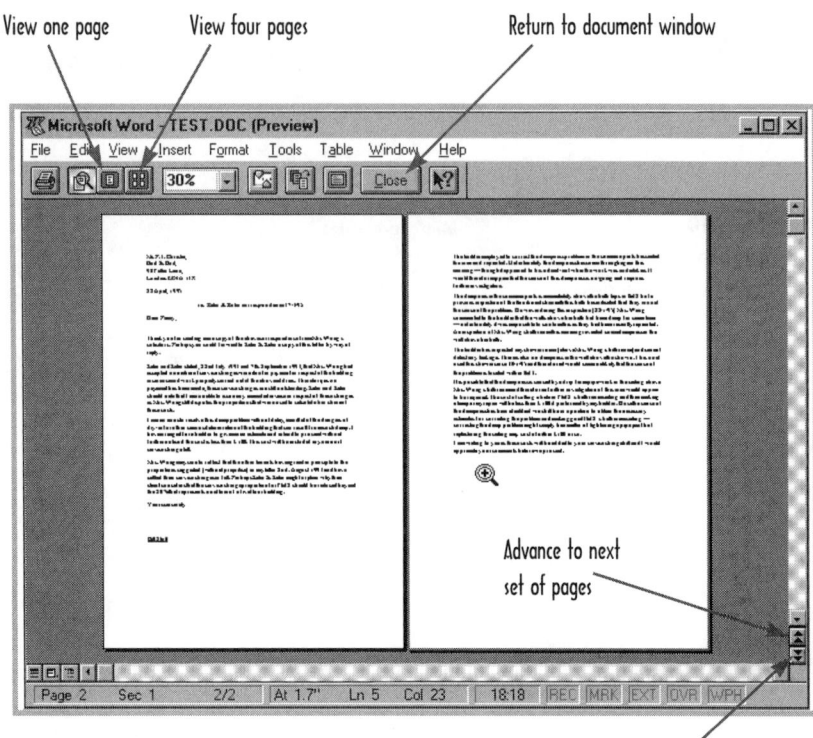

Labels on figure: View one page — View four pages — Return to document window — Advance to next set of pages — Return to previous pages

You now know more or less all there is to know about printing documents from Windows programs, so tidy up your Desktop before starting the next chapter.

14 *Close the Word document window containing your letter — press* **No** *in the message box that prompts you to confirm this action. Close Word's main window, tidy up your Desktop (described at the end of Chapter 2), then choose* **Start→Shut Down** *to shut down Windows 95 — this exercise is complete!*

Note

The same Print Preview facility is provided by many programs within their File menu

Summary

- Use a dialog box to qualify a particular action or review further choices that you might wish to apply.
- Obtain assistance completing a dialog box by pressing its **Help** button.
- Choose **File↪Print** from Word's menu bar then complete the various dialog boxes to specify your exact requirements for printing a document.
- Use property sheets to access many settings without navigating through a series of dialog boxes.
- Respond to message boxes arising during the execution of any action.

Tip

> Different programs often share the same dialog box when performing the same action

Chapter 5

Mouse and keyboard skills

Objectives

This chapter summarises the keyboard and mouse skills presented in previous chapters and adds some further techniques to help you get the most from Windows 95. In particular we look at:

▷ the way Windows 95 works — select something and then apply an action to it

▷ mouse skills — double-click to apply action, drag and drop actions, using the right mouse button

▷ mouse pointers — shapes reflect function, the hourglass, invalid drop zone, Help pointer

▷ keyboard skills — remove characters, align columns of text or figures, access the menu bar, keyboard shortcuts, keyboard locks, function keys

▷ using the keyboard to move and select — extended selection, cursor keys, keyboard selection, switching between programs.

This chapter contains information that you need to know if you are to use your programs and Desktop efficiently.

Chapter 5

The way Windows 95 works

Windows 95 and its application programs have a recognizable approach:

You select something on the Desktop or within a window then apply an action (or a sequence of actions) to it.

We have encountered this approach several times in previous chapters and will see it again and again in the future. For example:

- select some text in a document then apply an action to make it bold
- select a circle drawn in a document then apply an action to rotate it
- select an icon on your Desktop then apply an action to start a program and open a window.

Selection

Clicking something usually prepares it for action by:

- moving it into view if partly hidden behind something else
- making it active (if it is not already).

When you click on another object, it is prepared for action in place of the object you had previously activated. You can change the focus of your actions as many times as you wish — just click on something else. There is normally a visual clue when something is selected — it may be highlighted or painted in a different colour.

Table 5.1
How selection changes an object's representation

	window	icon	text
How selected	mouse left button clicked in window	mouse left button clicked on icon	mouse left button held down while pointer moved over text
Result	the window is made active — its title bar changes colour	the icon is made active — it is highlighted	the text is highlighted — ready for some further action

92   Chapter 5   Mouse and keyboard skills

*Start WordPad from your Taskbar (***Start⤻Programs⤻ Accessories⤻WordPad***) and type some text into its window. Practice selecting the things listed in Table 5.1 and investigate how different objects are prepared for action. Close the WordPad window (don't save changes) — this exercise is complete!*

> **Caution**
>
> When text is selected it will be replaced by the first character typed from your keyboard – a quick way to remove text prior to editing

Action

You do something with Windows 95 by applying actions to your selections:

- making a choice from a menu
- pressing certain buttons in your windows — buttons are often positioned on toolbars.

Nothing usually happens on your Desktop until you select something and apply an action to it. *You* drive the action.

> **Note**
>
> The actions supported by a particular object provide appropriate ways in which it can be used – its properties. A window can be restored, a program can be started, and so forth

Table 5.2
Select something then apply an action to it

	document window	program window
Select	mouse clicked in its window	mouse clicked in its window
Act	choose **File⤻Print**	choose **File⤻Exit**
Result	the document is printed	closes its windows and terminates the program

There are, however, ways to perform actions on your Desktop that do not involve *selection* followed by application of an *action*. You can make objects do something by using the mouse pointer to pick them up and drop them somewhere else — *drag-drop*. You can also activate an icon by *double-clicking*, as described later in this chapter.

Undoing actions — Edit↪Undo

Don't worry if you apply an action by mistake as most programs have an **Edit↪Undo** feature that can be used to back out of the previous action. Often you can back-track a whole *sequence* of actions by repeatedly choosing **Edit↪Undo**.

*Start Word from your Taskbar (***Start↪Programs↪Microsoft Office↪Microsoft Word***). Type some text into its document window then choose* **Edit↪Undo** *from its menu bar to remove the text you have typed. Close Word's main window (don't save changes) — this exercise is complete!*

Note

> A sequence of characters typed into a Word document window is considered a single action. Further actions are performed when you edit this text or use the menu bar to apply an action

Mouse skills

You can perform the following basic operations with your mouse:

- pointing — highlighting a menu choice or revealing a continuation menu
- clicking — selecting things, pressing buttons...
- dragging — moving windows, icons, scroll bars...
- double-clicking — applying the object's action.

You have already used the first three of these operations to navigate through menus, open windows and move objects on the Desktop. Here are some other ways of using the mouse to orchestrate the Windows 95 environment.

> **Note**
>
> The settings that determine the responsiveness and behaviour of the mouse can be adjusted (see page 398)

Double-clicking to apply an action

When you double-click on something the first click selects it while the second click applies its action. However the two clicks must be in swift succession for it to be interpreted as *select-act* and not as two separate single clicks: *select-select*.

1   *Double-click the* **My Computer** *icon on your Desktop to open its window.*

2   *Double-click the window menu icon at the top left of the* **My Computer** *window's title bar. The action associated with this icon (in any window) is to close its window — this exercise is complete!*

Figure 5.1
Double-clicking

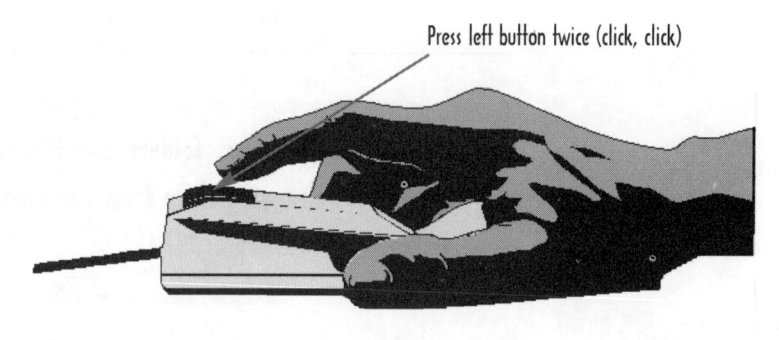

Press left button twice (click, click)

> **Note**
>
> Many objects in the Windows 95 environment have a menu containing the actions that can be applied to them – their default action (bold) is performed when you double-click them

Dragging operations

To drag something you must press and hold the mouse button, move the mouse pointer, then release the button. This is a routine way of manipulating objects on the Desktop, or within a window. For example, you can:

Chapter 5

- move a window by dragging its title bar
- operate objects (like a scroll bar's thumb) by dragging a handle
- apply an action to one object by dropping it on another — drag-drop (see Table 5.3)
- select things by dragging the mouse pointer around them — drag-select.

Table 5.3
Windows 95's common drag and drop facilities

	Document — Sales letter	Document — Sales letter	Document — Sales letter	Document — Sales letter
Dropped onto	printer (Shortcut to HP DeskJet 1200C)	folder (Pending)	Recycle Bin	program (Winword)
Default action	prints document	copies document into folder	deletes document (it may be recovered)	starts program and opens document

> **Note**
> Objects like printers, folders and files can be added to your Desktop by dragging them from the windows in which they are displayed (see Chapter 13)

1   Move (drag) the **My Computer** and **Recycle Bin** icons so that they are located next to each other in an empty area of your Desktop.

2   Position your mouse pointer on an area of the Desktop that is top-left of both icons then press (and hold down) your left mouse button while dragging the pointer to the bottom-right of the icons — a square appears as you move the mouse pointer. When you release the mouse button both icons are selected — this is drag-selection.

3   Drag the **My Computer** icon across your Desktop and the **Recycle Bin** will follow it. Click elsewhere on your Desktop to remove this multiple selection. The exercise is complete!

> **Note** — When more than one item is selected (multiple selection), actions that you apply to one object are also applied to the other objects that have been selected

Using the right mouse button

Windows 95 makes use of the right hand mouse button to reveal a pop-up menu attached to objects like the printer or document icons. Pop-up menus can be used in the following ways:

- actions can be selected from the pop-up menu that appears when something is dropped after being dragged with your right mouse button (see Figure 5.2a)
- pop-up menus often contain a **Properties** choice that may be used to modify the characteristics of an object. For example, the Taskbar's pop-up menu contains the choice **Properties** that can be used to change the way it behaves
- an object's actions are contained in its pop-up menu. For example, a Desktop icon's actions are listed in the pop-up menu that appears when it is right-clicked (see Figure 5.2b).

> **Note** — Right-click means use your right mouse button to click something rather than the left mouse button

*Use the right mouse button to drag the **My computer** icon across your Desktop. When you release the mouse button a pop-up menu appears with the actions that you can apply to the document. Select **Cancel** to restore the icon to its original position (the move action is cancelled). This completes the exercise!*

Chapter 5　Mouse and keyboard skills

Figure 5.2
Right button operations

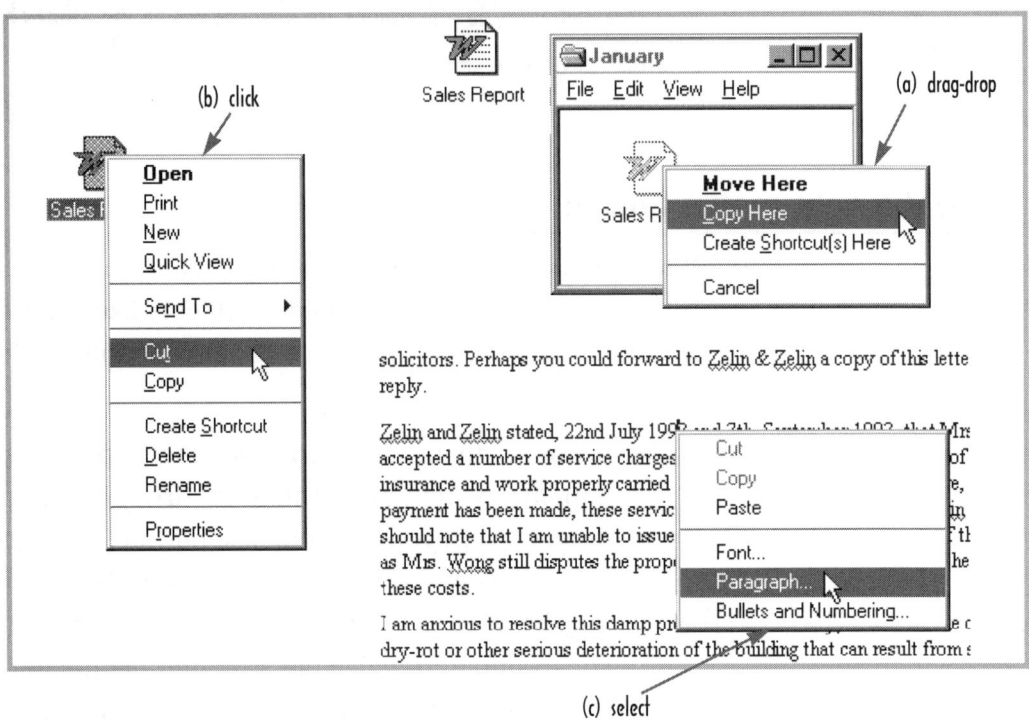

(b) click
(a) drag-drop
(c) select

Mouse pointers

The mouse pointer is most often used to direct where a selection or an action is applied on your Desktop or within a window. However the mouse pointer when moved over certain things can also bring about its own response.

Point to the **Start** *button on the Taskbar — after a few seconds a small box appears telling you what it does. Move the pointer and the box disappears.*

Figure 5.3
Start button and Word menu bar pop-up windows

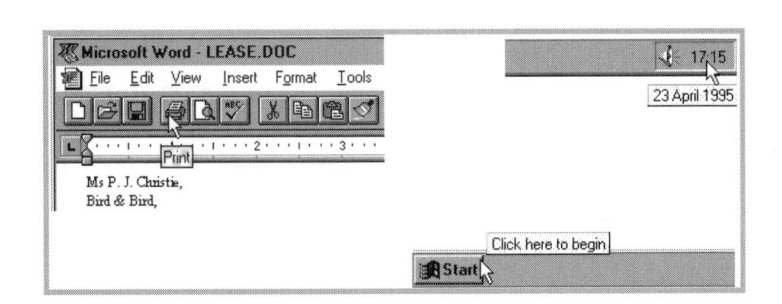

98   Chapter 5   Mouse and keyboard skills

> **Note**
>
> Many objects on your Desktop (or within its windows) have similar pop-up boxes to supply hints about their purposes

Mouse pointer shape reflects function

Moving the mouse pointer over other things on your Desktop changes its shape. The shape of the pointer reflects the type of action that can be applied to the object beneath it. Some common cursor shapes are shown in Figure 5.4.

> **Note**
>
> Some actions can only be performed when the pointer has assumed the correct shape — you cannot resize a window until the pointer has changed to a double headed arrow

1. *Open the* **Control Panel** *window from your Taskbar (***Start↪Settings↪Control Panel***) then double-click the mouse icon to open a property sheet, entitled* **Mouse Properties.** *Click the tab labelled* **Pointers** *to bring this page to the forefront then identify the various pointer shapes which are shown in Figure 5.4.*

2. *Close both the property sheet and* **Control Panel** *window — this exercise is complete.*

Figure 5.4
Common pointer shapes

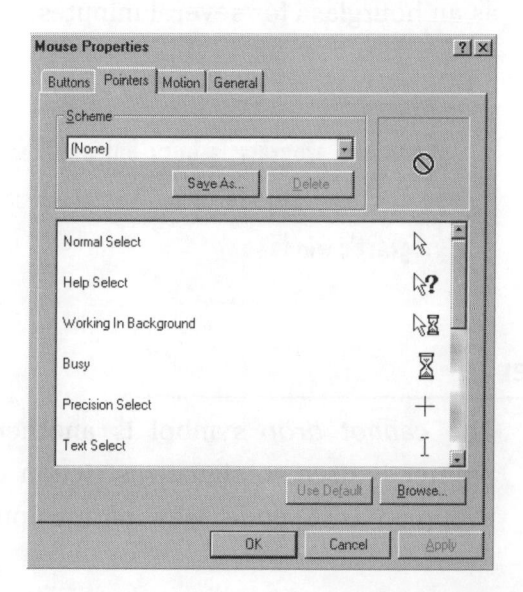

Chapter 5

> **Note:** The tip of the standard mouse pointer is called its hot-spot as it is the tip that activates the object beneath the pointer — this is useful when pointing or selecting small objects

Hourglass pointer

The mouse pointer indicates what sort of actions can be applied to things on your Desktop. When your system is busy and unable to perform any more actions, the pointer reflects this temporary situation by changing into an hourglass ⌛. Most modern PCs are so powerful that this busy state should not last for more than a few seconds.

The pointer sometimes assumes the shape of a pointer combined with an hourglass. This indicates that some of the actions you may wish to apply will have to wait for a part of the system that is currently busy — meanwhile other actions can be applied with immediate effect.

When a program performs a lengthy task it usually displays a message box rather than keeping the mouse pointer as an hourglass for several minutes.

> **Note:** When one program is busy but another is not, then the mouse pointer may change to an hourglass only while over the busy program's windows

Cannot drop pointer

The *cannot drop* symbol is another way that the mouse pointer is used to signal restriction of action. Dragging and dropping is a good way of manipulating things on your

Desktop or within windows, but what happens when you drag the object over something on which it cannot be dropped?

The cursor changes into the cannot drop symbol ⊘ when it is over an area that cannot accept the object you are dragging — the object is simply restored to its starting position if you release the mouse button at that point.

The help pointer

Many dialog windows provide a **Help** button that changes the mouse pointer into a help pointer ▷?. This pointer can be used to open a help window containing information about specific items within your window.

To obtain assistance about something in the window (or a dialog box) simply press the **Help** button, move the help pointer ▷? over the object, then press your left mouse button to open the Windows 95 help window. This will contain a topic relevant to whatever you were pointing at — *context-sensitive help.*

1   *Start Word from the Taskbar (***Start↪Programs↪Microsoft Office↪Microsoft Word***) and press the* **Help** *button at the far right of its toolbar — your mouse pointer changes shape into the* **Help** *pointer ▷?.*

2   *Move the* **Help** *pointer ▷? over the close button in Word's main window then click to open the Windows 95 help window with a topic describing how to use this button — the mouse pointer returns to its normal shape. Read the help topic as you would any other document in a window.*

3   *Close the help window then close Word's main window — this exercise is complete!*

Tip

Further details of using the Windows 95 Help window are given in Appendix A

Chapter 5

Keyboard skills

This section describes how you can use the keyboard to operate your programs and Desktop as well as enter text.

Note

> The control panel contains settings that allow you to adjust the responsiveness of the keyboard to your typing skills (see page 397)

Moving the focus between windows — [Alt] + [Tab]

Although your Desktop may contain many windows and controls, your actions are applied to a specific object — the one that has obtained the Desktop's input *focus*. In this way text is typed into just one window, pressing [Enter] operates only one push-button, and so forth.

Operating your Desktop with a mouse is easy — point at the object and click: the focus automatically moves to that object. However you can also use your keyboard to move the focus between different objects on your Desktop.

Open a number of windows on your Desktop (i.e. Word, WordPad, My Computer) then press the [Alt]+[Tab] keys to move your focus between them (see Chapter 2). Close the windows — this exercise is complete.

Note

> [Alt]+[Tab] means press and hold down the 'Alt' key while pressing the 'tab' key – release both keys when the action has been performed

Moving between controls — [Tab]

Pressing [Tab] by itself moves the focus in a defined order between the various controls in a dialog box or property sheet — usually left to right and from the top to the bottom. Each control has its own way of showing that it has the input focus.

You can reverse the normal direction in which the focus moves between control by holding down [Shift] while pressing [Tab].

> **Note**
>
> Pressing [Tab] in an edit box often moves the focus to another control rather than inserting a tab into the text

Aligning columns of text or figures — [Tab]

Documents sometimes contain things that must be vertically aligned e.g. figures forming the columns of a list. It is often difficult to correctly adjust the spacing of lines in such tables because each character has a different width. However by inserting tabs rather than spaces between the different columns, the items in your list can be aligned by their distance from the margin.

1 *Start Word from the Taskbar (***Start**↪**Programs**↪**Microsoft Office**↪**Microsoft Word***) and choose* **Format**↪**Tabs** *to open a dialog box that permits you to specify the position and alignment of each tab character in your current paragraph.*

2 *Enter* 1 *in the* **Tab Stop Position** *box then press the* **Set** *push-button to specify that the first tab in the line will move the cursor one inch from the left margin. Repeat this operation to define a tab location for the start of each column in your table. Press* **OK** *to close the dialog box and return to Word's document window.*

3 *Type the first line of your list, pressing* [Tab] *to separate the text into different columns. At the end of the line, press* [Enter] *and start the next row of the list — continue in this way until the table is complete.*

> **Tip**
>
> Other methods of aligning text in tables are described later in Chapter 9

Typing capitals — [Shift]

When [Shift] is pressed any letters typed from the keyboard will be entered into your document as capitals. Pressing any key in the main keyboard that has two symbols on its key top will cause the lower symbol to be entered into your document unless you are holding down [Shift] while striking the key.

> **Note**
> The upper symbols in the numeric keypad, located right of your main keyboard, are entered only when you press the key while *Num Lock* is active (see *Keyboard locks*)

Removing characters — [Delete] or [←]

The [Delete] key removes the character immediately in front of the cursor position. The *backspace* key [←] removes the character immediately behind the cursor position. The remaining characters shuffle back to fill the gap.

> **Caution**
> Selected text is replaced by any character typed at the keyboard — this is the default action of most of the keys on your keyboard

Pressing OK — [Enter]

The function of the [Enter] key depends on your context — while typing a document it inserts a new paragraph; while completing a dialog box it can have the same effect as pressing OK. The operation of push-buttons and other Windows 95 controls is described in Appendix B.

> **Tip**
> Dialog boxes often have a default push-button with a border that is bolder than other buttons — this is the button pressed when you press your keyboard's [Enter] key

Cancel — [Esc]

The [Esc] (escape) key is located at the top left hand side of your keyboard and often acts to cancel an action that you have started but not completed:

> when you have activated the menu bar by pressing [Alt], press [Esc] to return the keyboard's focus back to your document so that you can continue typing

> press [Esc] instead of pressing the **Cancel** button to close a dialog box without completing an action.

Accessing the menu bar — [Alt]

The problem of using the keyboard and mouse together is that moving your hands off the keyboard to operate the mouse will disturb the rhythm of your typing. There are two distinct ways of performing actions from the keyboard:

> pressing [Alt] to activate the menu bar followed by the keys that correspond to underlined letters in the menus and their headings (i.e. press [Alt]+[F] to open the **File** menu)

> using special key combinations to shortcut certain menu bar actions (i.e. press [Ctrl]+[P] to replicate **File↪Print** and print your document).

Almost all actions can be performed using either the keyboard or mouse. It is often much faster to use the keyboard if you are already typing.

4   *Press [Alt]+[E] to reveal Word's **Edit** menu then press [L] to select all the text in your document (both **e** and **l** were underlined). Remove this selection by selecting something else — click on an individual letter with the mouse.*

Tip

> Cancel a menu by pressing [Esc] once to hide the menu, then pressing it again to deactivate the menu bar and return the focus to your document window

Chapter 5

Keyboard shortcuts — [Ctrl]

Applying an action through the menu can be tedious, particularly if the action is commonly performed. Most menus provide shortcuts to such actions that can be applied directly from the keyboard. The keys that must be pressed to apply the shortcut are shown to the right of the equivalent menu action.

5   *Press [Ctrl]+[A] to select all the text in your document. Remove this selection by selecting something else — click on an individual letter with the mouse. Close Word's main window (don't save changes) to complete this exercise.*

Thus in Word's Edit menu the shortcut to **Edit↪Cut** is [Ctrl]+[X] — pressing both [Ctrl] and [X] at the same time will cut the text you have selected to the Windows 95 clipboard. Common shortcuts are shown in Table 5.4.

Figure 5.5
Activating the menu from your keyboard

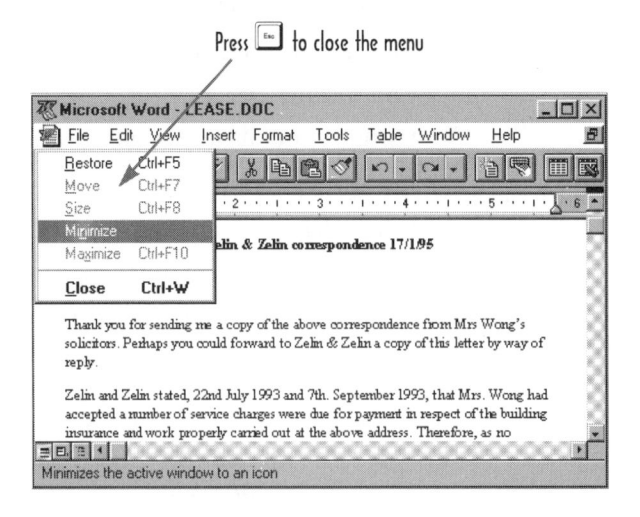

Press [Esc] to close the menu

> **Tip**
>
> Word allows you to add your own keyboard shortcuts for menu actions — choose Tools↪Customize — then reveal the Keyboard page

106   Chapter 5   Mouse and keyboard skills

Table 5.4
Standard keyboard shortcuts

Menu action	Shortcut	Description
File↪New	Ctrl + N	opens new document window
File↪Save	Ctrl + S	saves document to its file
File↪Print	Ctrl + P	prints document
Edit↪Cut	Ctrl + X	cuts selection to Clipboard
Edit↪Copy	Ctrl + C	copies selection to Clipboard
Edit↪Paste	Ctrl + V	copies Clipboard to document
Help↪Contents	F1	opens the help window

Keyboard locks — Shift Lock, Num Lock, Scroll Lock

There are three keyboard lock keys that set the keyboard into a special mode. They each have a indicator on your keyboard (as well as within the status bars of many windows) to show when they are active. You can avoid accidentally applying a keyboard lock by changing Windows 95 settings so that a distinctive beep is made by your PC whenever these keys are pressed.

Table 5.5
Keyboard locks

Key	Active	Inactive
Caps Lock	letter keys produce capitals unless Shift key is pressed	letter keys produce lower-case letters unless Shift key is pressed
Num Lock	keys in the numeric keypad type numbers	keys in the numeric keypad move the cursor
Scroll lock	using the cursor keys moves the document in its window, not the cursor	the cursor keys (↑, ↓, ←, → arrows) moves the cursor, not the document

1. Press and hold down the Num Lock key for more than five seconds to bring-up the **Toggle Keys** dialog box. Press Enter to close the box and apply the feature.

2. Remove the **Toggle Keys** feature by pressing the Num Lock key for more than five seconds — this completes the exercise!

> **Tip:** A lock is applied by pressing the key once and is released when the key is pressed again

Function keys — press F1 for help

You can usually start the Windows 95 help system simply by pressing the F1 key. The help topic displayed will depend on what you were doing when the button was pressed — it is context-sensitive help.

> **Note:** Windows 95 help system is described in Appendix A

Microsoft has reserved the F1 key for activing the help system so that this facility works from *all* application programs as well as from your Desktop.

Using the keyboard to move and select

While your mouse provides the primary means to move and select objects on your Desktop, there are occasions when the keyboard can assist with these tasks.

Extending selection — Ctrl and click

Selecting something with your mouse is a matter of placing the pointer over it and pressing one of the mouse buttons. However, selecting more than one object requires you to press the Ctrl key while clicking (or dragging) with your mouse — this stops the deselection of the first object when you select the second.

Cursor keys — ←, →, ↑ and ↓ arrow keys

The cursor keys are located between the main keyboard and the numeric keypad. These keys move the location of the cursor within a document.

> **Note:** When Scroll Lock is applied the cursor keys move the document within a window without changing the cursor position (see Chapter 2, *Scrolling*)

Keyboard selection — Shift and cursor keys

Pressing Shift while pressing a cursor arrow key selects text between the cursor position and the direction of the arrow on the cursor key. The ← and → cursor keys move this selection one character at a time, while the ↑ and ↓ cursor keys move the selection a line at a time.

Page scrolling — Page Up and Page Down keys

The Page Up (page up) and Page Down (page down) keys are located above the cursor keys, between the main keyboard and the numeric keypad. The Page Up key moves the document within its window so that information further up the page is displayed, while the Page Down key reveals information further down the page.

> **Note:** Each application determines how far Page Up or Page Down moves a document within its window

Switching between programs

Several keys, when pressed in combination, allow you to operate Windows 95 from the keyboard rather than by using the mouse. Some are listed in Table 5.6, and others are shown in Figure 5.6.

Table 5.6
Operating Windows 95 from the keyboard

Keys	Action
Alt + Tab	lists windows that are open on your Desktop
Ctrl + Esc	opens the Taskbar's **Start** menu

Figure 5.6
Key combinations that control your Desktop

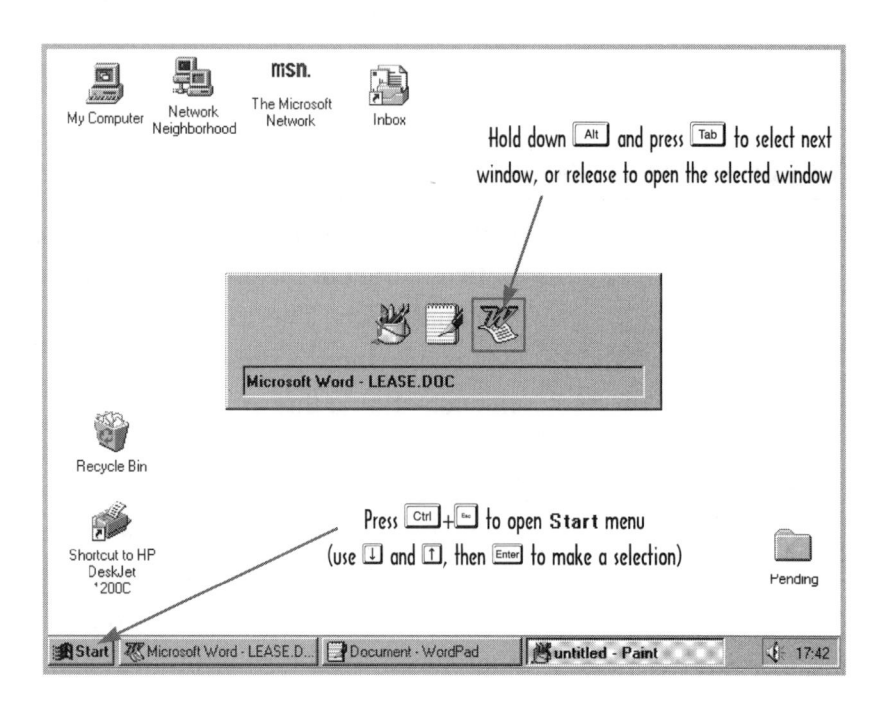

Hold down Alt and press Tab to select next window, or release to open the selected window

Press Ctrl + Esc to open **Start** menu (use ↓ and ↑, then Enter to make a selection)

> Appendix C lists the keyboard shortcuts which help you use Windows 95 more efficiently

Tip

You should now have a better understanding about the way you can use Windows 95, so tidy up your Desktop before starting the next chapter.

*Tidy up your desktop and shut down Windows 95 (***Start**↪**Shut Down***), as described in Chapter 2.*

What is better, mouse or keyboard?

The mouse may be the best means of manipulating and controlling things on your Desktop but it is not the *primary* means of entering information into your computer — this is the job of the keyboard.

Windows 95 always fits around the way you work, so while an author might prefer using the keyboard, a graphic designer might find it more convenient to use the mouse. They are both ways of using Windows 95 effectively.

Note

One of the features of Windows 95 is that there are often several ways to achieve the same goal

Chapter 5

Summary

- Use the mouse to select objects and apply actions to them — for instance, make text appear bold by first selecting it with your mouse then applying an action from the **Format** menu.
- Click the left mouse button once to *select* or *press* things, and twice in quick succession (double-click) to apply its default action.
- Hold the left button down while moving the mouse to drag something or select a group of objects. Release the mouse button to drop the object (and make something happen).
- Point at something then use the right mouse button to open a pop-up menu containing actions that can be applied to it. Drag objects using your right mouse button if you want to choose an action from its pop-up menu when it is dropped.
- The mouse pointer's shape reflects the type of operations that you can apply — the hourglass ⌛, say, indicates that your computer is busy.
- Your keyboard provides the means to enter text but it can also be used as a *shortcut* to many mouse operations. As examples, press [Alt] to activate the menu bar and [Esc] to deactivate it.
- Press [Ctrl] while clicking to select more than one object from a list or collection.

Chapter 6

Storing your work in files and folders

Objectives

You can store your work in the Windows 95 file system so that when you turn off your computer the information is not lost. This chapter covers the following:

- ▷ how documents are filed in Windows 95 — discover the way documents are arranged in files, folders and drives

- ▷ naming your files and folders — rules for naming drives, files and folders

- ▷ organising your own filing system — create folders for your documents

- ▷ storing a document in a file — use the **Save** dialog box to store documents as files on your hard disk

- ▷ restoring a document from a file — use the **Open** dialog box to restore a document from its file, wildcards

- ▷ protecting documents from alteration — read-only files

- ▷ recovering documents after a power-cut or disaster.

After reading this chapter you will know how to store documents created with programs like Word, so that you can recover them later.

Chapter 6

How documents are filed in Windows 95

Windows 95 allows you to store documents on your PC using files and folders much like an office filing system.

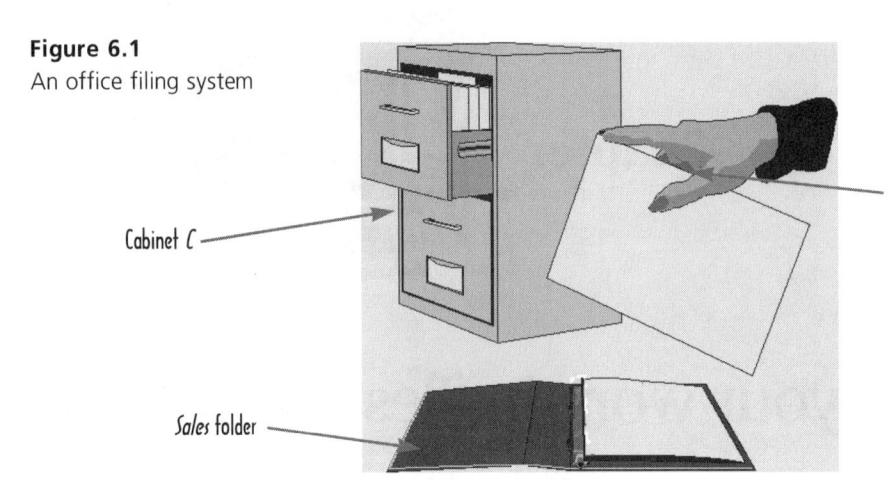

Figure 6.1
An office filing system

Cabinet C

Sales folder

Report named:
C\Sales\Summary July 94

A filing system is essentially a way of classifying information — the report in Figure 6.1 is called *C\Sales\Summary July 94* as it came from the *Sales* folder in filing cabinet *C*. Classifying files in this way has a number of advantages:

- the file reference describes a file's category and any sub-category — a file's location tells you something about its content
- a file can be easily found by looking in the appropriate folder, even if you don't know its precise name
- the filing system can be extended to create new categories and sub-categories simply by inserting fresh folders into the existing folders.

Complex collections of things are often much easier to use when they are grouped into such *hierarchies*. Everyday examples of hierarchies include; books in a library and people in an organization. The Windows 95 filing system is formed by combining the following basic components into a hierarchy that resembles an office filing system:

> drives — the physical devices where files and folders are stored. Each drive has at least one folder, its *root*
> folders — stacked one inside the other, they form a hierarchy to contain your collection of files
> files — contain individual documents classified according to the folders in which they are contained.

Figure 6.2
The hierarchical Windows 95 filing system

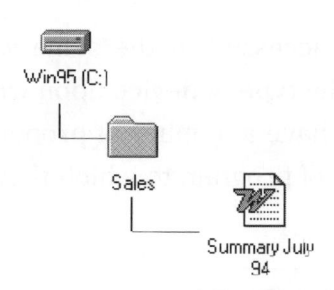

Win95 (C:)
 └ Sales
    └ Summary July 94

To make full use of the Windows 95 file system you need to understand the nature of its basic components — files, folders and drives.

Files

Definition

file . . . . collection of related data, like a document, that is recorded on storage devices such as floppy disk drives, hard disk drives or CD-ROM players (see *Storage devices*)

Files are used to store documents. They take many different forms, but fundamentally files are just an ordered collection of information.
> a letter or report is a collection of characters that form words, sentences and paragraphs
> a drawing is a collection of shapes (with attributes such as size and colour) that form the components of a picture
> a photograph is a collection of related coloured dots.

Therefore, as a document is no more than a sequence of data you can store it as a series of bytes within a computer file.

> **Note**
>
> Programs are also stored in files as a sequence of bytes — its instructions and data

All files are accessed in the same way, irrespective of the location or the type of device upon which they are physically stored. Files have a number of properties such as name, size and the type of program to which they belong.

Table 6.1 The properties of some documents stored on the authors' PC

Icon and label	File description	Document type	Size (kilobytes)
Sales letter	letter — 1 page	Word	20
Summary July 94	report — 50 pages	Word	60
Sales Analysis	spreadsheet (10 cols, 30 rows)	Excel	20
Sales Presentation	presentation — 10 slides	PowerPoint	30
Img0015	a colour photograph	Photo-CD	3,500

> **Note**
>
> The size of a file is measured in bytes. A single byte is just big enough to contain a single character. There are 1024 bytes in a kilobyte (Kb) and 1024 kilobytes in a megabyte (Mb)

The size of your files and their other properties can be viewed from the **My Computer** window, as described in Chapter 14.

Folders

Definition

> *folder* . . . . .container for files (or other folders) recorded on a storage device. Folders (also termed *directories*) provide the means to categorize your files into related groups

Files are contained within folders in your PC in the same way that related documents are kept together within a cardboard folder in an office filing cabinet. However the folders created on your computer have the advantage of being able to hold as many other folders and files as you wish; the only constraint is the capacity of the storage device. Thus, you can build a hierarchy of folders, one inside the other, in which you can classify all your documents.

Table 6.2
Properties of some folders found on the authors' PC

Icon and label	Folder description	Contents	
		Files	Folders
	root folder	25	3
Work	folder containing authors' working documents	45	0
Windows	folder containing Windows 95 programs and data files	1,242	47
Msoffice	folder containing Word, Excel and PowerPoint folders	142	8
Winword	folder containing Word's program files and data	114	5

Folders, like files, have a number of properties. Further information about the properties of a folder can be obtained from the **My Computer** View window, as described later in the book (see Chapter 14).

Chapter 6

> **Note:** *Directories* is an older term for *folders* and is often used in documentation — the two terms are interchangeable

Storage devices — drives

> **Definition:** *drive* . . . . a physical storage device for computer files that can be accessed by your PC (e.g. hard disk, floppy disk or CD-ROM)

Figure 6.3
My Computer window

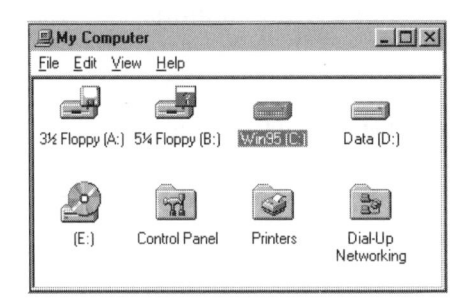

A list of the storage devices currently available to your computer is given in the **My Computer** window which can be opened from your Desktop. Depending upon how your computer was installed it may have different types and numbers of storage devices.

1. Double-click the icon labelled **My Computer** on your Desktop to open its window.

> **Tip:** Select a floppy disk drive (A or B) in the **My Computer** window then choose File→Format from its menu bar in order prepare a blank disk for storing files and folders

118 Chapter 6 Storing your work in files and folders

Some drives use media such as floppy disks or CD-ROMs that can be removed from your PC, but others contain disks that are fixed inside the drive mechanism — a hard disk. However, you do not need to understand the mechanics of each storage device in your computer — they are all operated from your Desktop in the same way.

Definition

CD-ROM . . . . .a compact disc (CD) that contains computer files rather than recorded music. Your computer's CD-ROM player looks like a normal CD player and even plays music CDs

Hard disk drives contain fixed disks which offer a much better performance than floppy disk drives (or CD-ROM players), and therefore are used for storing the files that you access most often — program files and the documents you are working on. However, when you have finished with a file on your hard disk you might wish to reclaim the space it occupies by moving the file onto a floppy disk which can then be removed from your PC.

Table 6.3
Properties of the drives in the authors' PC

Icon	Storage device	Capacity	
		megabytes	single page documents
3½ Floppy (A:)	Floppy disk 3.5"	1.44	75
Win95 (C:)	Hard disk	200	10,000
(E:)	CD-ROM	500	25,000

The capacity of a drive describes the amount of information that can be stored on a disk and is measured in megabytes. However you may find it more meaningful to consider the

Chapter 6 Storing your work in files and folders

number of documents that you can store on a disk. The figures given in Table 6.3 are based on the size of a single page Word document, like the one created in Chapter 3. Drives, like folders and files, also have properties that can be displayed from the **My Computer** View window described in Chapter 14.

Viewing the files and folders in your drives

Each drive contains a collection of files and folders arranged into a hierarchy. However, when you first open a drive's View window only the top level of this hierarchy is shown — to see the next level you must open one of the folders it contains.

2   *Double click drive* **C:** *in the* **My Computer** *View window to open a further View window displaying the contents of this drive's* root *folder — its top level folder.*

3   *Double-click any of the folders displayed within this top level View window to open further View windows containing files and folders stored at the lower levels of drive* **C:**.

Each View window belongs to a particular folder and displays the files as well as the folders contained at that level in the filing system hierarchy. Browsing through the contents of a particular drive is easy — just open each folder's View window as you progress from the upper to lower levels.

Definition   *root* . . . . the top level in a drive's folder hierarchy from which all other (lower level) folders form *branches* like an inverted tree

---

The branches needed to reach a particular file form a pathname which can be displayed in the title bar of its folder's View window.

Finding files on a drive is like climbing an apple tree. You start at the root of the tree and reach for the lowest branch, once on a branch you climb to further branches until you can grasp a particular apple. Once you have collected all the apples within reach from that branch you must climb down the tree and find another branch.

Each apple in the tree can be reached by climbing through a particular path of branches. The larger the tree, the more branches, then the more apples it will contain — but no one branch can be used to reach every apple!

All files and folders are ultimately contained within the root folder. You can find any file on the drive by starting at the root folder and searching down through each folder in turn until the file is found.

Figure 6.4
View window describes file names and location

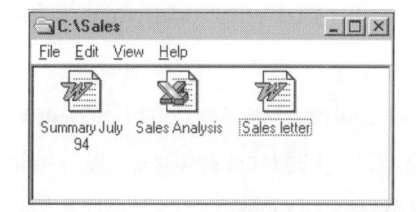

4   Choose **View→Options** *from any View window's menu bar to display its property sheet, then click on the* **View** *tab to show the page of view options. Insert a tick in the box labelled* **Display the full MS-DOS path in the title bar** *(in other words, just click it) and close the property sheet by pressing* **OK**.

You may have already realized that the location and name of a file can be described in a way that is very similar to the index system in an office filing system.

Figure 6.5
File and folder naming

C:\SALES\SUMMARY JULY 94

This naming system allows you to describe your files in terms of their position in a hierarchy of folders — irrespective of the type and location of the underlying drive mechanism. However there are some rules about the way Windows 95 names its files and folders that need further explanation.

Naming your drives, files and folders

Chapter 6

Windows 95 applies certain restrictions to the naming of drives, files and folders.

Note

> The \ character is used to separate the individual names of drives, folders and files, e.g. c:\folder1\folder2\file

Drive names — C:

Each drive that can be accessed by your computer has a name formed from a letter (A through to Z) followed by a colon. While the names allocated to drives need not be sequential, some letters have special significance:

- A: (or B:) always refers to the floppy disk drive, not the actual disk inserted into the device
- C: refers to your computer's hard disk drive.

Caution

> Do not confuse the label given to a drive (Win 95) with its name (C:). The label serves solely to help you identify the device whereas the name is used to access a file or folder

The drives located in your own computer, like drive C:, always keep the letter that was assigned to them during the set-up of your PC. Such drives are termed *local* drives to differentiate them from the *network* drives that may also be accessible.

Note

> If your computer is connected to other computers you may be able to access remote or network drives that are not physically located in your PC (see Chapters 15 and 16)

File and folder names — Summary July 94

A name is used to uniquely identify a file (or folder) in a given location. This gives rise to the first rule:

- names must be unique within a given context — two

files in the same folder cannot share the same name. There is, however, no reason why the same name cannot be used in *different* directories or drives.

Names are made up from a specific range of characters:

- any uppercase letter — A through to Z
- any lowercase letter — a through to z
- any number — 0 through to 9
- any of the following characters — ! # $ % ^ & ( ) - _ { } ~
- a space.

While names can include a wide range of characters (including spaces) there are a few symbols, such as the colon and backslash, that are reserved by Windows 95.

The maximum length of any file or folder name is 256 characters.

Windows 95 permits long names to be assigned to folders and files that are descriptive of their content, but there is an upper limit to the length of a name.

> **Note**
> When naming a file or folder try to use a name that is short but meaningful – a name that relates to its contents

The Windows 95 naming system for files and folders is more flexible than the system that applied in earlier versions, such as Windows 3.1. In particular, you can use longer and more meaningful names — some examples are shown in Table 6.4.

Table 6.4
File names — Windows 95 vs. Windows 3.1

Windows 95	Windows 3.1
C:\Sales\Summary July 94	C:\SALES\JULY94.DOC
Balance Sheet rev 09 — draft	BAL09D.XLS
Computer Contractors' Info.	COMPCONT

5 *Close all the View windows by clicking their close buttons* ☒ *at top right of each window — this exercise is complete.*

> **Note**
> Some knowledge of the MS-DOS naming convention is important if you need to use older files, or files created by people who are still using it

Chapter 6 Storing your work in files and folders   123

Chapter 6

Referencing files and folders — C:\Sales\Summary July 94

Referencing a file within a hierarchy of folders can produce an extremely long pathname as the various folder names are strung together.

The maximum length of a pathname is 256 characters, starting from the character after the drive name (e.g. **C:**) and ending before the terminating \ of the last folder's name. Therefore you must use less than 256 characters when describing a path to a file within a set of folders.

Figure 6.6
The format of a path and filename

Drive	Path	Filename
C:\Sales	.....\Summary July 94	....
1 .... .256		
	1 .... .256	
Win95 (C:)	Sales	Summary July 94

Note

> When you access a file or folder stored on another computer you must also specify the name of the computer — see page 334

The limit to the length of a pathname means that the depth of your file hierarchy is restricted by the names you have used for your folders — short folder names allow you to create more levels. However, it is rarely necessary to create more than four levels of folders, or use names longer than 64 characters.

Note

> The entire plant kingdom can be adequately classified within four levels of folders — *genus, sub-genus, species, varieties*

Organizing your own filing system

Your computer already has a number of folders that contain files related to Windows 95 and the other programs installed on your machine. However it is inadvisable to use these folders for storing your own files as they can quickly become cluttered with dozens of unrelated files — defeating the purpose of a filing system.

Creating your own system of classification allows you to group files into folders according to their content. For example, all the documents about bad debtors can be kept in the **bad debt** folder; this is good practice in any office.

Creating folders

You should give some consideration to the name and location of any new folder before inserting it into your existing collection of folders. It is not difficult to decide such matters once you have created a set of folders to reflect the way you work, for example you might structure your folders on the following basis:

- start your set of folders from the root folder of a drive containing similar files (e.g. **C:**)
- create a personal folder named after yourself (e.g. **bill**) if the **C:** drive is used by other people
- create working folders within your personal folder using names that correspond to natures of your work (e.g. *memos*, *special projects*, *reports*, *work*)
- within your working folders create further folders for files created over a particular period (e.g. *May 94, 21-11-94*) or for different copies of the same document (e.g. *Draft, Proof, Final*).

Windows 95 also allows you to create folders from your own Desktop, this is described in Chapter 13.

Tip

> Create a folder (e.g. *temp*) for storing copies of files you do not need to keep in the long term, so you can reclaim disk space by regularly erasing all the files in this folder

Chapter 6

The need to organize your files into separate folders should be balanced against the total number of files that you anticipate will be created. Start with a few basic folders and add more as the need arises, so that no more than twenty or thirty files are stored in any one folder.

1. *Open the **My Computer** View window from your Desktop then double-click the drive **C:** icon to open a further View window. Choose **File→New→Folder** from the menu bar of this second View window to make a new folder appear in its window — this folder is highlighted and labelled **New Folder**.*

2. *Rename this **New Folder** simply by typing **bill** then pressing [Enter] — text that has been selected is always replaced by your first keystroke.*

3. *Double-click the folder you have just created (**bill**) to open its View window. Now create a further new folder called **work** within the folder named **bill** (repeat steps 1 and 2).*

> **Tip**
>
> The new style Windows 95 **Open** and **Save As** dialog boxes allow you to create new folders from within a program when you are storing or retrieving a file

Chapter 13 contains further details about organising your files and folders from the Desktop.

Defining a program's working folders

You can often save yourself the trouble of locating your own set of folders with the Windows 95 file system hierarchy by changing a program's setting for its working folder — this is where it expects to find your documents.

4. *Start Word from your Taskbar (**Start→Programs→Microsoft Office→Microsoft Word**) then open its **Options** property sheet by choosing **Tools→Options** from the menu bar. Click on the tab **File Locations** to bring this page to the forefront, then select **Documents** from the list of **File Types**.*

Figure 6.7
Change the location for Word's documents

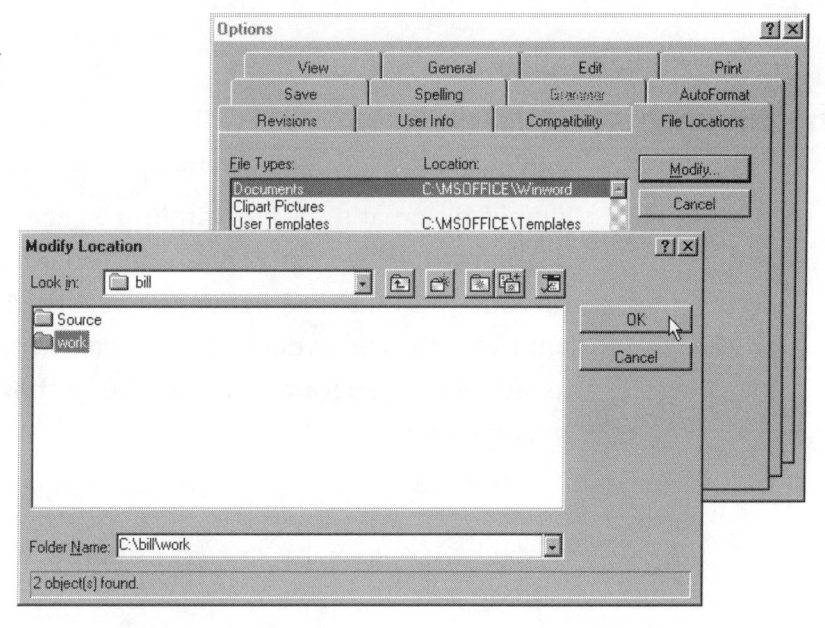

5   Press the **Modify** push-button to open the **Modify Location** dialog box (Figure 6.7) — it shows where Word expects to find your documents.

6   Type **C:\bill\work** into the box labelled **Folder Name** and press **OK** to close the dialog box. Finally press the **Close** push-button in the **Options** property sheet to return to your Word document window.

Henceforth whenever you bring-up the **Save As** or **Open** dialog boxes (described below) your folder **work** will be selected as the current folder in which to save or restore your files.

Definition

working folder . . . . . . the default folder used by a program for saving and restoring its files

Storing a document in a file

The Windows 95 file system provides the means for you to save and restore your work between sessions on the PC. This is a fundamental requirement for any computer and justifies the care we have taken to explain how files and folders are used.

Chapter 6

Saving documents — File↪Save As

You can save a document from a program such as Word simply by creating a file within a specific folder. Once the document has been stored as a file on a particular drive it is there for all time, like live music recorded on cassette tape, until you change or delete it. You can restore this document using your program's **Open** dialog box (see *Restoring documents*).

7 Type some text into Word's document window — this is the information that you will save in a file. Choose **File↪Save As** from Word's menu bar to open the **Save As** dialog box (see Figure 6.8).

Figure 6.8:
Word's **Save As** dialog box

Folder in which you are storing the document

Click to reveal a list of other folders

Look in Favorites

Commands and settings

Word's **Save As** options

Name of the file in which you are storing the document

You have previously set Word's working folder as **work** — a folder contained within your personal folder **bill** on drive **C:** and therefore this folder is automatically opened whenever you choose **File↪Save As** or **File↪Open**. You could create a file for your document within the **work** folder simply by following step 11 (over). However, in case you need to locate your file in a different folder, steps 8, 9 and 10 are provided.

> **Note**
>
> Windows 95 allows you to create folders on your Desktop so the hierarchy of folders extends beyond the drives displayed in your My Computer window back to the Desktop itself

128   Chapter 6   Storing your work in files and folders

8   Click the button at the right side of the control labeled **Save in** (top of the dialog box) to reveal a list of folders arranged as a hierarchy back to your Desktop. Click **Desktop** (top) to close the list and display its contents in your **Save As** dialog box.

9   Select the icon **My Computer** (click it) which is now displayed in the dialog box then press the button labeled **Open** (above **Cancel**). The dialog box then displays the storage devices located on your own computer (if an error is reported, remove all text from the **File Name** box and try again).

> **Tip**
>
> Select **Network Neighborhood** in place of **My Computer** to store your document on another computer (see Chapter 15)

10 Select the icon representing drive **C** and press **Open** to display the folders held within its root folder. Select **bill** and once more press **Open** to display your **work** folder. At last you have found the folder for your document, so select it and press **Open** again — **work** appears in the **Save in** control.

11 Type **Junk** into the **File Name** box — this names the file that will be created to store the contents of your document window. Press **OK** to close the dialog box and create the file.

> **Note**
>
> Your document has been stored in a file named **Junk** located in the folder **work** that is contained in your personal folder named **bill** on drive **C:**

A message box will appear if a file with the same name already exists in your selected folder. You may decide to overwrite this existing file, or cancel the action so that you can go back (step 11) and give your file an alternative name.

12 Close Word's main window — you will not be prompted to save changes. This exercise is now complete!

> **Caution**
>
> If you overwrite a file then its original contents are lost and cannot be recovered — a good reason to keep copies of files containing important documents (see Chapter 14)

Chapter 6   Storing your work in files and folders

Updating a file with changes to a document — File⇥Save

Once you have associated a file with a document it can be updated to reflect any changes to the document by simply choosing the action File⇥Save — there is no dialog box to complete. However, if you choose this action when the file has not been specified, then the Save As dialog box is brought-up for you to complete.

Tip

> Save your document as a file immediately after it has been created then regularly perform File⇥Save so that you can recover your file in case of a power-cut or other disaster

Using other features of the Save As dialog box

The Save As dialog box is used by many new Windows 95 programs and therefore provides a consistent way to store your documents. The standard Save As dialog box has a number of features beyond those you have already encountered:

▷ *Move up one level* — press this button to open the folder next highest in the hierarchy

▷ *Create new folder* — press this button to open a further dialog box that permits you to create a new folder (it is located within the folder whose contents are currently displayed in your Save As dialog box)

▷ *List and details* — the dialog box usually uses icons and file (or folder) names to list the contents of a given folder. However by pressing the details button you can also include information about the size, type and modification history of these files and folders (see Chapter 14)

▷ *Save as type* — you will normally want to save your documents in a specific file type — one appropriate for the program that created them. However by changing the setting in this control you can save your documents in a different type of file (see page 147).

Figure 6.9
WordPad's **Save As** dialog box

Folder name - My Computer

Move to the folder in which My Computer is stored

List

Details

Word's **Save As** dialog box builds on the features of the standard dialog box by providing the following additional controls:

▷ *Commands and settings* — press this button to reveal a pop-up menu that permits you to change such things as the order in which items are listed in the dialog box

▷ *Look in favorites* — Windows 95 provides a special folder which contains references (shortcuts) to the folders you use most often. Press this button to open the **Favorites** folder so you can quickly find (then open) the folder you need

▷ **File Name** *list* — press the button attached to the **File Name** box to reveal a list of the previous entries you have typed into this control

▷ *Options* — press this button to open the **Save** page of Word's **Options** property sheet (see page 136).

Tip

> Right click an item listed in the Save As dialog box to reveal a pop-up menu containing actions that can be applied to it (see page 291)

Restoring a document from a file

You can restore a document into your program's window by using the **Open** dialog box (**File**→**Open**) to locate then open the file in which it is stored. The contents of your **work** folder will be displayed in this dialog box when it is first opened (see

Chapter 6 Storing your work in files and folders 131

page 127) so you could go directly from step 1 to step 3 to restore your document **Junk**, created in the previous exercise. However the intermediate step is provided in case you need to find a Word document in a folder that contains many files.

Tip

> At the bottom of the **File** menu is a list of your most recently used documents – you may open any of these documents directly; just click the file name

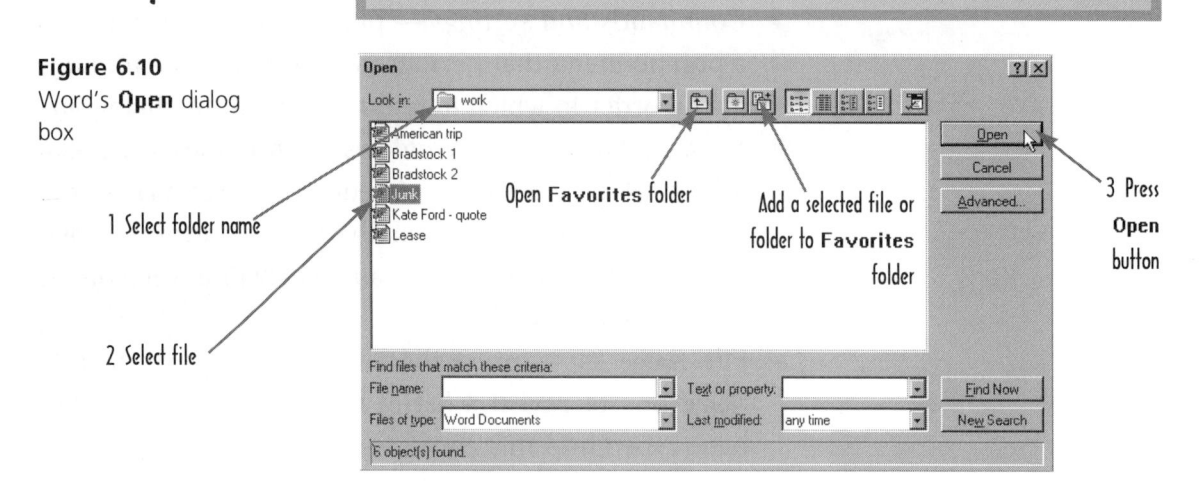

Figure 6.10
Word's **Open** dialog box

1 Select folder name

2 Select file

Open Favorites folder

Add a selected file or folder to **Favorites** folder

3 Press **Open** button

1   Start Word from your Taskbar (**Start↦Programs↦Microsoft Office↦Microsoft Word**) and choose **File↦Open** from its menu bar to bring up the **Open** dialog box.

2   Type **Ju*** into the **File Name** box at the bottom of the dialog box then press **Find Now** — you could also specify other criteria for the search such as the date it was last modified or the text it contains (see Figure 6.10).

When the search is complete the dialog box will display a list of the files in your **work** folder whose names start with **Ju** (* is a *wildcard*, see page 133). The **Advanced** button in the **Open** dialog box accesses a further dialog box from which you can conduct comprehensive searches for files in any folder available to your Desktop — you may wish to investigate this facility after reading Chapter 14.

> **Note**
>
> You can locate a file contained in another folder by following the same procedure as you used in the **Save As** dialog box

3 Select the file **Junk** (click it) then press the **Preview** button to display its contents. Press the **Open** button to restore this document into Word's document window.

You can change the document and store these changes in the file **Junk** simply by choosing **File↪Save** from the menu bar — there is no need to open the **Save As** dialog box unless you wish to create a new file for the revised document.

Matching names in a list — wildcards

It is quite easy to search through a short list of files in order to find the one you want. However when there are *many* files in a folder it can become quite tedious to scroll through a long list searching for your file.

> **Note**
>
> You can type a name directly into the **File Name** box but you must remember its *exact* spelling otherwise it will not be found

A better way of finding files in a long list requires the use of special *wildcard* characters in place of certain letters in your file's name — when you press the **Find Now** button the list is filtered so that only matching names are displayed. This reduces the length of the list to the number of files that share a similar name and therefore makes it much easier to select the file you want.

There are two wildcard characters (see Table 6.5):

▷ ? — any character will match at this position

▷ * — any character and any number of characters after this position will match.

Table 6.5
Wildcard characters

Filter	File Name list after search
*.doc	all files created by Word (or given a similar type name)
temp*	all files starting with the letters 'temp'
?emp	all files whose name has four letters ending with 'emp'
.	all files contained in the folder

> **Note**
>
> You can also find any document's file by searching through all the folders that can be accessed by your PC using the Taskbar's Find facility (see Chapter 14)

Protecting files

When your documents are restored from their files they can be protected against accidental alteration by opening them as *read only* — this means that any changes to the document cannot be written back to the file.

Definition

read . . . . the action of playing back or restoring information stored in a file is often described as *reading*

---

4 *Close the document window containing the contents of* **Junk** *(opened in step 3). Choose* **File→Open** *from Word's menu bar to bring up the* **Open** *dialog box — it displays the contents of your* **work** *folder. Use your right mouse button to reveal the pop-up menu belonging the file named* **Junk** *(right-click its icon) and select the menu choice* **Open Read Only**.

5 *Make some changes to the document then choose* **File→Save** *from Word's menu bar — a message box informs you that the file is read only. You must therefore store the changes you have made to this document in a new file.*

Definition

write . . . . the action of recording or saving information into a file is often described as *writing*. When you save a document into a file that already exists its contents are *over-written*

Word documents can be set so that you are prompted to open them as *read only* documents when restoring them from their files.

6   Open the **Save As** *dialog box by choosing* **File→Save As** *from Word's menu bar. Press the* **Options** *push-button in this dialog box to open a property sheet containing Word's options — it is open at the* **Save** *page. Check the box labelled* **Read Only Recommended** *at the bottom of this page and press* **OK** *to close the property sheet.*

7   *Save the revised document as* **Junk 2** *in the* **work** *folder then close the document window.*

> **Note**
>
> When a read only recommended document is restored, a message box appears asking you to confirm that the document should be opened as a read only document

You can further protect your documents by choosing the following passwords from Word's **Options** property sheet:

- **Write Preservation password** — changes cannot be stored in the file unless you know the password
- **Protection password** — the document cannot be restored unless you know the password. This protects the document from being read by an unauthorized person.

> **Caution**
>
> Once a password has been applied to a document it can only be removed by someone who knows the password – do not forget your passwords!

Recovering documents after a power-cut

Power-cuts and other disasters don't happen too often but when they do occur, you can be assured that it is the vital document that you were just about to **Save** that then makes this event a true catastrophe!

> **Caution**
>
> Frequently save your document in a file and make regular copies (backups) of the file to protect yourself against losing your work

Unless you save your work in a file it will be irretrievably lost when power is removed from your PC. However some programs, like Word, provide protection against such disasters by automatically saving your work on a periodic basis.

8   Re-open the property sheet containing Word's options by choosing **Tools→Options** from the menu bar. Click on the tab **Save** to bring this page to the forefront and insert a cross in the box labelled **Automatic Save** by clicking it. Close the property sheet by clicking **OK** to choose this new setting.

9   Close Word's main window and then tidy-up your Desktop before shutting down Windows 95 (**Start→Shut Down**) — this exercise is complete!

Henceforth, if Word abnormally terminates for any reason then the document you were working on when this calamity occurred will be automatically recovered, up to the last save, the next time you start-up Word.

Figure 6.11
Setting Word's options

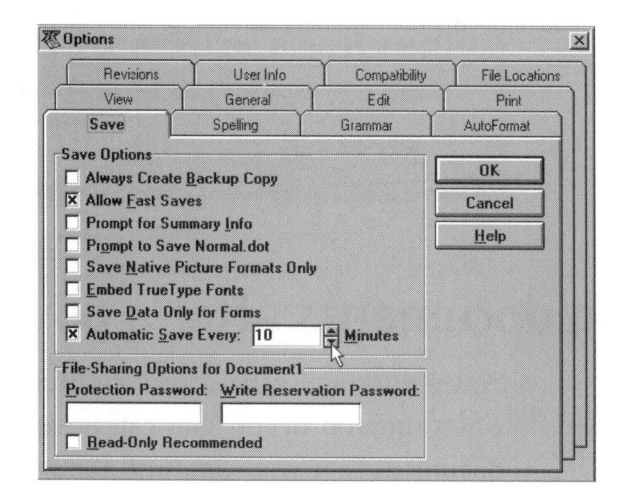

136   Chapter 6   Storing your work in files and folders

Summary

- Documents are stored in files and files are collected together in folders.
- Files and folders are stored on disk drives which may be located on your PC (local drives) or on other computers that are connected to your PC (network drives).
- Files, folders and drives are organized into a hierarchy — like a tree.
- Files can have names as long as 256 characters. Names can be composed of any letters or numbers and certain symbols.
- Create your own structure of folders in which to organize your documents.
- Store a document in a file by choosing **File↪Save** from the program's menu bar. Restore the file by choosing **File↪Open**.
- The wildcards * and ? can be used to find matching names from a list.
- Protect yourself against power-cuts by settings options within your programs that automatically save your documents every ten minutes or so.

Note

Word automatically saves its settings in an internal file so they can be restored between sessions on the computer according to the values you have set

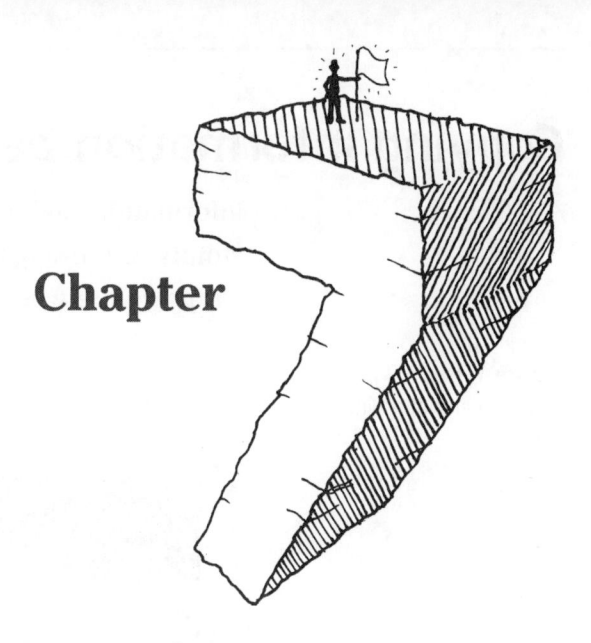

Chapter 7

Transferring information between documents

Objectives

This chapter is concerned with the various ways you can transfer information contained within your documents:

- copying information between documents — drag scraps of text from one document to another, cut and paste information using the Windows 95 Clipboard

- converting files created by one program so they can be opened by another

- embedding Excel files into a Word document — how to put different types of objects into your documents

- linking Excel files into a Word document — insert references to files in order to keep information up-to-date

- inserting pictures into your Word document, editing different types of information within a document

- adding sound to your documents — object packaging.

After reading this chapter you will know how to move and manipulate information between documents so that, for example, you can insert figures from an Excel spreadsheet into a Word document.

Chapter 7

Copying information between documents

Information can be transferred from one document to another simply by dragging it with your mouse (see Chapter 1, *Dragging*) between two windows on your Desktop.

Figure 7.1
Dragging and dropping text

Drag from here

Drop here

1 Use the Taskbar to open WordPad (**Start↪Programs↪Accessories↪WordPad**) and Word (**Start↪Programs↪Microsoft Office↪Microsoft Word**). Arrange the windows of these two programs on your Desktop so that they are both visible.

2 Type some text into the Word document window being careful to keep WordPad's window still visible below it.

3 Select the text you have just typed (drag your mouse across it) then drag it across your Desktop into the WordPad window — the text is copied between the two documents.

Tip

You can also drop the dragged text onto your Desktop to create an icon which can be later dragged into other documents or edited in its own right (see Chapter 13).

Transferring information between documents in this way is possible with some, but not all programs — it depends on their support for a technology called *object linking and embedding* — more usually known as just *OLE* (pronounced "oh-lay").

The Windows 95 Clipboard

Information can also be transferred from one document to another by storing it in an intermediate location — the Windows 95 Clipboard.

Definition

Clipboard . . . . .a storage area within Windows 95 that holds information from various types of documents. It is accessed by the **Cut**, **Copy** and **Paste** actions in a program's **Edit** menu

Because the Clipboard belongs to Windows 95 rather than any individual program, it provides a way of transferring information between different documents as well as between parts of the same document.

Figure 7.2
Cut and **Paste** in action

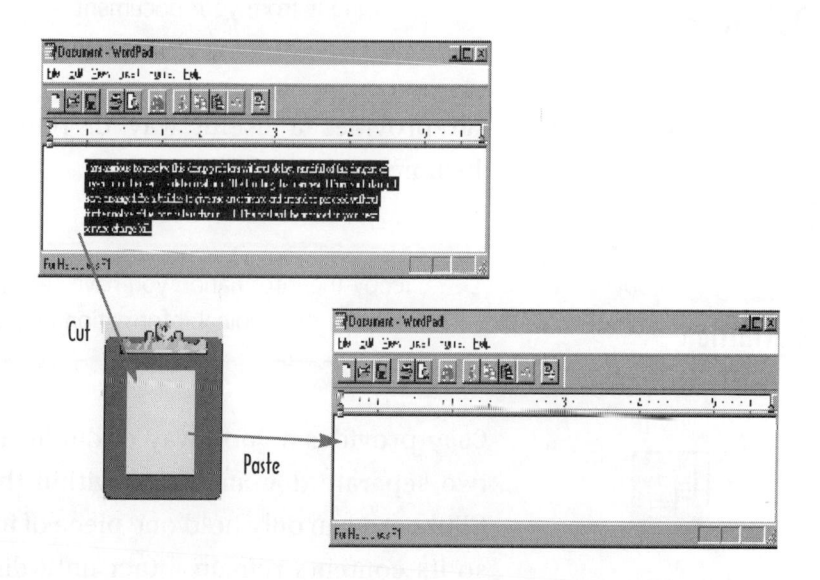

Chapter 7　Transferring information between documents

Chapter 7

> **Note:** The Paste choice is greyed (unavailable) when the Clipboard is empty. The Copy and Cut choices are greyed until you have selected something that can be transferred into the Clipboard

4 *Select part of the text in your Word document window by dragging the mouse across it (keep the left button pressed). Choose* **Edit↪Cut** *from the menu bar to transfer your selection to the Clipboard — it is removed from your document.*

5 *Move the cursor (insertion point) to the beginning of your document by clicking just before the first letter you typed, then choose* **Edit↪Paste** *to copy the contents of the Clipboard into your document at this point. Close Word's main window (don't bother saving the changes).*

6 *Activate the WordPad window (click it) then choose* **Edit↪Paste** *from its menu bar to copy the contents of the Clipboard into your document at its insertion point.*

Definition

cut . . . . .move the information you have selected into the Clipboard erasing it from your document — contrast with *copy*

Cut provides a useful way of removing things from your documents during editing.

Definition

copy . . . . .copy the information you have selected into the Clipboard leaving the original information in place — contrast with *move*

Copy provides a good way of duplicating something between two separate documents or within the same document. The Clipboard can only hold one piece of information at a time and so its contents remain intact until displaced by another **Cut**

(or **Copy**) action from one of your programs.

> **Definition**
>
> *paste* . . . . .copy the contents of the Clipboard into your document at its cursor position or current insertion point

Because the information is copied and not moved, the contents of the Clipboard remain intact ready for further **Paste** actions. It therefore provides an easy way of making several copies of something.

Programs such as Paint (**Start→Programs→Accessories→Paint**) have no obvious insertion point and therefore after a paste action, the object in the Clipboard is positioned at the top left of its window so it can be dragged into place.

What is the Clipboard?

The Clipboard has been defined as some form of storage that is internal to Windows 95 and this is a good description. You do not need to concern yourself with the form the storage takes, just consider it to be like a rubber stamp — cut and copy places information in the stamp, while paste presses it against a sheet of paper to make a copy.

> **Tip**
>
> Once something is held in the Clipboard it is available to every window that has a paste action in its menu bar

What sort of information can the Clipboard handle?

The Clipboard can hold more than just text from a Word document; it can accommodate graphics (in various formats) and figures from an Excel worksheet, as well as objects containing more diverse types of information.

Chapter 7

One of the easiest ways of putting graphics into the Clipboard is to press the [Print Screen] button on your keyboard (usually in the top row, next to the [F12] key). This copies the current image of your entire Desktop into the Clipboard from where it may be pasted into a document.

7   *Press the [Print Screen] key to copy everything you see on your screen into the Clipboard as a graphic image.*

8   *Start Paint from your Taskbar (**Start↪Programs↪ Accessories↪Paint**) then insert this image of your Desktop into its window by choosing **Edit↪Paste**.*

9   *Close both the Paint and WordPad windows — this completes the exercise.*

> **Tip**
>
> Pressing [Alt] + [Print Screen] copies an image of the active window into the Clipboard

Retaining connections between information

The problem with cutting and pasting information from one document to another is that it leaves no connection to the original data, or the program that created it. Often what we would like to do is copy the information from one document to another but leave a connection in place. This would present some interesting possibilities for data taken from an Excel spreadsheet then inserted into a Word document:

- ▷ if you needed to recalculate Excel data while editing the Word document you wouldn't need to go back and reinsert the information from the original file — the connection could tell Word how to edit the information in situ
- ▷ if you changed the Excel data then the connection could automatically update the Word document.

144   Chapter 7   Transferring information between documents

Retaining a connection to the source of the information that has been inserted into your document (and providing a number of services for that connection) represent the objectives of the Windows 95 OLE technology introduced by this chapter.

Figure 7.3
Embedding and linking Information between documents

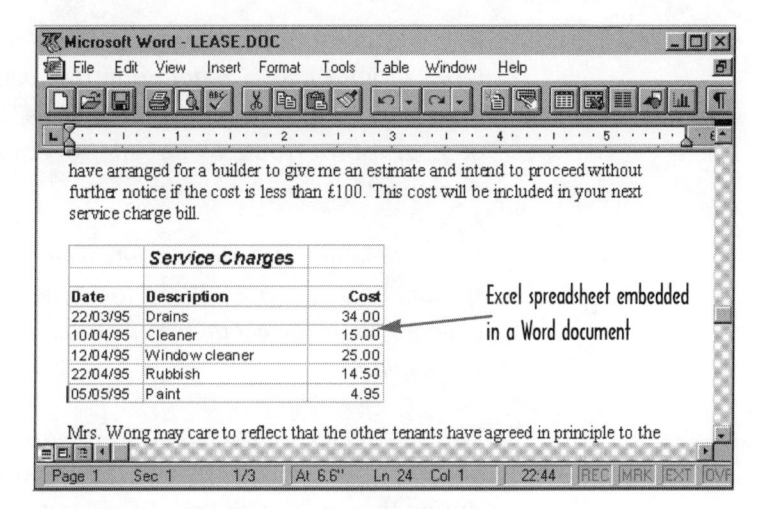

Object linking and embedding is the collective name for a group of technologies associated with handling diverse information on your computer. Microsoft is encouraging software producers to support OLE within their programs so that they can be tightly integrated with other OLE enabled programs on your Desktop.

Ingredients of OLE 2.0 include drop and drop, structured storage, object embedding, object linking, visual editing and automation. The remainder of this chapter describes the parts of OLE 2.0 that you are more likely to encounter while working on your documents.

What does OLE mean to you — how can it help you? Consider the following scenario.

> *You are employed by Deskbase Ltd. to prepare standard business plans for people starting a small business. These plans contain financial projections, site plans, demographic studies as well as written reports. Typically you assemble a business plan from a number of text, spreadsheet and graphic files into one integrated document by:*

Chapter 7

> ▷ converting the text and spreadsheet files produced by your client (using WordStar and Multiplan programs) into Word and Excel documents

> ▷ using your Word document as a container for the various types of information required in the plan. Drawings of the site plan, the results of financial projections, figures and charts from demographic studies can all be embedded into the one document

> ▷ linking your client's financial projections in the Excel spreadsheet to your Word document so that last minute changes to the projections will automatically update the figures in the plan.

> The final plans are contained within a single document that can be electronically sent around the Deskbase computer network during the review process. The Directors of Deskbase can open this document on their Desktop and record their comments next to particular parts of the plan — they use a microphone rather than a keyboard. Reviewing documents in this way avoids costly meetings and allows everyone's thoughts to be recorded directly into the document. Your clients are happy because the Directors give them an answer about their plan within days rather than weeks. You are happy because you get a bonus for each plan that succeeds!

The remainder of this chapter shows how such a scenario can be implemented on your own Desktop.

Converting files created by other programs

> ▷ converting the text and spreadsheet files produced by your client (using WordStar and Multiplan programs) into Word and Excel documents

Windows 95 programs tend to use their own native formats when storing their documents in files. A file's format determines the internal structure of the information it contains and is also a property of the file — its type.

> **Note**
>
> Filters installed with Word convert various foreign text and graphic files into a format that can be displayed by its document windows – refer to Word Set-up

Though each program is associated with a particular type of file, many programs offer the possibly of converting files of a different type into their own document formats. This conversion can be performed by an add-on component to the program called a filter or converter. Word can both save and restore files in foreign formats. The conversions are applied as shown in Figure 7.4.

Figure 7.4
Converting Files

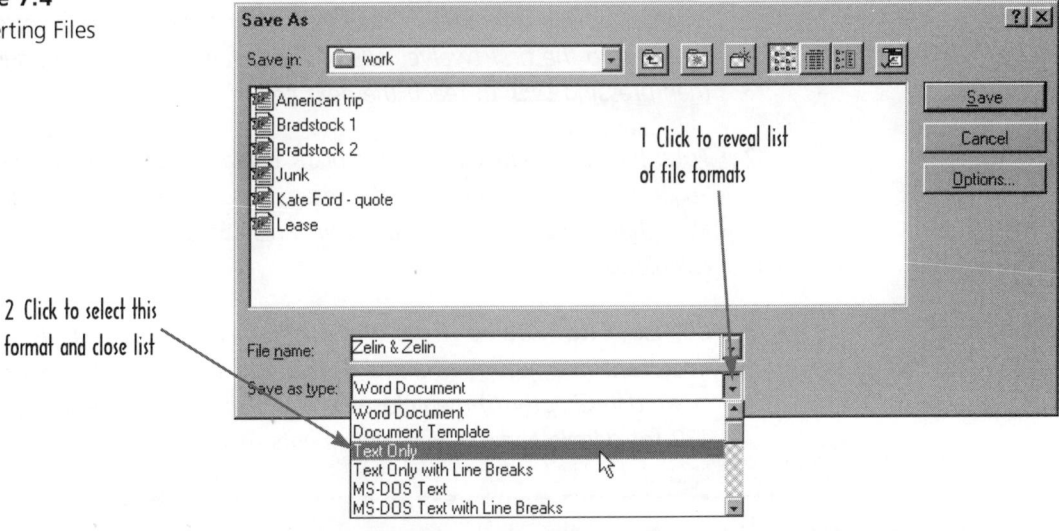

1 Click to reveal list of file formats

2 Click to select this format and close list

> **Note**
>
> When you use Word to open a file (File↪Open) in a foreign format it will automatically attempt to find the most suitable filter for the file – many other programs do the same

Chapter 7 Transferring information between documents 147

Chapter 7

Embedding Excel files in a Word document

> ▷ *using your Word document as a container for the other types of information required in the plan.*

In order to embed one document within another you must create two different types of document: a *container* and a *server*. First let's create a server document.

Definition server . . . . .a program which produces objects (documents) that can be stored in a container document. The actions of a server are made available to the container through its OLE connection

1   *Start Excel from the Taskbar (***Start➔Programs➔Microsoft Office➔Microsoft Excel***). Click the cell in its document window whose reference is column A, row 1. Now enter a set of figures into the first twelve cells of this column by typing a figure then pressing* [Enter] *to reach the next cell.*

2   *Total the column by clicking in a blank cell and typing the formula* =SUM(A1:A12) *where* A1 *is the reference of your first figure and* A12 *the reference of the last cell. Press* [Enter] *to complete the calculation.*

3   *Choose* **File➔Save** *from the Excel menu bar to store the document in a new file named* **Sales.xls** *(use the folder* **work** *created in Chapter 6) then close Excel's main window — see page 129 for details about saving documents as files.*

Definition container . . . . .a program which produces containers (documents) that can store objects produced by a server

You have now used a server (Excel) to create the information which can be embedded as an object in a container (e.g. a Word document).

Figure 7.5
The **Object** property sheet

Callouts on figure:
- 2 Press to locate the folder
- 1 Press **Browse** to open the **Browse** box
- 3 Click to select the file
- 4 Press to copy the file name and its location to the **Object** dialog box

4. *Use your Taskbar to start Word (***Start↪Programs↪Microsoft Office↪Microsoft Word***) and type some text into its document window. Click within this text to move the cursor (insertion point) to where you wish to insert the Excel data.*

5. *Choose* **Insert↪Object** *from Word's menu bar to open the* **Object** *property sheet. Click on the* **Create from File** *tab to bring this page to the forefront.*

6. *Press the* **Browse** *button to open a dialog box (similar to the* **Open** *dialog box) which can be used (see page 129) to locate* **Sales**, *the file you created in step 3. Press* **OK** *when you have found and selected* **Sales** *to copy its name and location into the* **Object** *property sheet.*

7. *Press* **OK** *to close the property sheet and insert the spreadsheet into your Word document. Finally, close Word's main window (don't bother saving the changes) — this exercise is complete!*

> **Note**
>
> Programs can be classified as either containers or servers. However some programs, including Word and Excel, act as both containers *and* servers

Chapter 7 Transferring information between documents

Chapter 7

Linking Excel files into a Word document

> ▷ linking your client's financial projections in the Excel spreadsheet to your Word document so that last minute changes to the projections will automatically update the figures in the plan.

Information can be linked to a container document in much the same way that it is embedded, you just need to check the box marked **Link to File** in the **Object** dialog box (Figure 7.9).

1 Start Word from your Taskbar (**Start↪Programs↪Microsoft Office↪Microsoft Word**) and enter some text into its document window. Move the insertion point to the location in this text where you want the Excel data inserted.

2 Choose **Insert↪Object** to bring-up the **Object** property sheet. Click on the tab **Create from File** to bring this page to the forefront and select the Excel file **Sales** as before but this time click the box **Link to File** before pressing **OK** to close the property sheet and insert the spreadsheet into your document.

3 Choose **File↪Save As** from Word's menu bar to store this document as a file named **Report** in your **work** folder. Close Word's main window.

Now if you change the figures in the Excel Sales document the values of the linked object in your Word document will alter.

4 Start Excel from the Taskbar (**Start↪Programs↪Microsoft Office↪Microsoft Excel**) and choose **File↪Open** from its menu bar to open the **Sales** document. Change one of your figures — just click in the cell and type a new value. Save the document (**File↪Save**) and close Excel's main window.

5 Start Word from the Taskbar and choose **File↪Open** from its menu bar to open the **Report** document. Observe that the Excel object has changed, then close Word's main window — this exercise is complete!

> **Note**
>
> You can use Word's Tools→Options to disable the automatic update of a document's links by changing the setting **Update Automatic links at open** in the **General** page settings

Updating links — Edit→Links

The link you establish between your documents is normally updated only when the Word document is opened — in most circumstances this is quite adequate. However, if you have disabled the automatic link update or otherwise require manual control over the link you must use the **Link** dialog box.

The **Link** dialog box allows you to select each link and apply an action such as update, break, open source and so forth.

1 *Start Word from the Taskbar (***Start→Programs→Microsoft Office→Microsoft Word***) and choose* **File→Open** *to open the document* Report *created in the previous exercise — the document containing the linked spreadsheet object.*

2 *Change the way Word treats the links contained in this document by changing a setting in its* **Options** *property sheet. — choose* **Tools→Options** *to open the property sheet and click the* **General** *tab to bring this page to the forefront. Click* **Update Automatic Links at Open** *to remove the tick in this box then press* **OK** *to close the property sheet.*

3 *Start Excel from the Taskbar (***Start→Programs→Microsoft Office→Microsoft Excel***) and choose* **File→Open** *to open the* Sales *document you created previously. Change one of the figures in this spreadsheet document then save this change by choosing* **File→Save** *from the menu bar. Close Excel's main window and return to your Word document.*

4 *Notice that your Word document's copy of the Excel spreadsheet (object) has not been updated — its links were not updated. However you can manually update the links by choosing* **Edit→Links** *from the Word menu bar, selecting the link, then pressing the* **Update Now** *push-button before closing the dialog box.*

Chapter 7   Transferring information between documents

Figure 7.6
Links dialog box

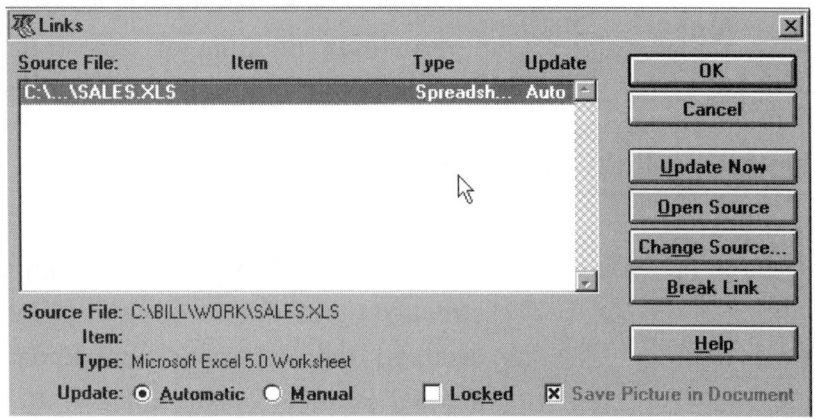

5   *Close Word's main window (don't bother saving your changes) — this exercise is complete.*

> **Note**
>
> Objects that have been embedded into a document are not automatically updated when you change the file from which they were sourced

Conserving disk space — save picture in document

Graphic objects, like drawings or Photo-CD images, often occupy several megabytes of disk space and can therefore dramatically increase the size of any document that contains them. It is not unusual for a five page Word document to occupy 10 megabytes or more after a few pictures have been added to it.

Large files are difficult to handle and much slower to load — they also take-up valuable space on your hard disk. However, you can still insert pictures into documents without creating these huge and unwieldy files by storing only the link information in a document rather than a copy of the data file.

> **Note**
>
> Whether you link or embed information in a document there is normally a copy of the data held in the file – choose Insert➔Picture if you want to store only the link information

Inserting Pictures

The special **Insert Picture** dialog box (Figure 7.7) has a setting that permits you to store only the link information in your document rather than a copy of the whole data file. This feature allows you to insert pictures into your document without significantly increasing its file size.

Figure 7.7
Insert Picture dialog box

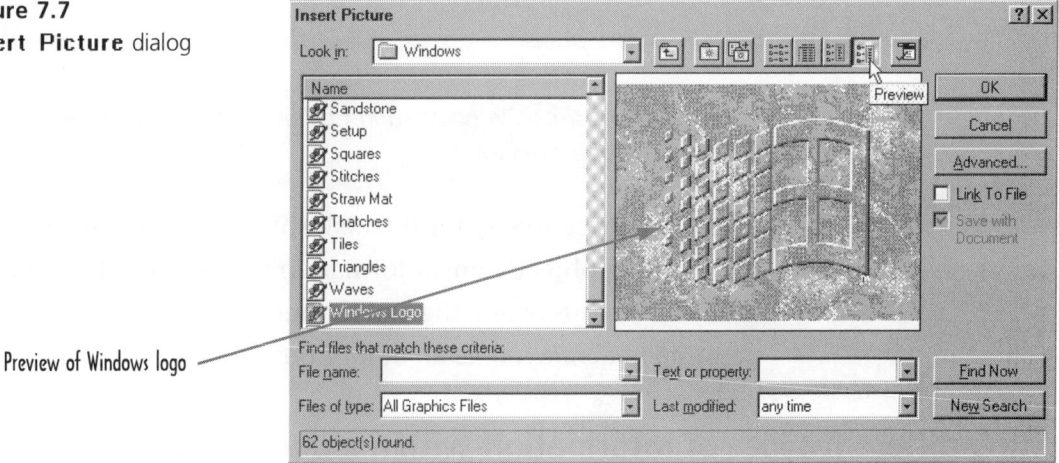

Preview of Windows logo

1   Start Word from your Taskbar (**Start➔Programs➔Microsoft Office➔Microsoft Word**) and type some text into its document window. Position the cursor at the point in your text where the picture is required then choose **Insert➔Picture** from the menu bar to open the **Insert Picture** dialog box (Figure 7.7).

2   The **Insert Picture** dialog box is almost identical to the **Open** dialog box and you should have no difficulty opening the **Windows** folder, usually located at the top level of drive **C** (use the same technique described on page 129).

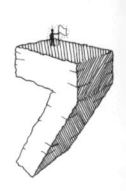

3   Select one of the graphics files (e.g. **Windows Logo**) that are stored in the **Windows** folder and press the **Preview** button in order to view it.

4   Insert a cross in the box **Link To File** (click it) and remove the cross from the box **Save with Document** (click it) before pressing **OK** to close the dialog box and insert a link to the picture into your document.

> **Caution**
>
> Once you have saved the picture in your document you will be unable to clear the **Save with Document** check box and reclaim the disk space

5   Close Word's main window (don't bother saving changes) — this completes the exercise.

There is a price to pay for the disk space saved by just storing the painting object's link information in your Word document — if, for any reason, the link cannot be resolved then the painting is displayed as an empty box.

Editing different types of information within a document

> *The Directors of Deskbase can open this document on their Desktop*

Once an object has been inserted in a document it can be manipulated and edited in much the same way as other native Word objects such as tables and bulleted lists (see Chapter 9). You edit a table by selecting it then applying actions — similarly you edit an object by selecting it and applying its actions. This is illustrated in Figure 7.11.

1. *Start Word from your Taskbar (**Start↪Programs↪Microsoft Office↪Microsoft Word**) and choose **File↪Open** from the menu bar to open **Report** (created in a previous exercise).*

2. *The document **Report** contains an embedded spreadsheet object which you can edit simply by double-clicking it — this opens an Excel window containing the spreadsheet **Sales** (also created in a previous exercise).*

3. *Change some of the figures in the spreadsheet then update **Report** by choosing **File↪Save** from the Excel menu bar before closing the Excel window.*

Figure 7.8
In-place editing of objects in a document

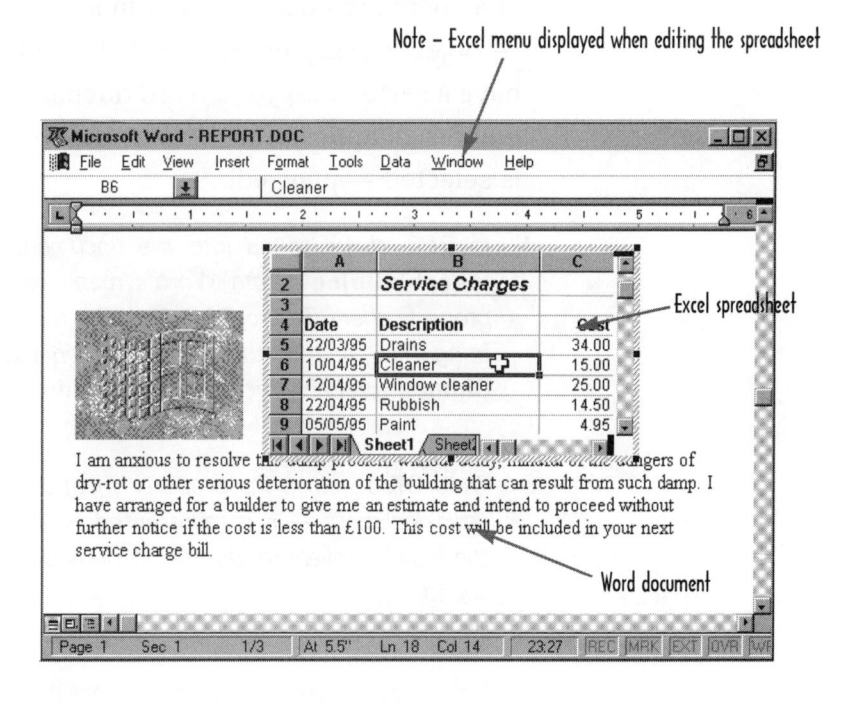

> **Note**
>
> **The Excel program, started by editing the worksheet information embedded into a Word document, remains open on your Desktop even after you have terminated Word**

Chapter 7 Transferring information between documents

Chapter 7

Adding sound to your documents

> ▷ record their comments next to particular parts of the plan — they use a microphone rather than a keyboard.

Many PCs are equipped with a sound adapter card that is connected to a set of speakers and a microphone so you can record and playback sounds attached to your documents. The following description applies to this type of *multimedia* PC.

Sound is a type of object that cannot be displayed directly in a container document and must be represented by an icon — object packaging. However, like all the other objects you have inserted into your Word document, a sound object has a number of appropriate actions that become available when it is selected — play, edit.

4   *Insert a chime sound into the document* **Report** *by choosing* **Insert→Object** *from Word's menu bar to open the* **Object** *property sheet (Figure 7.5). Click the tab* **Create from File** *to bring this page to the forefront then use it to select the file* **Chimes** *(probably located in* **C:\windows\media***).*

5   *Press* **OK** *to close the property sheet and insert this sound into your document — it is represented as an icon. Finally, right-click the icon to reveal its pop-up menu and select* **Play** *to hear the sound.*

Tip

> In addition to inserting existing objects into your Word document you can also create new objects. If you have microphone connected to your PC you can record your own voice in place of a pre-recorded sound – consult the appropriate manual for details about connecting a microphone to your computer's sound adapter card

Figure 7.9
The Sound Recorder

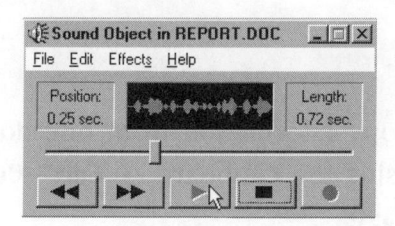

6   Open the **Object** property sheet by choosing **Insert→Object** from the Word menu bar and click the **Create New** tab to bring this page to the forefront. Select **Wave Sound** from the list of object types and press **OK** to close the property sheet and open the **Sound Object** window (Figure 7.9).

7   Press the **Record** button in the Sound Recorder and speak into your microphone. Press the **Stop** button after you have finished speaking. Close the Sound Recorder to insert your comments into the document as a sound object.

8   Double-click the sound icon that you have just added to your document to replay your comments.

9   Close Word's main window (don't bother to save changes), tidy-up the Desktop then use your Taskbar to shutdown Windows 95 (as described at the end of Chapter 2) — this exercise is complete!

One of the hallmarks of an efficient organisation is its ability to pool knowledge. Windows 95 provides the technology required to make this happen on your Desktop.

Chapter 7

Summary

- Copy information from one document to another by using the clipboard — **Edit↪Cut**, **Edit↪Copy**, **Edit↪Paste**.
- Convert files created by other programs so that they can be opened within your document window.
- Embed files into your documents to add pictures and other types of objects.
- Create links between documents so that changes in one document will be reflected in another.
- Put different types of documents into a single container document so that you can edit things with the appropriate program just by double-clicking them.
- Use a microphone and the sound card installed in your PC to record your own comments and to insert them into a document at a specific point.

Chapter 8

Working with Office 95

Objectives

This chapter provides a general introduction to application programs and Microsoft Office 95. It describes:

▷ what's an application program, what does it do?

▷ application windows — the different uses for windows belonging to different application programs

▷ learning to use a new application program — its windows, controls and dialog boxes are often quite familiar

▷ introducing Office 95 — how the information about its programs is arranged in this book, customizing the Office Bar to create and open documents as well as to start the programs you use most often.

Chapter 8

What's an application program, what does it do?

Note

> All the application programs on your Desktop are operated in a similar way. So once you have learnt how to use one program, the rest will be much easier to master

Definition

application . . . . a program that has been produced specifically for operation on your Desktop (e.g. Word)

The applications in your *Accessories* folder come packaged with Windows 95 while others, like Word, may be purchased separately then installed on your Desktop. The applications you might find on your PC can be broadly classified as follows:

- new Windows 95 applications that take full advantage of the power of your PC and its operating system — for example, Office 95
- older applications written for earlier version of Windows — they can still be used on your Windows 95 Desktop just like the new applications — for example, earlier versions of Office
- MS-DOS programs that require Windows 95 to create a window for them in which they can emulate the character-based screen of early PCs — for example, Word for DOS.

Note

> Application programs are produced by a wide variety of companies besides Microsoft

Application windows

An application program, once started, creates a window on your Desktop. It is the operation of the application's window (and the windows it contains) that best describes what the program does. A number of common application programs are listed in Table 8.1, together with the use they put to their document window or client area.

Figure 8.1
An application window

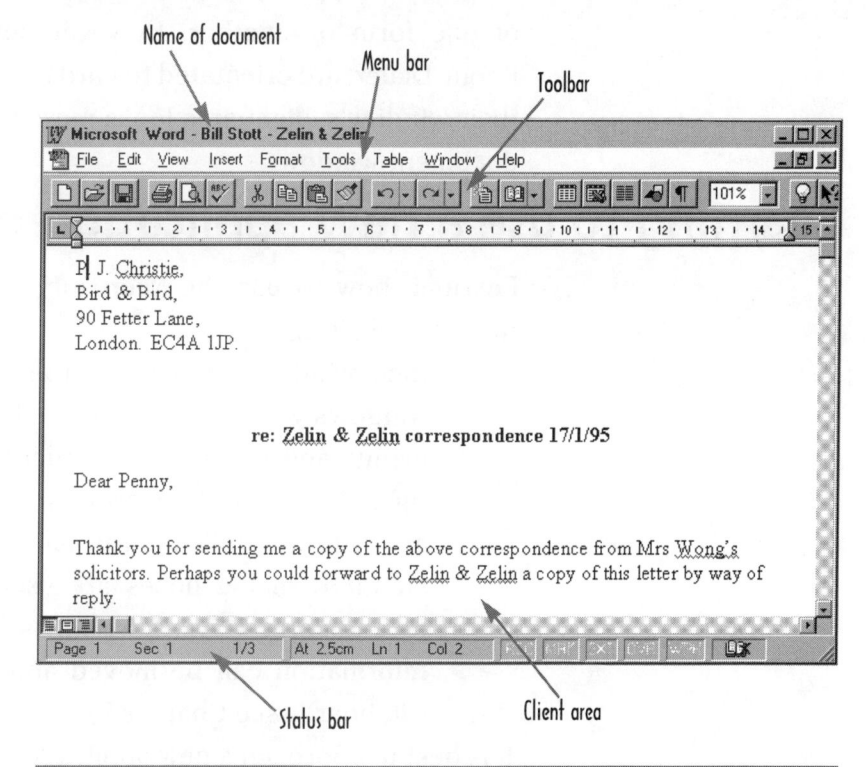

(Diagram of a Microsoft Word window labelled with: Name of document, Menu bar, Toolbar, Status bar, Client area)

Table 8.1
Uses for the windows belonging to different applications

Application	Window		
	Purpose	Document windows	OLE container
Word	editing text	yes	yes
Excel	calculating values	yes	yes
PowerPoint	editing a collection of slides	yes	yes
Access	accessing a collection of information — a database	yes	some
Schedule+	personal organiser	no	no
Binder	assembling documents	no	yes
WordPad	editing text	no	yes
Paint	drawing pictures	no	no
Phone Dialer	controls for dialing telephone numbers	no	no

Note

> An application's window is just another form of the general type of window introduced in Chapter 2 (see Figure 2.2)

Chapter 8

Most of the applications on your Desktop handle documents of one form or another. However some applications, like Phone Dialer, are orientated towards controlling something so their window's client area looks more like a dialog box than a document window.

Learning to use a new application program

Learning how to use the Microsoft Office programs is less difficult because:

- their windows are used in the same way as the other windows you have encountered (see Chapter 2)
- menus and toolbars are structured and operated like those found in other programs — things are selected and actions applied in the same way (see Chapter 3)
- standard dialog boxes are used to print documents (see Chapter 4), work with files (see Chapter 6)
- information can be moved and transferred using the Clipboard (see Chapter 7).

It is best to approach a new application program by first using the things that you already know how to operate — its windows, its menu bar, the way it stores and prints its documents. Once you have gained confidence you may wish to explore its specific features.

Introducing Office 95

Office 95 provides the programs you are most likely to need in a modern office — a word processor, a spreadsheet and a graphics package. You will understand how these programs may be used effectively after reading the following:

- Chapter 9: Word — creating a Word document, entering text and other objects, formatting.
- Chapter 10: Excel — creating an Excel spreadsheet, entering figures and formulae, formatting
- Chapter 11: Excel — designing lists, looking up information and performing calculations on your data

▷ Chapter 12: PowerPoint — creating a presentation, entering your material into slides, formatting

▷ Appendix E: Office Binder — linking a collection of Office documents together to form a report.

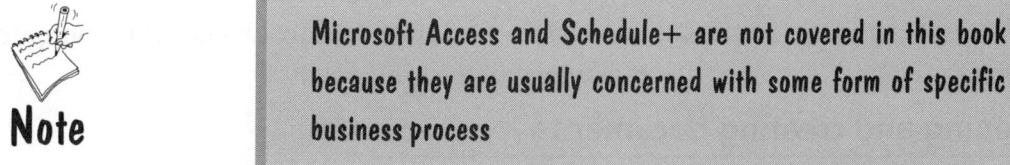

Note

> Microsoft Access and Schedule+ are not covered in this book because they are usually concerned with some form of specific business process

Office Bar

The Office Bar is a toolbar container — it can hold the Office 95 toolbar as well as any other toolbar that you might wish to define for providing convenient access to the documents and programs held within a particular folder.

Figure 8.2
The Office Bar and Office 95 toolbar

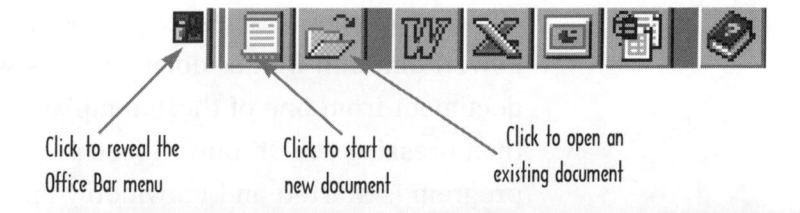

Click to reveal the Office Bar menu
Click to start a new document
Click to open an existing document

Tip

> Use the Office Bar as an alternative to the Taskbar to start programs and open windows on the Desktop for your documents

The Office Bar is normally attached to the top of your Desktop but it can be repositioned in the same way as a toolbar attached to the top of a window (see page 67). When you click the Office Bar's icon a menu is revealed — it behaves like the icon at the top left of a window (see page 42). Among the options provided by this menu are:

▷ **Auto Hide**[1] — when ticked the Office Bar can be obscured by other windows on your Desktop

▷ **Add/Remove Office Programs** — permits you to add or remove components of Office 95 such as import filters, clip art and so forth (you may need installation disks)

---

[1] You must also remove the tick from the **Always on Top** option in the **View** page of the **Customize** property sheet

> **Exit** — closes the Office Bar so it cannot be used until you restart its program (occurs automatically each time you switch on your computer)
>
> **Customize** — allows you to change the contents and behaviour of the Office Bar.

Opening and creating documents

The buttons provided in the standard Office toolbar include *open a document* and *start a new* document which open dialog boxes similar to those you have already used to open files (page 132) and create new documents (page 52), but without the prior need to start a program.

New documents are created from a number of standard templates. They can be used to create a wide variety of different document types; not just Word documents but Excel, PowerPoint and Binder documents as well. You can create a document from one of these templates simply by selecting it then pressing the **OK** button (see page 53) — the appropriate program is started and its window appears on your Desktop containing a document of the style you have selected.

Tip

> Create and access your documents directly from your Office Bar (or Desktop) rather than from a program's menu bar (see Chapter 13)

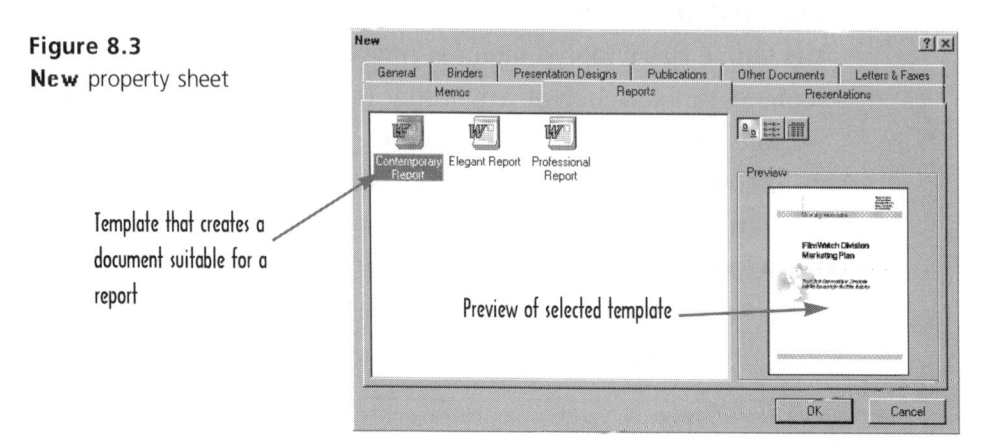

Figure 8.3
New property sheet

Template that creates a document suitable for a report

Preview of selected template

Some of the templates supplied by Office 95 have place holder text to describe the information that you must supply — just click and type to replace the place holder with your own text. Others create documents that are initialized by a Wizard — a series of dialog boxes prompt you for information which is then inserted into the appropriate part of the document. Microsoft provides three alternative styles for most of its templates (Professional, Contemporary and Elegant) so that all the documents issued by your office can have a consistent look in terms of their typeface and design.

Organizing templates

When you install Office 95 on your PC a number of folders are created for its templates so they can be categorized into groups such as **Letters & Faxes**, **Spreadsheet Solutions** and so forth. The **New** property sheet reflects this organization by displaying a page for each folder contained within the location specified for your user templates. The following exercise shows how to add a page to the **New** property sheet to provide your own template classification — in later chapters you will create the actual template files which are needed before this new page is displayed.

1   *Click the Office Bar icon and select* **Customize** *to open the property sheet shown in Figure 8.2. Click the* **Settings** *tab so you can write down the settings for your* **User templates location** *(e.g.* `c:\msoffice\templates`*) then press* **OK** *to close the property sheet.*

2   *Double-click the* **My Computer** *icon on your Desktop to open its window then double-click the* **C:** *drive to open a further window. Locate the folder* **msoffice** *in this second window then double-click its icon to open yet another window where you should find the* **templates** *folder.*

3   *Double-click the* **My Computer** *icon again then create a folder called* **Bill's templates** *within the folder* **Bill** *which was created earlier (see page 126).*

4   *Use your right mouse button to drag the* **Bill's templates** *icon (step 3) onto the* **templates** *folder (step 2) then select* **Create Shortcut** *from the pop-up menu which appears when you drop the icon. Close all the windows you have opened — this exercise is complete!*

Note: A shortcut is a reference to a file or folder so that it can be accessed from a different location without the need to create a separate copy (see page 293)

Customizing the Office Bar

The pages of the **Customize** property sheet permit you to change the Office Bar so that it conforms with the way you work. In particular you can:

- add your own toolbars to the Office Bar, each with their own set of buttons — **Toolbars** page
- change the buttons in your toolbars to provide short-cuts to specific files (or programs) and folders — **Buttons** page
- change the folders in which Office expects to find your template files (see page 52) — **Settings** page
- change the colour and presentation of the Office bar on your Desktop — **View** page.

TIP: Customize your Office Bar to provide shortcuts to files, folders and programs you use most frequently — just drag their icons from your Desktop and drop them on the Office Bar

Summary

- Applications are programs designed specifically for operation on a Windows Desktop.
- Windows 95 applications are consistent so once you have learnt how to do something, this skill can be applied to all the applications on your Desktop that have a similar feature.
- Microsoft Office contains a suite of programs that work on many of the types of documents found in an office environment.

Chapter 9

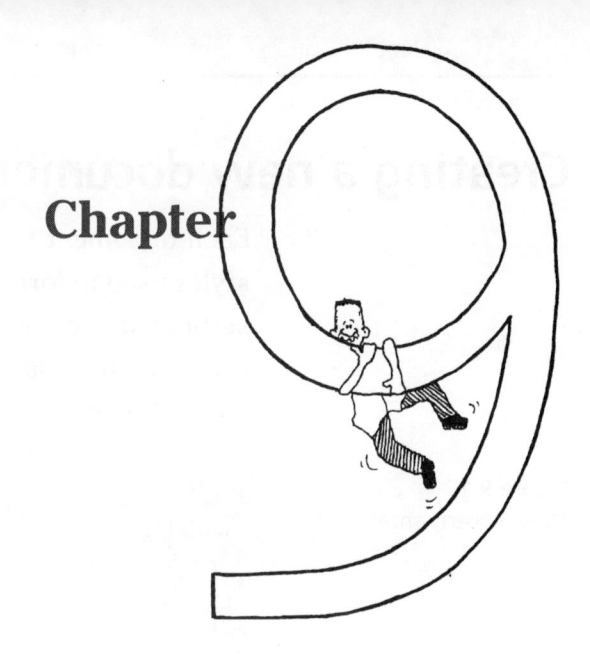

Word processing — Word

Objectives

Word is an application program that allows you to create letters, memos, reports, and even entire books. We look at the following in this chapter:

▷ creating a Word document — using a template

▷ features of Word's windows — display a document as it will appear when printed, edit page headers and footers

▷ producing the document — select text and choose actions such as *drag-and-drop*

▷ inserting things into your document — footnotes, bulleted lists, symbols, pictures, and tables

▷ finishing touches and important Word actions — how to set page margins, add sections, define formats

▷ reviewing and revising documents — check your spelling, add annotations, find and replace text.

When you have completed this chapter you will be able to produce a wide range of well composed documents that can appear like a typeset book.

Chapter 9

Creating a new document

Each document has a number of settings that determine the styles used to format its text, its page size, and so forth. These settings are copied from a template when the document is created (File↪New) so that you can start typing straight away without worrying about setting-up your new document.

Figure 9.1
New property sheet

Selected template

Create your own template based on selected template

Create a document from selected template

> **Note**
> The folder used to contain the template files on your PC is defined by the File locations page of Word's Options property sheet (Tools↪Options)

When Word is started a new document is automatically created in its document window — the settings for this document are copied from the default template (**normal.dot**). However you can also select a template from a list contained within the **Open** dialog box.

> **Note**
> Wizards take you step-by-step through the settings required to define documents derived from certain templates – the word Wizard usually appears in their name

Templates are themselves documents. In addition to defining settings, such as typeface and page size, you can also enter text (or graphics) into templates so that documents created from them will have the same initial content.

1. *Start Word from your Taskbar (**Start↪Programs↪Microsoft Office↪Microsoft Word**) and choose **File↪New** to open the **New** dialog box containing a list of templates. Click the **Template** button (above the **Cancel** button) and select **Normal** from the list of templates — it will be used as the basis for your new template. Press **OK** to close the dialog box and create a new template document.*

2. *Type your address and telephone number at the top of this document to create your letterhead — you may wish to choose a different typeface or other special formatting to this text (see Finishing touches — **Format↪Font**).*

3. *Choose **File↪Properties** from Word's menu bar to open the property sheet (Figure 9.2). Click the **Summary** page and type* template for my correspondence *into the **Title** box. Click the **Save preview picture** box before pressing **OK** to close the property sheet.*

Figure 9.2 **Summary** page of your document's property sheet

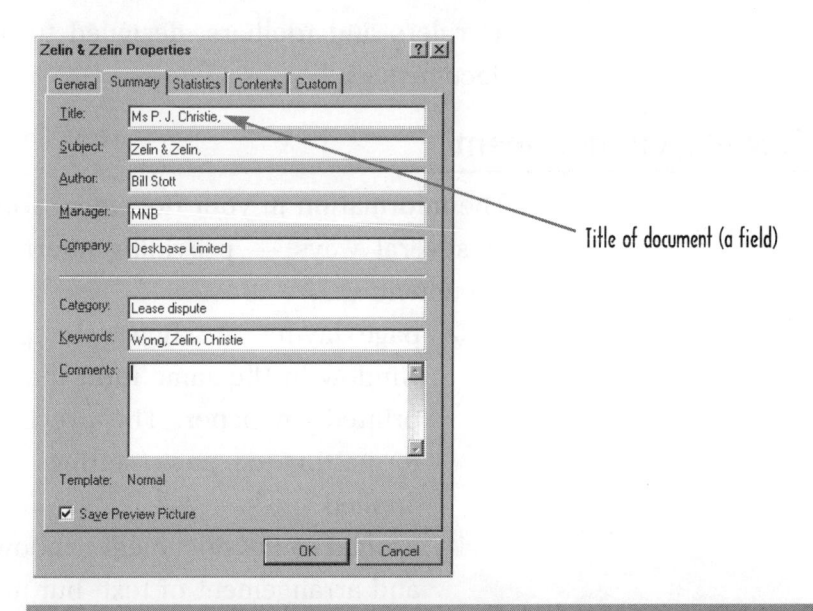

> **Note**
>
> **Summary information is attached to all Microsoft Office files (see page 116) — develop the habit of completing the Summary page before saving your documents**

4   *Choose* **File↪Save As** *from Word's menu bar to open the* **Save As** *dialog box. Locate your folder* **Bill's template** *in the* **Save in** *box, then type* `MyLetter.dot` *into the* **File Name** *box before pressing* **OK** *to store your template.*

5   *Close Word's main window — you have now successfully created your own template and thereafter it will be included in the* **Open** *dialog box's list of templates. This exercise is complete!*

You can create a template for each type of document that you need to produce so that your reports, correspondence and so forth all have a consistent appearance.

Features of Word's windows

Word's menu bar provides access to actions specifically for processing text documents as well as the more general-purpose actions that are often found in an application's menu bar. Word's windows also contain a number of features, such as rulers and toolbars, designed to help you process your documents.

Viewing your document

The information in your document window can be displayed in several ways — providing alternate views of the same document:

- page layout — shows the pages in the document window in the same form that they will appear when printed on paper. The precise effect of changes to formatting or page settings can seen as they are applied
- normal — the document window shows the formatting and arrangement of text, but not in the context of full size pages. It is easier (and quicker) to navigate through a document when it is viewed in this way
- outline — the document is shown only in terms of its headings. You can decide which headings are

Figure 9.3
Word's menu bar and window controls

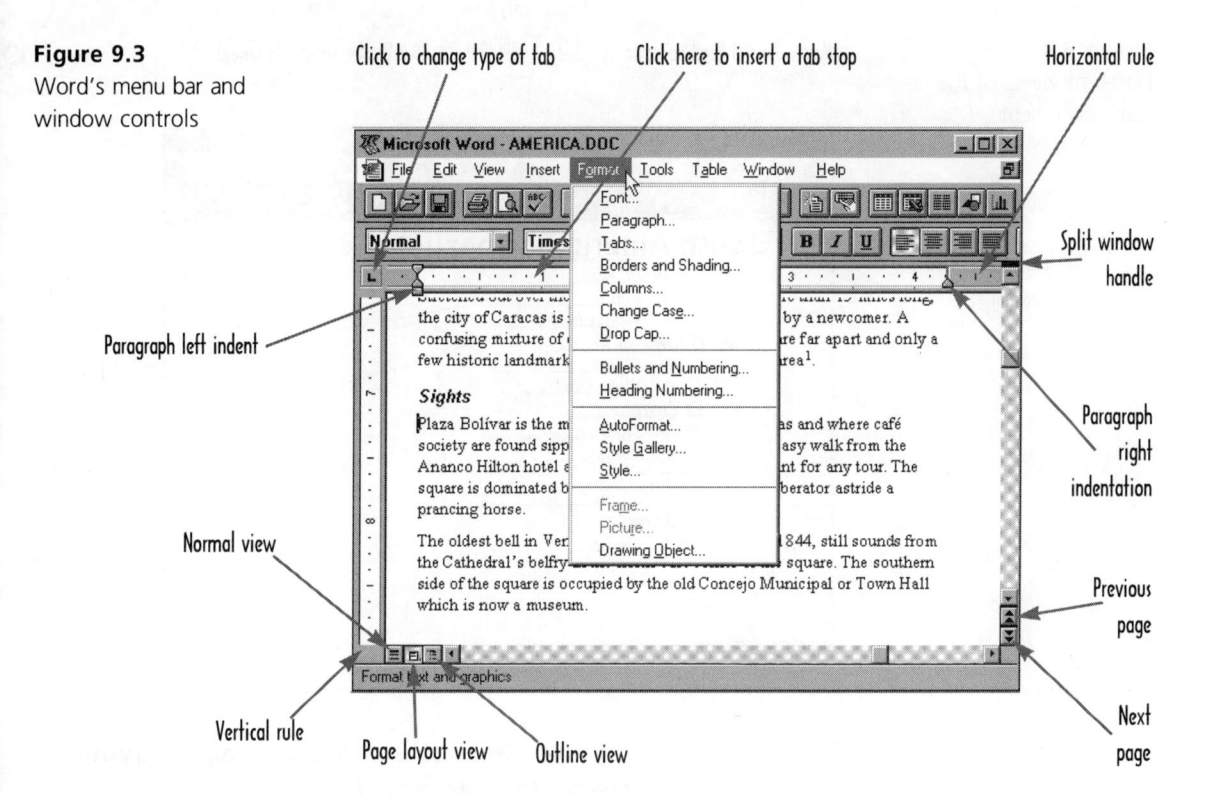

- Click to change type of tab
- Click here to insert a tab stop
- Horizontal rule
- Split window handle
- Paragraph left indent
- Paragraph right indentation
- Normal view
- Vertical rule
- Page layout view
- Outline view
- Previous page
- Next page

displayed then re-arrange the document simply by changing the order of these headings

> master document — a number of different documents (files) can be viewed together, as if they were combined into a single book.

1. *Start Word from your Taskbar (**Start→Programs→Microsoft Office→Microsoft Word**) and open an existing document by choosing **File→Open** from its menu bar — perhaps the document you stored as the file **Junk.doc** within your **work** folder (see Chapter 6).*

2. *Choose **View→Outline** from Word's menu bar to view your document so that each paragraph is a heading — the Outline toolbar also appears.*

3. *Click anywhere within the first paragraph of your document then press the button at the far left of the Outline toolbar to promote this paragraph to **Heading 1** (its style will alter). Investigate the actions of the other buttons in this Outline toolbar.*

Chapter 9   Word processing — Word   171

Figure 9.4
Different views of the same document

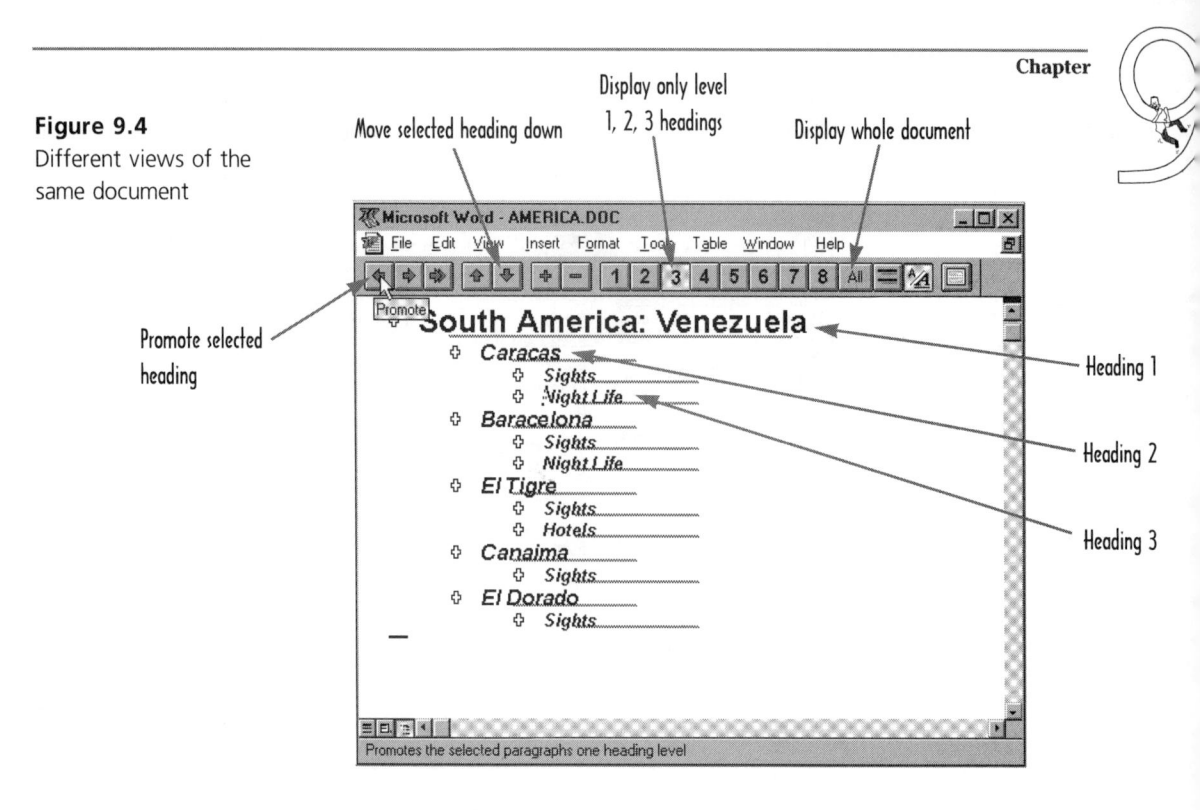

- Move selected heading down
- Display only level 1, 2, 3 headings
- Display whole document
- Promote selected heading
- Heading 1
- Heading 2
- Heading 3

4   Choose in turn **View→Normal** and **View→Page Layout** from Word's menu bar to display your document in other ways — judge for yourself the advantages of each view.

> **Note**
>
> Master documents are viewed like special Outline documents. Refer to the Word manual for further details

Page headers and footers

Printed documents allow space at the top and bottom of each page — specified by the margin settings (see **File→Page Setup**). Within this space you can add a *header* and *footer* that have a similar content on each page — useful for adding document titles, page numbers, and so forth to your documents.

5   Choose **View→Header and Footer** from the Word's menu bar — the **Header and Footer** dialog box appears (Figure 9.5) and your view of the document changes from the main body of the text to the header area of the page.

**Figure 9.5
Header and Footer**
dialog box

Choose **Format→Borders
and Shading** to add a border to
the page header

Page field value

Switch between header and footer   Page number field   Date field   Time field

6   Type `Page-` in the dotted header box then press the dialog box's page number button to insert the page number (see *Inserting fields*) into your document's page header. Close the **Header and Footer** dialog box to return to page Layout view of your document — this header appears (greyed) at the top of each page.

7   Choose **View→Normal** from Word's menu bar to hide the page header and display only the main text of your document. Close Word's main window (don't bother saving changes) — this exercise is complete!

Tip

> Your document can divided into sections, each with its own page header and footer information

Other views of your document that can be activated from the **View** menu include:

▷ footnotes — you can insert a footnote reference[1] within your text, then type a description of the reference at the bottom of the page (see *Inserting footnotes*)

---

[1] Footnotes are often used in academic text to provide a reference for information

- annotations — when reviewing a document you may wish to add a comment rather than amending the original text (see *Revising and reviewing documents*)
- zoom — you can change the size of the document as it appears in the document window. The standard Word toolbar also contains a zoom control.

> **Note**
> A different view is just a different way of presenting the same material — changing your view of a document does not change its contents

Producing the document

Word's document windows are specifically adapted for entering and manipulating the type of text used in correspondence, reports and so forth. You can enter and edit your text using the techniques introduced in Chapter 4 — use your mouse or keyboard to move the cursor, then type to enter text at that point in your document.

1   *Open Word from the Taskbar (***Start↪Programs↪Microsoft Office↪Microsoft Word***)to create a fresh document window and type some text into this window.*

Once you have created some text you can start manipulating it — select something and apply an action to it.

Selecting text

Selection is generally performed in any window by pointing at something then pressing the left mouse button — click to select. However Word's document window also provides a number of special selection techniques that reflect its role in manipulating your text.

You can select text (or objects) using your mouse or keyboard then choose an action from your menu bar to apply this text — cancel a selection simply by selecting something else or pressing [Esc].

Table 9.1
Text selection in Word's document windows

Select what	Mouse	Keyboard
word	double-click on any character	[Shift]+cursor key
line	click opposite line in left margin	–
sentence	[Ctrl]+click on any character	–
block of text	click at start of block then [Shift]+click at end of block	–
text within a box	[Alt]+drag to the bottom right of the text you wish to select	–
paragraph	triple-click on any character or double click next to paragraph in left margin (selection bar)	–
from cursor to end of paragraph	–	[Ctrl]+[Shift]+[↓]
document	triple-click in left margin	[Ctrl]+[A]

Table 9.2
Object selection

Select what	Mouse	Keyboard
table	click in table then choose Table↪Select Table	[Alt]+[5]
table row	click in row then choose Table↪Select Row	–
table column	click in column then choose Table↪Select Column	–
frame (or picture)	click in frame (or picture) so that a box with eight *handles* appears	–

Note

> Word's document windows also support drag-select, where a number of items can be selected by dragging the mouse pointer around them (keeping left button pressed)

Replacement

The default action applied when you press a key after selecting some text is *replacement* — the selected text is replaced by the letter you have typed.

2   Select an occurrence of the word `the` in text you have typed in your document window. Press Ⓐ to replace the definite article with the indefinite article — `the` is replaced by `a`.

> **Caution**
> Pressing a key when text is selected can result in unwanted replacements — however you can choose Edit↪Undo (or press the undo toolbar button) to recover your text

Drag-and-drop

Word, like many application programs, supports *drag-and-drop*. Selected text can be dragged to a new location then dropped — often the quickest way to move it.

3   Select the last word in the text you have typed in your document window then drag it to the beginning of the text.

When dragging text the mouse pointer adopts a different shape — and a bar moves through your text (like a bomb sight) showing where the text would land.

> **Note**
> Moving the mouse pointer just above, or below, the client area of the document window while dragging text has the effect of scrolling the document in the window

Inserting things into your document

Word documents can contain many other things besides simple text:
- footnotes
- fields

- lists and bullet points
- pictures
- symbols
- tables of information.

You can put any of these elements into your own document by following the descriptions provided in the remainder of the chapter.

Inserting footnotes — Insert↪Footnote

Footnotes were introduced earlier in this chapter as a means for providing references within text. Once you have attached a footnote to a piece of text it will always appear at the bottom of its page — even if you subsequently move the text or otherwise change its page number. The numbering of footnotes is automatically adjusted to reflect their order within the document, so if you add a further footnote (above one that already exists) the reference numbers change accordingly.

4   *Change your document view to* **Page Layout** *(***View**↪**Page Layout***) and move the cursor to the word in your document to which you wish to attach a footnote reference.*

5   *Choose* **Insert**↪**Footnote** *from Word's menu bar to open the* **Footnote and Endnote** *dialog box, click the boxes* **Footnote** *and* **Autonumber***, then press* **OK** *to close the dialog box and move the cursor to the footnote area of the page.*

6   *Type your footnote then scroll back to the main body of your text and continue working on the document. A number appears next to the word you had selected and a corresponding number appears in the footnote at the bottom of the page.*

Note

> Footnotes are displayed in your document window only when View↪Page Layout has been applied from the Word menu bar

You can edit a footnote simply by clicking the text within the footnote area of your document. Remove your footnote by deleting the reference mark within the main body of your text — drag-select the mark then press [Delete].

> **Note**
>
> Endnotes serve the same purpose as footnotes but are placed at the end of your *document* rather than at the bottom of the page

Inserting lists — Format↪Bullets and Numbering

Bullet points provide a good way of formatting a list within your document — each item in the list is prefixed with a special *bullet* symbol. Traditionally the bullet symbol is a large dot (●) but you may select almost any other character or symbol within the fonts available to Windows 95.

7   Type a list in your document, pressing [Enter] after each item so that it appears in its own paragraph. Select all the paragraphs in your list and choose **Format↪Bullets and Numbering** from the menu bar to open the dialog box in Figure 9.6. Now press **OK** to close the dialog box and apply the selected bullet formatting to your list.

8   Remove the bullets by selecting your list once more, opening the **Bullets and Numbering** dialog box then pressing its **Remove** button.

> **Tip**
>
> Bullets can be applied to (or removed from) your list by pressing the bullets button in Word's toolbar – a similar numbering button creates numbered lists

**Figure 9.6
Bullets and
Numbering** dialog box

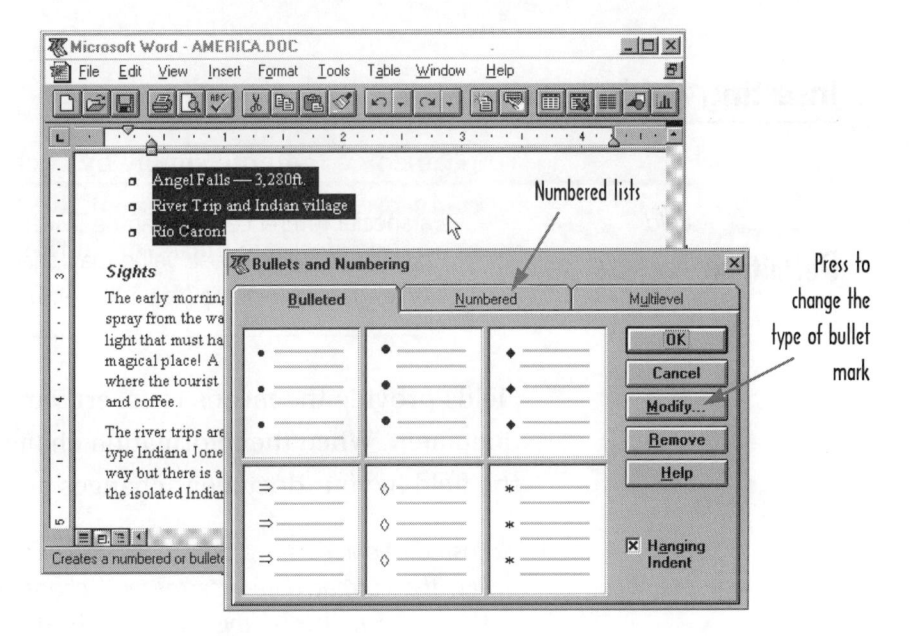

Inserting symbols — Insert↪Symbol

The typefaces supplied with Windows 95 contain symbols such as ©, in addition to the normal number and letters of the alphabet that correspond to the keys on your keyboard. It is very easy to insert such symbols into your text.

9   *Position your cursor at the point in your text where you would like a symbol to be inserted then choose* **Insert↪Symbol** *from Word's menu bar — this opens the* **Symbol** *property sheet.*

10 *Click the button attached to the* **Font** *control in this property sheet (or press* Alt+F *keys) to reveal a list of fonts installed on your PC. Select* **Symbol** *from this list so that the squares at the bottom of the property sheet display its symbols.*

11 *Click the square at the bottom of the property sheet that contains a copyright symbol (©) then press the* **Insert** *button to put the symbol into your text. Press the* **Close** *push-button to close the property sheet and return to your document.*

> Press the Shortcut key button in the Symbol property sheet to open a further property sheet that permits you to define a keyboard shortcut for inserting particular symbols into your document

Tip

Inserting fields — Insert↪Field

Definition

field . . . . a special reference that can be inserted into a document to display an item whose value may change — a variable such as *time*, *date*, *file name* (see Table 9.3)

Fields provide the means to insert variable information into a document. When the information changes then the content of the field in your document changes as well.

12 *Position your cursor at the point in your text where you would like the current date inserted and choose* **Insert↪Field** *from Word's menu bar — this opens the* **Field** *dialog box.*

13 *Click* **Date and Time** *from the list of categories (left side of the dialog box) to display (right side) a list of fields related to date and time information. Click the field* **CreateDate** *then press* **OK** *to close the dialog box and insert this field into your document.*

Tip

> Insert the CreateDate field in a template document so you can automatically date the documents created from this template (File↪New)

Table 9.3
Common fields

Category	Field	Description
Date and Time	PrintDate	date the document was printed
	Date	current date
	CreateDate	date the document was created
Document Info	Filename	document's file name
	Author	see of **File↪Properties (Summary, Author)**
	Title	contents of **File↪Properties (Summary, Title)**
	Subject	contents of **File↪Properties (Summary, Subject)**
	NumPages	the number of pages in the document
User Info	UserName	name of the person using Word **Tools↪Options↪(UserInfo, Name)**

> **Tip**
>
> The Printing page of Word's Options property sheet (Tools→Options) has a setting (print page) that causes fields to be updated whenever the document is printed – press F9 to update your fields at other times

Inserting pictures into your document

Pictures inserted directly into your text (see Chapter 7) are difficult to move and adjust, as they are treated by Word as a huge single character — the surrounding text is simply fitted on the same (or following) line. However, inserting a picture into a *frame* makes it much easier to handle. Word treats frames differently to its normal text in the following ways:

> frames fit into the middle of a block of text so that the lines flow around it — your picture can fit into a box in the middle of the text

> frames have a *border* that can be used to position the picture on the page as well as *handles* that allow you change its height or width

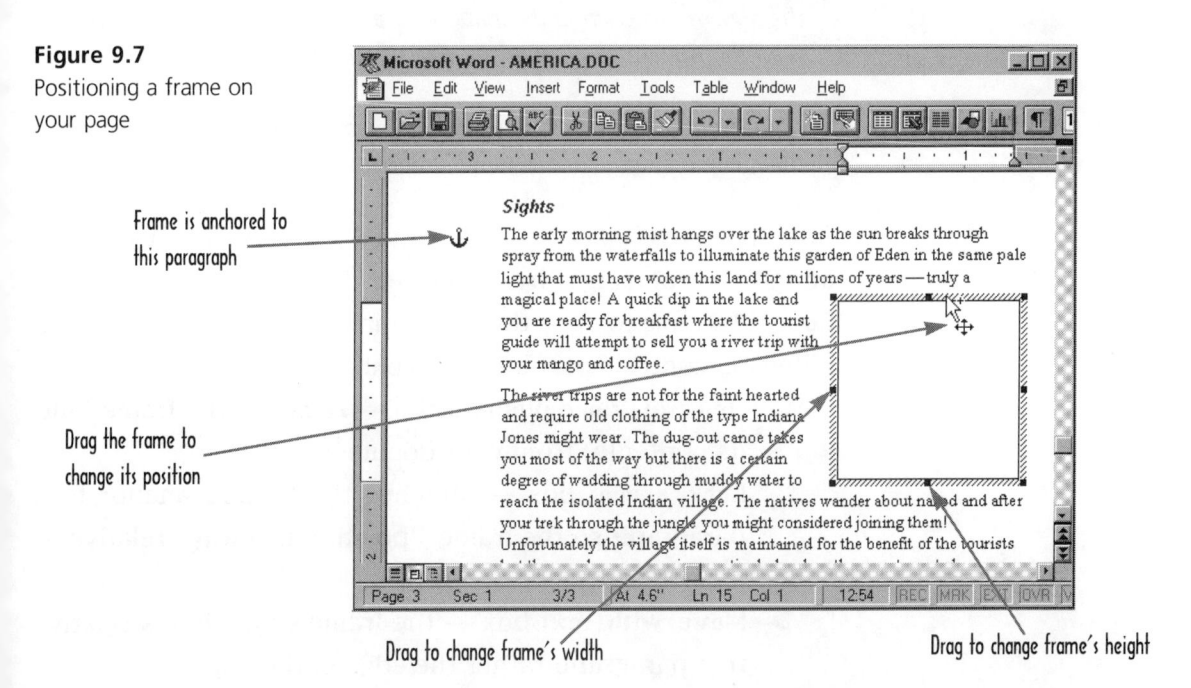

Figure 9.7
Positioning a frame on your page

Frame is anchored to this paragraph

Drag the frame to change its position

Drag to change frame's width

Drag to change frame's height

▷ frames can be anchored to a piece of text so that it moves with the text. Display these anchors by choosing **Tools→Options** and changing the **Object Anchors** setting in the **View** page.

Tip

> Word's Options property sheet has the setting **Picture Placeholders** in its **View** page that permits the frame to be displayed

14   *Choose* **Insert→Frame** *from the menu bar to change your mouse pointer into a small cross. Place the mouse pointer at the position on your page that will mark the top left of the frame, press the left mouse button and drag the mouse down to the location of the frame's bottom right corner. When you release the mouse button the frame is inserted into your document.*

15   *Click within the frame to reveal its border and click on the border to reveal six small squares. Move the mouse pointer over one of the squares to change its shape into a double headed arrow and drag this square to change the size of the frame.*

16   *Reposition the frame within the page by dragging its border in the same way you would move a window on your Desktop.*

After you have inserted a frame into your document you can adjust its settings by selecting it and then choosing **Format→Frame** to open the **Frame** dialog box. You may find the following controls particularly useful:

▷ **Remove frame** push-button — removes the frame (and its contents) from your document

▷ **Lock anchor** box — attaches the frame's anchor to a paragraph so the frame's position is always relative to a particular piece of text

▷ **Move with text** box — the frame's position is relative to a paragraph rather the edge of the page.

17 Click within the frame and choose **Insert→Picture** *from the menu bar to open the* **Insert Picture** *dialog box. Select a graphic file (see page 153) and press* **OK** *to close the dialog box and insert the picture into your frame.*

18 *Stretch or reduce the image by dragging one of the frame's handles. Crop the image by pressing* ⎡Shift⎦ *before dragging the frame's handle.*

Definition

crop . . . . .cutting the edges of your picture to fit a given space (or to remove unwanted parts of the image) as opposed to stretching or reducing an image to fit a space

Tip

> Use frames to contain tables, charts, drawings and any other items whose position on the page must be controlled separately from the surrounding text

Inserting tables of information

There are two ways to correctly align columns of figures (or text) in a Word document:

- set-up a *tab* stop for each column — a line of figures can be entered by pressing ⎡Tab⎦ before typing the number in each column (see page 103)
- insert a table into your document — figures can be entered into its rows and columns. This is described below.

You can insert a table into your document to contain any type of tabular information — it is often easier to manipulate a table, rather than tab stops, in a paragraph.

19 *Move Word's cursor to the position in your document where a table is required. Choose* **Table→Insert Table** *from the menu bar to open a dialog box that permits you to select the number of rows and columns required for the table.*

Chapter 9

20 When you have defined the table, press **OK** to close the dialog box and insert it into your document. Choose **Table→Gridlines** from Word's menu bar to show 'gridlines' within your table — they will not be printed but help you manipulate the table.

> **Tip**
>
> Select the whole table and choose Format→Borders and Shading from Word's menu bar. This opens a dialog box that permits you to put printable lines between the table's rows and columns

`Tab` is used to move the cursor from column to column in the table, moving to the next row when required. Pressing `Tab` at the end of the table creates a new row.

21 Click in the first column of the first row of the table and type a figure. Press `Tab` to move the cursor into the next column and type a second figure. Press `Shift`+`Tab` to move the cursor back to the previous column.

Rows and columns can be deleted from, or inserted into, a table by selecting the row or column and choosing the appropriate action from the **Table** menu. The various elements of the table can be selected as shown in Table 9.1.

Table 9.4 Selecting parts of a table

Select what	Menu	Mouse
Row	click within the row and choose **Table→Select Row**	click in the margin at the left of the table
Column	click within the column and choose **Table→Select Column**	click immediately above the column (the mouse pointer changes shape)
Whole table	click within the table and choose **Table→Select Table**	drag-select the table

> **Definition**
>
> cell . . . . .the intersection of a particular row and column is termed a cell; it can contain a figure, text or some other object

The width of a column (or height of a row) can be adjusted by selecting it and choosing **Table↪Cell Height and Width** from the menu bar.

Alternatively, you can adjust the settings directly by dragging the column gridlines (or the markers within the *rulers* at the edge of the document window).

22 *Select a column from your table and move the mouse pointer over a vertical gridline in your table — the pointer changes shape into a small double-headed arrow. Drag the gridline to the left or right to change the width of the column.*

Other actions that can be applied to a table include:

- convert table to text and vice versa — for instance, you can select a group of paragraphs and convert them into rows of a table. Alternatively, a table can also be converted into a set of paragraphs
- sort — you can change the order of rows in a table to reflect the alphabetic (or numeric sequence) of a particular column's contents
- split table — you can split a single table in two by selecting a row and choosing **Table↪Split Table**
- formula — apply a formula to a cell that displays the result of a calculation, like an Excel worksheet (see Chapter 10)
- Autoformat — a number of pre-defined formats can be applied to your table.

23 *Close Word's main window (don't bother saving changes) — this exercise is complete!*

Tip

> Insert a table into a frame if you need to adjust its position on your page

Chapter 9

Finishing touches and important Word actions

Word provides a wide range of settings and facilities that can improve the presentation of your document before it is printed. The most common finishing touches that you may wish to choose are:

- starting a new topic
- page settings
- adding boxes and shading
- changing the typeface
- altering the layout of a paragraph
- choosing a style for your document.

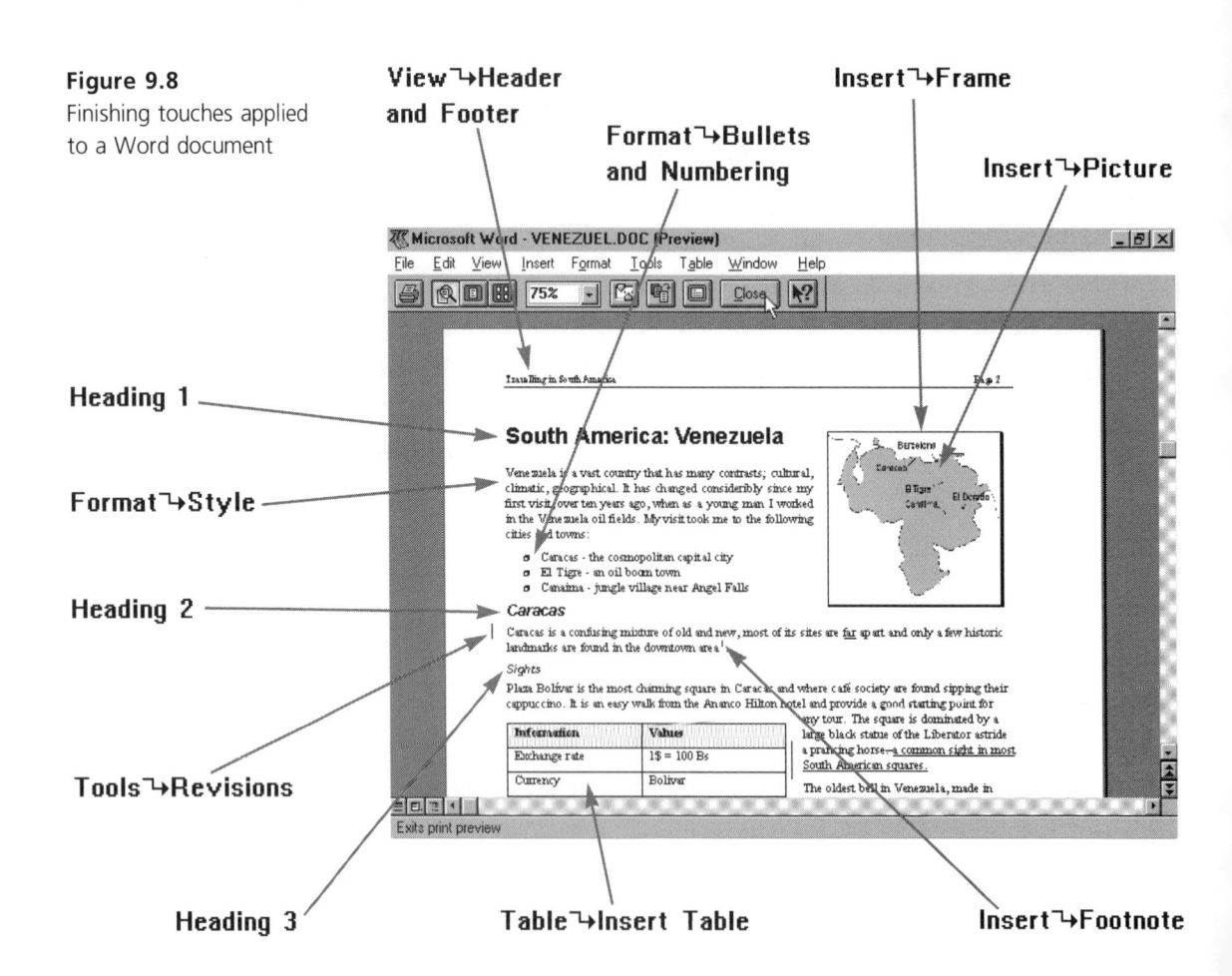

Figure 9.8
Finishing touches applied to a Word document

Callouts: View→Header and Footer; Format→Bullets and Numbering; Insert→Frame; Insert→Picture; Heading 1; Format→Style; Heading 2; Tools→Revisions; Heading 3; Table→Insert Table; Insert→Footnote

186 Chapter 9 Word processing — Word

> **Tip** — Make a copy of your document (File→Save As) before choosing extensive formatting, so you can recover the original file and start again if you are not satisfied with the results

Starting a new topic — Insert→break

While your document might appear in a document window as text on a continuous roll of paper (**View→Normal**), it is actually printed on separate sheets of paper by your printer. Therefore after typing a certain number of lines you will reach the end of one page and start the next. Word recognizes when you have reached the end of a page and automatically inserts a *page break* into your document, so that you can continue typing on the next page.

> **Tip** — Choose View→Normal to display page breaks as a simple dotted line running across a continuous roll of paper. Choose View→Page Layout to display your document as separate pages

You may insert your own page breaks into the document to start new pages at appropriate points in the text — at the start of a new topic, for example. You can also define new sections in your document so each topic can have its own settings, page header, and so forth.

1 *Start Word from your Taskbar (***Start→Programs→Microsoft Office→Microsoft Word***) and type some text into its document window.*

2 *Move the cursor to an appropriate point in the text then choose* **Insert→Break** *from Word's menu bar — this opens the* **Break** *dialog box. Click the* **Page Break** *option then press* **OK** *to close the dialog box and insert a page break into your document.*

Figure 9.9
Break dialog box

Start new page at cursor position

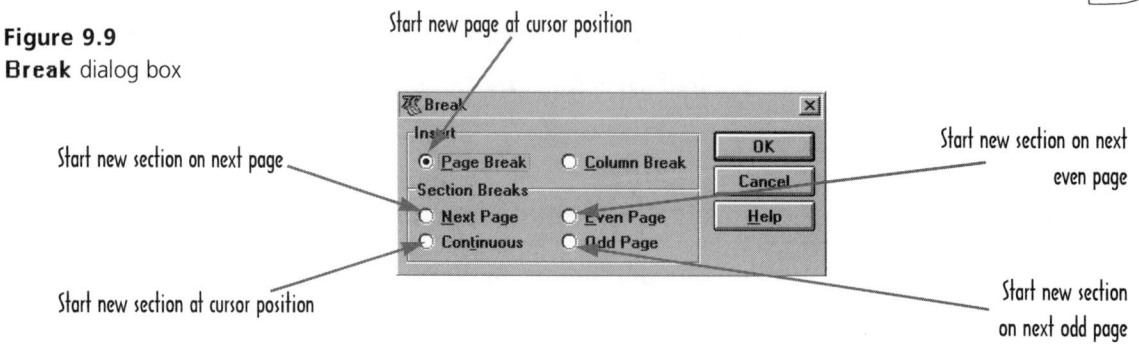

Start new section on next page

Start new section on next even page

Start new section at cursor position

Start new section on next odd page

Dividing your document into a number of separate sections allows you to apply different settings to each part. Therefore, should you need to print a piece of your document differently — perhaps to fit a wide table that must be printed side-on to the page (landscape orientation) — simply insert a new section and apply the appropriate settings.

Page settings — File ↪ Page Setup

Word's **Page Setup** property sheet contains settings that control the way your document is printed:

- **Margins** — defines the size of the page margins, as well as the distance between the edge of the page and your header and footer
- **Paper Size** — usually the page size will correspond to the size of the paper in one of your printer's trays (e.g. A4). There is also a setting to change the orientation of the page between landscape or portrait
- **Paper Source** — some printers provide more than one paper tray or have a manual feed facility. Change the settings in this page to specify the source of the paper used to print your document
- **Layout** — defines where new sections of your document should start, as well as permitting a different header and footer to be used on odd and even pages — useful if you are printing on both sides of the paper.

3   *Choose* **File→Page Setup** *from Word's menu bar to open the* **Page Setup** *property sheet. Click the* **Paper Size** *tab to bring this page to the forefront, then click the* **Landscape** *control (bottom left) to change the orientation of your document. Press* **OK** *to close the property sheet and apply this setting — your page rotates through 90°.*

Each of these page settings can be applied to the whole document, or just a part of it. Thus, if your document is divided into a number of sections, each can have its own **Page Setup** settings.

Adding boxes and shading

You can draw a box around a paragraph to provide emphasis for a title or page header. You can also choose shading to a paragraph, or insert lines to any of its four sides. These effects are particularly useful for formatting rows and columns within tables, in order to give them a professional appearance.

4   *Select a paragraph from your document window by triple-clicking it (that is, clicking your left mouse button three times in rapid succession in the paragraph). Choose* **Format→Border and Shading** *from Word's menu bar to open a property sheet with two pages —* **Borders** *and* **Shading**.

5   *Click the* **Borders** *tab to bring this page to the forefront and select a* **Style** *and* **Color** *for the line before clicking the pre-set border labelled* **Box**. *Adjust the separation of text from this border by changing the setting* **From Text**.

6   *Click the* **Shading** *tab to bring this page to the forefront then select* **10%** *(click it) before pressing* **OK** *to close the property sheet — your paragraph will be shaded and surrounded by a box.*

Note

> Colours may be applied to the foreground (ink colour) and background (paper colour). Auto colour provides a contrast with any other colours that might be used in the paragraph

Chapter 9

Changing the typeface — Format↪Font

Word gives you control over the typefaces used throughout your document. A typeface with a particular font, style and size can be applied to a single character, the entire document, or any selection of text in-between. The typeface of the text in your document window closely corresponds to way it will appear when printed.

Figure 9.10
Font property sheet

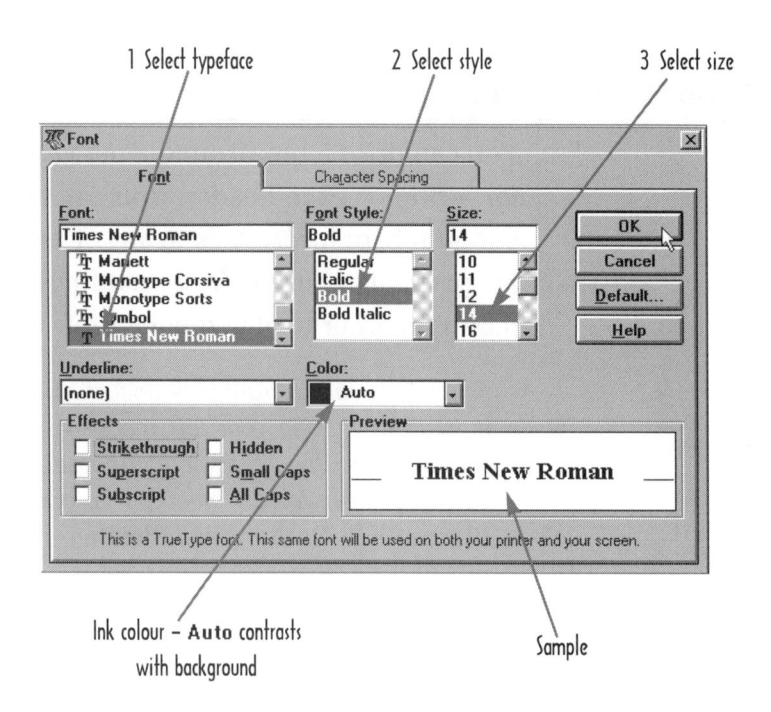

1 Select typeface   2 Select style   3 Select size

Ink colour – **Auto** contrasts with background

Sample

7   Select some text then choose **Format↪Font** form Word's menu bar to open the **Font** property sheet. Make a selection from the list of fonts on the left side of the **Font** page then choose the required **Font Style** and **Size**. Press **OK** to close the property sheet and choose the typeface for your text.

> The size of a typeface is specified in *points* which approximate to 1/72 inch. Most fonts are available in sizes between 8pt and 72pt – normal text is typically set in 10pt

190   Chapter 9   Word processing — Word

Altering the layout of a paragraph

Each time you press the enter key a hard return is inserted into the text and a new paragraph is formed. Paragraphs have settings that determine their horizontal position and alignment from the margins, as well as their vertical position from each other. These settings are stored in the hard return that terminates each paragraph.

Definition

justified ....lines of text are justified when each line begins and ends a set distance from the edge of the page, so avoiding the ragged edges of *centred*, *right*, or *left* aligned text

The hard carriage return symbols are normally hidden from view, but they can be shown in your document if you press the paragraph mark button in the toolbar. When you delete a paragraph mark its text is joined to the next paragraph and adopts its style, forming one (long) uniform paragraph.

Figure 9.11
Paragraph settings

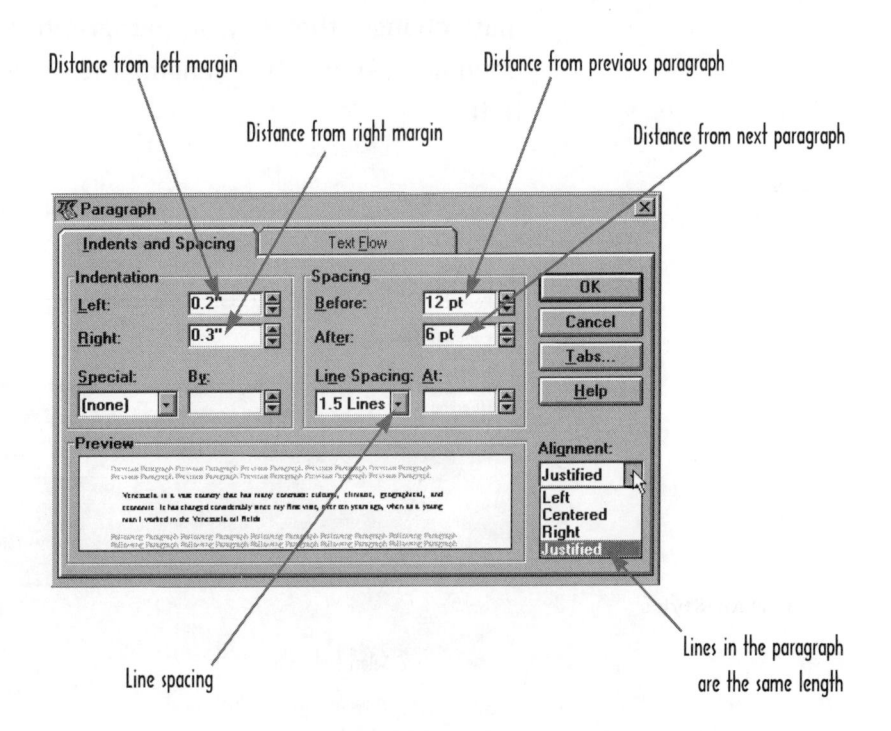

- Distance from left margin
- Distance from right margin
- Distance from previous paragraph
- Distance from next paragraph
- Line spacing
- Lines in the paragraph are the same length

8   Click within a paragraph then choose **Format→Paragraph** to open the **Paragraph** property sheet. Click the **Indents and Spacing** tab to bring this page to the forefront. Type 1982 into the **After** box then press **OK** to close the property sheet and increase the spacing between this paragraph and the next.

> **Note**
>
> Word's Options property sheet contains a setting (View page) that permits paragraph marks (and other hidden characters) to be displayed in your document window

Applying a style to your document

Each paragraph in your document has a particular *style* that is contained, together with other settings, in its paragraph mark. This style setting determines the default presentation of the paragraph — its typeface, alignment and so forth. You may change the way a paragraph is presented in your document, simply by changing the style that has been applied to it.

Figure 9.12
Style dialog box

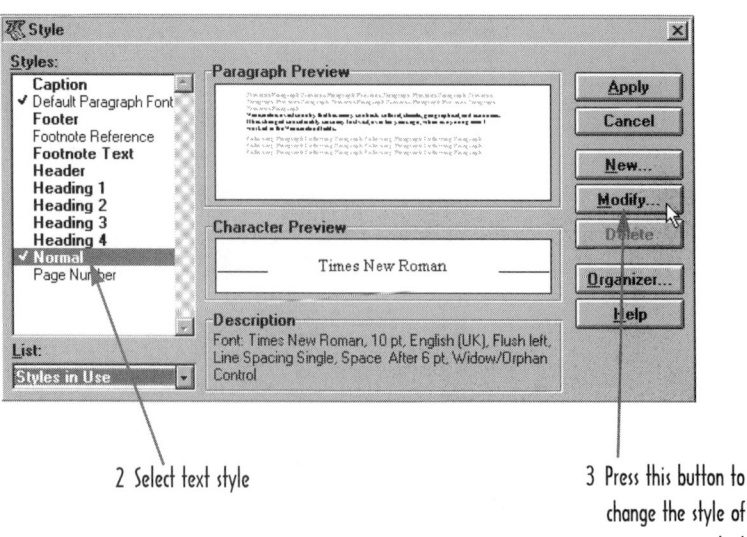

1 Set to **All Styles**

2 Select text style

3 Press this button to change the style of **Normal** text

192   Chapter 9   Word processing — Word

9   Move the cursor to a paragraph in your text then choose **Format→Style** from Word's menu bar to open the **Style** dialog box. Select **Heading 1** from the **Styles** list (left side) and press the **Apply** button to close the dialog box and change the style of this paragraph.

> **Tip**
>
> Give your document a consistent look by applying the same style for each heading, footnote, caption, and so forth

A collection of styles is copied into your document when it is created — these standard styles are contained in its template. However, you may define your own styles by pressing the **New** push-button in the **Style** dialog box — there is also button that permits you to modify an existing style.

10 Open the **Style** dialog box by choosing **Format→Style** from Word's menu bar. Select the **Normal** style from the **Styles** list then press the **Modify** push button to open a further dialog box entitled **Modify Style**.

11 Press the **Format** button in the dialog box to reveal a menu containing the choice **Font**. Click this choice to open the **Character** property sheet (Figure 9.10), then define a new typeface for the style **Normal** (see step 7). Press **OK** to close the property sheet, then press **OK** again to close the **Modify Style** dialog box.

12 You may alter other styles in the same way you changed **Normal**. When you have finished defining styles for your document, press the **Close** push-button to return to the document window — all paragraphs with the style **Normal** now have a different typeface. Close Word's main window — this exercise is complete!

> **Note**
>
> A paragraph's default style is Normal — this is the style that usually applies to the main body of your text

Reviewing and revising documents

Word provides various tools and features that help you review and revise your document prior to its final publication. These include:

- checking your spelling
- adding reviewer's comments
- finding and replacing words and phrases.

Note

> A red wavy line appears automatically under misspelt words — right-click to display a pop-up menu from which you can correct the spelling

Checking your spelling — Tools↪Spelling

The spelling of each word in your document can be checked against a number of dictionaries that are supplied with the Microsoft Office programs. You can also check words against your own dictionary for proper nouns, names and other words that are specific to your business.

Note

> The Spelling dialog box is modeless (see Chapter 4) so you can find a misspelt word, edit the document at that point, and then return to you spelling check

1. Start Word from your Taskbar (**Start↪Programs↪Microsoft Office↪Microsoft Word**) and type some text into its document window (include a few misspellings). Choose **Tools↪Spelling** from Word's menu bar to check the spelling in your document — the dialog box shown in Figure 9.13 opens at the first misspelt word.

2. The unrecognized word is displayed in the box labelled **Not in dictionary**. The **Change To** box displays the spell checker's best guess at the word that you were attempting to spell.

Figure 9.13
The **Spelling** dialog box

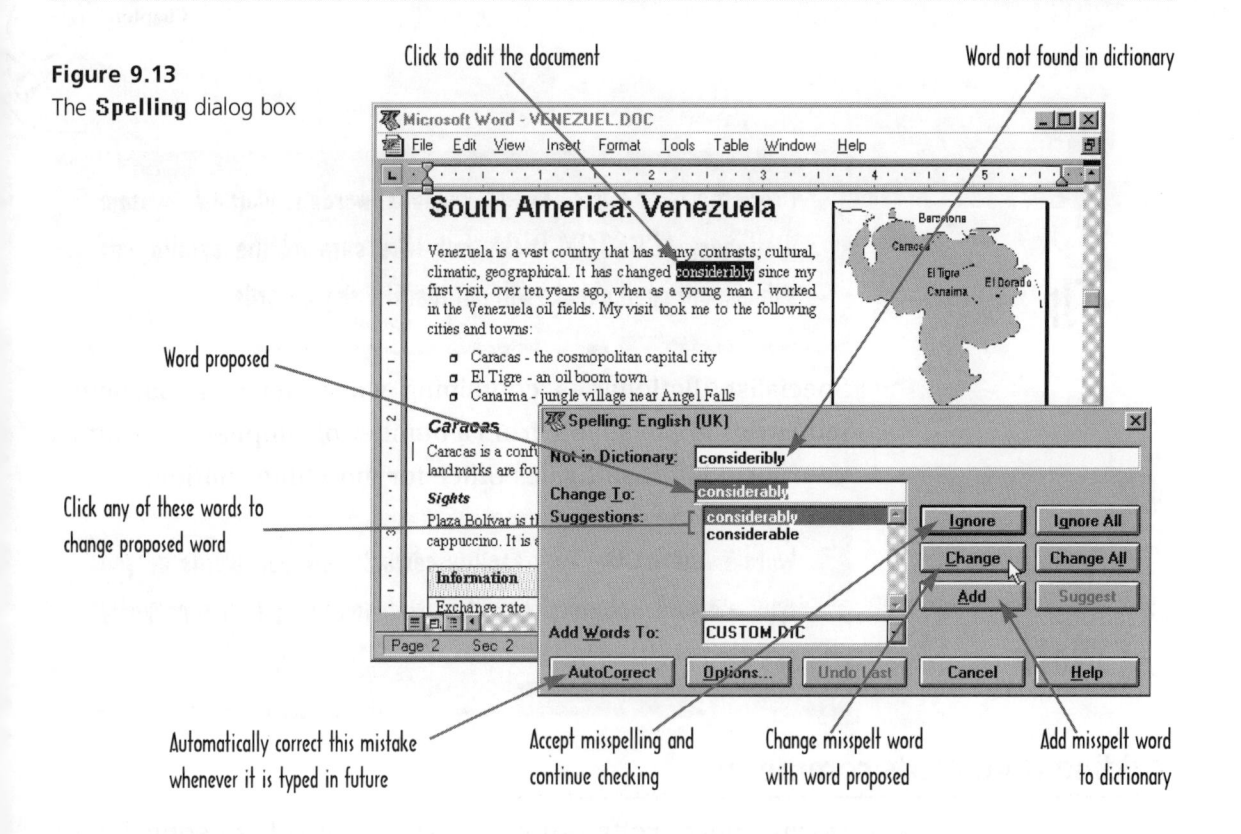

Callouts:
- Click to edit the document
- Word not found in dictionary
- Word proposed
- Click any of these words to change proposed word
- Automatically correct this mistake whenever it is typed in future
- Accept misspelling and continue checking
- Change misspelt word with word proposed
- Add misspelt word to dictionary

3   You can amend the word in the **Change To** box by clicking on a word in the **Suggestions** list. Alternatively, you can type a new word in the **Change to** box then press **Suggest** to update the **Suggestions** list.

4   Press the **AutoCorrect** button to add the misspelt word (and its correct spelling) to a list that will be used to automatically correct words as you type.

5   Press the **Change** button to replace the word in your document with the word in the **Change To** box. Alternatively, you may click in your document window and change the word yourself — click in the **Spell Check** dialog box to resume your spell check (press the **Start** push-button).

When the spelling of every word in your document has been checked, a message box is displayed — **Spelling check complete**. However you can stop the spelling check at a particular unrecognized word by pressing the dialog box's **Cancel** button.

Chapter 9   Word processing — Word   195

> **Tip:** Press the Add button to add specialist words to your own custom dictionary (CUSTOM.DIC), but take care of the spelling as subsequent spell checks will not identify these words

Specialist dictionaries containing words used in particular industries are available from a number of suppliers — contact your local Microsoft sales office for more information.

> **Note:** Word's AutoCorrect facility corrects misspelt words as you type – disable it by changing its setting in the Options property sheet's Spelling page

Adding reviewer's comments

Documents are often subject to review by other people before they are finally printed and distributed. Word provides two facilities that can assist this review process:

- when reviewing a document you can add comments to the text that will not appear when it is printed — annotation. Each reviewer can select a different annotation colour or style so that their comments can be uniquely identified
- when changing a document you can mark alterations to your document, so that people who have read the previous version can quickly identify the parts that have changed — revision marks.

Annotations are added to a document in a similar way to footnotes — a reference is inserted into the text so that the reviewer can attach a comment.

6 Choose **Tools→Options** *from Word's menu bar and click on the page* **User Info** *to confirm that your name and initials are correctly set — they will be used to identify your annotations (and revision marks). Close the property sheet by pressing* **OK**.

7   Select the text within the document to which you wish to add a comment then choose **Insert→Annotation** from Word's menu bar. Type your comment in the window that appears at the bottom of the document window then press its **Close** button — neither the annotation reference or your comment will be displayed in the document window.

8   Choose **View→Annotations** to display the document complete with any annotations that have been added. You may also print the annotations that have been attached to a document by choosing **File→Print** and selecting **Annotations** from the **Print What** box.

> **Tip**
>
> Dictate your annotations rather than typing them by pressing the Record button in the annotation window — your PC must be equipped with a microphone

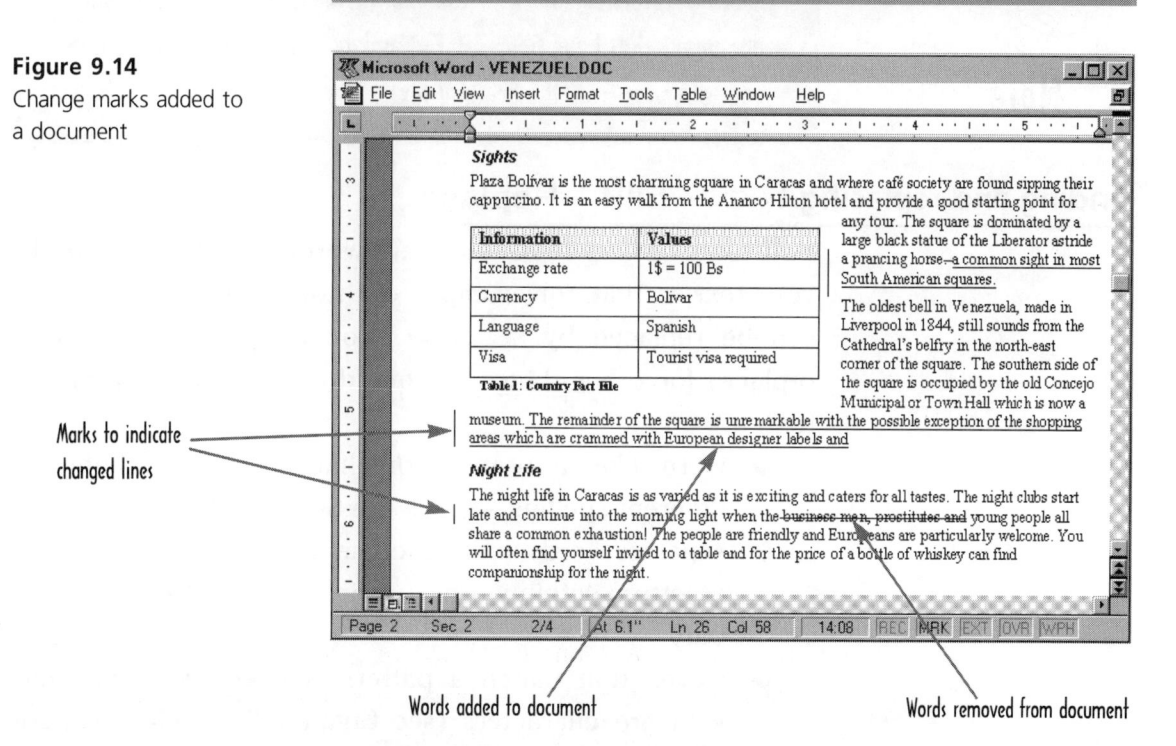

Figure 9.14
Change marks added to a document

Marks to indicate changed lines

Words added to document

Words removed from document

Words added or removed from a document can be underlined, or struck through, in a colour that is associated with the person specified in the **User Info** page of Word's **Options** property sheet — revision marks.

Chapter 9   Word processing — Word   197

9   *Choose* **Tools→Options** *from Word's menu bar and click the* **Revisions** *tab to bring this page to the forefront so you can adjust its settings. Press* **OK** *to close the property sheet.*

10 *Choose* **Tools→Revisions** *from Word's menu bar to open the* **Revisions** *dialog box. Insert a cross in the boxes* **Mark Revisions While Editing** *and* **Show Revisions on Screen** *(click them to do this), so that subsequent changes to the document will be marked as revisions within your document window. Press* **OK** *to close the dialog box.*

11 *Type some more text into the document window and also remove some existing words — these changes will be marked as revisions according to your settings in the* **Options** *property sheet.*

> **Note**
>
> Adding a vertical mark in the margin next to the lines in your document that have been altered makes it easier to differentiate your changes from the original text

Finding and replacing text — Edit→Replace

You can find and replace certain words (or phrases) within your text so that, for example, each occurrence of `Mr. Smith` can be replaced by `Mr. Jones`. You can also search (and replace) for other things in your document besides simple text:

- words like *Cathy* and *Kathy* that sound similar but have different spelling — click the **Sounds Like** check box
- separate words in the document rather than sequences of letters within words — click the **Find Whole Words Only**
- words that match a pattern defined by letters and wildcard characters (see Chapter 6) — click **Pattern matching**
- special characters like tabs, paragraph marks — press the **Special** button
- words or phrases with a particular format (e.g. italic text) or style — press the **Format** button

▷ different forms of the same word (e.g. past, present tense — **Find All Word Forms**).

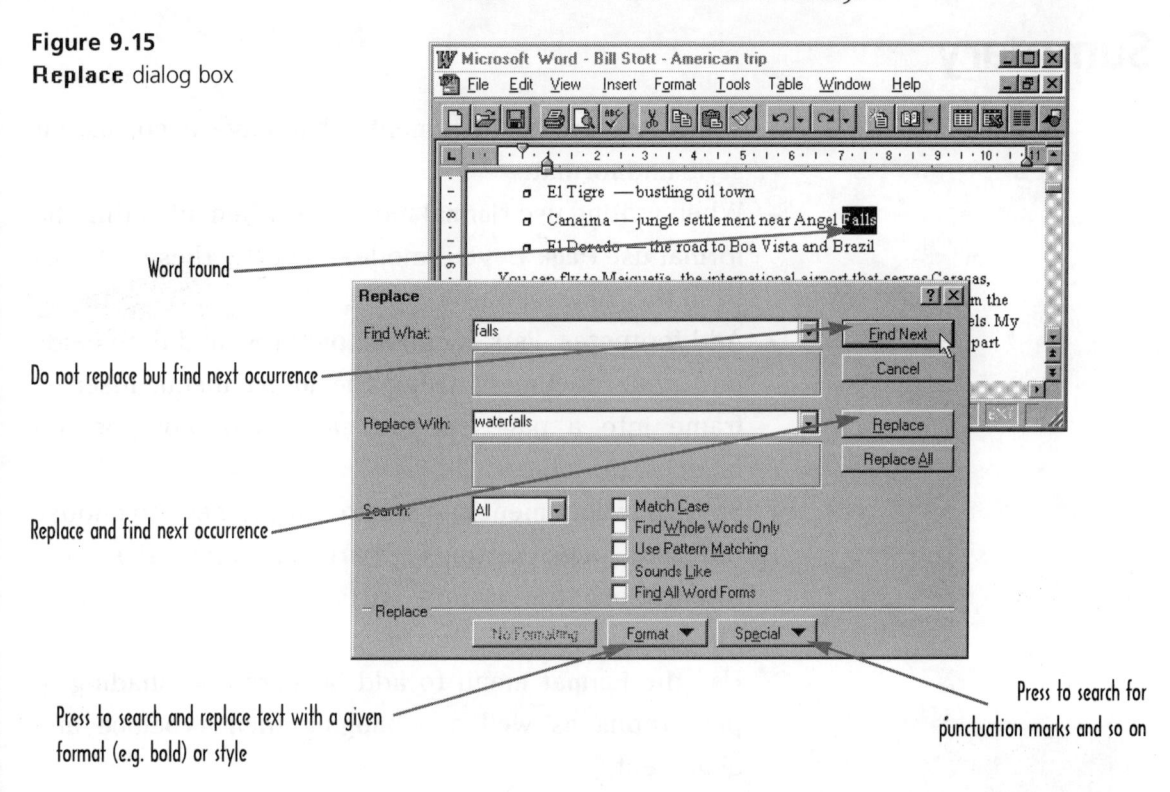

Figure 9.15
Replace dialog box

Word found

Do not replace but find next occurrence

Replace and find next occurrence

Press to search and replace text with a given format (e.g. bold) or style

Press to search for punctuation marks and so on

The search for text defined in the **Find What** box normally starts from the cursor position and proceeds to the end of the document. You can change this behaviour by changing the option for the **Search** box — **All**, **Up** or **Down**.

12 Choose **Edit→Replace** from Word's menu bar to open the dialog box shown in Figure 9.15. Type the word or phrase you wish to find in the **Find What** box. Type the word or phrase that should replace this text in the **Replace With** box. Finally press the **Replace** push-button to replace the first occurrence of your **Find What** text.

13 Continue pressing **Replace** until all the occurrences of your **Find What** text have been replaced. You may press the **Find Next** button to avoid replacing a specific occurrence of your **Find What** text, or press **Replace All** if you know that each occurrence needs replacing.

14 Close the **Replace** dialog box then close Word's main window before tidying-up your Desktop and shutting down Windows 95 (described at the end of Chapter 2).

Summary

- Templates create documents that have a consistent style and format.
- When writing use **Normal** mode and when adjusting the format use **Page Layout** mode — choose these settings from the **View** menu.
- Add footnotes, lists, symbols, pictures, and date fields into your document using the **Insert** menu. Insert a frame into a page so you can accurately position objects and tables.
- Split your document into sections if you need to choose different page settings (margins, paper size, and orientation) to various parts of the document — **File↪Page Setup**.
- Use the **Format** menu to add borders and shading to paragraphs as well as changing their typeface and alignment.
- The **Tools** menu allows you to proof your document before printing — it also is used to insert annotations and mark changes when reviewing a document (**Tools↪Revisions**).
- Find and replace words, phrases or special characters in your document by choosing **File↪Replace** from the menu bar.

Chapter

Spreadsheets — Excel

Objectives

Excel works with documents that are adapted for storing and analysing tables of information. In this chapter we consider:

▷ what is a spreadsheet? — an introduction to Excel's workbooks and worksheets

▷ creating a document — using a template to define the content and format of a workbook and worksheet

▷ features of Excel's windows — how they are adapted for processing workbooks

▷ producing a worksheet — selecting information, entering text and figures, moving and manipulating your data

▷ applying names to cells — referencing groups of cells by name, defining and managing names

▷ finishing touches and important Excel actions — worksheet page settings, formatting cells and worksheets.

When you have completed this chapter you should understand enough about Excel to create simple lists and perform basic calculations on information stored in a workbook.

What is a spreadsheet

A spreadsheet is simply a document that contains tables of information arranged into rows and columns of individual cells. A cell is the basic unit of information in a spreadsheet and may contain text, figures, formula or a reference to other cells.

Definition

column . . . . .a collection of information about a category of items in a list, i.e. the cost of each item in your *June* expenses claim is contained in the *price* column

Figure 10.1
A typical spreadsheet

	A	B	C	D	E
1					
2		June Expense Claim - Bill Stott			
3					
4		Details	Price		
5		Paper	4.30		
6		Train fare	15.75		
7		Breakfast	7.34		
8		Taxi	4.50		
9		Taxi	4.50		
10		Lunch	13.76		
11		Taxi	2.30		
12		Total	52.45		
13					
14					

Definition

row . . . . .a collection of information about the same item in a list, e.g. the first entry in your *June* expenses claim relates to *paper* bought for £4.30

The unique feature of a spreadsheet is its ability to relate groups of cells to each other then apply an operation to them. In Figure 10.1 the second column in the table forms a group of cells containing the cost of your expense items. At the bottom of the column is a cell that displays the *sum* of all the cells in this group.

Extending this basic concept allows spreadsheets to serve a wide variety of purposes, including:
- sorting and arranging information — create lists by entering and manipulating text or figures in groups of cells
- performing calculations — enter formula into a cell to display the results of operations on a group of cells.

Almost any information that you need to collect, manipulate or organize can be a put into a spreadsheet. Excel provides the facilities you need to create and perform operations on this type of document.

Workbooks and worksheets

Excel refers to worksheets, rather than spreadsheets, and groups of related worksheets together within a single workbook. Each workbook is contained in its own file and is therefore comparable with an individual Word document — worksheets within a workbook are like different sections of a Word document.

> **Note**
>
> The settings defined by Excel's File→Page Setup apply only to the currently selected worksheet just like Word's File→Page Setup settings apply to a selected section (see Chapter 9)

There's a number of advantages to organising a spreadsheet into workbooks and worksheets, for example:
- you can consolidate a number of individual expense accounts by summing the total given on each worksheet
- information that is only loosely related can still be held together in the same file — client notes, accounts and so forth
- special sheets can be added to your workbook for containing charts or a special type of program (*macro sheets*, *Visual Basic modules* and so forth).

> **Tip**
>
> You will generally want to start a new workbook when there is no relationship between the information you are adding and the information that already exists

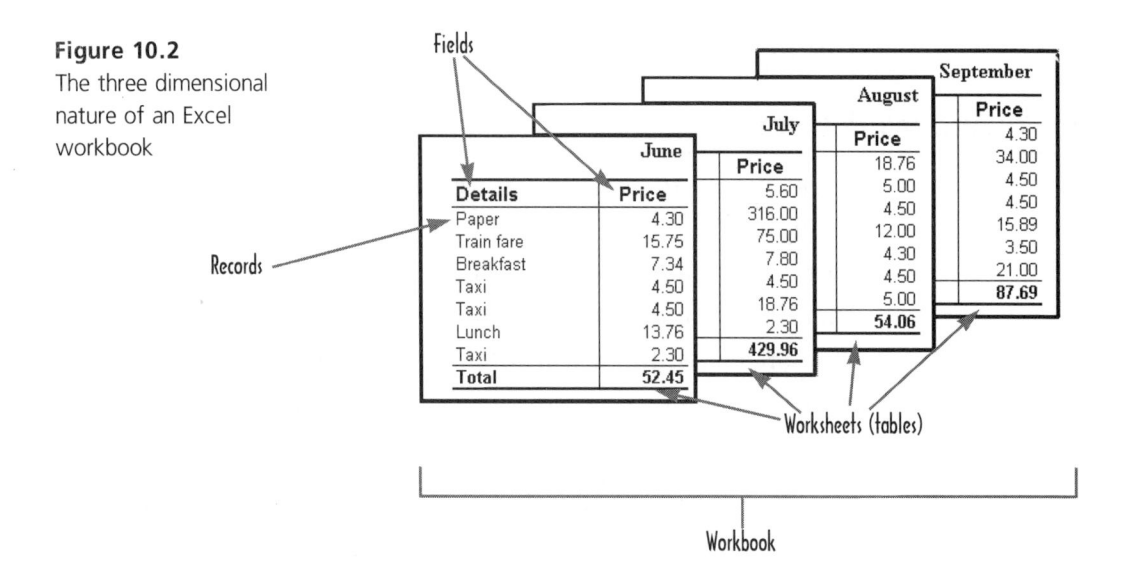

Figure 10.2 The three dimensional nature of an Excel workbook

Details	Price
Paper	4.30
Train fare	15.75
Breakfast	7.34
Taxi	4.50
Taxi	4.50
Lunch	13.76
Taxi	2.30
Total	**52.45**

June — Fields, Records

July Price: 5.60, 316.00, 75.00, 7.80, 4.50, 18.76, 2.30, **429.96**

August Price: 18.76, 5.00, 4.50, 12.00, 4.30, 4.50, 5.00, **54.06**

September Price: 4.30, 34.00, 4.50, 4.50, 15.89, 3.50, 21.00, **87.69**

Worksheets (tables) — Workbook

Creating an Excel document

When Excel is started **Book1** is automatically created in its document window, in the same way that **Document1** is created when Word is first started (see Chapter 9). The settings used to create **Book1** are copied from within Excel, unless you have created your own template to define the format and content of this initial workbook.

1   *Start Excel from your Taskbar (***Start↪Programs↪Microsoft Office↪Microsoft Excel***) to create a new workbook containing sixteen worksheets —* **Book1**.

> **Note:** Excel's initial workbook may be defined by a template file named BOOK.XLT located within the XLSTART folder (C:\MSOFFICE\EXCEL)

2 Choose **File→Save As** from Excel's menu bar to open the **Save As** dialog box. Click the box labelled **Save as type** and select **Template** from the list of file types — you want to store the contents of the document window as a template rather than a workbook file.

3 Type BOOK into the **File name** box and select the folder **xlstart** from the list of directories (normally located in c:\msoffice\excel). Press **Close** to close the dialog box and save your document as Excel's default template.

> **Note:** The file BOOK.XLT is called Workbook when displayed in the General page of the New property sheet

BOOK.XLT is Excel's equivalent of Word's NORMAL.DOT. Once you are more familiar with the operation of Excel you may decide to replace the contents of BOOK.XLT, so that a more appropriate initial workbook is produced whenever you start the program.

Creating a workbook from Excel templates

You can create other templates besides BOOK.XLT and store them in the **Bill's templates** folder (see Chapter 8). They then may be selected from the **New** property sheet whenever you decide to create a new Excel document. A template is formed by saving any workbook as a template file (see step 2).

> **Note:** Open the New property sheet from the Office toolbar (see page 165) or by choosing **File→New** from Excel's Menu bar

Chapter 10 Spreadsheets — Excel 205

Figure 10.3
Properties of your document

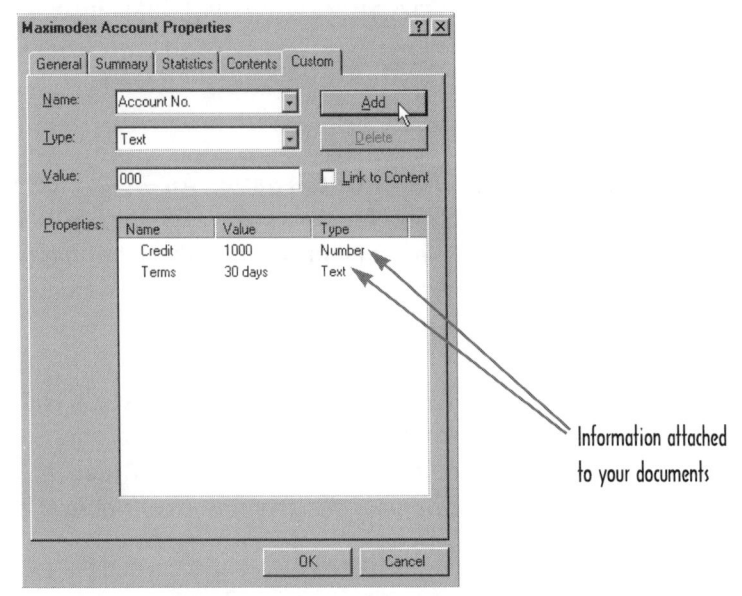

You can modify an existing Excel template simply by opening its file (**File↪Open**), making some changes, then storing it back in the file (**File↪Save**). One of the things you might wish to change in an existing template is its **author** setting— information which is held in the file's properties (see page 116).

4   Choose **File↪Properties** from Excel's menu bar to open the property sheet shown in Figure 10.3. Click the **Summary** page and complete the boxes which will contain information common to every workbook created from this template.

5   Click the **Custom** page and create your own categories of information for workbooks based on the template — type `Account No.` in the **Name** box, `000` in the **Value** box, then press **Add**. Close the property sheet by pressing **OK** then choose **File↪Save** to update the template file (**BOOK.XLT**).

> **NOTE:** Excel provides a number of standard templates (msoffice\templates) which you can modify for the specific needs of your business — see the Spreadsheet Solutions page of the New document property sheet

Creating a new worksheet

A workbook is normally created with sixteen worksheets. However you can add further worksheets to your workbook, up to a maximum of 255 worksheets, by applying **Insert→Worksheet** from Excel's menu bar. New worksheets are inserted just before the currently selected worksheet and given a default name like **Sheet17**.

Figure 10.4
Workbooks and worksheets

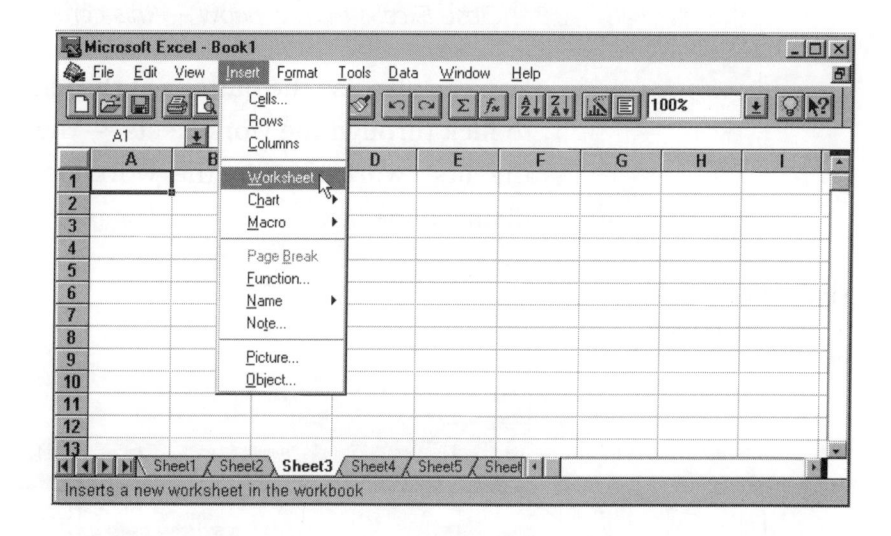

> You can also insert a worksheet by right clicking on a worksheet's tab – this reveals a pop-up menu from which you can choose **Insert**

Tip

Moving worksheets within a workbook

The order of worksheets within a workbook can be changed as easily as if they were held in a ring-binder. Each worksheet has a tab that serves both as a label to identify it, and as a handle to drag it between its neighbouring worksheets.

6   *Drag the tab* **Sheet2** *so that it is located between* **Sheet4** *and* **Sheet5** — *the order of the worksheets in your workbook is altered.*

7   Right-click the tab **Sheet2** to reveal a pop-up menu. Select **Move or Copy** from this menu to open a dialog box containing a list of the worksheets in your current workbook (as well a list of other workbook files stored in the same folder). Click **Sheet3** in the list labelled **Before Sheet** then press **OK** to close the dialog box and restore the position of your worksheet.

8   Close Excel's main window — this completes the exercise.

You can also use the buttons at the left of the workbook's tabs to flick through the worksheets — the far left button displays the first worksheet in the workbook, the far right button displays the last.

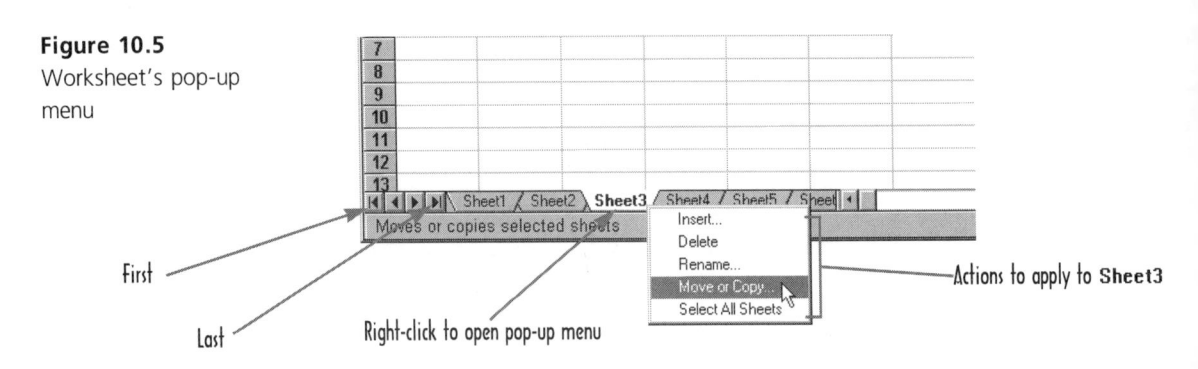

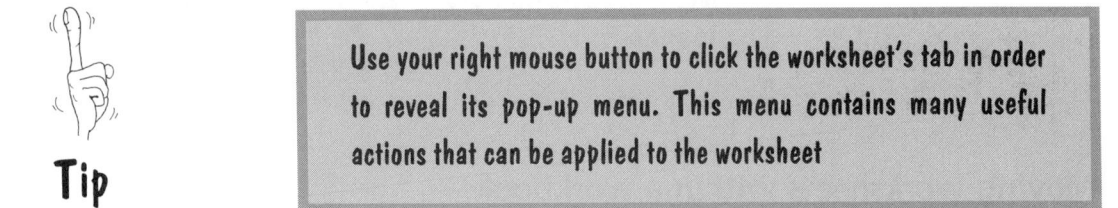

Figure 10.5
Worksheet's pop-up menu

First

Last

Right-click to open pop-up menu

Actions to apply to **Sheet3**

> **Tip**
>
> Use your right mouse button to click the worksheet's tab in order to reveal its pop-up menu. This menu contains many useful actions that can be applied to the worksheet

Features of Excel's windows

Excel's menu bar provides access to actions specifically for processing worksheets and workbooks, as well as the more general-purpose actions that are often found in an application's menu.

Figure 10.6
Excel's window

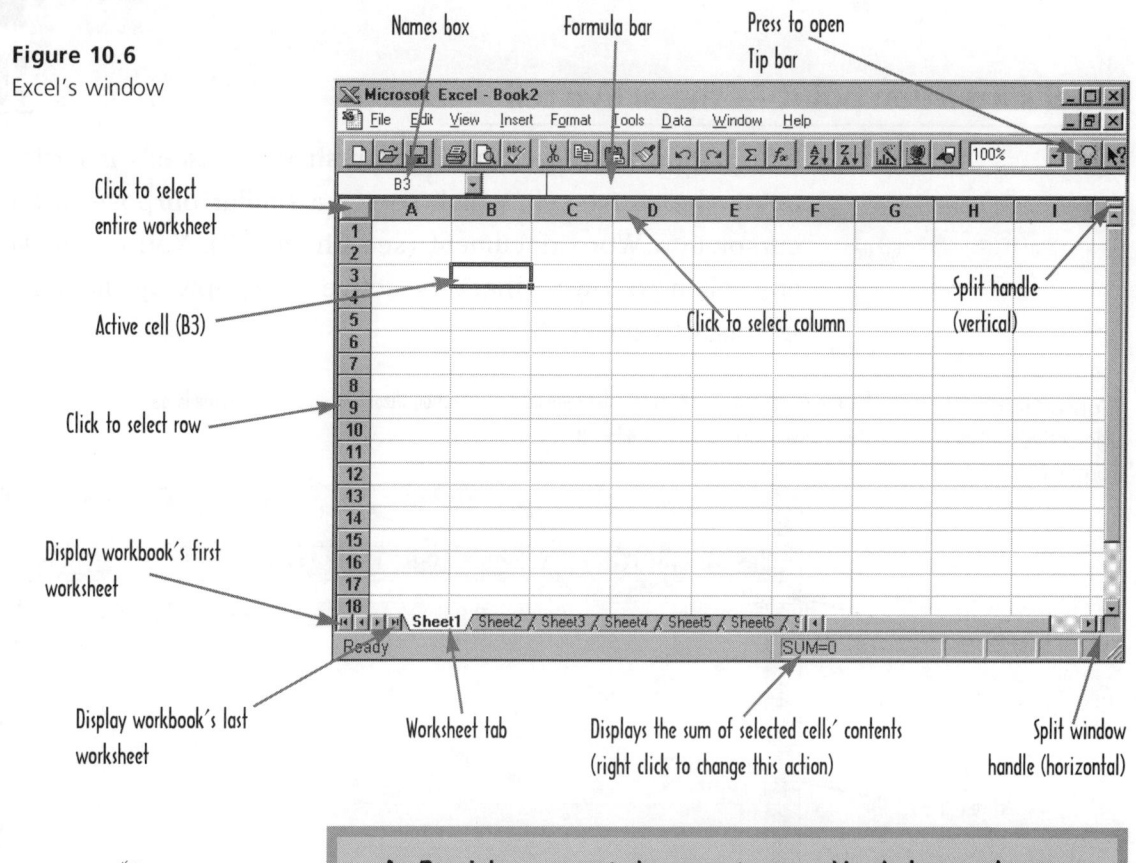

Callouts on figure:
- Names box
- Formula bar
- Press to open Tip bar
- Click to select entire worksheet
- Active cell (B3)
- Click to select row
- Click to select column
- Split handle (vertical)
- Display workbook's first worksheet
- Display workbook's last worksheet
- Worksheet tab
- Displays the sum of selected cells' contents (right click to change this action)
- Split window handle (horizontal)

> **Note**
> An Excel document window contains a workbook that can have as many as 255 worksheets. A worksheet has 256 columns and 16384 rows of cells — each holding up to 255 characters

Producing a worksheet

Excel's document windows are specifically adapted for entering and manipulating tables of information. You enter information into a cell simply by selecting it (click the cell) then typing some text or figures from your keyboard — each cell may contain as many as 255 characters.

> **Note**
> Cells in a worksheet are independent containers of information that can be arranged as you wish — very different to lines in a Word document whose order is always significant

Chapter 10 Spreadsheets — Excel

Chapter 10

Excel's insertion point — the *active* cell

Information is entered into a worksheet at Excel's insertion point, the *active* cell, which serves a similar purpose to the cursor in a Word document (see Chapter 3). You can make any cell in your worksheet the active cell simply by clicking it — this also selects it.

Figure 10.7
The active cell and Formula bar

Labels: Press to cancel and clear Formula bar; Press to enter formula into cell; Function Wizard; Formula bar; Name box; Active cell

> **Note**
> The reference D5 in the Name box describes the cell that intersects column *D* and row *5*. The Formula bar shows the contents of the active cell

1. Start Excel from your Taskbar (**Start⇝Programs⇝Microsoft Office⇝Microsoft Excel**) to create a new workbook — **Book1**. Click the cell that intersects column D and row 5 in the worksheet labelled **Sheet1**. Type shopping list then press [Enter] to move to the next cell in the same column (**D6**).

2. Type a description for a series of ten shopping items into different rows within column D, pressing [Enter] after typing each item to move to the next cell. The list should occupy cells in the range **D6** to **D15** (i.e. **D6:D15**).

3   Double-click the cell **D5** *to make the cell into an* edit *box (see Appendix B) with its own cursor. Use this edit box to change the contents of the cell into uppercase then press* [Enter] *to restore the cell to its normal form and make* **D6** *the active cell.*

Typing information into a cell is like typing a line of text into a Word document — you can use many of the skills learnt in Chapter 3. However, there is no defined order in which a worksheet must be completed (unlike lines in a Word document) and often information is distributed throughout its collection of cells.

> **Note**
>
> You can also alter the contents of your active cell by editing its text as displayed in the Formula bar (Figure 10.7), which is another type of edit box

Entering figures

Figures are entered into a worksheet just like text — select the cell and type the value.

4   *Click the cell* **E6** *(opposite the first item in your list), type* `1.20` *(its price) and press* [Enter]. *Repeat this operation to price all the items in your list.*

You will notice that figures, like `1.20`, have their terminating zero removed when you press [Enter] — this is because figures are given a default format by Excel. However you can display monetary values in an appropriate way by changing the *format code* of the cells from the **Format Cells** property sheet.

5   *Click the label* **E** *at the top of your document window to select the whole of column E then choose* **Format→Cells** *from Excel's menu bar to open the* **Format Cells** *property sheet. Click* **Currency** *from the list of* **Categories** *(within the* **Number** *page) then press* **OK** *to close the property sheet and change the format of the prices in column E.*

Figure 10.8
Format Cells property sheet

Precede your numbers with a currency symbol

Select the number of decimal places for your numbers

Select to display your negative numbers in this format

> **Note**
>
> A more complete description of format codes and other ways to change the presentation of information within cells is given at the end of the chapter

Changing the size of cells

The descriptions of some items in your shopping list are probably too long to fit inside their cells. Before you added the pricing figures this extra text simply overflowed into adjacent cells, however now that column C has its own information some of your descriptions will be truncated.

6   Move your mouse pointer slowly over the line that separates column label D from column label E. When the pointer changes into a double-headed arrow drag the line to your right then release the mouse button to increase the width of column D.

The width of the column containing the active cell can also be altered from the dialog box that is opened when you choose **Width** from the **Format→Column** continuation menu.

> **Note**
>
> ##### is displayed when a cell containing a figure is not wide enough for the number — avoiding the value being misread (see page 252)

Producing a total — AutoSum

The next step of producing this worksheet involves tying together the rows within a column, in order to produce a total for the items in your shopping list. This is where the power of a spreadsheet lies — the ability to relate groups of cells to each other and then apply an operation to them.

In addition to text and figures, cells can also contain formulas that express relationships between groups of cells. Typically the cell containing the formula will also display the result, so you can easily express something of the nature:

Make this cell display the total of the values contained in column E, row 6 through row 15, i.e. =SUM(E6:E15)

Totalling columns is a common requirement and, fortunately, there is a toolbar button that avoids the need to type this formula directly into the cell.

7   *Click the cell E18 that is beneath the column of prices for the items in your shopping list. Press the AutoSum button (in the standard toolbar) then press* Enter *to insert a formula into this cell — it displays the total cost of your shopping.*

You will recall that the contents of the active cell are displayed in Excel's Formula bar — a form of edit box. Therefore when a the active cell contains a formula, its text (i.e. =SUM(E6:E15)) is displayed in the Formula bar while the cell itself displays the result. You may use the Formula bar to edit the parameters of the formula or even type an entirely new formula (see Chapter 11).

Figure 10.9
Summing a column of figures — AutoSum button

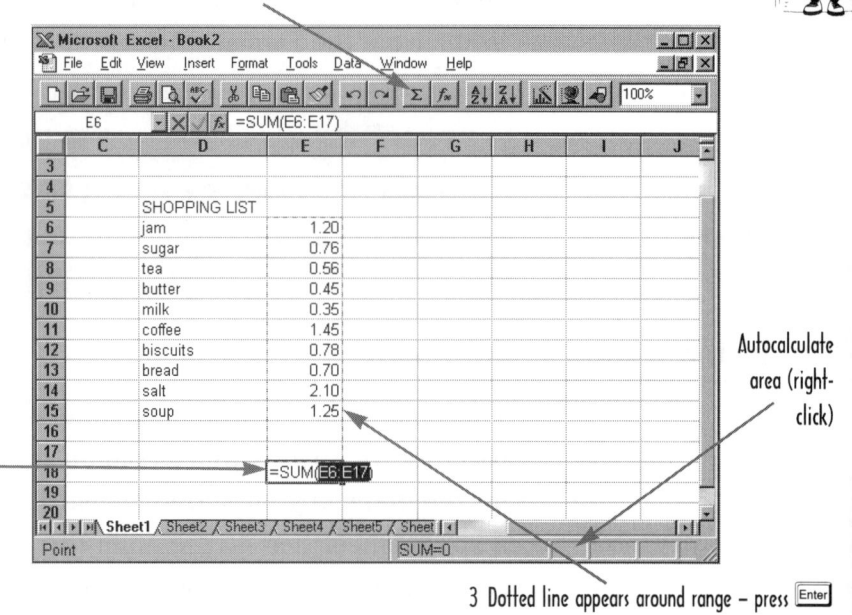

2 Click here to insert sum formula into selected cell

1 Click here to select cell

Autocalculate area (right-click)

3 Dotted line appears around range – press Enter

Note

The AutoCalculate area of the status bar will display the SUM, AVERAGE or COUNT of the selected areas

Filling cells with the same value — drag-fill

Frequently you will need to fill a range of cells with the same value. Your shopping list, for example, might have a discount column with a 10% discount applying to most items.

Figure 10.10
Drag-filling with a cell's fill handle

Drag-fill handle down to end of range

214   Chapter 10   Spreadsheets — Excel

8   Enter `10%` in cell F6 — the same row as the first item in your list. Point to the handle in the bottom right hand corner of this cell (your mouse pointer turns into a black cross). Drag this fill handle to the row that marks the bottom of your list then release the mouse button, so that these cells fill with the figure in the first cell — 10%.

> **Note**
>
> You can also fill a range of cells by first selecting the range of cells (Table 10.1), then typing the number to be duplicated, and finally pressing `Ctrl` + `Enter`.

Filling cells with a series of values — Edit↪Fill

You can also fill a range of cells with different values, such as a sequence of numbers starting from *1* — this can save a lot of typing!

7   Type `1` in cell C6 — opposite the first item in your list. Point to the handle in this cell so that your mouse pointer turns into a black cross. Drag the fill handle down to C15 in order to fill these cells with the value `1` — the cells remain selected so further actions may be applied to them.

8   Choose **Edit↪Fill** from Excel's menu bar then choose **Series** from its continuation menu in order to open the **Series** dialog box. Type `1` in the **Step Value** box and select **Linear** from the **Type** options, before pressing **OK** to close the dialog box and apply this series to your data — each item in your shopping list now has its own number.

> **Tip**
>
> Use your right mouse button to drag-fill a range of cells in order to reveal a pop-up menu, from which you can open the **Series** dialog box (or otherwise qualify the action)

Figure 10.11
Series dialog box

Increase values in linear series

Only one column has been selected

Increase values by 1

Values will not exceed this value

> **Note**
>
> The Series dialog box can be used to fill cells with series of numbers (or dates) that increase at different rates and between defined ranges

Selecting information

Actions applied from the menu bar operate on cells that have been selected in your current worksheet. Selecting a single cell is simple — just click it. However you can select cells in other ways, as described in Table 10.1.

> **Tip**
>
> Press [Tab] to move the active cell forward in a selection of cells and [Shift]+[Tab] to move it back

Table 10.1

Selecting cells in a worksheet

Select what	Mouse	Keyboard
individual cell	click the cell	use the cursor keys
column of cells	click the column heading	`Ctrl`+space
row of cells	click the row heading	`Shift`+space
whole worksheet	click the button at the intersection of the column and row headings (top left)	`Ctrl`+a
continuous range of cells	click at the start of the range then hold down the left mouse button while dragging to the end of the range — drag-select	press `Shift` and use the cursor keys
collection of cells	press `Ctrl` while clicking each subsequent cell	–

Definition

drag-select . . . . by moving the mouse pointer (a thick white cross) into the middle of a cell, pressing the left-mouse button then moving the mouse pointer into the next cell you drag-select the cells. When you release the mouse button both cells are selected

Moving information within a worksheet

You can move information in an Excel document in much the same way that other (selected) objects are moved within the Windows 95 environment:

▷ dragging — a general description of dragging is given in Chapter 1

▷ cutting and pasting — a general description is given in Chapter 7, specific details are given below.

Caution

The contents of any cells in the destination area are overwritten when information is moved (or copied) onto them – see *Inserting cells*

Cutting or copying and pasting

In Excel the cut and paste action is slightly different as information is not removed from your document until you apply the paste action. Cells that have been cut (or copied)

Figure 10.12
Moving information in a worksheet

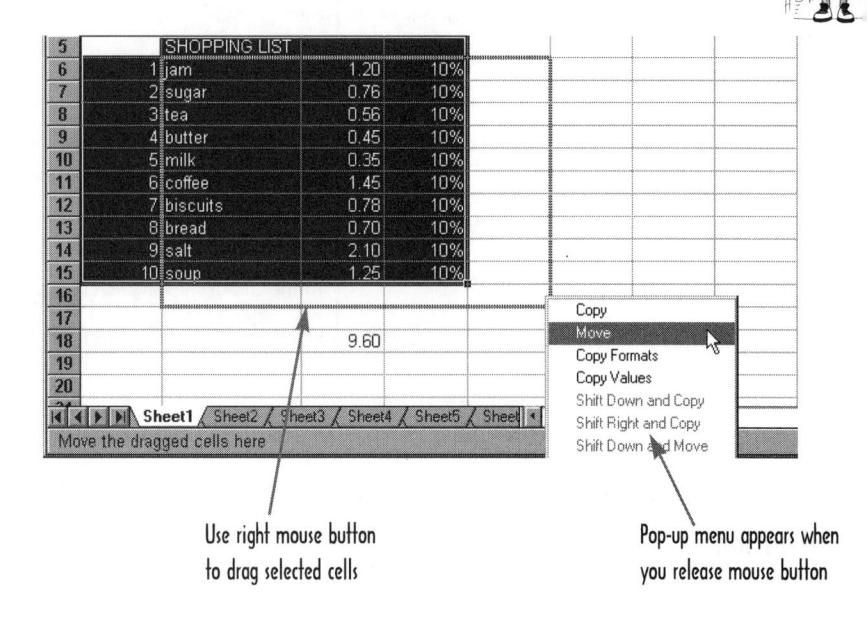

Use right mouse button to drag selected cells

Pop-up menu appears when you release mouse button

are marked with a moving border which remains until the action is complete, or until you press [Esc].

In other respects cut and paste is the same as found in other programs — information can be cut and pasted between different documents, as well as between worksheets and workbooks.

Clearing cells — Edit↪Clear

A cell's contents are overwritten when you select it and type anything at your keyboard. You can also delete the contents of a selected cell or range of cells by making a choice from the **Edit↪Clear** continuation menu.

9 *Select the group of cells in column C (opposite the description of the items in your shopping list). Choose* **Edit↪Clear↪Contents** *from Excel's menu bar to remove the contents of these cells.*

The **Edit↪Clear** continuation menu allows you to clear cells in the following ways:

▷ clear contents — remove anything you might have typed into the cell

- clear format — restore default format information to cell
- clear notes — remove notes that you have added to a cell with **Insert↪Note**. Adding a note to a cell can help remind you as to how its value was obtained
- clear all — remove all of above from selected cell or range.

> **Note**
>
> Clearing only removes things contained in the cell and not the cell itself — see deleting cells

Deleting cells — Edit↪Delete

When you delete a cell or range of cells it is the cell rather than its content that is removed from your worksheet. The gap that this leaves will be filled by:
- moving up the cells from the same column (below)
- moving across the cells from the same row (left)
- deleting the rest of the row or column.

> **Caution**
>
> Deleting cells from part of a list might alter the arrangement of the remaining information, as one column (or row) is moved relative to the others

Inserting cells — Insert↪Rows

Normally, when you drag-and-drop a range of cells they overwrite whatever they land on. However you can insert information into the middle of an existing range without overwriting its contents, by creating a suitable gap before moving or copying your information.

10 Click the cell F6 then choose **Insert↪Columns** from Excel's menu bar to add a further column in the middle of your shopping list.

> Hold down [Shift] during a drag-and-drop operation to move a selection of cells. This avoids overwriting the cells onto which they are dropped

Summary of manipulating cells

The following figure summarizes the most important ways in which you can manipulate the cells in your worksheet.

Figure 10.13
Summary of manipulating cells

Applying names to cells

Referring to a cell by a name such as *list_total* is far more intelligible than a reference like *E16*. Names have other advantages too:

- names make formulas easier to read and provide a degree of documentation. For instance,

    =SUM(expense_items)

    is much clearer than

    =SUM(E6:E15)

220   Chapter 10   Spreadsheets — Excel

- using the name *BaseRate* (=5.6%) throughout your workbook, rather than a specific value, means that when *BaseRate* varies you need change only the definition of the name rather than each cell where it is used
- names are often more convenient to use than references like *Sheet1!E6:E15*.

> **Using names rather than references improves the structure of your worksheets, making them easier to use and maintain**

Tip

Names can be used almost anywhere that a column, row reference (called A1 reference style) can be used. They are defined by choosing **Insert▸Name**.

11 *Drag-select the range of cells E6:E15. Choose* **Insert▸Name▸Define** *from Excel's menu bar to open the* **Define Name** *dialog box.*

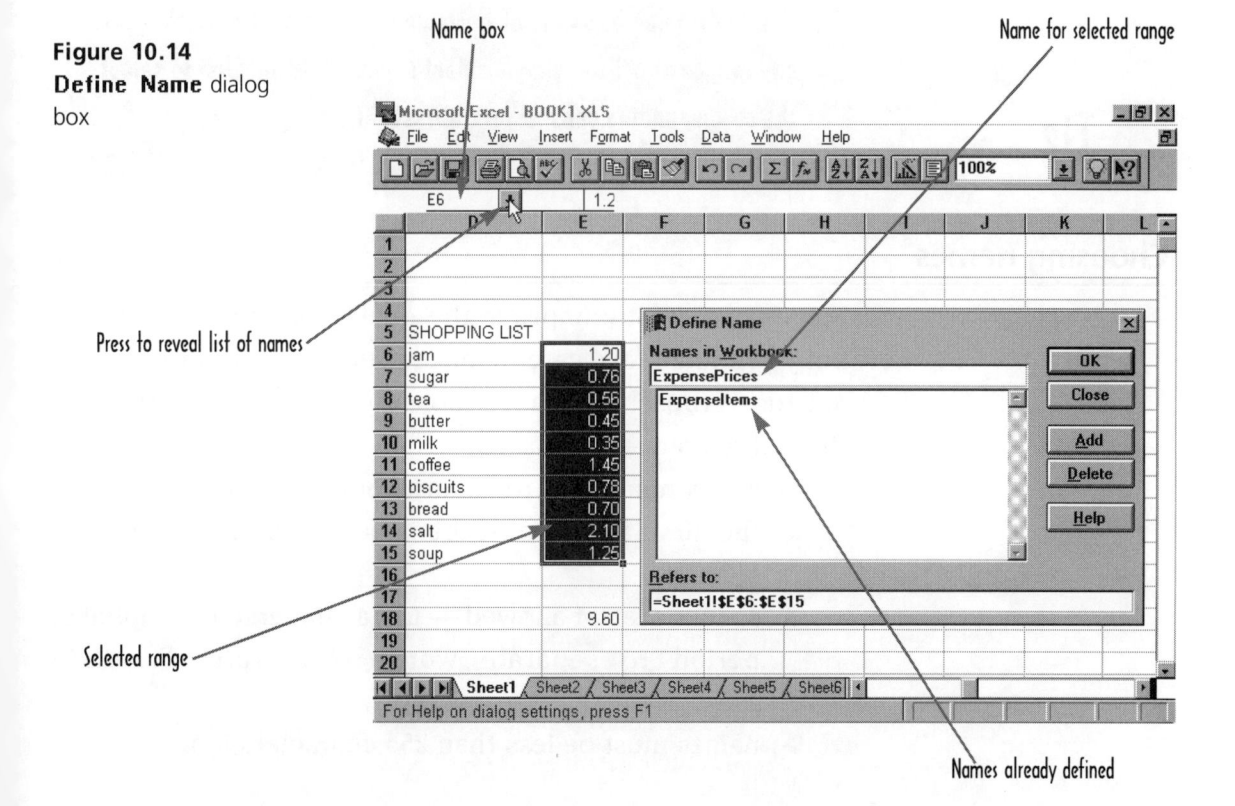

Figure 10.14
Define Name dialog box

Name box

Name for selected range

Press to reveal list of names

Selected range

Names already defined

Chapter 10 Spreadsheets — Excel 221

> **Note** — The Define Name dialog box can be used to both add and delete names for cells in your workbook

12   Type the name ExpensePrices into the edit control at the top of the dialog box then press **Add** to insert it into the list of names defined for your workbook. Press **OK** to close the dialog box.

13   Click the cell G17 and type =SUM(into your Formula bar — the first part of the SUM formula. Press the button attached to the Names box (left of Formula bar) to reveal a list of the names defined for your workbook and select **ExpensePrices** to copy this name into your Formula bar — the second part of the SUM formula. Type) and press Enter to complete the formula — its result is displayed in G17.

> **Tip** — Use the Names box (left of Formula bar) to select specific cells and ranges of cells — simply select a name from this list to select the corresponding cells in your worksheet

Choosing names

Names can greatly improve the quality of your spreadsheet but you should take care to make your names descriptive and not too verbose — a badly chosen name can be worse than the cell reference it replaces.

There's a number of rules for choosing names:

- the first letter must be a letter or an underscore (_1stQrt)
- spaces are not allowed — use an underscore, capital or period to separate words (*base_rate*, *BaseRate*, *base.rate*)
- names must be less than 255 characters long.

You are free to use any numbers and uppercase or lowercase letters that might be needed to compose an appropriate name. However you should consider the following:

- make names meaningful — avoid codes and cryptic abbreviations such as *EEI09DSK*. Will you remember what it means six months or ten years later?
- use names with exact meanings that are consistent throughout all your workbooks. Base rate may not have an exact meaning if your spreadsheet is used in several countries.
- consider prefixing a lower case character to the start of a name to reflect the type of information in the cell(s) — *n* for a number (*nBaseRate*), *l* for a list (*lExpenseItems*), *f* for a formula (*fTotal*), and so forth
- names over four characters long should differ by at least two characters — avoid names that are so similar they can be easily confused or mistyped.

Note

> #NAME? appears in a cell that contains a reference to an invalid name — check the name in this cell against the list in your Names box. (see Chapter 11 *Troubleshooting*)

Cell references

There are occasions when you might need to reference a cell that hasn't been given a specific name. Excel uses the following conventions for referencing cells within your formulas:

- *A1* — a relative reference is calculated as a number of rows and columns from the cell that contains the formula. The reference remains valid while the cells maintain the same relative position to each other
- *$A$1* — an absolute reference is calculated as a number of rows and columns from the top left of the worksheet. The reference is invalidated if you subsequently move the cell

- *A1:B5* —range of cells between cell A1 and cell B5
- *A1,B5* — a list of cells that includes A1 and B5 (but not cells between them)
- *Sheet2!$A$1* — a cell in the worksheet named *Sheet 2*. Use this form of reference when addressing cells on other worksheets
- *[ABC.XLS]Sheet1!$A$1* — a cell in the worksheet *Sheet1* in the workbook *ABC.XLS*. Use this form of reference when addressing cells in other workbooks
- *'C:\work\[ABC.XLS]Sheet1'!$A$1* — use quotation marks to reference a worksheet in a workbook file located within a specific folder.

> **Note**
>
> #REF! appears in a cell that contains an invalid reference — deleting a cell often causes this type of error (see Chapter 11 Troubleshooting)

Moving a cell that contains a relative reference will **result in** the reference being adjusted to compensate for the movement. Thus, moving a range of cells will also update the reference in any cell that refers to them.

14 Select all the cells in your shopping list then drag them to a different part of the worksheet (first move the mouse pointer to the border beneath the block of selected cells so it changes into an arrow).

15 Open the **Names** box and click **ExpensePrices** to select the group of cells that contain the prices of your shopping list. Close Excel's main window (don't bother saving changes) — this exercise is complete.

> **Tip**
>
> While editing a formula you can enter a cell's reference simply by clicking on the cell within its worksheet — this even applies if the cell is located in a different workbook

Finishing touches and important Excel actions

Spreadsheets are often used simply as scratchpads — for working-out ideas, storing information and producing results from calculations. However they can also be used, with great effect, to present information both on your computer's screen and in paper form as a report:

- defining how worksheets are printed
- removing page gridlines and headings
- hiding rows, columns and worksheets
- using predefined formats
- formatting groups of cells.

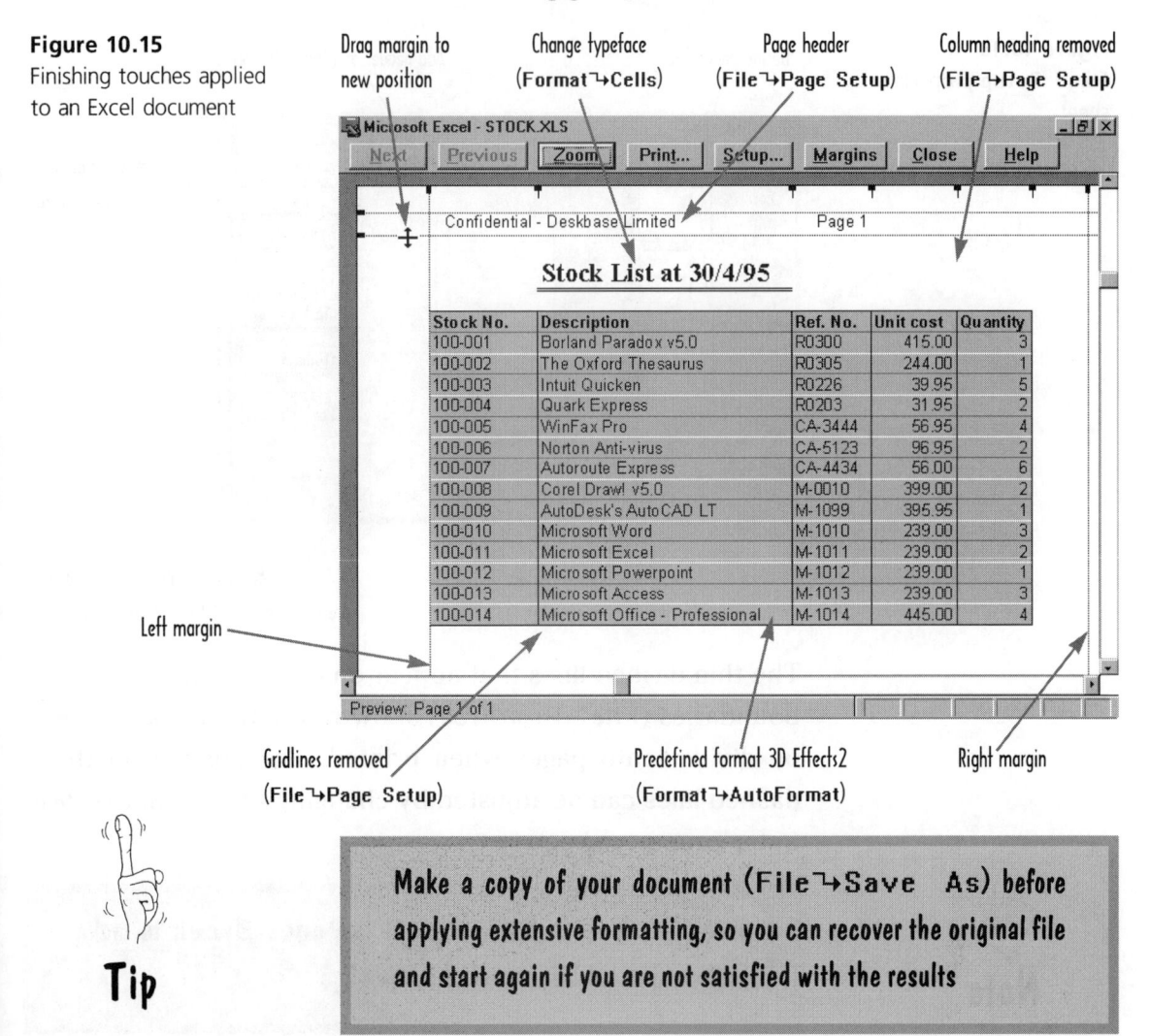

Figure 10.15
Finishing touches applied to an Excel document

Callouts:
- Drag margin to new position
- Change typeface (Format→Cells)
- Page header (File→Page Setup)
- Column heading removed (File→Page Setup)
- Left margin
- Gridlines removed (File→Page Setup)
- Predefined format 3D Effects2 (Format→AutoFormat)
- Right margin

Tip: Make a copy of your document (File→Save As) before applying extensive formatting, so you can recover the original file and start again if you are not satisfied with the results

Defining how worksheets are printed — File↪Page Setup

When a worksheet is viewed in a document window it appears as a huge sheet of squared paper, but when it is printed this single sheet must be cut up into a number of pages which corresponds to your printer's standard paper size — the more cells have been completed, the more pages are printed.

The **Page Setup** property sheet contains the settings that determine how a particular worksheet will be represented on paper. Each worksheet has its own settings.

Figure 10.16
Page Setup property sheet

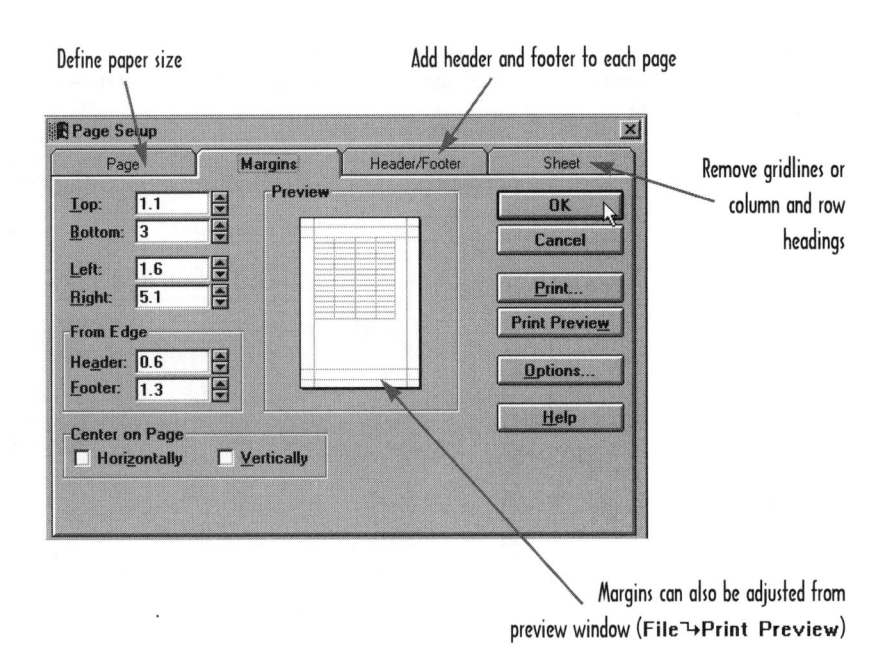

Define paper size

Add header and footer to each page

Remove gridlines or column and row headings

Margins can also be adjusted from preview window (File↪Print Preview)

The thin dashed lines that appear on certain row and column boundaries (File↪PrintArea) show where the worksheet will be divided into pages when printed. The position of these dashed lines can be adjusted by changing settings in the **Page Setup** property sheet.

Note

> Select a cell then choose Insert↪Page Break to make that cell the top left corner of a new page

1   Start Excel from your Taskbar and enter a table of information into its initial workbook — Book1. This table should occupy the range of cells, C3:G17.

2   Choose **File↪Page Setup** from Excel's menu bar to open the **Page Setup** property sheet. — click the **Page** tab to bring this page to the forefront. Press [Alt]+[Z] and select **A4 210×297mm** (or the size of paper in your printer) from the list displayed in the **Paper Sizes** control. Press **OK** to close the property sheet and apply this new setting.

> **Tip**
>
> The Page Setup property sheet's Sheet page contains the setting Print Area which permits you to specify the printable range (i.e. E6:E16) of the worksheet

Removing gridlines and headings

The gridlines that form the borders to the rows and columns of cells in the worksheets are often redundant after you have formatted your information. Likewise the column headings (**A**, **B**, **C**...) and row headings (**1**, **2**, **3**...) might not be needed if your worksheet already has meaningful titles for the rows and columns in its various tables.

3   Choose **File↪Page Setup** from the Excel's menu bar and click the tab **Sheet** to move this page to the forefront of the **Page Setup** property sheet. Remove the cross from the boxes labelled **Gridlines** and **Row and Column Headings** (just click them) then press **OK** to close the property sheet.

The settings in the **Sheet** page of the **Page Setup** property sheet only apply to the worksheet when it is printed, or viewed in **Print Preview** (see Chapter 4). However you can remove gridlines from the document window by changing a settings in Excel's **Options** property sheet (**Tools↪Options**) **View** page.

Chapter 10   Spreadsheets — Excel   227

> **Note**
>
> Repeat particular rows at top on each printed page by entering their reference into the **Print titles** box within the **Sheet** page of the **Page Setup** property box

Hiding rows, columns and worksheets

Your worksheets sometimes contain things that you do not want printed (or displayed) — intermediate workings or confidential information. You can hide a selection of rows, columns or even entire worksheets, by making the appropriate choice from the continuation menus within the **Format** menu.

4   Select row **3** then choose **Format↪Row↪Hide** — row **3** disappears!

5   Select row **2** and row **4** (either side of the row your have just hidden) then choose **Format↪Row↪Unhide** — row **3** reappears! Deselect these cells by clicking elsewhere.

> **Note**
>
> You can protect your workbook so that **Format↪Row** and other parts of the menu are disabled unless the correct password is used to unprotect the workbook (see Chapter 11)

Using predefined formats — Format↪AutoFormat

Excel provides a number of predefined formats that can be applied to tables of information on your worksheets.

6   Select the range of cells containing your table (C3:G17) and choose **Format↪AutoFormat** from Excel's menu bar to open the **AutoFormat** dialog box. Select **Classic3** from the list in **Table Format** then press **OK** to close the dialog box and reformat your table — select another cell to see the effect (removes the highlight).

Figure 10.17
AutoFormat dialog box

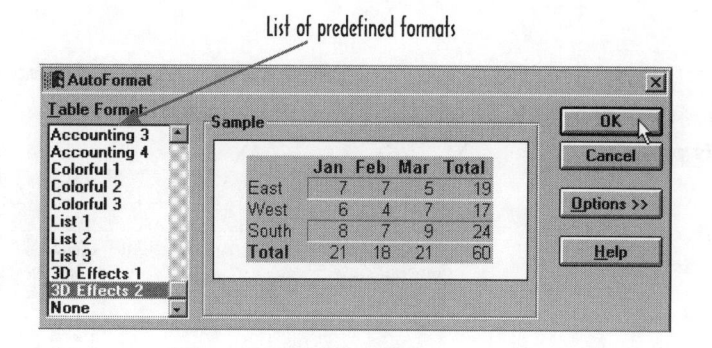

List of predefined formats

> **Tip**
>
> The Format Painter button copies formats from one cell to another — select the cell whose format you wish to copy, click the Format Painter button, then drag through a range of cells to change their format

Formatting groups of cells — Format↪Cells

The **Format Cells** property sheet allows you to apply your own formatting, to change the way information is presented in the cells you have selected.

> **Note**
>
> You have previously applied a format to a group of cells that contained price information in a shopping list — this caused the figures to be displayed as currency rather than numbers

7   Select the range of cells containing your table (C3:G17), choose **Format↪Cells** from Excel's menu bar, then click the **Patterns** tab to open the **Format Cells** property box at the **Patterns** page.

8   Click the light blue square inside the **Cell Shading** box to define the background colour for your cells. Press **OK** to close the property sheet and apply this setting to your cells — select another cell to see the effect (removes the highlight).

Figure 10.18
Format Cells property sheet

Labels on the dialog:
- Format for numbers
- Change typeface
- Add border
- Change background
- Protection options
- Adjust height of cell to fit the text

Note: formatting applies to selected cells

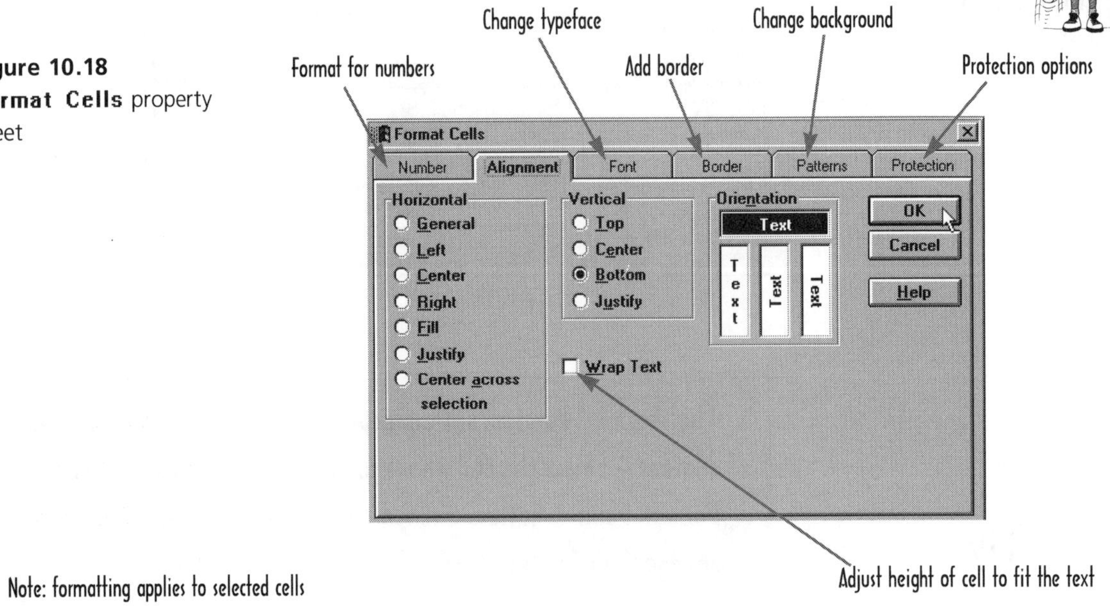

The **Format Cells** property sheet can operate on a selection of cells in a variety of other ways:

- **Alignment** — align the contents of each cell to the left or right, top or bottom of the cell
- **Font** — specify the typeface of the cells' contents in the same way that you change the typeface of text in a Word document (see Chapter 9)
- **Border** — define the type of line that surrounds the cells; dotted, solid, thick, thin or none at all
- **Patterns** — control the background (paper) colour and pattern within the cells
- **Protection** — display the results of formulas but not the formulas themselves, or make cells read only so they cannot be changed (see Chapter 11).

9 *Experiment by applying other types of formatting to your table. After you have finished, close Excel's main window and tidy-up your Desktop, before using your Taskbar to shut down Windows 95 (see Chapter 2) — this exercise is complete!*

Format codes applied to numbers

The **Number** page of the **Format Cells** property sheet permits you to apply specific *format codes* to figures contained in the cells that you have selected. These format codes present numbers in standard forms that reflect the nature of the underlying information (i.e. scientific data, monetary values, and so forth).

You can define your own formats by selecting the category **Custom**, then typing your own format codes into the **Type** box. The basic syntax of a format code is:

- ▷ # — a digit placeholder; the number is rounded to fit the number of # characters after the decimal place (i.e. #,###.##)
- ▷ 0 — always displays a digit in this position (even if its zero), but otherwise it behaves like # (i.e. 0.00)
- ▷ [red] — defines the colour (red) that will be applied to the figures
- ▷ ; — divides the format code into the format that is applied to: positive numbers; negative numbers; zero value (i.e. +0.00;-0.00;0).

Therefore to specify the form of a number such as *($1,959.56)* you might use the format code:

$#,##0.00;($#,##0.00)

Your Excel manual gives full details of numbers formatting.

Summary

- Excel refers to worksheets rather than spreadsheets. Groups of related worksheets are held together in the same workbook which is stored as a file on your hard disk.
- Templates create workbooks that have a consistent style and format.
- The **Insert** menu permits you to add further worksheets into a workbook — change the order of the worksheets by dragging them with their name tabs (right-click to reveal a menu).
- Insert a formula into a cell to make it display the results of an operation on other cells — use the Formula bar to edit a formula in your active cell (the worksheet's insertion point).
- Use names (e.g. *expense_items*) to refer to cells rather than column and row references such as *E6:E15*.
- Change the settings for pages in an Excel document (**File↪Page Setup**) in order to scale the worksheet so that it fits the printed page.
- Choose **Format↪Cells** to change the way information is presented in a selected cell — set its alignment, font, border and the format codes used for numeric values.

Chapter 14

Lists & calculations — Excel

This chapter explains how Excel allows you to perform calculations on your data or arrange it into a collection of related lists. In particular the chapter shows you how to go about:

- ▷ putting information into lists — how to design lists and use them to look-up information, copying information into lists from other documents

- ▷ finding information — how to find information in long lists, sorting and filtering a list

- ▷ performing calculations on your data — how to apply arithmetic operations and formula to your data

- ▷ protecting worksheets and workbooks — hide your formula and prevent people from altering your work

- ▷ troubleshooting — handling common types of errors.

After reading this chapter you should have a better understanding of how Excel can help you use and manage information within your own organisation.

Objectives

Chapter

Putting information into lists

The shopping list you created in Chapter 10 is a very simple example of a list. Large and intricate lists can be created with Excel to which you can apply powerful data management functions. To take full advantage of these features you must give some thought to the design of your list — see Table 11.1.

Definition

list . . . . .a group of cells whose boundaries are formed by empty rows and columns. The first row of a list usually contains a set of labels for its columns

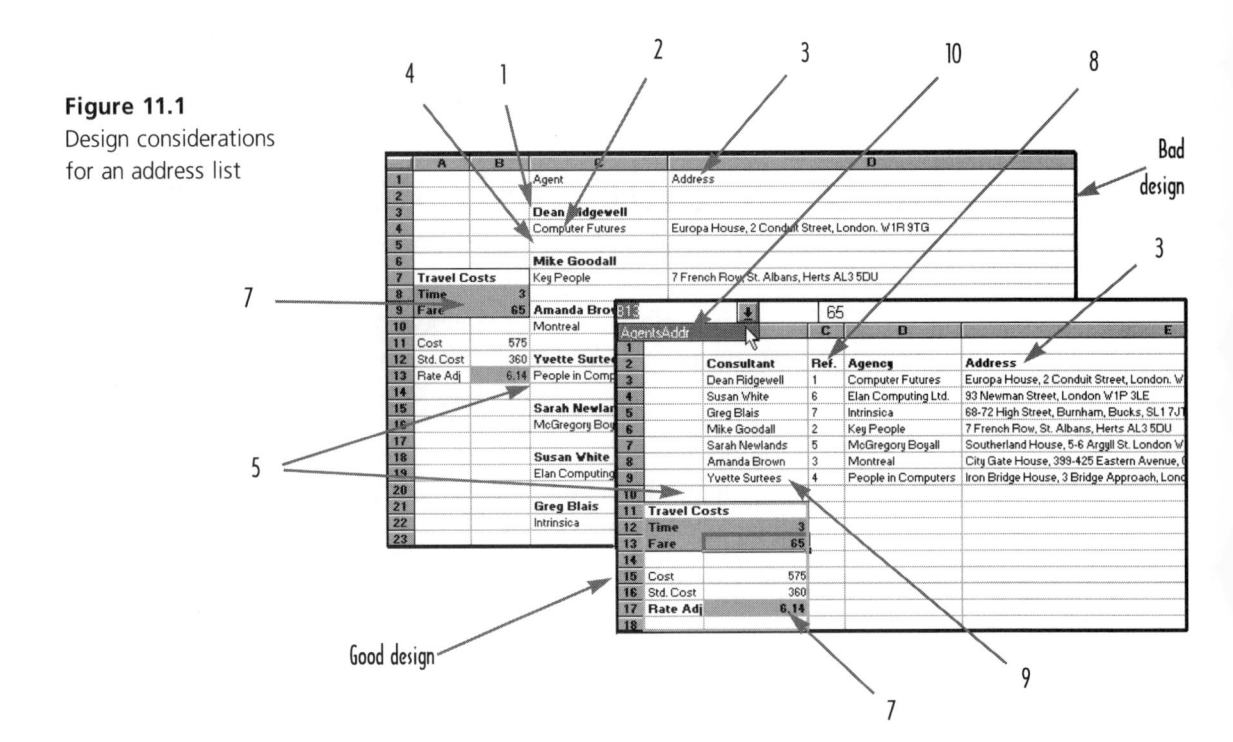

Figure 11.1
Design considerations for an address list

Bad design

Good design

Your list may have 255 columns and 16,384 rows — with each cell containing up to 255 characters! Although a workbook can contain up to 255 such lists (each on a separate worksheet) you should keep the overall size of your workbooks within manageable limits — there are better ways to store large volumes of information.

Table 11.1
Ten tips for producing a well designed list

Tip		Explanation
1	don't use rows to sub-divide a table	your address list has columns for surnames, telephone numbers, address and so forth. Do not split the list by putting surnames in their own row above each address and telephone number — this makes it very difficult to manipulate the list
2	don't mix information in the same column	always put information in the correct column in case the list's columns are re-arranged. Think carefully before using the same column for storing more than one type of information, i.e. including postcode in the address column means you will be unable to sort your address list by postal area
3	use a different style for column headings	a number of Excel list management facilities rely on headings having a different format to members of the list. It is also easier to differentiate labels from items in the list if another typeface is used
4	don't insert blank rows	blank rows can be mistaken for the boundaries of your list — don't even put blank lines between column labels and the data
5	leave space around the list	the list's boundaries are formed by the blank rows and columns separate it from any other information in the worksheet
6	put each list in its own worksheet	several of the facilities provided by Excel to help manage your lists rely on each worksheet holding only one list. However, you can use other areas of a worksheet to store information that will not be used as a further list (e.g. Travel Cost calculator)
7	reserve each row used by the list	if you hide (or filter) some of the rows in your address list, any other information in these rows will also be hidden — only use cells above or below the list for storing information that doesn't belong to the list
8	apply a unique sequence number	you can restore the order of your address list after it has been reorganized by re-sorting the list, using the sequence number column
9	put look-up data in the first column	putting surnames (or other look-up values) in the first column of your address list allows you to use Excel's lookup function to access any other information related to a given name
10	name the table	make your list easy to select by defining a name for the range of cells that its occupies

Looking-up information in different worksheets

Columns of information are often shared between different lists — for example, the part number in a stock list column might also be used to identify items in the purchases column of a customer's invoices. You can save yourself a lot of typing by looking-up information from a list rather than entering it by hand into each invoice.

Figure 11.2
Looking-up information in other worksheets

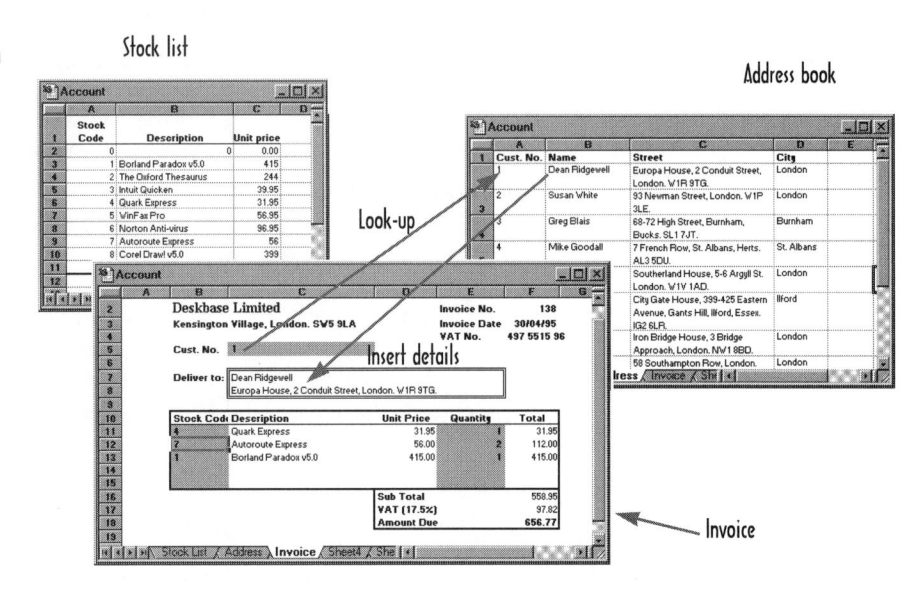

Keeping a separate list of your customers' names and addresses means that a customer number can be used to automatically provide an address on another worksheet (see Figure 11.2). This has a number of other advantages:

- information is easier to maintain when located in one place. For example, a change to an address requires only a single alteration to your *address list* in order to update every worksheet (or workbook) where it is used
- typing errors are avoided by using Excel to look-up the information directly from the address list
- the size of the workbook is reduced as information is not duplicated in each worksheet — addresses displayed in your invoices are actually stored as references to your address list worksheet
- storing information in separate lists makes your worksheets more flexible to any changes in requirement that may arise

The following exercises create a *stock list* and address list to provide information for your sales invoice — these are all worksheets within the same workbook.

1 Start Excel from your Taskbar (**Start**↪**Programs**↪**Microsoft Office**↪**Microsoft Excel**). Create a stock list in **Sheet1** of **Book1** by labelling columns A, B, C of row 1 as **Stock Code**, **Description** and **Unit price** then inserting details of various stock items into rows 2 to 10 beneath these headings (see Figure 11.2).

2 Create an address list in a separate worksheet by clicking the tab of **Sheet2** and repeating the above step — but label columns A, B, C, D of row 1 as **Cust. No.**, **Name**, **Street**, **City** and enter address details in rows 2 to 10 (see Figure 11.2).

3 Define a name for your stock list by selecting cells A1 through C10 (**Sheet1**), clicking the name box immediately to the left of the formula bar, then typing StockList before pressing [Enter]. Repeat this procedure to name your address list (**Sheet2**, cells A2 through D10) as **AddressList**.

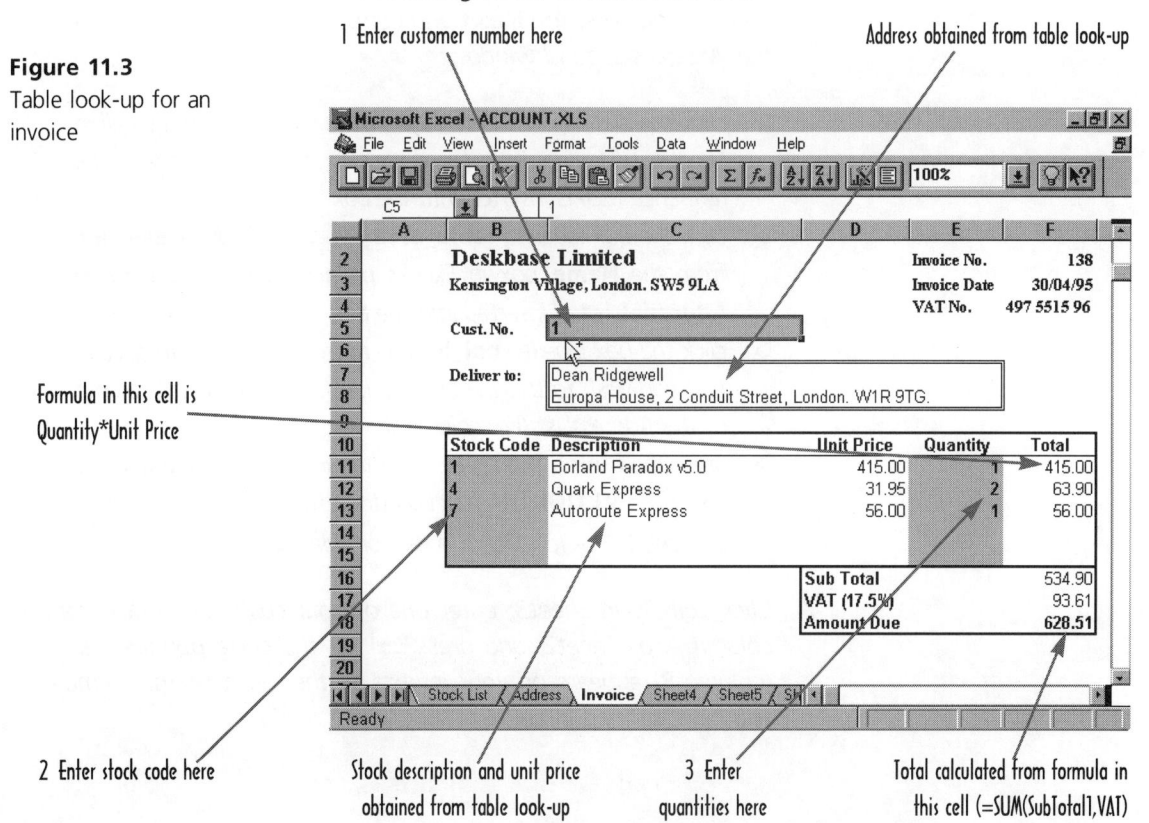

Figure 11.3
Table look-up for an invoice

1 Enter customer number here

Address obtained from table look-up

Formula in this cell is Quantity*Unit Price

2 Enter stock code here

Stock description and unit price obtained from table look-up

3 Enter quantities here

Total calculated from formula in this cell (=SUM(SubTotal1,VAT))

> **Note:** The customer's number must be in the left hand column of the address list in order for it to be used as a value for a lookup function

4   Create an invoice form in Sheet3 that duplicates Figure 11.3. Type a customer's number (taken from Sheet2 column A) into the cell C5.

5   Select cell C7 then choose **Insert→Function** from Excel's menu bar to open the **Function Wizard** window which helps you define a formula for this cell. Select **Lookup and Reference** from the **Function Category** list in this window, then scroll through the **Function Name** list to locate and select **VLOOKUP**.

6   Press the push-button **Next** and complete the following boxes in the Wizard's second window:

   ▷ click the box labelled **look_up value** then click on the cell in Sheet3 that contains the customer number — the cell's reference (C5) is inserted into the box
   ▷ click the box labelled **table_array** then select **AddressList** from the **Name** box in Excel's main window — the name **AddressList** is inserted into the box
   ▷ click the box labelled **col_index_num** then type 2 to specify that you wish to use the information from the second column of the AddressList (i.e. column B)
   ▷ press the **Finish** button to close the **Function Wizard** and insert the **VLOOKUP** function (together with its parameters) into cell C7 — it appears in the formula bar.

7   Click cell C5 in Sheet3, enter one of your customer codes from column A of Sheet2, and press [Enter] — the corresponding name (column B) appears on your invoice as the result of the formula you have defined in cell C7.

8   Repeat the above steps for all the information that you wish to lookup from the **AddressList** and **StockList** worksheets in order to complete your invoice. Save your workbook in a file (**File→Save As**) then close Excel's main window — this exercise is completed!

> **Tip**
>
> Copy the invoice worksheet to a new workbook then save this workbook as a template, so you can create new invoices simply by selecting it from the New property sheet (see page 205)

Database or spreadsheet?

A workbook used for listing information serves a similar purpose to a database — it holds a structured collection of data. There's a number of application programs that specifically create, maintain and manipulate databases; Microsoft's Access, Borland's Paradox, IBM's DB/2 to name but a few.

What does a typical database management program provide that Excel does not? A database will generally:

- hold more than 16,384 rows (or records) of information
- have the ability to index information using more than one column — this improves the speed of searches for specific information in large collections of data
- provide a more formal way of storing information to give better security and performance — particularly when data is shared across a network
- allow its lists of information (tables) to be joined by common columns to provide different views of the various relationships that exist in your data
- provide a more suitable basis for systems that are critical to the operation of your business.

Excel, on the other hand, is better for:
- storing a small amount of informal data — it is usually much quicker and easier to use a spreadsheet rather than designing a database
- changing and restructuring data
- performing calculations and applying formulas to your data
- keeping all the information together in one file — easier to backup .

Excel provides the facility to both supply and retrieve information held by a variety of database management programs — see your Excel User Manual for details.

> **Note:** In terms of a relational database terminology, a list in an Excel worksheet equates to a table, while its columns correspond to fields, and its rows form records — see Figure 10.2

Entering data into a list

There's a number of ways that information can be inserted into an Excel worksheet using its menu bar actions:
- **File↪Open** — files created by other programs can be imported into a worksheet with the assistance of the Excel **Import Wizard**
- **Data↪Get External Data** — imports data directly from databases like Paradox, dBase and Access as well as other external data files and workbooks
- **Edit↪Cut, Edit↪Paste** — text and figures can be copied from other programs by using the Clipboard. Data separated by tabs (or within a Word table) will be put into a sequence of cells.

When a list is properly designed you can use a standard *data entry* form to enter and edit information into your worksheet.

> **Tip**
>
> Choose Data↪Text into Columns in order to separate text that is contained in a single cell. This feature is useful when imported data is not separated by tab characters

Figure 11.4
A data entry form

Add new entry to bottom of table

Remove this entry (row) from the table

Display other rows in the table

> **Note**
>
> A data entry form requires the active cell to be located within a list whose first row contains column labels that are formatted differently to the other rows in the list

1. *Start Excel from your Taskbar (***Start**↪**Programs**↪**Microsoft Office**↪**Microsoft Excel***) and create an address list in* **Sheet1** *of* **Book1** *(see Figure 11.2). Select the first row of your list (contains column headings) and alter its format by pressing the bold button in the Excel standard toolbar.*

2. *Click within the second row of the list then choose* **Data**↪**Form** *from Excel's menu bar to display a* **Data Entry** *dialog box which contains the values in this row — you can alter them simply by typing a new value into the appropriate box. Press the* **Find Next** *and* **Find Previous** *push-buttons to display the contents of other rows in your list.*

3   Add a row to the bottom of your list by pressing the **New** push-button then entering values into the appropriate boxes. When you have completed your modifications to the list close the dialog box then close Excel's main window — this exercise is complete!

When you are entering batches of information into your worksheet it is more convenient to use a data entry form, rather than attempting to type the information directly into the appropriate cells.

Finding information

While it is possible to find a certain piece of information in a list by searching each row in turn, this approach becomes tedious when the list contains a large number of items. Excel provides two mechanisms to facilitate the location of information contained in long lists:

- Sorting the list so that columns are arranged in alphabetic or numeric order (ascending or descending). Sort your address list by postcode so that all the addresses in the SW5 postal district are placed together
- filter the list so that only those rows which contain matching items are displayed. Filter your address list by the postcode value SW5 to display only those addresses found in this postal area.

Sorting and filtering provide efficient ways of finding specific information in long lists.

Sorting lists

A list can be sorted to rearrange the items in an order that is determined by one of their values — the shopping list you created in Chapter 10 is sorted by item number but it could also be sorted by price or discount.

A list can be sorted in terms of increasing or decreasing values such as:

- text values — arrange a list of names alphabetically, say
- numeric values — arrange a list of prices by their value
- date or time values — arrange a list of appointments chronologically
- logical values — arrange a list of customers so that the ones who have a tick mark (a logical value, yes or true) are listed before those who have not
- other values — arrange a list by blanks in a particular column or errors when the value is calculated by formula that does not compute.

> You can regain the original order of a list that has a *sequence number* column simply by using the values in this column to re-sort your list (see Figure 11.1)

1 *Start Excel from your Taskbar (***Start↪Programs↪Microsoft Office↪Microsoft Excel***) and create an address list in* **Sheet1** *of* **Book1** *(see Figure 11.6).*

2 *Select a cell in the* **Names** *column of your address list then choose* **Data↪Sort** *from Excel's menu bar to open the* **Sort** *dialog box. Press* **OK** *to accept the default settings in this dialog box and re-sort your list by the ascending alphabetical order of its* **Names** *column.*

Note

> Lists can be sorted by using the values in a single column, but more intricate sorts can be performed by combining the values in a several columns

Filtering lists

When you filter a list some of its rows are hidden so that you can find items without changing the list's order. A filter is more flexible than a sort because you can specify criterion, such as displaying only those rows whose price column

Figure 11.5
Sort dialog box

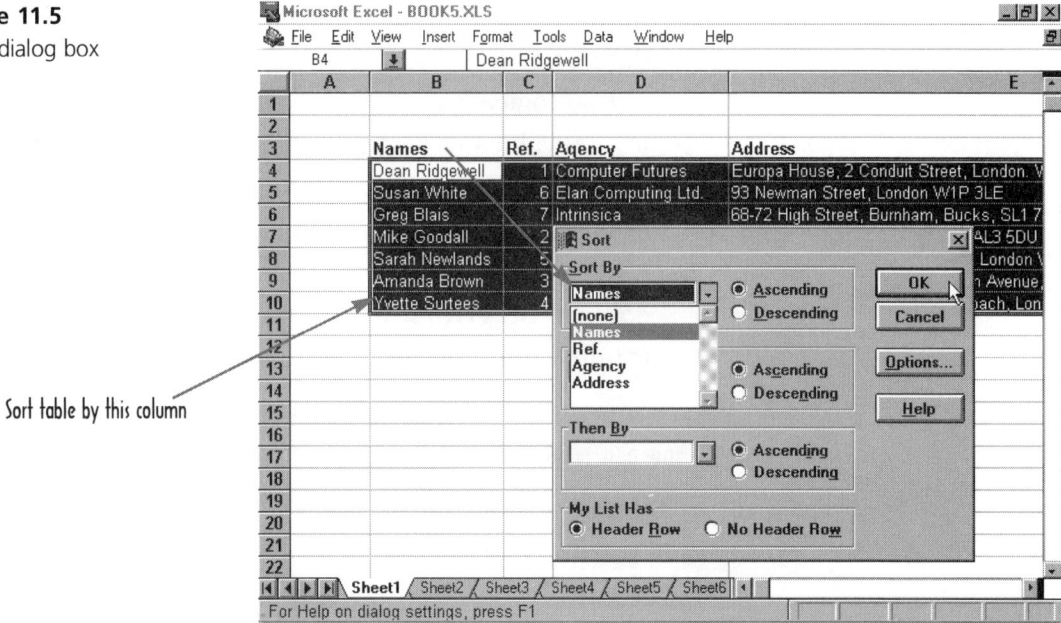

Sort table by this column

contains a value greater than 50p. Excel supports two types of filter:

- **AutoFilter** — this filters a list according to values contained in special controls that appear in the column headings of your list
- custom filters — these filter according to criteria specified by a range of cells in your worksheet.

Figure 11.6
Autofilters

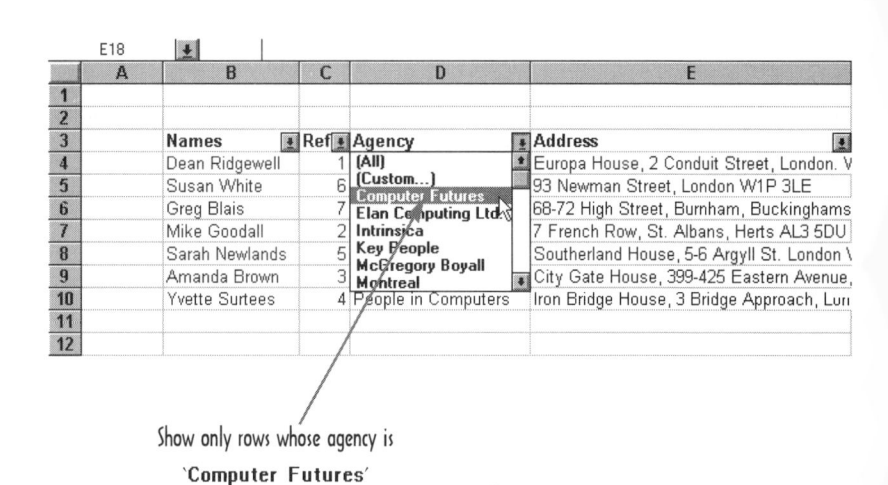

Show only rows whose agency is
'Computer Futures'

> **Note**
>
> When a row is filtered the entire row is hidden — you cannot view any other information that might be contained in cells to the left or right of your table

3   Select a cell in your address list then choose **Data↪Filter↪Autofilter** from Excel's menu bar to insert a special button in the column headings of your list.

4   Press the button attached to the **Names** column heading to reveal the unique items in this column. Select one of these items to hide any rows in your list that do not contain this value. Press the button again then select the first value (All), to remove the filter you have just applied.

5   Press the button attached to the **Ref** column heading and select the second value (Custom). This opens a dialog box that permits you to define comparison values for the column, rather than an exact matching value.

6   Click the box containing = within the dialog box in order to reveal a number of symbols. Select > from this list then type 3 into the adjacent box. Then press **OK** to close the dialog box and apply your custom filter.

Table 11.2 Comparison symbols

Symbol	Meaning	Example
>	greater than	>18 *means* values of 19 and more
>=	greater than or equal	>=18 *means* values of 18 and more
<	less than	< 18 *means* values of 17 and less
<=	less than or equal	<=18 *means* values of 18 and less
=	equal	=18 *means* values equal to 18
<>	not equal	<>18 *means* all values but 18

7   Close Excel's main window (don't bother saving changes) — this exercise is complete!

> **Tip**
>
> Construct compound filters by adding further filter criteria to additional columns – i.e. filter by both *Ref greater than 3* and name matching *Thompson*

Performing calculations on your data

You have already used the following formulas to perform operations on the data contained within your worksheets:

- `AutoSum` was used to totalize the values contained within a range of cells (see page 213)
- `VLOOKUP` was used to copy a selected piece of information from a table into a cell according to a supplied look-up value (see page 238).

These formulas are only two of many of the formulas (called functions) provided by Excel to perform a calculation upon data in your worksheets. A function has the general form shown in the Formula bar of Figure 11.7 — where `Fn` is the function name and the parameters qualify the way its action is perfomed.

Figure 11.7
General form of an Excel function

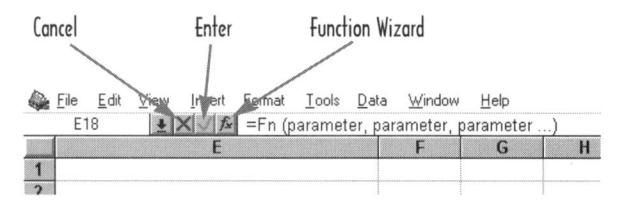

The Function Wizard (**Insert→Function**) takes you step-by-step through the process of selecting a formula and supplying the required parameters. However you can also construct your own formula by typing it directly into the formula bar.

1. Start Excel from your Taskbar (**Start→Programs→Microsoft Office→Microsoft Excel**) then type the numbers 5, 4, 7 into cells C3, C4 and C5, respectively. Select cell C6 and type the formula =C5+C4+C3 into Excel's formula bar. Finally, press Enter to display the result **16** in cell C6.

Note: The result of a formula is usually displayed by the cell in which it is contained — the formula itself is displayed in the formula bar only when this cell becomes the active cell

Formulas start with = and contain both *values* and *operators*, as described in Table 11.3 and Table 11.4

Table 11.3
Values used in formulas

Values	Example	Explanation
Cell references	C5	refers to the contents of the cell — it may contain text, numeric values, dates, times
Numeric values	3.17	refers to a specific value — a constant
Names	BaseRate	refers to the value returned by a cell reference, formula, numeric value

Table 11.4
Operators used in formulas

Operators	Example	Explanation
Arithmetic	+, –, /, *	perform add, subtract, divide, multiply operations between values to produce a result
	^, %	exponential, percent operations applied to a value
Comparison	=, >, <, >=, <=, <>	compare values to produce a true or false result (see Table 11.2)
Text	&	joins text values in different cells together to form a single piece of text as a result (i.e. A1&A2)

The order in which operators are applied follows the standard algebraic convention of evaluating multiplication and division before addition and subtraction, though the order can be altered using parentheses.

2 *Select cell C7, type* =C5*(C3+C4), *and press* Enter *to display the result* **63** *in cell C7. Select the cell C8, type* =C5*C3+C4, *then press* Enter *to display the result* **39** *in cell C8.*

3 *Select cell D5 and type* Freedom is. *Select cell D6 and type* Slavery. *Select cell D7, type* =D5&D6, *then press* Enter *to display both pieces of text in cell D7.*

Chapter 11   Lists & calculations — Excel   247

Note: You can build more complex expressions by including Excel functions into your formulas — just press the Function Wizard button in the formula bar

Calculation accuracy

Excel normally stores (and calculates) numbers accurately to 15 digits. However, the precision with which they are displayed on your worksheet is dependant on the format of the cell that contains them. Excel performs calculations on the basis of the stored number's precision rather than its displayed value. Rounding errors in displayed numbers may effect your calculations.

Definition

precision . . . . the number of decimal places used to contain a figure that is not a whole number. Numbers are rounded-up (or down) to fit their precision, so 9.1276 becomes 9.128

The difference between the accuracy of the stored and displayed number can yield some unexpected results.

Consider two invoices whose VAT values are stored as £54.344 and £23.784 but displayed as values rounded to the nearest penny, £54.34 and £23.78. The total VAT due from these invoices is £78.12, though because the fractions of pennies are retained in the stored values Excel would mistakenly round the total of £78.128 to £78.13

When you are dealing with currency values you may wish to store values to the same accuracy as they are displayed so as to avoid *rounding errors*. You can set the accuracy of the stored values in your workbook so that they match the displayed values by changing the **Precision as displayed** setting in the **Calculation** page of Excel's **Option** property sheet.

> **Note** — Change the displayed precision of numbers contained in a selection of cells by choosing Format➔Cells then choosing a suitable format code from the Number page of the property

Protecting worksheets and workbooks

Spreadsheets can form very powerful business tools that have considerable value in terms of the information and knowledge they contain. This creates a need to safeguard your investment beyond the normal requirement of making regular back-up copies of workbook files. You can safeguard your workbook in the following ways:

- protect the workbook file
- protect the structure of a workbook
- protect individual cells.

> **Caution** — You should keep a note of any passwords that you apply to a worksheet (or workbook) in case you forget them. You can lose all your work by forgetting a password!

Protect the workbook file

The file protection facilities described in Chapter 6 can be applied to a file containing a workbook document, so that it cannot be opened without the correct password. You can also specify that the file cannot be updated without a write password.

4   Choose **File➔Save As** from Excel's menu bar to open the **Save As** dialog box. Define a file name and folder for your workbook (see Chapter 6), then press the **Options** push-button to open a further dialog box containing settings for this file.

5   Click the **Read Only Recommended** box in the **Save Options** dialog box (so that when subsequently you open this file a message box will prompt you to open this workbook as a read-only document). Press **OK** to close this dialog box then press **Save** to close the **Save As** dialog box.

Protect the structure of a workbook

When preparing a workbook for other people it is often desirable to protect its worksheets so that they cannot be accidentally deleted (or other worksheets inserted).

6   Choose **Tools↪Protection↪Protect Workbook** to open the **Protect Worksheet** dialog box. Insert a tick in the box labelled **Structure** then press **OK** to close the dialog box and prevent any alterations to the structure of the worksheets.

7   Choose **Tools↪Protection↪Unprotect Workbook** to remove the protection applied in the previous step — a dialog box will prompt you for any password that was entered in the **Protect Worksheet** dialog box.

Protect individual cells

Individual worksheets can be protected in terms of their content. When you have protected a worksheet in this way, individual cells can be locked and the text of your formulas hidden.

8   Select the cells in Sheet1 that contain the formulas and values entered at the start of this exercise (C3:D9), then choose **Format↪Cells** from Excel's menu bar to open the **Format Cells** property sheet. Click the **Protection** tab to bring this page to the forefront, then check the **Locked** and **Hidden** check boxes before pressing **OK** to close the property sheet.

9   Choose **Tools↪Protection↪Protect Sheet** from Excel's menu bar to open the dialog box in Figure 11.8. Type `microsoft` into the **Password** box, then press **OK** to protect all the cells in the worksheet according to their individual protection settings — another dialog box will prompt you to confirm your password.

Figure 11.8
Protecting and unprotecting a worksheet

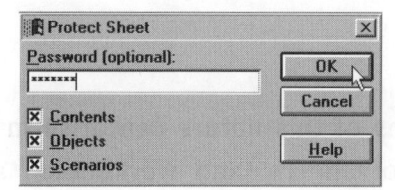

10   Select cell C6 — its formula is not displayed in the formula bar because the cell's protection is set to hidden. Select cell C4 and attempt to enter a new value — a message box warns you that the cell's protection is set to locked.

11   Choose **Tools→Protection→Unprotect Sheet** from Excel's menu bar to open a dialog box prompting you for a password — type microsoft into this box then press **OK** to remove the protection from this worksheet.

12   Close Excel's main window and tidy-up your Desktop before shutting down Windows 95 from your Taskbar (as described in Chapter 2) — this exercise is complete!

Tip

> Protect cells in the workbook that contains your invoice template to prevent accidental alteration of the address information — only permit changes to the customer code cell

Troubleshooting

When using Excel you can generate an error simply by changing the value in a cell — it may be valid within the context of the individual cell but produces an error when used by a formula in another cell.

Note

> A formula that divides the contents of cell C4 by 10 will produce an error whenever cell C4 contains the value zero — divide by zero is an illegal mathematical operation

Problems of this nature can arise in many cells throughout your worksheets (and workbooks) as a result of a single operation, like moving a group of cells. Accordingly, Excel often handles errors simply by inserting an *error value* into the appropriate cell — see Table 11.5.

Table 11.5
Excel error values

Cell's error	Description	Recover by
#####	numeric value too long to fit in a cell	increase width of cell
#REF!	refers to a cell that is not valid	alter references in the cell's formula
#VALUE!	the value of a function's parameter is invalid	alter the function's parameters
#N/A	refers to a value that is no longer available	make the reference available (undo a delete)
#NAME?	uses a name that does not appear in the **Name** box	define the name (see Chapter 10)
#NUM!	incorrect use of a number	change cell's number format or use of the number
#NULL!	refers to the invalid intersection of two areas	change the cells' references to a valid intersection
#DIV/0!	invalid operation — divide by zero	change the value or reference of cell's divisor

KISS — *keep it simple stupid*

Excel gives you the power to develop some very complex worksheets that can save you from many hours of tedious number crunching work. When used correctly Excel provides a tool that can significantly improve your efficiency, but you should be aware it can also create its own set of problems.

▷ You might easily find yourself replacing hours of number crunching with hours of designing, building and maintaining spreadsheets.

▷ Check that your worksheet is working correctly by using a set of data whose result is known to you — just because you are using a computer doesn't mean that errors can't creep into a worksheet.

- Constructing a worksheet that will be used by someone else requires much more skill than building one for yourself — other people might fail to appreciate the limitations of your worksheet and use it incorrectly.
- Worksheets can quickly proliferate within an organization and become a critical part of its business systems. There remains a need to manage and control these worksheets as for any other type of system.
- You should always apply common sense when evaluating results — do they make sense?

Once you have grasped how to use Excel you will doubtless think of many new applications for it within your own business. The best advice to keep in mind while you develop these new worksheets is KISS — *keep it simple stupid.*

Summary

- Take the trouble to design lists properly, so that you can look-up information from another worksheet and use Excel's data entry forms to update them.
- Sort lists, by increasing or decreasing values in a particular column, by choosing **Data↪Sort** from the menu bar.
- Filter lists, in order to display only values that match certain criteria, by choosing **Data↪Filter** from the menu bar.
- Use the Formula Wizard to insert one of Excel's built-in formulas into a cell, together with any necessary parameters — you may also type your own formula directly into a cell.
- Protect the contents of your worksheets from alteration, or hide your formulas from view, by choosing **Tools↪Protection** from the menu bar.
- Identify problems with the contents of a particular cell from the various Excel errors codes.

Tip

Programs often do only one job well — use **Access** to store your data securely, **Excel** to manipulate the information, and **Word** to present it in a report

Chapter 12

Presentations — PowerPoint

Objectives

PowerPoint is a program which you might use to make a graphical presentation — its document can form a set of slides, speaker's notes and handouts. This chapter considers:

▷ creating a presentation — using a template to create an appropriate type of presentation

▷ menus and controls — how PowerPoint's window is adapted for producing a presentation. View your presentation in terms of an outline document, individual slides, handouts, and speaker's notes

▷ preparing the presentation — how to plan an outline, provide speaker's notes, then arrange your collection of slides

▷ inserting things into your presentation — how to insert objects into your slides; ClipArt, Word tables, Excel worksheets, and so forth

▷ finishing touches and important actions — how to copy a format from another presentation, or define your own master slides to provide consistency between each slide.

When you have completed this chapter you will be able to give your own presentation using slides for display on a PC screen, overhead foil projector, or traditional 35mm projector.

Creating a presentation

You can easily produce an initial collection of material for your presentation by selecting a suitable template from the **New** property sheet — choose **File→New** from PowerPoint's menu bar or simply press the **Start a New Document** button in your Office toolbar (see page 164). Microsoft provides a number of standard templates which may be used to create documents for many common types of presentations — **Reporting Progress, Training, Selling a Product** and so forth.

Figure 12.1
New property sheet

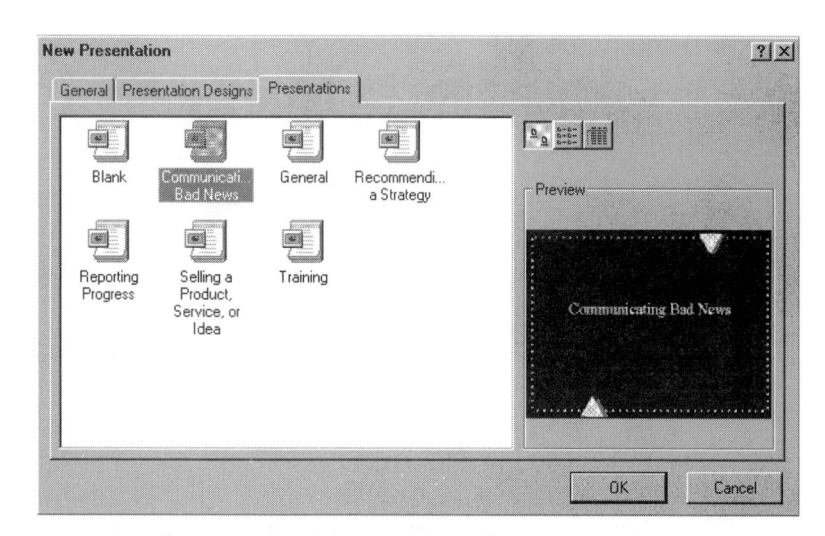

Note

> PowerPoint presentations are created in the same way as Word or Excel documents – templates define the initial style and content of a new document

1. Start PowerPoint from your Taskbar (**Start→Programs→Microsoft Office→Microsoft PowerPoint**). Close any dialog boxes that might appear when the program is started (e.g. **Tip of the Day**). Choose **File→New** from PowerPoint's menu bar to open the **New** property sheet.

2. Select the **Training** template from the **Presentations** page of the **New** property sheet then press **OK** to create your document. Choose **View→Outline** from PowerPoint's menu bar to display the structure of the presentation in its document window.

> **Tip**
>
> A special program will guide you step-by-step through the initial setup of your presentation if you select a template with the word Wizard in its name

It is always a good idea to store a new document in a file soon after you have created it. You can regularly save your work on the PC's hard disk simply by choosing **File→Save** from the menu bar — this way you don't lose the entire document if there is a power-cut!

3. Choose **File→Save As** from PowerPoint's menu bar to bring up the **File Save** dialog box. Select a suitable folder for your document in the **Save in** control (e.g. **work**, created in Chapter 6) then type a name for your file into the **File Name** box. Press **Save** to close the dialog box and create the file that will store your presentation.

Figure 12.2
Properties of your presentation

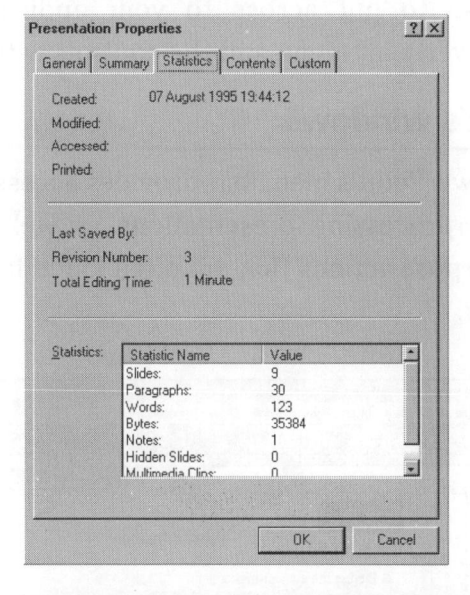

> **Note**
>
> You can create a PowerPoint template from your presentation by changing the **Save as type** control to Design Templates before creating its file — locate the file in your Bill's templates folder so that it will appear in the New property sheet (see page 165)

Information about your presentation can be attached to the file in which it is stored by changing the file's property settings. You can add your own custom property values (see page 206) as well as insert values for the standard settings — title, author, subject and so forth.

4   *Choose* **File↪Properties** *from PowerPoint's menu bar to open the property sheet shown in Figure 12.2. Click the* **Summary** *page and complete the various boxes to define the properties that will be attached to your presentation's file. Press* **OK** *to close the property sheet and return to your document.*

You are now ready to start modifying the initial document that has been provided by the PowerPoint template. However before fleshing-out this material with the information that you wish to put across to your audience, let's look at the PowerPoint menu and the controls within its main window.

Features of PowerPoint's windows

PowerPoint's menu bar provides access to actions specifically for processing presentations as well as the more general purpose actions that are often found in an application's menu bar.

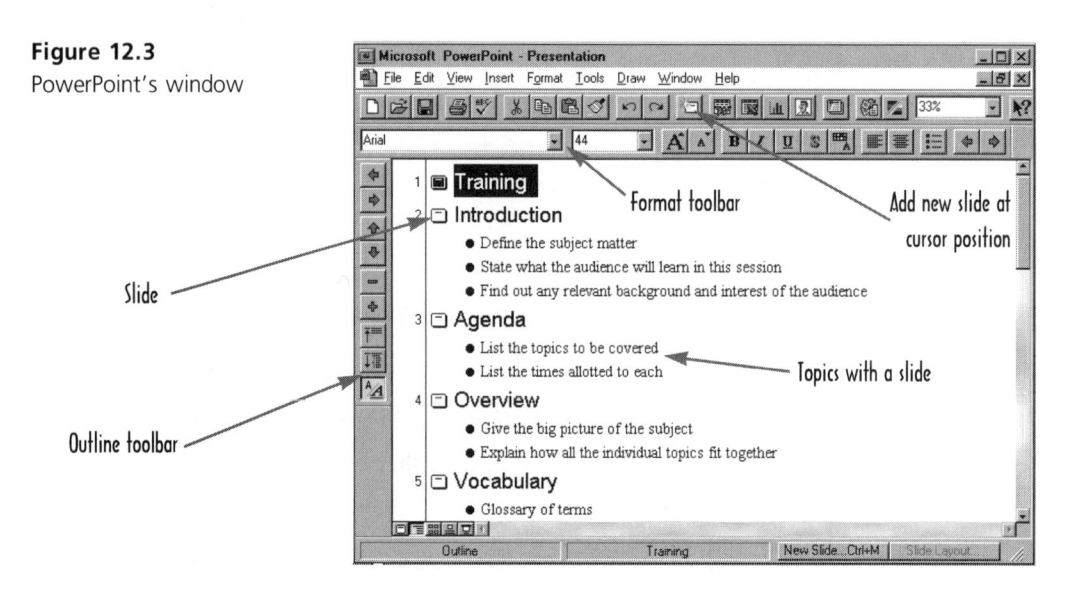

Figure 12.3
PowerPoint's window

Viewing your slide collection

The outline, slides, handouts and speaker's notes produced by PowerPoint are in fact the same information presented in different ways. The View buttons at the bottom of the document window can be used to show these different views of your presentation within its document window.

Figure 12.4
View buttons at the bottom of the document window

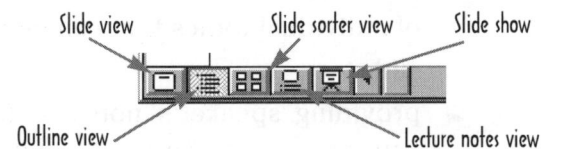

(Labels: Slide view, Slide sorter view, Slide show, Outline view, Lecture notes view)

The ways in which you can view your presentation are shown in Figure 12.5 — *Slide Show* is not shown in this diagram as this view gives a full screen slide show.

5   Choose **View→Slide Show** *from PowerPoint's menu bar to open the* **Slide Show** *dialog box. Press the* **Show** *push-button to start the slide show on your PC's monitor.*

6   *Press your space bar to advance each slide. Press* [Esc] *to return back to PowerPoint and the Windows 95 Desktop. Choose* **View→Outline** *from PowerPoint's menu bar to ensure that the presentation appears as an outline in its document window.*

Figure 12.5
Different views of a presentation

(Labels: Outline view, Slide view, Slide sorter)

Chapter 12   Presentations — PowerPoint

Preparing the presentation

There's a number of distinct steps to preparing a successful presentation:

- planning the outline — dividing the talk into a sequence of individual topics that can be summarized by a single slide
- providing speaker's notes — filling out your outline with what you want to say while the slide is displayed
- sorting and arranging the slides — confirm the information is presented in the best order. Mark optional slides that may be required to illustrate answers to questions from your audience.

Planning an outline

The objective of an outline is to create, then manipulate, the structure for your document. This structure is composed of a list of headings, each with its own order of importance (shown in Figure 12.6). You can rearrange the structure by demoting or promoting the importance of a particular heading, as well as changing its order in the document.

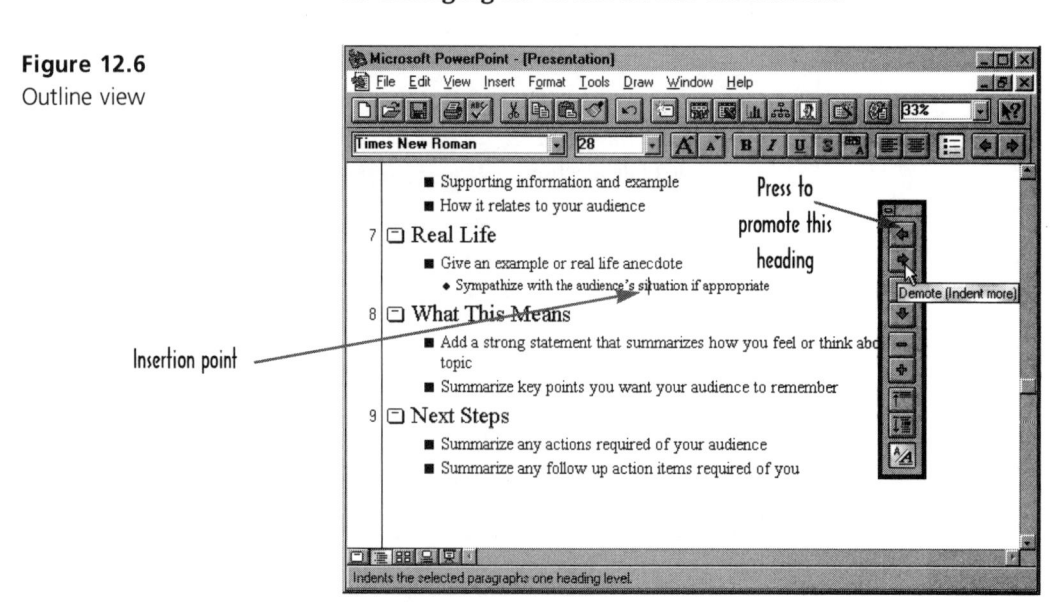

Figure 12.6
Outline view

> **Tip:** You can import a Word document into PowerPoint then promote or demote its text to form the required headings and slides — choose **Insert↪Slides from outline**

7. Choose **View↪Toolbars** from PowerPoint's menu bar to open the **Toolbars** dialog box. Put a tick in the box **Outlining** (click it) before pressing the **OK** button — this attaches the toolbar (see Chapter 3) to the left edge of PowerPoint's main window.

8. Move your cursor to the text `Define the subject matter` in PowerPoint's document window (click it) then press the button in the **Outline** toolbar that has a downward pointing arrow — this moves the text down the document. Restore the position of the text by pressing the button in the **Outline** toolbar that has an upward pointing arrow.

9. Promote the text `Define the subject matter` by pressing the button in the **Outline** toolbar that has an arrow pointing to the left. Demote this text by pressing the toolbar button that has an arrow pointing to the right.

The basic techniques required to enter and manipulate text in a document window are described in Chapter 3 — they apply as much to a PowerPoint document (displayed in outline) as they do to a Word document.

> **Tip:** Insert extra slides into your presentation by typing text on a new line (press `Enter`) then promoting it until a slide heading is formed

Once you have planned the outline of your presentation, defining the order and content of each slide, you can consider the points that should be made when the slides are displayed — your speaker's notes.

Providing speaker's notes

Speaker's notes are not displayed on the slides shown to your audience, but provide a useful prompt for the issues you wish to raise about each slide.

Figure 12.7
Speaker's notes

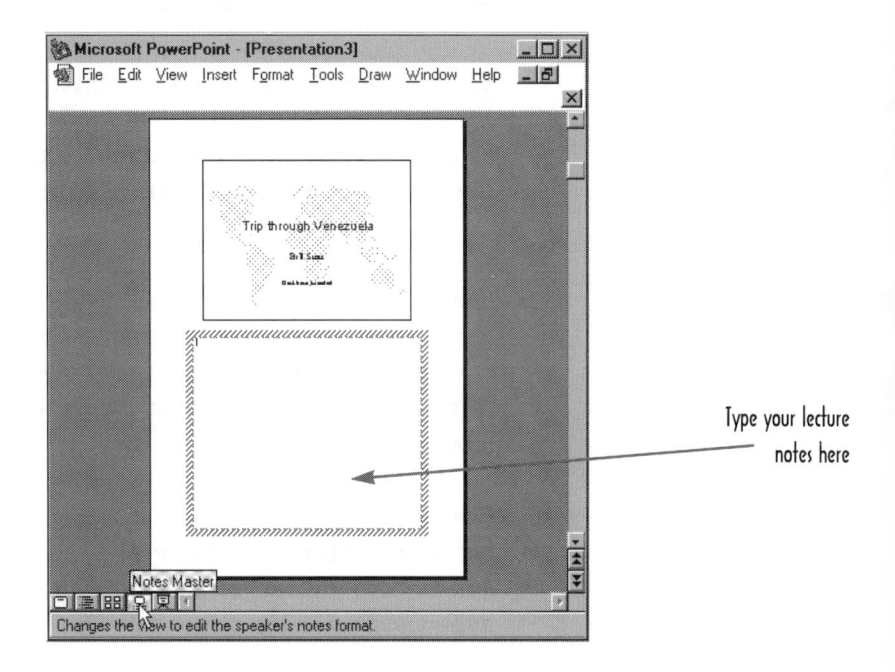

Type your lecture notes here

10 Move the cursor to a heading for a slide that requires some speaker's notes then press the **Notes Page** button at the bottom of the document window. The view of your presentation changes to a page that contains both a picture of the slide and an area in which notes can be added.

11 Choose **View→Zoom** from PowerPoint's menu bar to open a dialog box that contains a number of options for the magnification given to the document window. Select **100%** then press **OK** to close the dialog box and gain a better view of the area for your speaker's notes.

12 Click within the box that contains the prompt **Click to add text** in order to make it behave like a window's document area. Type your comments into this box as if it was a Word document window (see Chapter 3)

13 When you have finished the notes for one slide, proceed to the next slide by pressing the button with the double-arrow head at the bottom of the document window's vertical scroll bar.

> **Note**
>
> Choose Tool→WriteUp from PowerPoint's menu bar to open a dialog box that permits you to use Word to compose the notes for your slides

Sorting and rearranging slides

The *Slide Sorter* allows you to look at your presentation as a whole. You can also use the toolbar displayed in this view for:

- marking slides so that they will not appear in the handouts
- re-arranging the order of your slides
- timing the length of your presentation
- specifying effects used in Slide Show view when advancing from one slide to another.

Figure 12.8
Slide Sorter view of your presentation

14 *Press the Slide Sorter button at the bottom of the document window to display your presentation as a sequence of slides. Choose* **View→Zoom** *from PowerPoint's menu bar to open the* **Zoom** *dialog box so you can change the window's magnification to 33% — this allows you to see all the slides.*

15 Press the Show Formatting button (right side of Slide Sorter toolbar) so the title of each slide can be clearly seen — this removes the background and formatting. Use your mouse to drag and drop individual slides within the document window until you are satisfied with the order of your presentation.

16 Press the Rehearse Timings button in the Slide Sorter toolbar to start the presentation and record the time taken to talk through each slide. Press your space bar to advance to next slide — press ⎋ to return to Slide Sorter view.

> **Tip**
>
> Preparing a good presentation is rarely a step-by-step process — often as you finish one stage you will want to go back and change a previous one

Inserting things into your document

Graphics are often the most effective way of adding interest to a slide. PowerPoint contains a gallery of pictures (called ClipArt) that can be used to illustrate your slides.

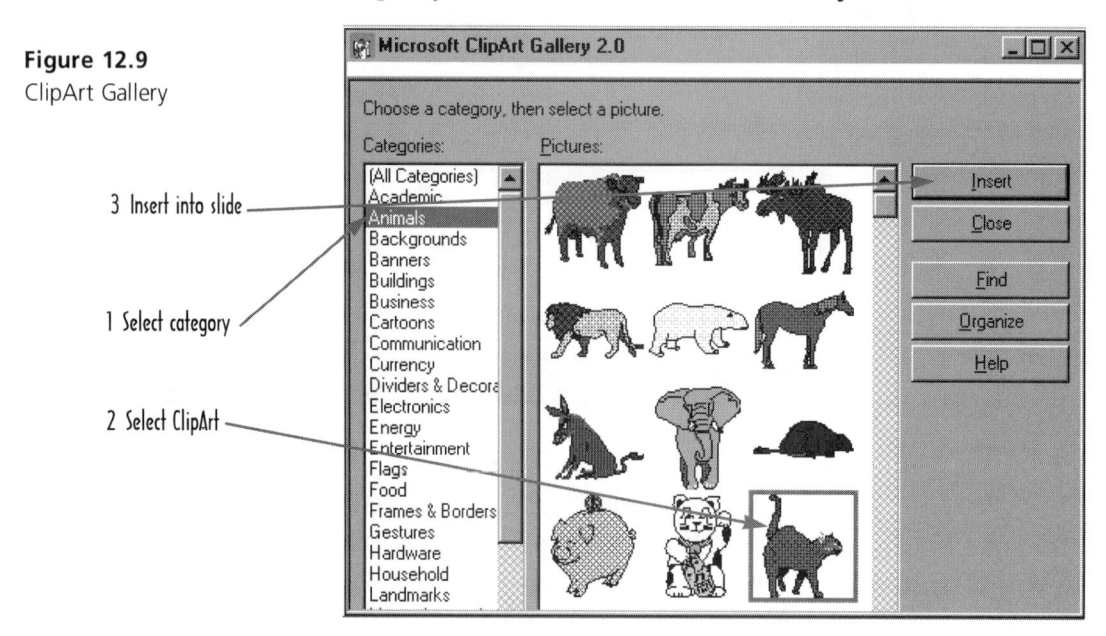

Figure 12.9
ClipArt Gallery

3 Insert into slide
1 Select category
2 Select ClipArt

17 Choose **View→Slides** from PowerPoint's menu bar to view your presentation as a collection of individual slides — press the buttons with the double-headed arrows at the bottom of the vertical scroll bar to move between slides.

18 Choose **Insert→ClipArt** from PowerPoint's menu bar to open the ClipArt gallery — it may take a few minutes to initialize itself. Select **Animals** from the list of picture categories at the top of the dialog box, click the picture of a cat from the bottom of the dialog box then press **Insert** to close the dialog box and add this picture to your slide.

19 Click the picture you have just inserted into your slide to display the eight handles that can be used to stretch and crop the image. Position the image within your slide by dragging and dropping it with your mouse (see page 181).

Tip

> Graphic objects in any Office 95 document are moved, stretched and cropped in the same way (see page 181)

The drawing toolbar provided by the Slide (and Notes Pages) view of the presentation can be used to add your own drawings to the slides.

Figure 12.10
The Drawing toolbar

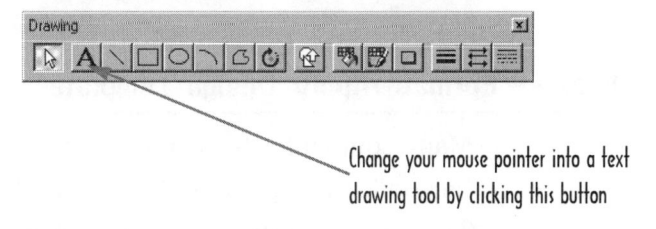

Change your mouse pointer into a text drawing tool by clicking this button

20 Click the Text tool button in the Drawing toolbar — the mouse pointer changes into a vertical bar. Click within the slide to locate the starting point of the text then type CoCo.

21 Click the Rectangle tool button in the drawing toolbar — the mouse pointer changes into a cross. Click within the slide, to locate the top left of the rectangle, then drag down to the bottom right to form a square.

You can insert the following items into your slides using the appropriate buttons in the standard PowerPoint toolbar:

- Word tables — add a table to a slide which is used in the same way as a table in a Word document
- Excel worksheets — insert a number of cells into your slide that act like cells in an Excel worksheet
- a graph — use a special tool to produce a graph of your data within a slide.

Note

> A wide range of objects can also be inserted into your documents using the Clipboard and other techniques explained in Chapter 7

Finishing touches and important actions

PowerPoint has many features that improve the visual impact of your presentation and this can help retain your audience's attention even if you aren't a natural communicator.

Tip

> Avoid the temptation to start adding finishing touches until you are certain about what you want to say. Don't waste time dressing-up material that will eventually go in the waste bin

Defining a look — Format➔Apply Design Template

Many companies have a well-defined corporate image that can be applied to a presentation to create a consistent impression. The style of your presentation can be copied from any other presentation, so you can apply the corporate stamp with one simple action — **Format➔Apply Design Template**.

22. Choose **Format➔Apply Design Template** from the menu bar to open the dialog box shown in Figure 12.12. Locate and select a PowerPoint file whose format you wish to copy then press **Apply** to close the dialog box and give your slides a similar look to this presentation.

Figure 12.11
Defining a corporate image

Background copied from another presentation

Company name

A logo added to each slide
(Define master slide)

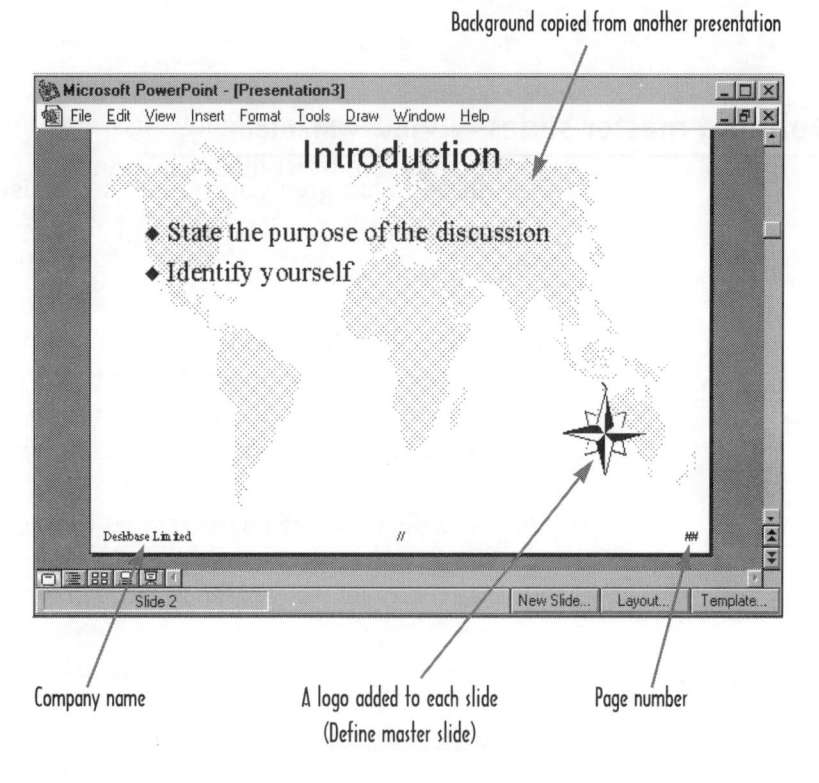

Page number

Figure 12.12
Apply Design Template dialog box

1 Locate folder

2 Select presentation

3 Copy master slides to your presentation

Note

Only the *style* of the file selected from the Apply Design Template dialog box is copied, not the content of the presentation itself

Chapter 12   Presentations — PowerPoint   267

Defining master slides— View↪Master

You can also give your slides a consistent look by creating a master slide whose format and content is applied to each slide in your presentation.

23 Choose **View↪Master↪Slide Master** to display a special master slide that forms the basis for all other slides in your presentation. Add the information to this slide that you wish to replicate in each of your own slides — a piece of ClipArt perhaps.

24 Choose **View↪Slides** from PowerPoint's menu bar to return back to the view of individual slides in your presentation — they each contain the content of the master slide.

Figure 12.13
View of the master slide

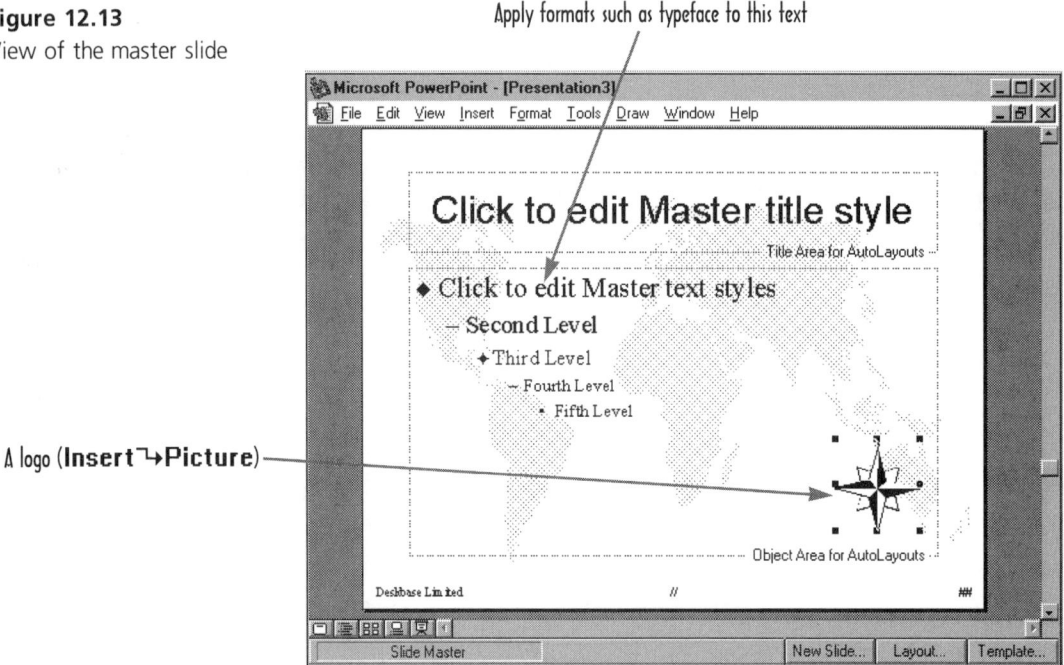

> **Note:** Applying the style of another presentation to your PowerPoint document (Format↪Apply Design Template) simply copies the master slide information between the two documents

Giving the presentation

You can print out your PowerPoint document as a series of slides which then can be made into foils for an overhead projector. You may also deliver the presentation directly from your computer screen — an option that allows you to use the transition and build effects provided by the Slide Sorter toolbar.

> **Tip**
>
> Prepare 35mm slides by attaching a special camera to the PC's monitor and running the Slide Show, or ask a specialist service bureau to produce the slides directly from a file (File↪Send to Genigraphics)

Presenting a Slide Show

The Slide Show view of your presentation fills the entire area of your screen — it even covers the Taskbar. You can then control the presentation from your mouse or keyboard (see Table 12.1) so that each slide is advanced when required. Alternatively, the slide show can be run automatically so that the slides advance after a preset period — insert sounds and video clips to give added impact!

Figure 12.14
Slide Show dialog box

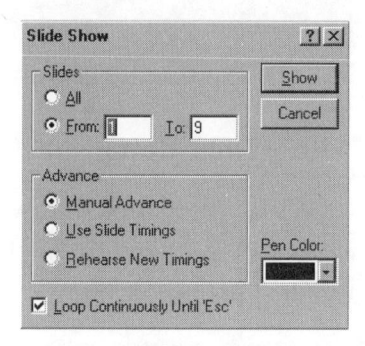

25. Choose **View↪Slide Show** from PowerPoint's menu bar to open the **Slide Show** dialog box. Click **Rehearse New Timings** then press the **Show** button to start. Press the space bar after talking through each slide and press ⎋ when you have finished — the timings are displayed in the **Slide Sorter** view.

Tip

> Choose File→Pack And Go to start a Wizard that guides you through the process of copying your presentation, together with all the files needed to deliver it from another computer, onto a floppy disk

Table 12.1
Controlling a slide show

Key	Effect	Key	Effect
F1	Help	B	Blacks (or unblacks) the screen
Esc	Stops the slide show and displays your Desktop again	W	Whites (or unwhites) the screen
Space	Advances to next slide	A	Shows (or hides) the mouse pointer
Cursor	Changes the slide displayed on your screen	S	Starts (or restarts) the automatic slide show
Home	Return to the first slide	Ctrl + P	Changes mouse pointer to pen tool
End	Display the last slide	Ctrl + A	Changes mouse pointer to arrow
5 (Enter)	Displays the fifth slide	E	Erase drawing on screen

Tip

> Double-click your left mouse button to advance each slide, or right click to reveal a pop-up menu from which you can also control the slide show

Matching screen to printer — File→Slide Setup

Slides can be set-up to ensure that what you can see on your screen is what will be printed on the paper (or overhead transparency film) in your printer.

Note

> The aspect ratio is the length of a slide's height in relation to its width. Letter paper has a 4:3 aspect ratio, a 35mm slide has a 2:3 aspect ratio

Figure 12.15
Slide Setup dialog box

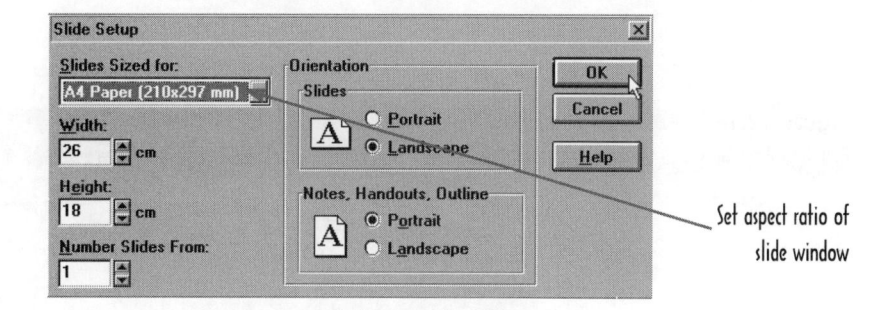

Set aspect ratio of slide window

26 Choose **File↪Slide Setup** to open the dialog box shown in Figure 12.15. Select the type of paper in your printer, then press **OK** to close the box and change the aspect ratio of the slides in your document window.

If the aspect ratio used to display slides in your document window does not match the aspect ratio of the paper in your printer, then you might gain an ugly blank space when the slide is printed (or lose part of it) — just like a Cinemascope film being shown on a domestic television. You can select **Scale to fit** in the **Print** dialog box to ensure that the slide fills the page — but this may distort your image.

Printing the material — File↪Print

The **Print** dialog box is very similar to those found in other programs and allows you to print your presentation in the following stages:

- **Slides**
- **Notes Pages**
- **Handouts** (2,3,6 slides per page)
- **Outline** view.

You can select the whole range of slides in your presentation or just one.

27 Choose **File↪Print** from PowerPoint's menu bar to open the **Print** dialog box. Click the button attached to the box labelled **Print what** and select **Notes Pages** from the list of material in the presentation. Press **OK** to close the dialog box and send this component of your presentation to the printer.

Figure 12.16
Print dialog box

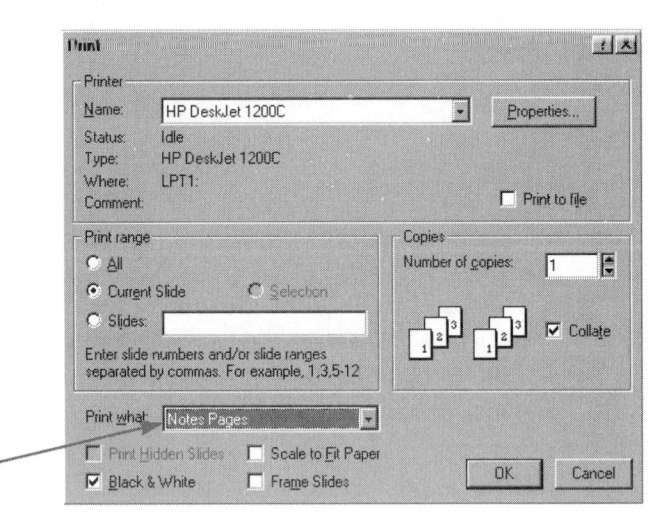

Select component to print

28 Close PowerPoint's main window (don't bother to save changes) then tidy-up your Desktop before shutting down Windows 95 from your Taskbar (as described at the end of Chapter 2). The exercise is now complete!

Note

When printing an outline, the size of the text on the printed page depends on the view size on the screen. Use View ⤳ Zoom – 100% to print material the same size as it is displayed

Summary

- The PowerPoint Wizard provides a quick way to start your presentation — use the outline document to plan its structure.
- The **View** menu settings permit you to prepare speaker's notes and handouts, as well as displaying individual slides.
- Choose **View↪Slide Sorter** from the menu bar in order to re-arrange the order of your slides. Choose **View↪Slide Show** to rehearse the presentation and check your timings.
- Use the **Insert** menu to add Clip Art and so forth to your slides — pictures makes a presentation more interesting!
- Give your presentation a consistent look by copying the style and format of another presentation (choose **Format↪Apply Design Template**) — insert a company logo into each slide.
- Use the **Print** dialog box to print-out the various components of your presentation; overhead slides, handouts, speakers notes.

Chapter 13

The Windows 95 Desktop

Objectives

> This chapter takes a close look at the Desktop, for this is what makes Windows 95 so visibly different from its predecessors. Following topics are considered:
>
> ▷ the steps you need to take before switching-off your PC
>
> ▷ the Desktop — an introduction to the facilities provided on the Windows 95 Desktop
>
> ▷ the Windows 95 Taskbar — program selector, event indicator and menu system
>
> ▷ the Taskbar's **Start** Button — access to programs, settings, documents, help and so forth
>
> ▷ working from your Desktop — how Windows 95 makes it easier to organize your documents and work more efficiently.
>
> This chapter provides a good starting point for someone upgrading to Windows 95 from earlier versions of Windows.

Don't forget to shut down

You may have developed the bad habit of simply switching-off your computer after you have completed (and saved) your work for the day. This was never advisable with Windows 3.1, and is even less advisable with Windows 95 because there is every likelihood that some information will be lost. The correct procedure for shutting down your PC is:

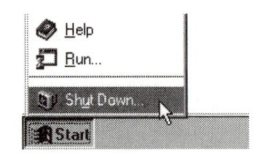

Press the **Start** *button at the bottom left of your screen and click* **Shut Down** *to display the* **Shut Down Windows** *dialog box — press the* **OK** *button within this box to prepare your PC before you switch-off.*

Always shut down Windows 95 from the Taskbar (see page 25) and wait for the instruction to switch-off your computer

Windows 95 is designed to automatically recover after an unforeseen power-cut, but relying on this mechanism each time you wish to shutdown your machine might eventually prove disastrous.

The Desktop

A few minutes after you switch-on your PC the screen is filled with the Windows 95 Desktop — usually it contains the **Welcome** window, a number of icons and the *Taskbar*. The main components of the Desktop in Figure 13.1 are:

> **Welcome** window — permits you to register the product (modem required) and gives you some hints about using Windows 95

> Taskbar's **Start** button — reveals a series of menus that open windows to perform specific tasks on your Desktop

> Taskbar — controls the windows displayed on your Desktop

Figure 13.1
The Windows 95 Desktop

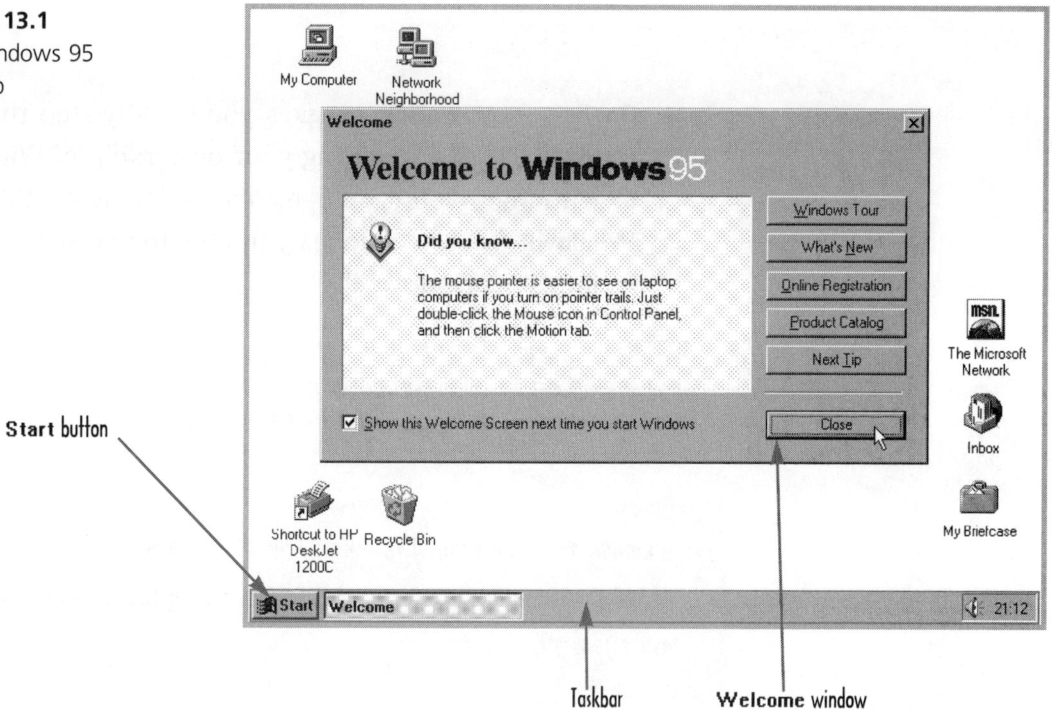

Start button →

Taskbar — *Welcome window*

- program and document icons — start programs and open windows for specific documents
- the Desktop itself — allows you to arrange the icons, create new documents and folders.

The Windows 95 Desktop provides the means for you to interact with your PC. Many tasks such as creating, printing and filing documents, can be performed directly from your Desktop. However, other tasks require you to open a window by double-clicking an icon on your Desktop.

Welcome window

The **Welcome** window is useful to people who are new to Windows 95, particularly if they are upgrading from Windows 3.1 There's a number of push-buttons in this window, including:

- **What's New** — opens a help window containing answers to some question often asked by people who are upgrading from Windows 3.1

Chapter 13 **The Windows 95 Desktop** 277

Chapter 13

- **On-line Registration** — takes you step-by-step through the process of registering your ownership of Windows 95 with Microsoft (you'll need a modem to do this)
- **Windows Tour** — teaches you how to use some of the facilities of Windows 95.

1 *Switch-on your PC and wait for the Windows 95 Desktop to appear (log on to your computer network, if required). Close the* **Welcome** *window by pressing its* **Close** *push-button.*

> **Tip**
>
> Remove the tick from the small box at the bottom left of the **Welcome** window to prevent it from opening the next time you start your PC

The Windows 95 Taskbar

The Taskbar's principal function is to control the presentation of the various windows on your Desktop.

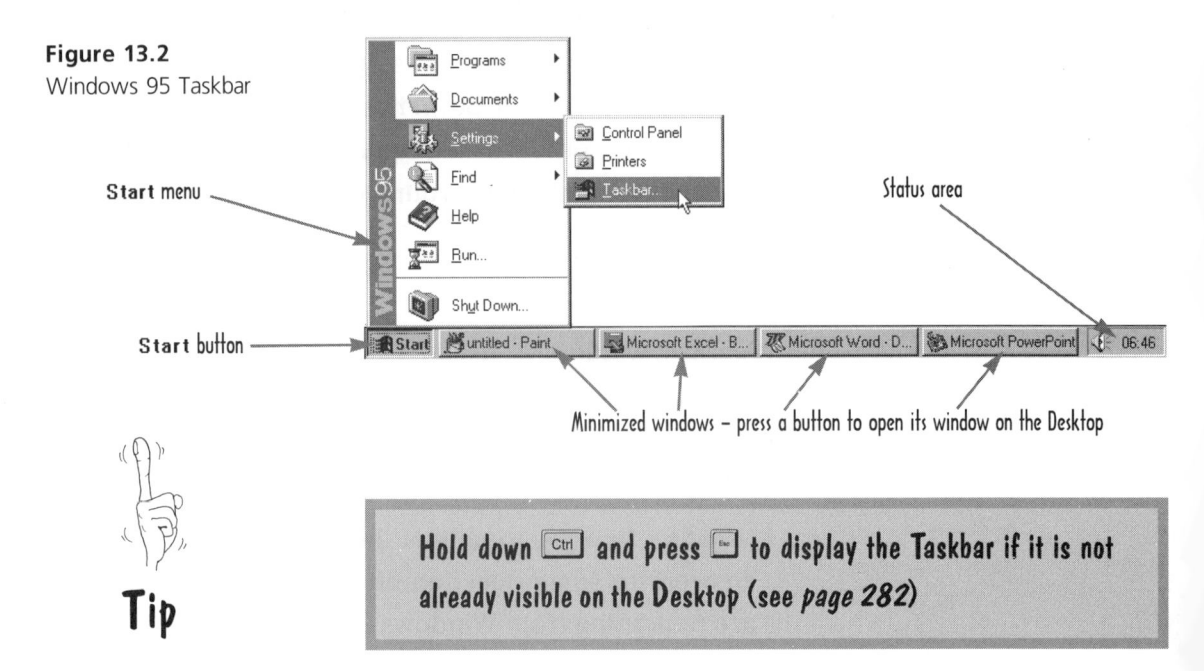

Figure 13.2
Windows 95 Taskbar

Start menu

Start button

Status area

Minimized windows – press a button to open its window on the Desktop

> **Tip**
>
> Hold down [Ctrl] and press [Esc] to display the Taskbar if it is not already visible on the Desktop (see *page 282*)

278   Chapter 13   The Windows 95 Desktop

You may have a remote controller for your television, now you have a controller for your computer — the Taskbar! At the press of a button the Taskbar hops between windows just like hopping between the channels on your television. Each time a window is opened on your Desktop a further button is added to the Taskbar. Whenever a window is closed (rather than just hidden) its button is removed from the Taskbar.

2   *Double-click a number of icons (**MyComputer** and the **Recycle Bin**, say) to open some windows on your Desktop. The active window is the one that overlays the other windows on your Desktop — its Taskbar button is also depressed. Press the Taskbar button belonging to another window to make it the active window on your Desktop.*

3   *Use your right mouse button to click (right-click) one of the buttons in the Taskbar so that the window's menu pops-up from the Taskbar. Use your left mouse button (click) to select **Minimize** from this menu and remove the window from your Desktop — it is hidden not closed. Repeat this operation for all the windows on your Desktop.*

4   *Press one of the buttons on your Taskbar to restore its window to your Desktop — alternatively use your right mouse button to reveal its menu then select **Restore**. Repeat this operation for the other window buttons on your Taskbar.*

Note

> The Taskbar's buttons list all windows currently open on your Desktop — these windows may be visible or hidden

Windows 95 allows you to have more than one program's window on your Desktop at once, but why would you want to do that? Consider the following scenario:

> *You are editing a letter on your computer when you need to look-up some thing in your address book. You start the Address Book program, find what you are looking for, then copy the information into Windows 95's Clipboard so that you can paste it directly into your letter.*

> *However, before you can return to your letter the telephone rings — a customer returning your call about an unpaid bill. Your invoices are held in a spreadsheet so you must start a third application, Excel, to obtain the relevant details. The customer accepts that the money is due, but claims he has not received your invoice; perhaps it's lost in the post! Fortunately your Address Book is already on your Desktop, but it is covered by the window containing your client's account details. You press the **Address Book** button on your Taskbar and the **Address Book** window comes into view. Your client has recently changed address so you update your Address Book and promise to send a copy invoice in the next post.*
>
> *Resolving to finish your letter without further interruption you press the **Letter** button on your Taskbar. Just then a symbol appears on your Taskbar to inform you that a fax has been received by your computer's modem. You start the **Fax Viewer** application...*

This sequence of events provides some justification that Windows 95's multi-tasking capability is worthwhile — although you may wish that you didn't have to work with so many interruptions in the first place!

Tip

> Hold down [Alt] while repeatedly pressing [Tab] to change the active window on your Desktop — the selected window appears when both keys are released

Changing the Taskbar's position and size

The Taskbar is normally located at the bottom edge of your screen. However, you can also drag it to the top, left or right edge of the screen and change its height so that it occupies more (or less) of the screen.

5   *Move your mouse over the Taskbar's top edge until the pointer changes into a double-headed arrow, then drag the edge of the Taskbar pointer towards the top of the screen to increase its height.*

6   *Move your mouse over a blank area of the Taskbar (where there are no buttons) then drag it to the left, right, or top edge of the screen — when dragging the Taskbar move your mouse pointer all the way to the edge of the screen before dropping it.*

> **Note**
> Increasing the height of the Taskbar normally reduces the area of the screen available to your Desktop — it also reduces the area of a maximized window

Uses of the Taskbar — tiling and cascading, minimizing all

A Taskbar button provides a pop-up menu that allows you to change the appearance of its window. However the Taskbar *itself* has a pop-up menu that permits you to rearrange all the windows on your Desktop.

7   *Position your mouse over a blank area of the Taskbar and press your right mouse button (right-click) to reveal the Taskbar's pop-up menu. Select* **Cascade** *from this menu (left-click) to rearrange all the windows on your Desktop as shown in Figure 13.3 . Repeat this exercise but select* **Tile Horizontally** *to arrange the windows without an overlap — like tiles on a roof.*

> **Note**
> Other selections in the Taskbar menu permit you to minimize all windows on your Desktop and change the way it behaves (see Taskbar properties)

Taskbar Properties

Your Taskbar is normally set so that it is always visible and, therefore, provides a constant reference point while you manipulate the various windows on your Desktop. However

Chapter 13   The Windows 95 Desktop   281

Figure 13.3
Windows arranged in cascade on your Desktop

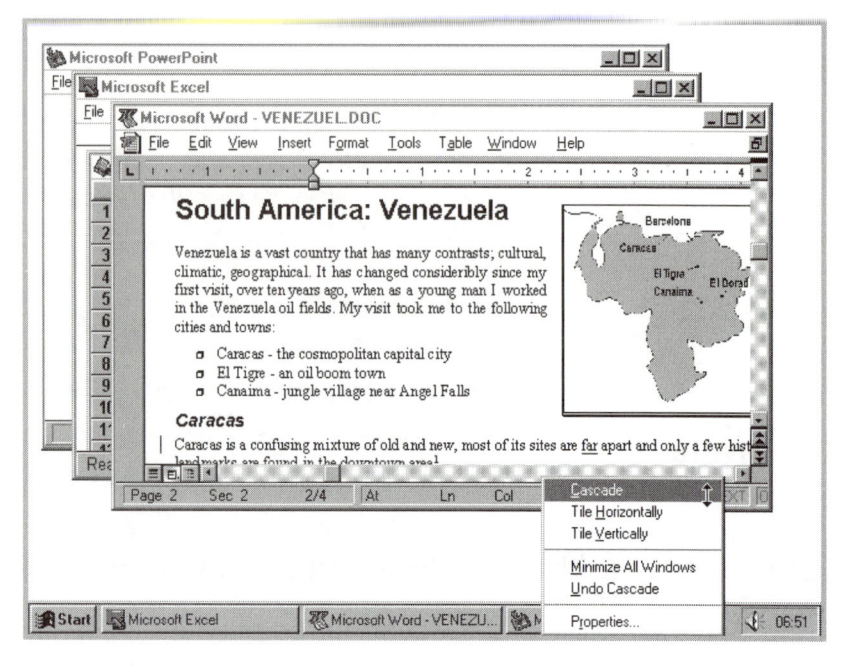

this reduces the size of your Desktop as the part of the screen it occupies cannot be used for any other purpose. You may regain the full area of your screen for the Desktop by changing the Taskbar's properties from its pop-up menu.

8   *Right-click over a blank area of the Taskbar to reveal its pop-up menu then left-click* **Properties** *to display the* **Taskbar Properties** *window. Click the box* **Autohide** *in the* **Taskbar options** *page to add a tick so that the Taskbar will disappear (almost) when the mouse pointer is moved away from it.*

> **Tip**
>
> The Taskbar will reappear when you move the mouse pointer to edge of the screen where its located — you see only the very edge of the Taskbar when it is hidden

9   *Clear the tick from the box* **Always on top** *(click it) so that your windows can overlay the Taskbar. Press the* **OK** *button to close the window and apply your new settings. Observe the effects of these settings on the behaviour of your Taskbar.*

10 *Restore the original Taskbar settings (repeat the previous steps) then close all the windows you have opened — use the pop-up menu from the Taskbar buttons and select* **Close**. *This exercise is now complete!*

> **Note**
>
> The settings in the Start Menu Programs page of the Taskbar's property sheet permit you to change the contents of the Start button's menu (see page 392)

The Taskbar's Start button

The **Start** button at the left side of your Taskbar provides access to a series of menus that allow you to start programs, open your documents, and so forth. The first level of this menu system is shown in Figure 13.4.

> **Note**
>
> When you open a document, Windows 95 automatically starts the appropriate program then loads your document into its window on the Desktop

Some of the choices in Figure 13.4 have a small arrow-head to indicate that a further menu will be displayed when they are selected. This type of *continuation* menu allows a large number of choices to be categorized under a variety of headings — making it easier to find the one you need.

Figure 13.4
The **Start** menu

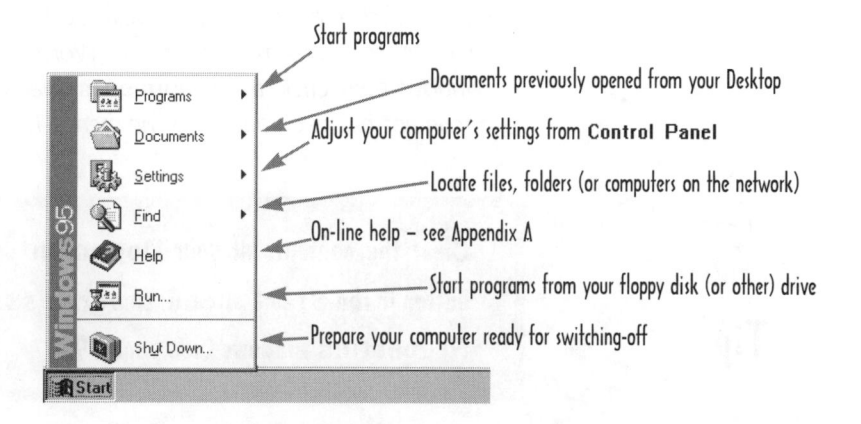

- Programs → Start programs
- Documents → Documents previously opened from your Desktop
- Settings → Adjust your computer's settings from **Control Panel**
- Find → Locate files, folders (or computers on the network)
- Help → On-line help – see Appendix A
- Run... → Start programs from your floppy disk (or other) drive
- Shut Down... → Prepare your computer ready for switching-off

Programs menu

All of the programs installed on your PC can be accessed from the **Programs** menu.

1 Use your mouse to press the **Start** button and reveal the menu shown in Figure 13.4. Move the mouse pointer to the **Programs** choice and its continuation menu will be displayed — there is no need to click. Point to the **Accessories** choice to reveal a further continuation menu then click **Paint** to start Microsoft Paint — a program supplied with Windows 95.

2 Explore the other continuation menus accessed from **Programs** and start a few other programs. Try to obtain an idea of the way that programs have been categorized within the menu system. Finally, close all the windows you have opened by starting these programs — this exercise is complete!

> **Note**
> The short-hand Start↪Programs↪Accessories refers to the continuation menu Accessories accessed from the Start button's Programs menu

Documents Menu

You are probably less interested in starting programs than working on the documents they create. A list of the most recent documents opened from your Desktop is contained in the Taskbar's **Documents** menu.

Double-click the icon on your Desktop labelled **Release Notes** to open this document within a WordPad window. Close the window then click the **Documents** menu — the name of the document has been added to the menu. This exercise is complete!

> **Tip**
> Clear the contents of your Documents menu by pressing a button in the Start menu programs page of the Taskbar Properties windows (see page 393)

Settings menu

Windows 95 provides a number of settings that determine the behaviour of your PC and the devices to which it is attached — printers, modems, networks and so forth. These settings are accessed through the **Start** button's **Settings** menu:

- **Control Panel** — opens a View window containing a number of programs and folders that permit you to add programs and devices to your Desktop, as well as change the properties of your system
- **Printers** — opens a View window containing the printers that have been installed on your PC
- **Taskbar** — displays the **Properties for Taskbar** window, that is also revealed when you point to a blank area of the Taskbar and press your right mouse button (see earlier in this chapter).

1   Choose **Start↪Settings↪Taskbar** and click the tab **Start Menu Programs** to bring this page to the forefront. Press the button **Clear** in this page to remove the contents of your Document menu. Finally press **OK** to close the window — this exercise is complete!

Note

> Further details of the Control Panel and Start menu settings are given in Chapter 18

Find menu — files or folders

The sheer amount of material that is available to your PC can make it very difficult to find the things you need. However you can quickly search for a particular document (or group of documents) in all the folders and drives at your disposal by opening a special **Find** window from the **Start** button's **Find** menu.

Chapter 13

1   *Choose* **Start→Find→Files or Folders** *to open a* **Find** *window on your Desktop (Figure 13.5). Click on the tab* **Name & Location** *to bring this page to the forefront (if it is not already visible).*

2   *Type* `ReadMe` *in the box labelled* **Named** *and select* **My Computer** *from the list that is revealed when you press the button attached to the* **Look in** *control. Insert a tick in the box labelled* **Include subfolders** *(click it) then press* **Find Now** *to start the search.*

3   *All the files named* **ReadMe** *will be displayed in the list that appears in the bottom half of the* **Find** *window. Use the scroll bar attached to this list in order to find the file whose* **Type** *is given as* **Text Document** *then drag its icon onto your Desktop. Close the* **Find** *window.*

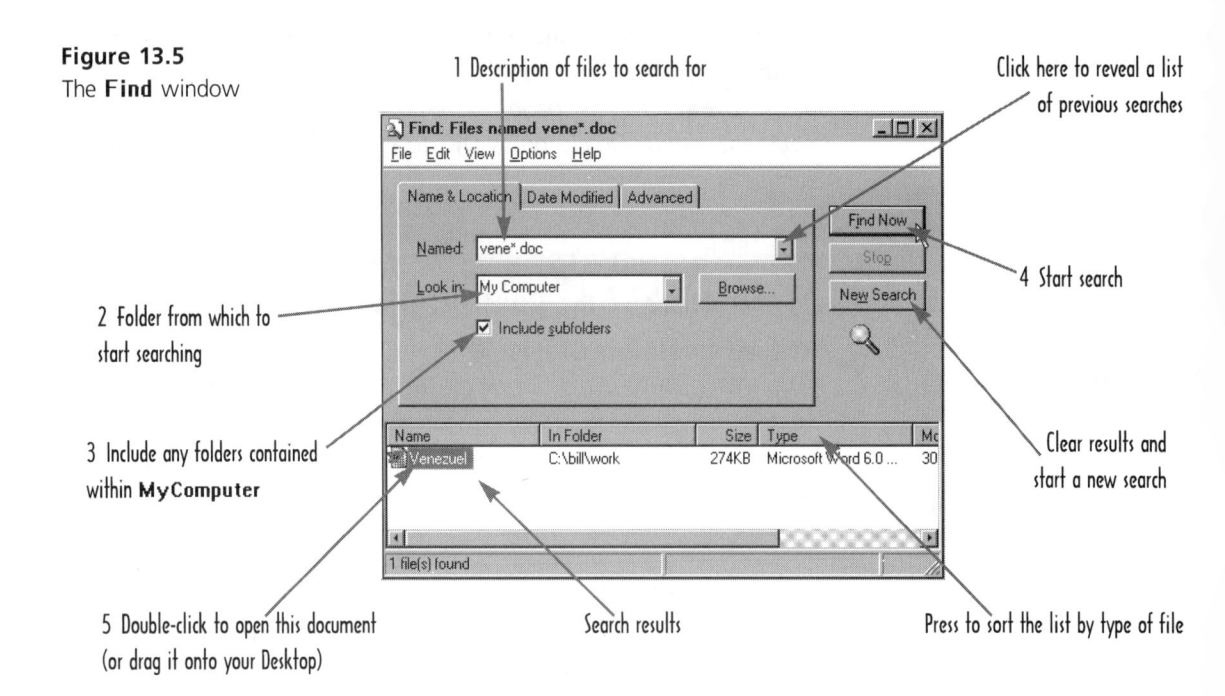

Figure 13.5
The **Find** window

1 Description of files to search for

Click here to reveal a list of previous searches

2 Folder from which to start searching

4 Start search

3 Include any folders contained within **MyComputer**

Clear results and start a new search

5 Double-click to open this document (or drag it onto your Desktop)

Search results

Press to sort the list by type of file

286   Chapter 13   The Windows 95 Desktop

> **Tip**
>
> Searching is quicker if you specify (Look in control) a folder or drive from which to start your search— use the Browse button

You may search for files and folders that:

- share some *part* of a name. For example: `tvr*` typed into the **Named** box searches for all files and folders whose name starts with the letters *tvr* (see page 133)
- were created or modified *between certain dates*. For example: typing 7 into the **Previous day** box searches for all files created during the previous week (**Date Modified** page)
- contain specific text. For example: typing `Dear James` into the **Containing text** box searches for all files containing a letter addressed to James —the search is much quicker if you specify a particular folder or type of file (**Advanced** page).

> **Tip**
>
> When using the Advanced or Date Modified pages of the Find window, check that appropriate settings for your search are also provided in the Name & Location page

The **Find** window is similar to a View window (see Chapter 14) and permits you to apply actions from its menu bar to the files you have selected as a result of your search. You can also apply **File→Save Search**, in order to save the results of a particular search as an icon on your Desktop — double-click the icon to re-open the **Find** window complete with its list of results.

Find menu — Computers, On the Microsoft Network

When your computer is connected to an office network (see Chapter 15) you can open a **Find** window from the **Start** button's Find menu, In order to locate any computer to which you have access.

1. *Choose* **Start→Find→Computers** *from the Taskbar to open a* **Find** *window on your Desktop — it only has a single* **Computer Name** *page. Type* * *(a wildcard character) into the* **Named** *box then press* **Find Now** *to search for all the computers to which you have access.*

2. *Double-click one of the icons in the results list to open a View window (see Chapter 14) containing the folders, files and resources available to you on that machine. Close this window then close the* **Find** *window — this exercise is complete!*

> **Note**
>
> The **Find** menu contains an option that opens a similar **Find** window, so you can locate services on the Microsoft Network

Help — obtain assistance

You can obtain assistance while using the Desktop by choosing **Start→Help**. This opens a help window containing the following pages that permit you to locate an appropriate help topic:

- **Contents** — a list of help topic titles arranged under a number of common headings, like the contents page of a book
- **Index** — an index of help subjects arranged alphabetically, so that you can obtain a reference to the title of the help topic
- **Find** — an alphabetical list of all the words that are used in the help topics.

> **Note**
>
> Appendix A gives further details about using the Windows 95 help system

Run — start a program

You are sometimes given the following instruction on the label of a floppy disk when installing a program on your PC:

Insert Disk 1 into Drive A and run setup.exe

Choosing Start↪Run opens a dialog box that permits you to find a program's file then apply the **Run** action to it — this is the same as starting a program.

Figure 13.6
Running programs

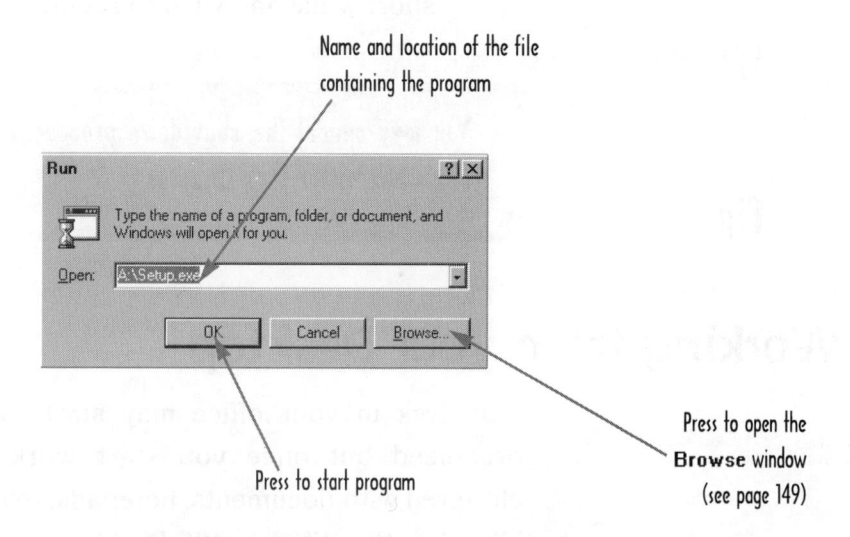

Name and location of the file containing the program

Press to start program

Press to open the Browse window (see page 149)

Note

> The Start button's Run choice is the same as that provided by the Windows 3.1 Program Manager's menu choice File↪Run

Shutting down Windows 95

Choosing Shut Down is the way to prepare your PC before switching-off the power — the Desktop dims and a dialog box appears giving you the following options:

▷ **Shut down the computer** — make this choice at the end of the day when you wish to switch-off your PC

▷ **Restart the computer** — select this option if you have been instructed to restart Windows 95

> **Restart the computer in MS-DOS mode** — choose this option only if you have experienced problems operating an old style program that worked before you upgraded to Windows 95. Return to Windows 95 by typing `win` at the MS-DOS prompt

> **Close all programs and log on as a different user** — make this selection if you are leaving your PC for a short while and wish to secure your Desktop.

Tip

> You may cancel the shut down process by pressing the dialog box's No button (see Chapter 1)

Working from your Desktop

The desk in your office may start the day tidy and well organized but once you start work it usually becomes cluttered with documents, notepads, telephones, and so forth. Likewise, the Windows 95 Desktop may be almost empty at the start of the day but will rapidly fill-up as you:

> open windows to view the files and folders holding the documents you need

> drag various files and folders from these windows onto your Desktop for easy access — they are represented as individual *icons*

> create new documents and folders directly from the Desktop by right-clicking (clicking your right mouse button) — this creates more icons on your Desktop.

Unlike a real desk your Windows 95 Desktop can be quickly re-organized with a few clicks of your mouse — see page 295. The Windows 95 Desktop reflects the fact that most people work with documents rather than computer programs. Therefore, most of the actions you might wish to perform on a document can be applied directly from your Desktop.

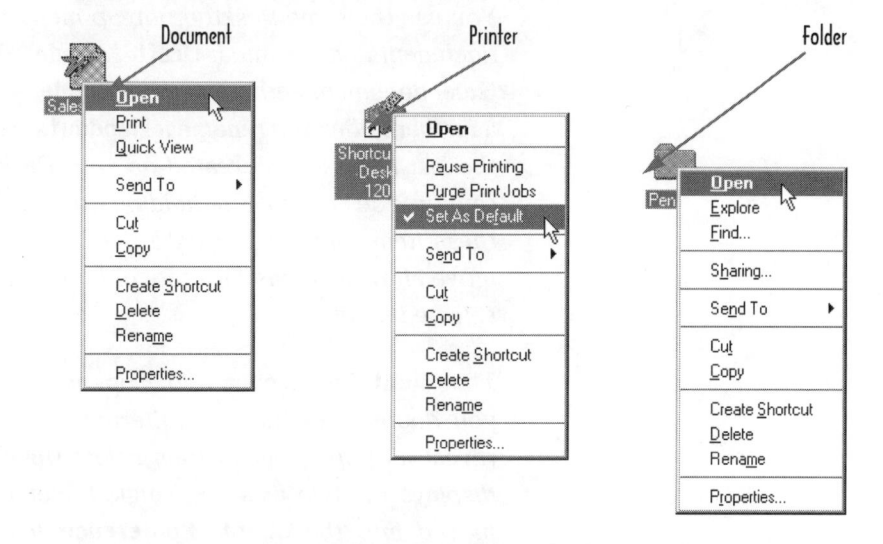

Figure 13.7
Right-click to reveal a pop-up window

Document

```
Open
Print
Quick View
Send To         ▶
Cut
Copy
Create Shortcut
Delete
Rename
Properties...
```

Printer

```
Open
Pause Printing
Purge Print Jobs
✓ Set As Default
Send To         ▶
Cut
Copy
Create Shortcut
Delete
Rename
Properties...
```

Folder

```
Open
Explore
Find...
Sharing...
Send To         ▶
Cut
Copy
Create Shortcut
Delete
Rename
Properties...
```

Tip

> Point to an icon and press your right mouse button to reveal its pop-up menu containing actions such as Open, Copy, Rename, Delete, Print and so forth

A typical session with your Desktop might run as follows:

> *You have just been given responsibility for a new project — organising a Client conference. This task requires you to produce an agenda and the necessary handouts.*
>
> *Your Desktop is untidy so you right-click on a blank area of the Taskbar — this reveals its pop-up menu from which you select* **Minimize all windows** *to give yourself space to work. You then create a folder for the new project by selecting* **Folder** *from the Desktop's pop-up menu (right-click on the Desktop and point at* **New** *to reveal its continuation menu). A new folder appears on your Desktop with its name highlighted so you rename it simply by typing* Client Conference *and pressing* Enter *— you are not restricted to eight letter names for these files and folders.*

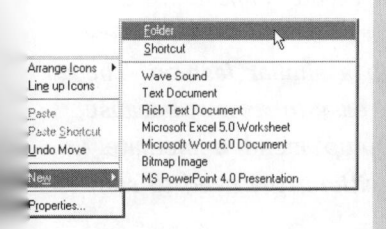

```
                    Folder
                    Shortcut
Arrange Icons  ▶
Line up Icons       Wave Sound
                    Text Document
Paste               Rich Text Document
Paste Shortcut      Microsoft Excel 5.0 Worksheet
Undo Move           Microsoft Word 6.0 Document
                    Bitmap Image
New            ▶    MS PowerPoint 4.0 Presentation
Properties...
```

Draft Agenda

Client Conference

Shortcut to HP DeskJet 1200C

You use the same Desktop pop-up menu to create a new Word document and rename it **Draft Agenda**. You then create a new Excel document and rename it **Attendees List**. You also create a further folder and rename it **Handouts**. Pressing `Ctrl` you select the last three items created on your Desktop by clicking them (multiple selection). Still holding down `Ctrl` you drag any one of these items and drop it onto the **Client Conference** folder to move all three items into the folder — the action applies to all selected items.

The **Client Conference** folder opens into a View window when you double-click its icon (alternatively you can right-click to reveal its pop-up menu then select **Open**). This View window displays the two files and single folder that you created then moved into the **Client Conference** folder. You double-click **Draft Agenda** to start Word with this document in its window — it's empty! You now type the conference agenda into the document then choose **File→Save** before closing the window. Next, you print **Draft Agenda** by dragging its icon from the folder and dropping it upon the Desktop's printer icon — this copies the file into the print queue, where it will be sent to the printer then deleted.

You check the progress of the print job by right-clicking on the printer icon then selecting **Open** from its pop-up menu (alternatively you could double-click the icon, as open is the default action — **Open** is emboldened in the pop-up menu). The printer's View window lists the documents waiting to be printed together with their status. You could delete all waiting documents in your local printer's queue simply by choosing **Purge Print Jobs** from its pop-up menu.

Having finished the draft agenda you create some more new documents from your Desktop (and also from the folder's View window) so they can be prepared in a similar fashion. The content of any of these documents is easy to review, because choosing **Quick View** from its pop-up menu immediately displays the document in a window without the need to start Word.

Discussions about the conference details continue over several weeks, but meanwhile you have other work to do so you drag the **Client Conference** *folder into your Desktop's* **Pending** *folder. Whenever someone telephones to discuss the conference you open* **Pending** *and drag the* **Client Conference** *folder back onto your Desktop. However because the draft agenda is the subject of many last minute telephone calls you decide to keep the document to hand. How can this be done while also keeping the document correctly filed? The solution involves creating a shortcut (or reference) to the document that can be kept on your Desktop — the file itself is stored within the* **Client Conference** *folder.*

A shortcut icon behaves just like the icon belonging to the document it references. You create a shortcut to **Draft Agenda** *by using your right mouse button to drag the file from its folder onto the Desktop then selecting* **Create shortcut Here** *(rather than* **Move***) from the pop-up menu that appears when the mouse button is released. The drop action is always specified from a pop-up menu whenever you drag something with your right mouse button.*

Eventually management is happy about your conference arrangements so you can finalise the documents. You use each document's pop-up menu to rename them as required — finals rather than drafts. You also delete files and folders you no longer need — deleting a shortcut removes the reference and not the actual file. It is very easy to organize and change the properties of your files directly from the Desktop.

You are just about to send out the invitations when the telephone rings; it's the Chairman and he wants to discuss some details in a document that you have just deleted! Fortunately you open the **Recycle Bin** *on your Desktop, locate the file and restore it (***File→Restore***), before he starts asking awkward questions. You answer the Chairman's questions and finally he tells you to send the agenda to your clients.*

You locate the **Agenda** *document in your folder and use the* **Send to** *option in its pop-up menu to reveal a further menu with the choice* **Fax Recipient***. Selecting this choice starts*

Microsoft Exchange and creates a new fax message form containing the **Final Agenda** *document. You click on the* **To** *button in the fax form and select the client list from your Personal Address Book. Your task is finally complete as you press the* **Send** *button from the Exchange toolbar — Windows 95 will now transmit this fax message to each of your clients while you make yourself a cup of tea and have a well earned rest!*

> **Tip**
>
> Try to repeat the above session on your own PC to get a better understanding of the way in which your Desktop can be used

Many types of document can be created from your Desktop then moved into appropriate folders simply by dragging and dropping. Thus you can organize your work just like a standard office filing system. The document icon's pop-up menu contains many of the actions you might wish to apply to the document:

- **Open** — starts the program that creates a window for the document on your Desktop
- **Print** — sends the document to the *default* printer
- **Quick View** — opens the document in a **Quick View** window on your Desktop (useful for a quick review of its content)
- **Send To** — copies the document to a floppy disk, fax and so forth. You can add your own folders to this menu by adding a shortcut to them in the **SendTo** folder
- **Cut**, **Copy** — moves or copies the document from its current location into the Windows 95 clipboard so that it can be pasted into a folder (or Desktop)
- **Create Shortcut** — makes a reference to the document that can be moved into another folder (or your Desktop)

- **Delete** — moves the document into the **Recycle Bin** where it is eventually destroyed
- **Rename** — changes the name of the document
- **Properties** — reveals statistics and summary information about the document and changes file attributes that make it read-only.

> **Note**
>
> The pop-up menu is revealed when you point to the icon and press your right mouse button (right-click) — the bold item in this menu is the default action applied when you double-click

Tidying your Desktop

At the end of a busy day your Desktop is covered with documents, windows, icons and so forth — its just as messy as a real desk. However with no more than a few mouse clicks you can make it tidy again ready for the morning start.

1 *Right-click on a blank area of the Taskbar to reveal its pop-up menu — select* **Minimize All Windows** *in order to clear your Desktop.*

2 *Use your right mouse button to click, in turn, each button in the Taskbar, then select* **Close** *from its pop-up menu to remove the window from your Desktop and the button from your Taskbar.*

3 *Choose* **Start↪Shut Down** *to dim your Desktop and display the* **Shut Down** *dialog box. Click the option* **Shut down the computer** *then press* **Yes**. *Wait until you are informed by a message on the screen that it is safe to turn off your PC before finally switching-off — this exercise is complete!*

A summary for the usage of many Desktop objects is shown in Table 13.1.

> **Note**
>
> The state of your Desktop can be preserved when you shut down, so that it can be restored next time you switch-on the PC (see page 399)

Chapter 13

Table 13.1
Features of the Windows 95 Desktop

Object	Use
Desktop	❑ placeholder for your program and documents
	❑ placeholder for windows
	❑ right-click to reveal its pop-up menu — create new documents and folders, change its properties, rearrange icons
Document or folder icons	❑ move its location by dragging and dropping it into another folder (or drive)
	❑ drag with right mouse button to reveal pop-up menu when it's dropped — specifies the action that will be performed
	❑ right-click to reveal its pop-up menu
Document icon Sales letter	❑ double-click to open document
	❑ print document by dropping it onto a printer
Folder icon Pending	❑ double-click to display its contents in a View window — files and other folders
	❑ add other folders and documents by dragging and dropping them on this folder
Program icon Winword	❑ double-click to start the program and create a window on your Desktop. Close the window to stop the program
Shortcut icon Shortcut to Draft Agenda	❑ a reference to a program, document or folder kept within your file system, rather than on the Desktop
Printer icon HP DeskJet 1200C	❑ drop document icons on the printer for them to be printed
Recycle Bin icon Recycle Bin	❑ double-click to open its View window — holds the files and folders deleted from your Desktop before they are destroyed
	❑ drop a document on the **Recycle Bin** for it to be deleted

Summary

- The **Welcome** window allows you to register your copy of Windows 95 and provides a quick tour of its new features.
- The Taskbar controls the various windows that have been opened on your Desktop (screen) — right-click a blank area of the Taskbar to change its properties.
- Don't forget to use the Taskbar to shut down before switching-off your PC.
- The Taskbar's **Start** button provides a series of menus from which you can start your programs, open your documents, change the settings for your PC, and find things.
- Create new folders and documents directly from your Windows 95 Desktop by making selections from its pop-up menu — right-click a blank area of the Desktop.
- Right-click an icon in order to reveal its pop-up menu — permits documents to be printed, folders to be opened, printers to be set as the default, and so forth.

Tip

> Press the Advanced button in your Open dialog box (File↪Open) to find documents in the same way as in the Windows 95 Find window

Chapter 14

Exploring files and folders

Objectives

This chapter explains how you can use View and Explorer windows to manage your computer's files and folders as well as its other resources. There are several concepts for you to understand:

▷ **View windows** — provide a simple way to access the contents of your PC and the computers to which it is connected

▷ **Windows Explorer** — a single window which permits you to administer the hierarchy of folders that start from your Desktop

▷ **Toolbars** — View windows and the Windows Explorer share a common toolbar that supplements the actions found in their menu bars

▷ **Recycle Bin** — a special folder that provides a temporary repository for deleted files before they are permanently destroyed

▷ **Printers** — a folder from which you can open the special View windows that are used to manage your pending print jobs.

After completing this chapter you will understand how to make full use of the various View and Explorer windows that appear throughout the Windows 95 environment.

VIew windows

A View window provides a uniform way of displaying the contents of any folder that can be accessed from your Desktop.

1. *Double-click the icon* **My Computer** *on your Desktop to open its View window (alternatively, right-click the icon and choose* **Open** *from its pop-up menu).*

2. *Double-click the icon labelled* **C:** *in the* **My Computer** *window to open another View window that displays the contents of the drive* **C:** *root folder. Double-click the* **Windows** *folder in this window to open a further View window — use its scroll bars to review the files and folders it contains.*

Figure 14.1
My Computer window

- Described in this chapter
- Chapter 18
- Click to select a different folder
- Details about selected drive
- (see Chapter 16)

Note

Each document accessed from your PC is stored in a file, located within a hierarchy of folders, that originates from the *root* folder of a particular disk drive (see Chapter 6)

The **Windows** folder contains many files and other folders — most of them have significance only to your system. Closing the View window hides these mysterious files so you no longer need worry about them.

3   *Close the View windows you have opened by choosing* **File↪Close** *from their respective menu bars. This exercise is complete!*

People often find it difficult to grasp the concept of locating files within a hierarchy of folders that stems back to the root of a particular disk drive. You should persevere, for once the concept has been grasped you have the key to organising your own files and folders.

> **Tip**
>
> Write down the name of each folder as you open its View window and arrange these names into a list like a family tree starting from the disk drive's root folder (C:)

Creating folders — File↪New

It is not a good idea to add your own documents into the **Windows** folder because you would have to search through a mass of unnecessary detail to find them again. It is a much better idea to create your own folder.

1   *Double-click the Desktop icon* **My Computer** *to open its View window then open the View window for your Desktop (use the Toolbar's list of folders control (see page 313) to select the folder at the top of the list). Choose* **File↪New↪Folder** *to create a new folder within the window.*

2   *Rename this new folder by typing* My Files *then pressing* Enter *— its name (***New Folder***) is initially highlighted so it will be replaced by your first keystroke.*

You have now created your own folder named **My Files** that is contained on your Desktop. This single folder may suffice while there are only a small number of files for your documents, but as your collection of files grows so does the need to organize them into different folders.

Figure 14.2
Set of folders for your documents

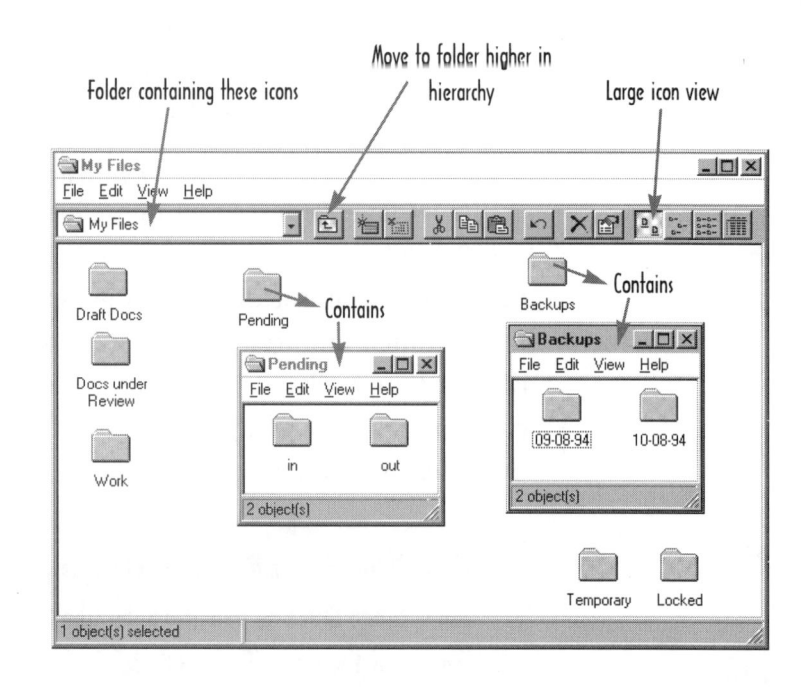

[Figure shows a "My Files" window with folders: Draft Docs, Pending, Docs under Review, Backups, Work. The Pending folder is opened showing "in" and "out" subfolders. The Backups folder is opened showing "09-08-94", "10-08-94", Temporary, and Locked subfolders. Annotations point to: "Folder containing these icons", "Move to folder higher in hierarchy", "Large icon view", and "Contains".]

It is advisable to start with a simple structure then add to it as your needs expand. You might consider creating an initial set of folders as shown in Figure 14.2.

3 *Open* **My Files** *(the folder you have just created) and repeat steps 1 and 2 in order to create a hierarchy of new folders like those shown in Figure 14.2 — in future you can use these folders to store your documents.*

The way Windows 95 allows you to classify your files into a hierarchy of folders provides a very powerful and flexible way for you to organize your documents. However, storing files within a hierarchy of folders has a number of other advantages, besides making it easier for you to locate your documents:

▷ new folders can be created to accommodate new projects and accounts — keep related files together

▷ operations can be assigned to particular folders — copy its files to a floppy disk, delete its contents and so forth

▷ backup and maintenance of your files is greatly simplified — you only need to concern yourself with files and folders within **My Files**, your own top level folder.

> **Note**
>
> Folders are only one of the many different types of objects that can be created from the File→New continuation menu in a View window's menu bar (see Chapter 13)

Operating on files and folders — the File menu

A number of common operations can be performed on the files and folders in a View window, by first selecting them, then applying an action from the menu bar. For example, if you have selected a folder you may wish to apply one of the following actions from the **File** menu:

▷ **Open** — open a further View window to display the contents of the folder

▷ **Explore** — open an **Explorer** window to display the folder within the context of all the other folders that can be accessed from your PC (see later this chapter)

▷ **Find** — open a **Find** window (see Chapter 13) that can be used to search the folder for particular files (or folders)

▷ **Sharing** — open a properties sheet that permits the contents of the folder to be shared with other computers connected to your PC (see Chapter 15)

▷ **Send To** — copies the folder and its contents to a floppy disk or other folder

▷ **Delete** — move the folder and its contents into the **Recycle Bin** folder (see later this chapter).

> **Tip**
>
> Right-click an item in a View window, or the window area itself, to reveal a pop-up menu containing the actions you can apply

Renaming Items in a View window

You can rename an item selected in a View window by applying File→Rename from its menu bar then typing the new name.

4   *Select the* **My Files** *folder (created previously) from the* **My Computer** *View window. Choose* File→Rename *from the menu bar of this window in order to change the label of your folder into a small* edit *box — the text* **My Files** *is highlighted.*

5   *Replace the highlighted text simply by typing a new name then pressing* Enter *— this renames the item and restores the label to its normal state. Complete this exercise by closing the various View windows you have opened.*

Note

> Text in an edit box can be changed and manipulated in the same way throughout the Windows 95 environment — it is a common control (see Appendix B)

Properties of items in a View window — File→Property

Files and folders have properties, such as size and the date they were created. These are displayed in a property sheet opened from your View window.

1   *Open your* **My Computer** *window then open a number of other View windows to display the contents of various folders. Select a file from one of these folders then choose* File→Properties *from the window's menu bar in order to open its property sheet.*

2   *Press* **OK** *to close the property sheet then close the other windows opened in the previous step — this exercise is complete!*

The following attributes can be set from the property sheet belonging to a file (or folder):

- **Read only** — tick this box to prevent further alterations to the file and any document it contains
- **Archived** — this box is cleared by programs like Backup when the file has been archived. It is then set again whenever you alter the file
- **Hidden** — tick this box to hide the file from view. You may change a setting in your **Options** property sheet to display hidden files and folders
- **System** — this box is checked if the file is an internal Windows 95 file.

Note

> The settings you gave your Office 95 documents (see page 169) are displayed in the Summary page of the file's property sheet

Devices such as disk drives have a different set of properties to those belonging to files and folders. The properties of a disk drive selected from the **My Computer** window are shown in Figure 14.3.

Figure 14.3
Properties of a drive —
File→Properties

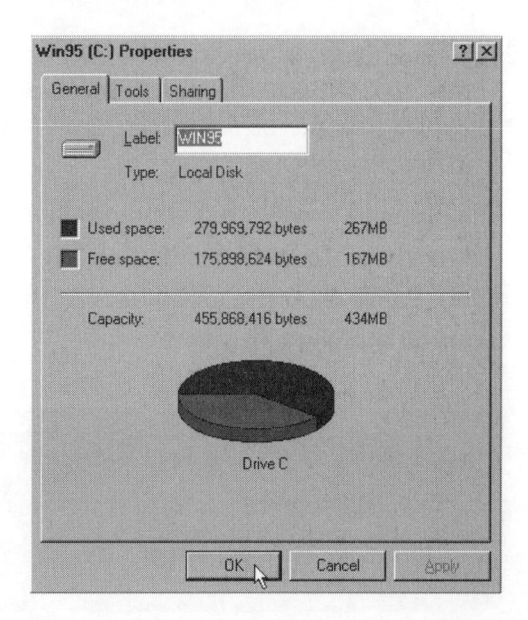

Chapter 14 Exploring files and folders 305

Chapter 14

Selecting and manipulating items — Edit menu

The standard way of selecting something is to click it with your left mouse button. However you can also use the **Edit** menu to select groups of files and folders within your View window, in the following ways:

- **Edit↪Select All** — selects all files and folders displayed in the window'
- **Edit↪Invert Selection** — selects all files and folders except for those currently selected

> **Tip**
>
> Select more than one item from a View window by holding down `Ctrl` while clicking subsequent files and folders — multiple selection

1. *Double-click the **My Computer** icon on your Desktop to open its View window. Next, choose **Edit↪Select All** from its menu bar (or press `Ctrl`+`A`) in order to select the items in this window — they are all highlighted.*

2. *Click a folder to select it (this cancels your previous selection) then choose **Edit↪Invert Selection** to select all the items in the window except this folder. Cancel this selection by clicking the folder again.*

Once you have selected some items in a View window you can move them to another folder, by choosing **Edit↪Cut** and **Edit↪Paste** from the menu bars of the source and destination window — see Figure 14.4.

> **Tip**
>
> You can also move files (and folders) by dragging them from one View window to another using your mouse — this moves the items between the corresponding folders

306 Chapter 14 Exploring files and folders

Figure 14.4
Copy and paste items from one folder to another

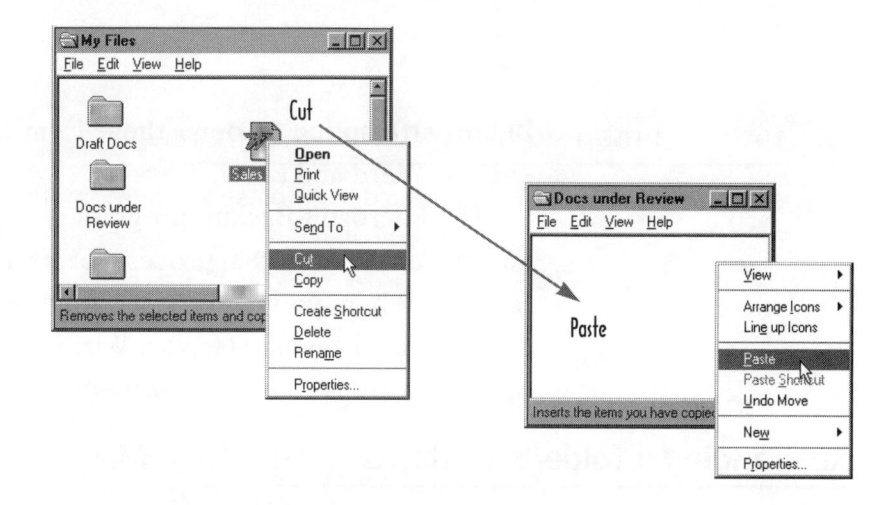

You will often find yourself moving files into the same folder, for example:

> *You have created a folder to contain all the files (and folders) relating to a certain project. When the project is complete you need to move the folder onto a floppy disk so that you can reclaim space on your hard disk.*

The need to regularly move items into the same folder can be met by adding the folder to your **Send To** menu — **File→Send To**. The contents of this menu is determined by shortcuts placed in the **Send To** folder, located within the **Windows** folder in drive **C:**.

Archiving and backup

Moving files between folders is particularly useful when archiving or backing-up important documents. You should always keep at least one backup copy of significant files in case your working copy becomes corrupted or accidentally deleted. Do not leave this until the document is complete — do it at the end of each day!

Floppy disks are useful for storing backups because they can be physically removed from your computer. However floppy disks are too slow to be used for holding files while they are being used — always move files to your hard disk before attempting to open them from application programs such as Word and Excel.

The Microsoft Backup program is supplied with Windows 95 and automates the process of archiving your files and folders. When you start this program (**Start↪Programs↪ Accessories↪System tools**) a Wizard takes you through the necessary steps to backup, or restore, your work.

Rearranging a folder's contents — the View Menu

The contents of your folders can become rather messy as more files (and folders) are added and moved around between them. At first you can overcome the problem by enlarging the View window, but eventually you will need to reorganize its contents.

Figure 14.5
View↪Arrange Icons continuation menu

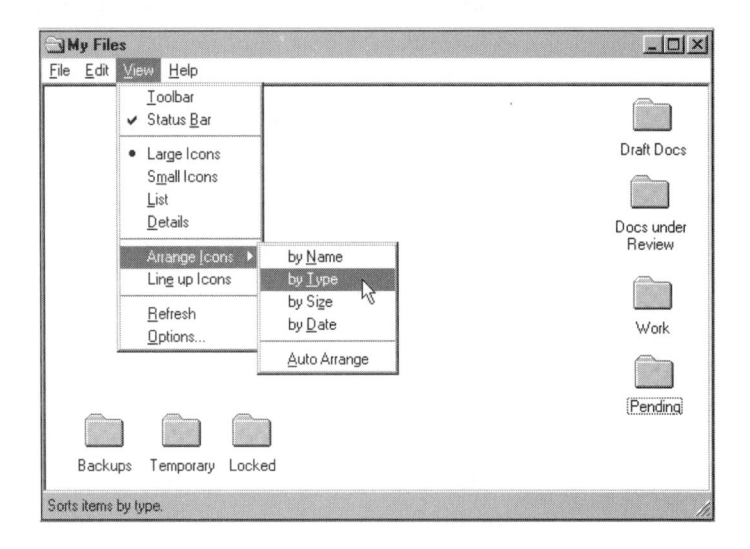

The contents of a View window can be sorted by choosing one of the options, described in Table 14.1, from the continuation menu provided by **View↪Arrange Icons**.

3   *Choose* **View↪Arrange Icons↪By Name** *from the* **My Computer** *window's menu bar — this rearranges the icons in the window according to their label name (see Table 14.1). Complete this exercise by closing the View windows you have opened.*

Table 14.1
Arranging icons

Sort By	Appearance of icons
Name	arranged in rows, alphabetically A through to Z, by their label name
Type	arranged in rows according the program to which they belong (e.g. Word, Excel)
Size	arranged in order of the sizes of the things they represent
Date	arranged by the creation date of the things they represent
Auto Arrange	automatically arranged by Windows 95 — you can't reposition the icons within the window when this choice is ticked

> **Note**
> The choices in the View↪Arrange Icons continuation menu depends on the type of objects that are contained in the View window

Alternative views of information — the View menu

The large icons in the View windows can be replaced by smaller icons or even a list of files. This permits more information to be displayed in the window as shown in Figure 14.6.

Figure 14.6
Options for presenting information in a View window

Press to sort list by file type

Name	Size	Type	Modified
Draft Agenda	5KB	Microsoft Wor...	02/03/95 12:00
Attendees List	6KB	Microsoft Exce...	02/03/95 12:00
Work		Folder	01/05/95 22:03
Temporary		Folder	01/05/95 22:02
Pending		Folder	01/05/95 22:01
Locked		Folder	01/05/95 22:03
Draft Docs		Folder	01/05/95 22:01
Docs under Review		Folder	01/05/95 22:02
Backups		Folder	01/05/95 22:03

9 object(s)   10.0KB

> **Note**
> The View window's toolbar contains buttons that duplicate the menu actions for changing the way items are displayed in its window area

The View menu also contains two standard actions that effect the display of its status bar and toolbar.

- **View⤷Status bar** — displays a bar at the bottom of the window that provides hints to help you perform each action
- **View⤷Toolbar** — displays a bar beneath the menu that contains buttons providing shortcuts to actions.

Tip

> Choose View⤷Refresh to update the contents of the View window after its folder has been altered by some external event, i.e. a change of the floppy disk on which it is stored

The Windows Explorer

The Windows Explorer allows you to administer the hierarchy of folders that start from your Desktop — it's a more powerful alternative to using View windows.

Note

> Folders are arranged into hierarchy that is similar to a family tree — all folders share the common ancestor of your Desktop and form branches of related folders (see Chapter 6)

1 *Open the Windows Explorer from your Taskbar (***Start⤷ Programs⤷Windows Explorer***). Identify the important components of the Explorer window marked in Figure 14.7, then use the vertical scroll-bar attached to the left half of the window to move through the list of folders.*

2 *Locate, then select (click) the* **Desktop** *folder at the top of the hierarchy in order to display its contents within the right side of the Explorer window.*

Figure 14.7
The Explorer window

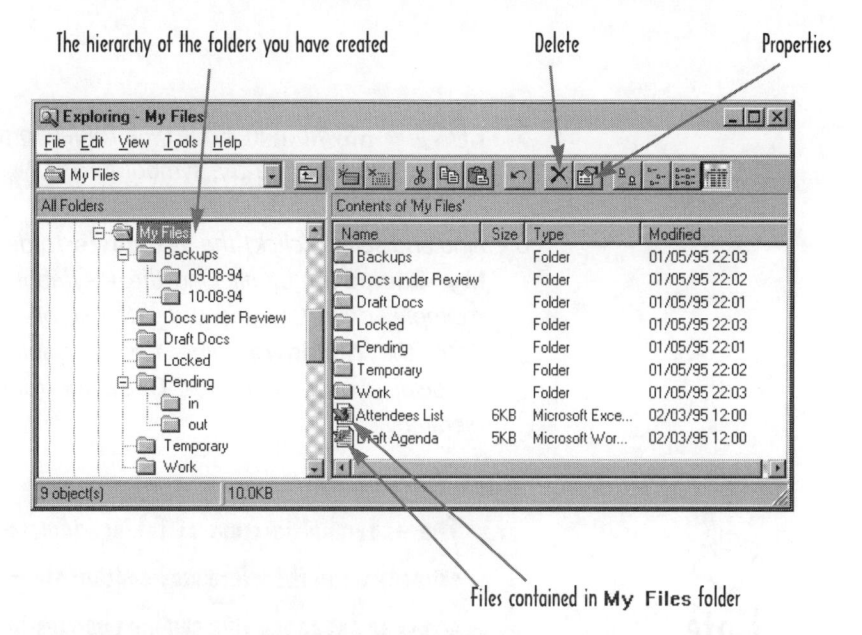

The hierarchy of the folders you have created — *Delete* — *Properties*

Files contained in My Files folder

The Windows Explorer menu is similar to the menu in a View window and this reflects the common purpose of both windows. However, the division of the Explorer window area into two separate halves makes it easy to identify and defines its particular character. Each half of this window has a different use:

- **All folders** — locates a particular folder from the hierarchy of folders that can be accessed from your PC
- **Contents of...** — displays the contents of the folder that has been selected in the other half of the window.

3 *Move your mouse pointer over the bar that separates the two halves of the window — it changes into a double-headed arrow. Drag the bar to alter the space available to each side of the window.*

It much easier to move files and folders using the Windows Explorer, because you can locate the item within the right side of the window then simply drag it onto the desired folder on the left side of the window.

4 *Click the + symbol in front of a folder on the left side of the Explorer window to reveal the folders contained at the next lower level (the symbol becomes − when these folders are revealed).*

5 Click the – symbol in front of a folder to hide the folders that it contains and change the symbol into +.

6 Find and select (click) the **Windows** folder that is located within **My Computer** by clicking the + symbol in front of a drive (for example, drive **C:**) and using the scroll-bar to scan its folders. After the **Windows** folder has been selected use the scroll-bar to display once more the **Desktop** folder at the top of the hierarchy.

> **Note**
>
> The + symbol in front of folder indicates that it has not been expanded and therefore may contain other folders. When a folder has been expanded this symbol changes to –

7 Locate the file **Calc** (a program file) within the contents of the **Window** folder as displayed in the right side of the Explorer, then drag it to the **Desktop** icon on the left side — this creates a shortcut that can be used to start the program from your Desktop.

8 Close the Explorer window and minimize any other windows on your Desktop — the exercise is complete!

> **Note**
>
> Use your right mouse button while dragging files within an Explorer window in order to reveal a pop-up menu — just like moving files between View windows

View windows are easier for a beginner to master, but as you gain experience the Windows Explorer becomes more appealing, because it helps you to quickly locate items that are stored within a hierarchy.

Toolbars — Explorer and View windows

The toolbars belonging to Windows Explorer and View windows are identical and contain the following controls that supplement actions in your menu bar:

▷ *list the folders* — press the button attached to this control to display a list of all the folders available to your PC. Select one of these folders to display its contents in the window area

▷ *move up a level* — press to display the contents of the next highest folder in the hierarchy

▷ *undo last action* — undoes the last action you applied to the folder

▷ *details, list, large and small icon views* — press any of these buttons to change the way the contents of the folder are displayed

▷ *map, disconnect network drives* — press one of these buttons to associate a network folder with a drive name (e.g. F:), then press the other button to break such associations.

Figure 14.8
Explorer toolbar
View↪Toolbar

Note: Other windows appear on your Desktop (Open, New, Browse) that have a similar function to Explorer and View windows

Chapter 14

Recovering deleted files — Recycle Bin

Every file deleted from your Desktop is moved into the **Recycle Bin** folder before it is permanently destroyed. Windows 95 destroys the oldest files in the **Recycle Bin** when there is a shortage of space in your hard disk drive, but until then, a deleted file can be recovered simply by dragging it out of this folder.

Just like any other folder on your Desktop the contents of your **Recycle Bin** can be displayed in a View window (or in Windows Explorer) — the contents of its menu bar reflect the special nature of this folder.

Double-click the **Recycle Bin** *icon on your Desktop to open a View window containing the files that you have previously deleted. Drag a file from this window onto your Desktop — it can be used like any other View window. Close the* **Recycle Bin** *window now that your file has been recovered — this exercise is complete!*

Note

> The amount of space allowed on each hard disk for the Recycle Bin is determined by settings in the Global page of its property window (right-click the icon to reveal its pop-up menu)

Managing your print jobs — Printers folder

Each of the printers installed on your PC is represented by an icon in the **Printers** folder, which can be opened from your Taskbar (**Start↪Settings↪Printers**). These printer icons open the special View windows that are used to manage your pending print jobs (Figure 14.9).

314   Chapter 14   Exploring files and folders

Note

> A print job is a special file that contains all the information needed for the printer to reproduce the document — it is automatically deleted after being transmitted to the printer

When you send a document to your printer it is actually dispatched as a print job to the appropriate printer window. It then joins the queue of other print jobs waiting to be sent to the printer (see page 85). Windows 95 is responsible for taking print jobs from this queue and transmitting them to the appropriate printer (or device) so that your program can continue with other tasks — as far as your program is concerned, once the document has joined a print queue it has been printed.

Figure 14.9
Printers folder and a Deskjet 1200C printer window

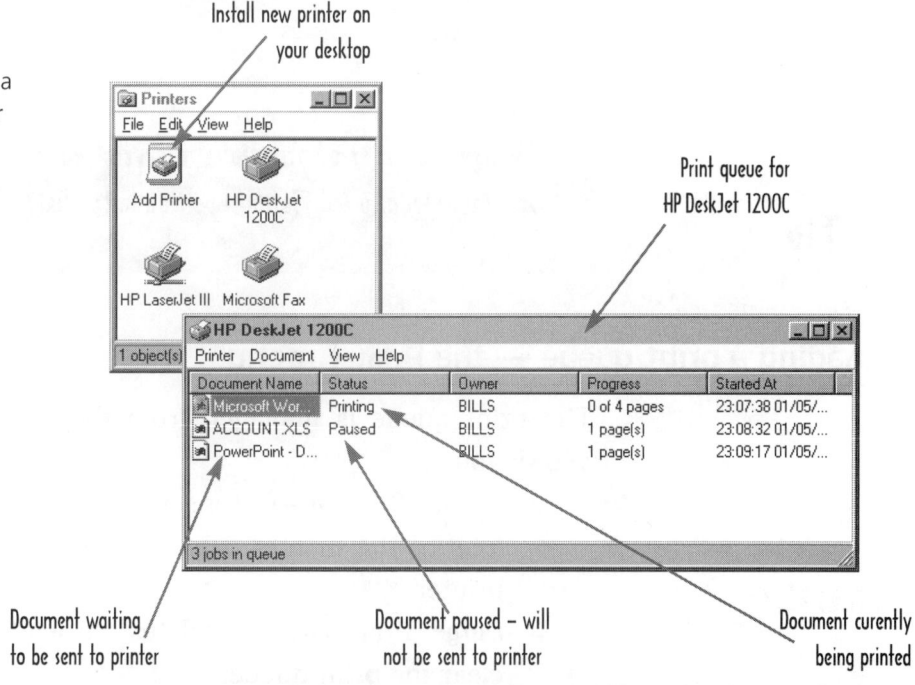

Install new printer on your desktop

Print queue for HP DeskJet 1200C

Document waiting to be sent to printer

Document paused – will not be sent to printer

Document curently being printed

Tip

> Right-click a printer icon to reveal a pop-up menu containing many of the actions that can by applied to the printer and its pending print jobs

Chapter 14　Exploring files and folders

The printer window serves to display and manage print jobs waiting in the queue for a particular printer. These print jobs are listed in order and have a number of attributes:

- **Name** — the file name of the document and the name of the program that created the print job
- **Status** — the print job at the top of the list is usually printing while the remainder are either pending or suspended (paused)
- **Owner** — the user name (see page 323 of the person who requested the print job
- **Progress** — the number of bytes that are still awaiting transmission to the printer
- **Started At** — the time and date the print job was created.

> **Tip**
>
> Change the order of print jobs in a print queue by dragging the document icon to a different position in the list

Managing a print queue — the Printer menu

The print queue is managed from the **Printer** menu which allows you to:

- **Pause Printing** — stops the transmission of its print jobs to the printer, suspending all printing from this printer
- **Purge Print Jobs** — deletes all pending print jobs to clear the print queue.

1 *Open the* **Printers** *folder from your Taskbar (***Start**↪ **Settings**↪**Printers***) and double-click a printer icon to open its printer window (Figure 14.9). Choose* **Printer**↪**Pause Printing** *to suspend transfer of print jobs to the printer.*

2   Start WordPad from your Taskbar (**Start↪Programs↪ Accessories↪WordPad**) *and type some text into its window to form a document. Print several copies of this document by choosing* **File↪Print** *before closing WordPad's window — a number of print jobs are now waiting in your (paused) print queue.*

You can also use the **Printer** menu to change the properties of the printer as well as making it the Desktop's default printer — the one selected whenever you print anything.

> **Note**
> The print queues of network printers (see Chapter 15) are not located on your PC and accordingly there are some restrictions to the actions that you can perform on its print jobs

Managing print jobs — the Document menu

The individual print jobs are managed from the **Document** menu whose actions choose to the items selected in the window:

▷ **Pause Printing** — temporarily stops a particular print job from being sent to the printer

▷ **Cancel Printing** — deletes a print job from the print queue.

3   *Select a print job from the print window's queue then choose* **Document↪Pause Printing** *to suspend printing of that document. Print the other documents in the queue by choosing* **Printer↪Pause Printer** *to remove the tick applied in step 1.*

4   *Choose* **Printer↪Purge Print Jobs** *to delete the print job which you suspended in the previous step of this exercise — it also removes any other print jobs from the queue.*

5   *Close the windows you have opened in the previous steps then tidy-up the Desktop before using your Taskbar to shut down Windows 95 — the exercises in this chapter are complete!*

Tip

> A printer icon appears in the Taskbar's status area (far right) whenever its print queue is not empty – double-click this icon to open the printer window so you can manage the print jobs

The **Printers** folder and the various printer windows provide the means to control your print jobs, but you should not forget that it is often much easier to print documents directly from your Desktop.

> *You need to write a letter to your accountant, Jeffrey Zinkin. You click your right mouse button while pointing at a blank area of the Desktop in order to reveal a pop-up menu which allows you to create a new Word document. This document appears as an icon on your Desktop and you can compose your letter simply by opening its window. When you have finished your letter, you close the window and save your changes in the document's file — it is stored in your Desktop folder.*
>
> *You can now print the letter by dragging its icon across your Desktop onto a printer icon labelled* **Letterheads** *— it's set-up to use the letterheads in your printer's top paper tray. A file copy of the letter is printed by dragging the document icon onto another printer icon labelled* **Plain paper** *— it corresponds to the same physical printer but is set-up (see page 81) to use the bottom tray containing plain A4 paper.*

Tip

> Printers often provide more than one paper tray so that documents can be printed on different types of paper – choose Printer↪Properties to specify your printer's tray settings.

Summary

- Open the **My Computer** window to access all the things contained within your PC.
- Insert things into an existing folder by choosing **File↪New** from the menu bar of its View window to create a new folder, document, and so forth.
- Review the properties of something you have selected in a View window by choosing **File↪Properties**.
- Select the entire contents of a View window by choosing **Edit↪Select All**.
- The Windows Explorer shows everything that is accessible to your PC — arranged as a hierarchy of folders from your Desktop.
- The View and Windows Explorer windows share the same toolbar — reflecting the common purpose of these two types of windows.
- Recover deleted files by dragging them from your **Recycle Bin** window — double-click its icon on your Desktop to open this window.
- The **Printers** folder contains an icon for each of the printers that have been installed on your Desktop — double-click a printer icon to open a View window showing its print queue.
- Manage the print jobs created by your programs from the View windows of the printer queues to which they have been sent.

Note

> The printer installation Wizard takes you step-by-step through the process of installing a printer on your Desktop (see page 337)

Chapter 15

Working with an office network

> This chapter explains how connecting your PC to an office network or local area network (LAN) makes it easier to share information and resources with other people in your organization. We consider:
>
> ▷ connecting your PC to an office network — log on to the network, change your password, preserve your Desktop layout and settings, log off
>
> ▷ browsing for network resources — how to find the folders and printers that are shared across the network
>
> ▷ sharing files with other people on the network — network files and folders can be used as if they were found on your own Desktop
>
> ▷ sharing devices across the network — printers attached to other people's computers can be used to print your documents. How to install a printer on your Desktop
>
> Connecting your PC to an office network allows you to communicate with people inside your immediate office or building — though some LANs connect offices in different continents!

Objectives

Connecting your PC to an office network

Networks are formed by inter-connecting a group of computers. A simple network can be established by linking together the PCs within your office — this might involve:

- plugging a network cable into the special socket located at the back of each PC
- *logging on* to the network when you switch-on your PC to start Windows 95 (see Chapter 1).

> **Note:** You will need to install a network adapter in your PC before it can be attached to a network — ask a technician to complete this task or refer to the appropriate manuals

A local area network (LAN) is a private network that links together computers within a small geographical area — typically an office or building. A wide area network (WAN), on the other hand, links computers over much larger distances and usually offer some form of public access (see Chapter 16).

There are a bewildering variety of different technologies used to implement office LANs; Ethernet, Token Ring and ATM to name but a few. Fortunately, you do not need to concern yourself with these technical matters in order to use the network facilities provided on your Desktop.

Once your PC has been set-up for connection to a network the **Enter Network Password** dialog box appears immediately before the Desktop is activated — this box allows you to log on (connect) to the network.

1 *Switch on your PC and wait for the* **Enter Network Password** *dialog box to appear (Figure 15.1). Enter your user name, password, and office* domain *name (if required) before pressing the* **OK** *button — if you press* **Cancel** *the Desktop will still appear, but your PC will not be connected to the network.*

Figure 15.1
Enter Network Password dialog box

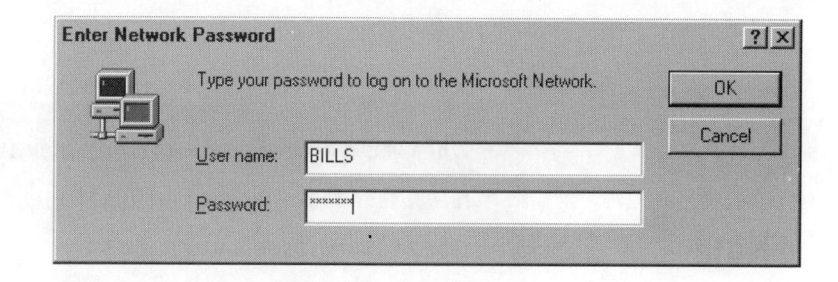

2   Wait for the Desktop to fill with objects like **My Computer**, **Network Neighborhood** and the Taskbar.

> **Note**
>
> The network in your organization may have a different Logon box – ask your *network administrator*

User name — the name by which you are known

Each person in your organization must be identified when they connect to the office network. A user name provides this identifier and might be formed from your surname, nickname or payroll number — Bill Stott's user name is *Bills* and is known to everyone in his office. Depending on how your network is administered you may select your own user name or have one assigned for you.

Password — a secret code known only to you

A password is associated with each user name and should not be known to anyone apart from the person to whom the user name belongs — the password used by *Bills* is secret. Your password stops other people connecting to the network under your name, therefore you should avoid such simple passwords as:

- *password*
- *26-07-59* (or your birthday)
- *BillStott* (or your user name).

Chapter 15   Working with an office network   323

Note: When you type your password an asterisk appears in the edit box rather than the letter you have typed – this prevents people from reading your password as you log on

Administration of larger networks

A large network requires careful management to ensure that everyone using it has adequate access to the resources they need for their job. This role is normally performed by the *network administrator*, whose responsibilities may also include policing access to the network by its users.

Large networks usually impose restrictions on the way new people may join the network. Typically, a new member of staff will ask the network administrator for a user name and temporary password before they can connect to the network. The user name determines the resources that they can use, while the temporary password permits them to log on so that they can change their password to something more appropriate.

Tip: You should change your password frequently in case anyone has discovered it by chance – most large networks force you to change your password at least monthly

Changing passwords

You can change your password simply by double-clicking on the appropriate icon in the **Control Panel** folder.

Passwords

3   *Open the* **Control Panel** *from your Taskbar (***Start↪Settings↪Control Panel***) and double-click the icon labelled* **Passwords** *to open the* **Passwords** *property sheet .*

4   Press the button labelled **Change Windows Password** to open the dialog box shown in Figure 15.2. Type your current password and your new password in the appropriate boxes, then press **OK** to close the dialog box and change your password.

**Figure 15.2
Passwords
Properties** dialog box

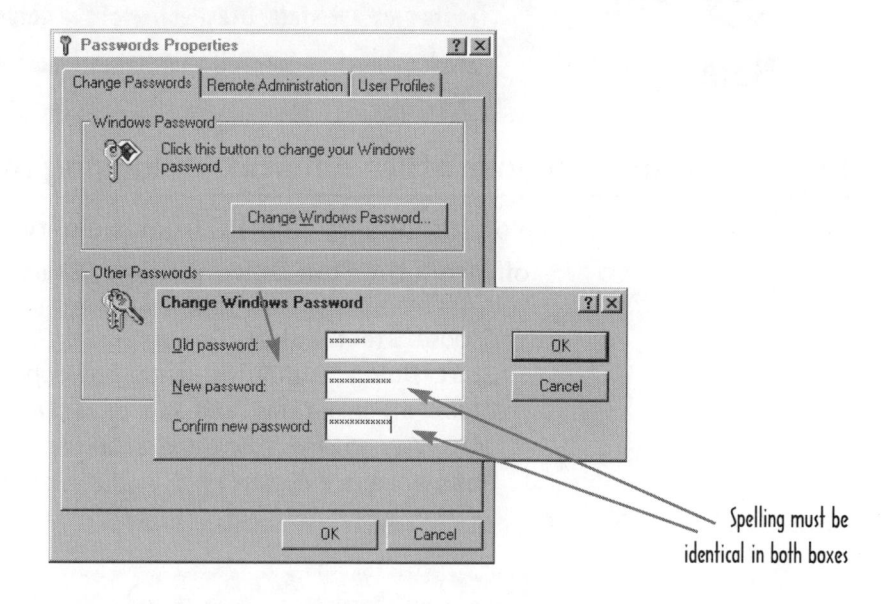

Spelling must be identical in both boxes

Note

> Depending on the features of the network used in your organization there may be other ways to change your password — consult your network administrator for details

Preserving your Desktop layout

You can stop other people who might use your PC from changing the arrangement of your Desktop, by preserving your settings so that they can be automatically restored each time you log on (see page 399) — this can be useful if several people use the same PC.

5   Click the **User Profiles** tab in the **Passwords Properties** window. Click the button labelled **Users can customize their preferences...**, then insert a tick in the two check boxes before pressing **OK** to close the property sheet and apply your settings. Close the **Control Panel** window.

Note: Certain networks also provide the facility to restore your Desktop to its previous state, irrespective of the actual PC from which you are logging-on — consult your network administrator

Disconnecting from your office network — logging off

You disconnect your PC from the network (known as logging off) from the Shut Down window (Start↪Shut Down).

6 Choose **Start↪Shut Down** — *the Desktop darkens and the* **Shut Down Windows** *dialog box appears. Select the option* **Close all programs and log on as a different user**, *then press* **Yes** *to clear your Desktop and open the* **Enter Network Password** *box (Figure 15.1) — this exercise is complete!*

Note: Once you have disconnected from the network any shared resources (printers, folders, files) on other computers will no longer be available to you

Browsing for network resources

Resources are the physical devices attached to a PC, like a printer, CD-ROM or a hard disk drive. However, the term is often extended to include files and folders shared on a network. You can browse through the network's resources in much the same way that you can browse the files and folders physically located in your own PC (see Chapter 14).

Note: Disk drives located on your own PC are termed local drives, whereas those physically located in other people's PCs are called network drives

1   Switch on your PC and wait for the **Enter Network Password** to appear. Enter your user name, new password and domain name (if required) before pressing **OK** in order to log on and populate your Desktop with icons and so forth.

2   Double-click the icon **Network Neighborhood** to open the View window shown in Figure 15.3 — it is empty if you have not successfully connected to the network. Use this View window to explore the resources that have been make available to you from other computers.

The **Network Neighborhood** window displays the computers within your immediate area that are currently connected to the network and which may have resources you can share. The network in our office is shown in Figure 15.3 — it consists of just three PCs.

Figure 15.3 Network Neighborhood

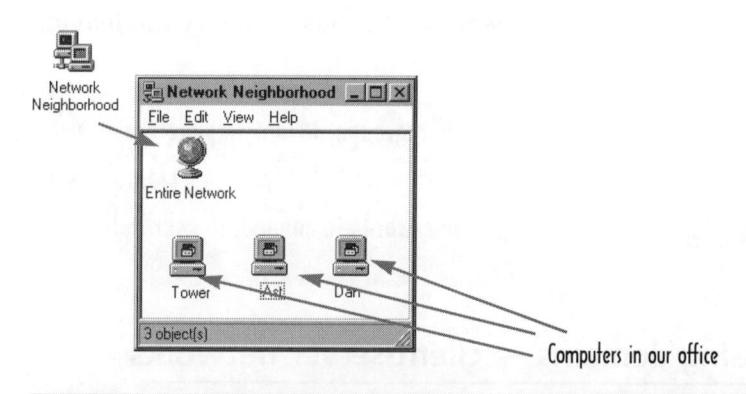

Note

The exact content of your Network Neighborhood window will depend on how your organization's LAN is arranged — each network is different in this respect

Participating in a workgroup — peer-to-peer networks

The LAN shown in Figure 15.3 reflects the way that a number of PCs would be connected together in a small business with just a single office. Each PC has a similar function and status with resources and information being shared among the people who are connected to the network. Networks having this type of arrangement are called *workgroups* or *peer-to-peer* networks.

> **Note**
>
> Workgroups offer few restrictions on your use of the network. While this may be acceptable in a small office it might cause problems in the context of a large network.

The limitations of peer-to-peer networks become evident once the size of your office grows. The resource belonging to a particular PC can only be shared when it is connected to the network — to access Mark Brearley's marketing survey (a file in his shared folder) you first must switch-on his PC. Sharing resources in this way can become difficult in a large office, because it relies on everyone leaving their PCs switched-on.

> **Note**
>
> Workgroups do not impose restrictions on who can log on to a particular PC — you can create any number of user names and passwords to connect to your network

Accessing domains — client-server networks

The needs of much larger businesses can be met by connecting together the networks in each office. This means resources and information can be shared within the context of the organization as well as the individual office. This is where the concept of a domain can help in the organization of a large network.

Definition

domain . . . . .a collection of PCs belonging to a particular group within an organization. Your company might have a *Sales Office* domain, *Service Department* domain, and so forth

Each domain has at least one PC that serves to manage your connections to other domains (offices) in the organization.

Such a PC is termed a *server*, while the computers to which it is connected (perhaps via other servers) are termed *clients*.

3   *Double-click the icon* **Entire Network** *in the* **Network Neighborhood** *window to view other domains to which you may have access. Double-click a domain in the* **Entire Network** *window to open a further window containing the computers (servers) connected to that domain — this window can be used just like the* **Network Neighborhood** *window.*

4   *Close the various View windows that you have opened in this exercise — it is now complete!*

Note

> A server PC is seldom switched-off; this means it is always ready to provide resources whenever a client PC connects to the network — a good place to locate the domain's shared resources

The resources and information available to your client PC depends on the access rights that have been granted to you, within the context of your own server, as well as any rights you might have in another domain's server. This might sound complex but in practice it means that your network View window shows only the resources that you can use on the network.

> *Andrew, the Chief Executive of XS Ltd., requires access to a report prepared by Christopher in Sales; information that is physically located in a file within a shared folder in the* Sales Office *server PC.*
>
> *After Andrew logs on to the network his* **Network Neighborhood** *window contains all the PCs connected to the CEO domain — including the CEO domain server. However there are a number of other domains to which he has access and these are displayed when he opens the* **Entire Network** *window. Double-clicking on the* **Sales Office** *icon in this window opens a further window containing all the PCs connected to the Sales Office domain — including the Sales Office server PC. Andrew can*

Chapter 15   Working with an office network

> display all the shared resources in this PC by simply opening its View window (by double-clicking its icon). To take a copy of Christopher's report Andrew just opens a folder within this View window, then drags the appropriate file onto his own Desktop.
>
> Christopher has only just joined XS Ltd and therefore has no need to access computers outside the Sales Office domain. After he logs on to the network his **Network Neighborhood** window contains all the PCs in his office but his **Entire Network** window contains only one entry — the Sales Office domain.

Domains and client-server networks allow the network administrator to permit only particular individuals (or groups of users) access to specified network resources.

Note

> Networks not only permit the sharing of resources like files, folders and printers, but also give you access to message services (see Chapter 17)

Sharing files with other people on the network

The properties of selected folders in your local disk drive can be altered so that other people can access the files they contain directly from their own Desktops.

1. *Double-click the* **My Computer** *icon on your Desktop to open its View window, then open a further View window for drive C (double-click its icon). Select a folder in this window then choose* **File⇾Sharing** *to open its property sheet (Figure 15.4).*

2. *Click the* **Sharing** *tab to bring this page to the forefront. Select* **Shared As** *then select* **Full (Access Type** *option) in order that any computer connected to the network may have read and write access to the contents of this folder. Finally press* **OK** *to close the property window. Close the drive C window.*

330   Chapter 15   Working with an office network

Figure 15.4
Folder's property sheet

1 Click here to share this folder

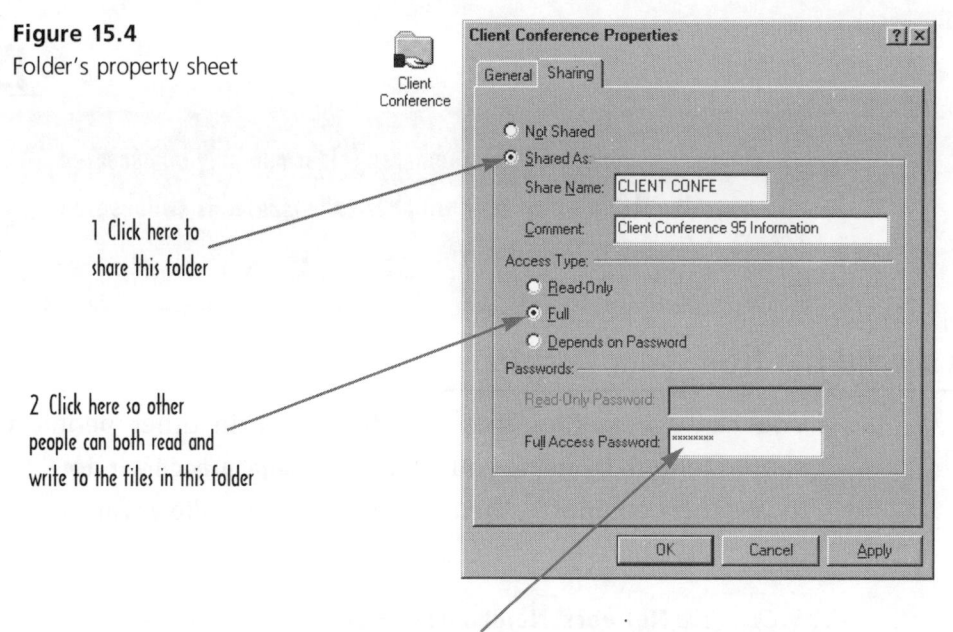

2 Click here so other people can both read and write to the files in this folder

Any password typed here must be supplied by anyone wishing to access your folder

> **Tip**
>
> Create a special folder on your Desktop and make it a shared network resource, so you can share your documents simply by copying the associated files into this folder

You can specify that your folders are shared with other people connected to the network in one of the following ways:

- **Read-only** — the files it contains cannot be modified or removed from the folder, but can be opened by a program for reading. If a read-only password is given then anyone wishing to access the folder must supply the correct password before it can be opened
- **Full** — the files it contains can be modified or moved without restriction. If a password is given then anyone wishing to access the folder must supply the correct password before it can be opened
- **Depends on Password** — the type of access to the files it contains depends on the password that is supplied by anyone wishing to use them.

> **Note**
>
> The files contained within a shared folder can only be accessed when the PC in which they are physically located is switched-on and attached to the network

Accessing a shared file from your Desktop

You can access files that are stored within other people's shared folders by using your **Network Neighborhood** window, to locate their computer, then opening a further View window to display its shared resources.

1 Open the **Network Neighborhood** window and double-click the icon that represents the computer which has granted you shared access to a number of its folders — this opens a further View window.

2 Open a shared folder within this View window just as if it was located on your own PC. Double-click one of its document files to start a program on your Desktop that will create a window for the document.

3 Change the document from within your program's window, in the same way that you would alter a document that was contained in a file on your local hard disk. Choose **File→Save** from the program's menu bar to update the file on the network drive.

> **Note**
>
> The Network Neighborhood window contains an icon for each of the computers in your workgroup – double-click this icon to open a View window containing its shared resources

The network View windows are just the same as the View windows used to manipulate the files and folders in your local drives (see Chapter 14). Accordingly, you may drag a file from a shared folder onto your Desktop in order to make your own private copy.

Figure 15.5
Sharing a file across your network

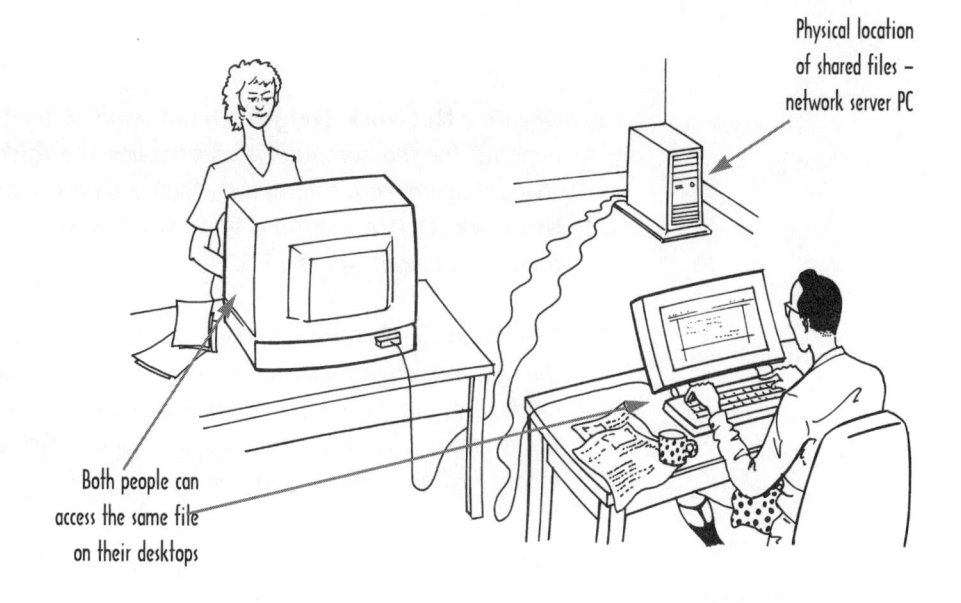

Physical location of shared files – network server PC

Both people can access the same file on their desktops

4   Close the various windows you have opened — this exercise is complete.

> **Tip**
>
> You can also access network resources from an `Explorer` window (see Chapter 14) — it displays everything available to your PC within a hierarchy starting from your Desktop

Accessing shared files from your programs — File→Open

The **Open** dialog box used by new style Windows 95 programs can open the **Network Neighborhood** folder (and its contents) in the same way as any other folder that is available from your Desktop (see Chapter 6). However older style **Open** dialog boxes can only open folders on specific drives — you must therefore assign a drive name to your shared folder.

> **Tip**
>
> Assign a drive name (`d:` through `z:`) to a folder that is located on another computer, so you can access its files simply by using this name as part of the pathname (i.e. `h:\share.doc`)

Chapter 15

1. *Open the **Network Neighborhood** window then open the View window for the computer that contains the folder you want to share. Locate and select this folder then choose **File→Map Network Drive** from the View window's menu bar to display the dialog box in Figure 15.6.*

2. *Use the **Map Network Drive** dialog box to select a name for the network drive that will be assigned to the shared folder. This name (a single letter between* d *and* z*) will be used to access the folder from your PC as if it was a* local *disk-drive physically located within your own machine.*

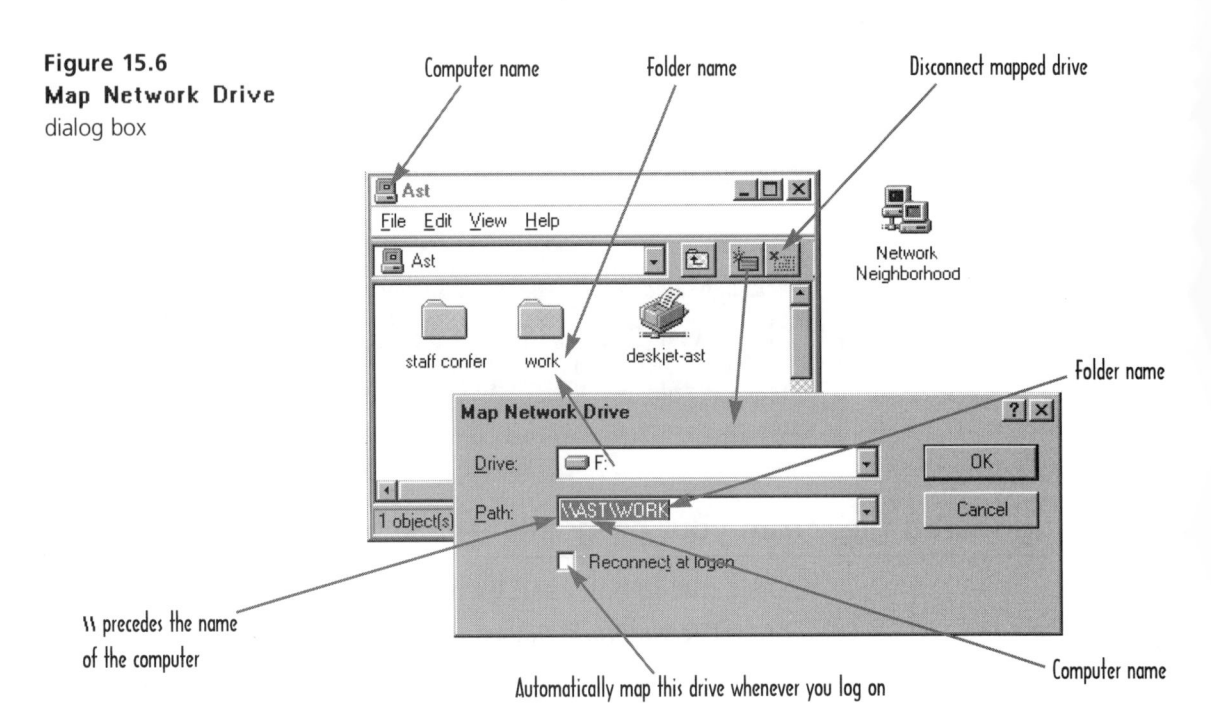

Figure 15.6
Map Network Drive dialog box

Computer name — Folder name — Disconnect mapped drive

\\ precedes the name of the computer

Automatically map this drive whenever you log on

Folder name — Computer name

3. *Click the box **Reconnect at Log on** if you want this drive mapping to be automatically re-established each time you log on to the network from this PC. Press **OK** to close the dialog box and map your drive name to the folder you have selected.*

The *path* displayed in the **Map Network Drive** dialog box is the name of the computer and folder in a format that can be typed directly into your program's **Open** dialog box — without the need to assign a network drive.

334 Chapter 15 Working with an office network

> **Note:** The characters \\ at the beginning of a path name indicate that the following characters (before the next \) form the name of a computer

4   Start Word from your Taskbar (**Start**↪**Programs**↪**Microsoft Office**↪**Microsoft Word**) then choose **File**↪**Open** to display the **Open** dialog box. Click the **Lookin** button and select the network drive you have just assigned from the list of drives — you may need to use the scroll-bar.

5   Open a file within this shared folder just like you would a file on your own PC — click on the file name then press **OK** to display it in Word's document window. Finally, close Word's main window as well as any View windows opened during the course of this exercise — it is now complete!

> **Note:** You can also grant access to files located in your shared folders to people who have connected to your PC by modem – see Chapter 16 *Remote access*

Sharing devices across the network — printers

You can allow anyone to use the printer attached to your PC by making it a shared network resource — simply change its properties from within your **Printers** folder. Other people can then use this network printer to print their documents in exactly the same way as a local printer that is physically attached to their own PC (see Chapter 4).

deskjet-ast

> **Note:** Before using a network printer it must be installed on your Desktop by the **Printer Wizard** so that your programs are made aware of its facilities

Chapter 15   Working with an office network   335

Figure 15.7
Sharing a printer across the network

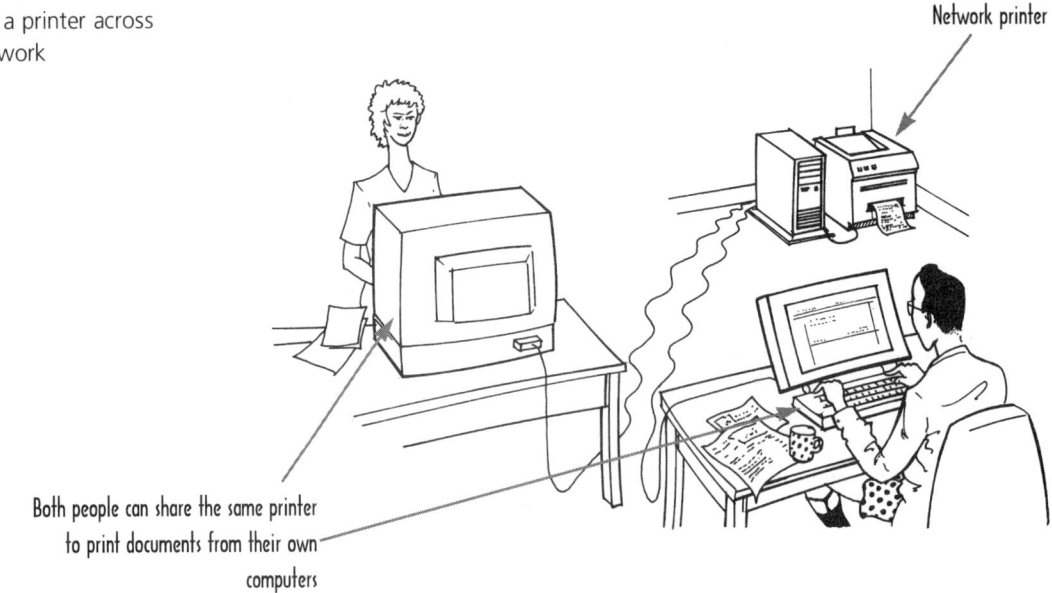

Network printer

Both people can share the same printer to print documents from their own computers

1 *Double-click the icon* **My Computer** *on your Desktop to open its View window. Open the* **Printers** *folder (double-click its icon) from within this window to open a further View window containing the printers that have been installed on your PC.*

2 *Select (click) the printer that you wish to make available to the network then choose* **File↪Sharing** *to open its property sheet. Click the* **Sharing** *tab to bring this page to the forefront.*

3 *Click the button* **Shared As** *then type the printer's name into the edit box labelled* **Share Name** *before pressing* **OK** *to close the property sheet and make this printer a shared network resource — this exercise is complete.*

Note

You can also add a comment and password to the printer's properties that will apply when it is used by other people as a network printer

336   Chapter 15   **Working with an office network**

Figure 15.8
Print installation Wizard

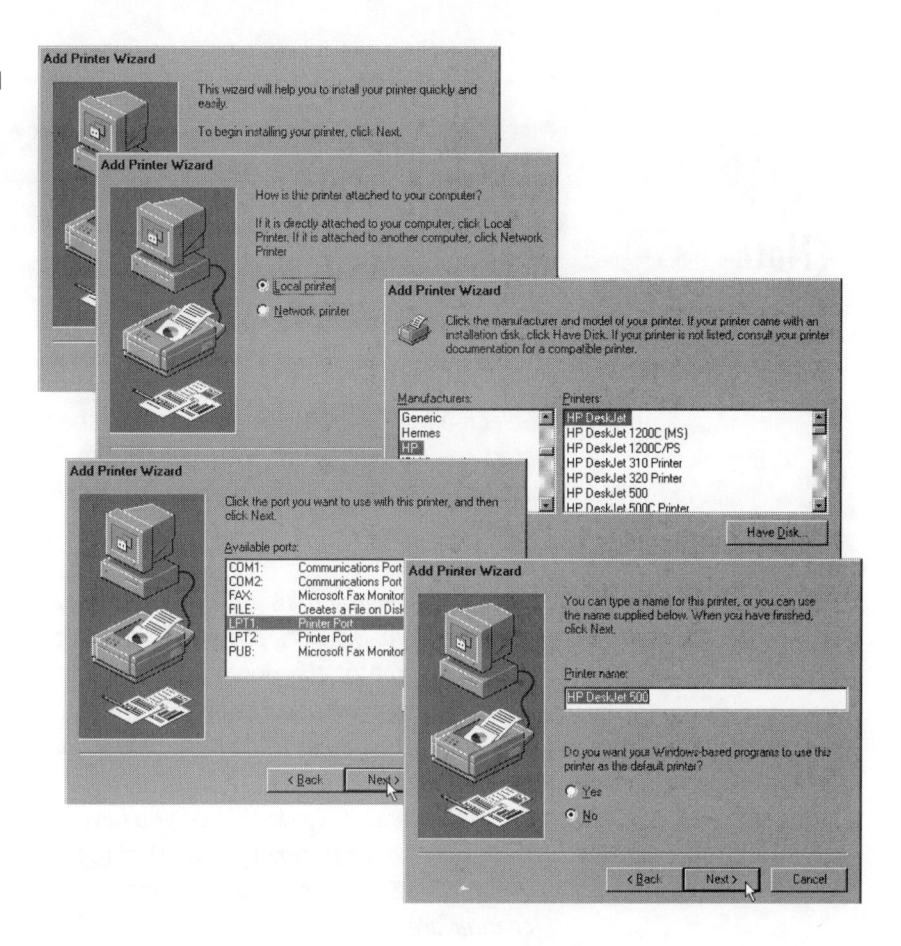

Installing a printer on your Desktop

Installing a new printer on your Desktop is not difficult because the **Add Printer Wizard** guides you through the process (which is the same whether it's a network printer or a local printer). Once you have installed a network printer on your Desktop it can be used to print your documents just like a local printer (see Chapter 4) — however, you may need to walk across the office or down the corridor in order to collect your print-out!

1   *Open your* **Network Neighborhood** *window to display the computers currently attached to the network. Open the View window belonging to one of these computers to display its shared resources — including any network printers that are physically attached to this machine.*

> **Note:** You can print your documents on this network printer by changing the default printer —select the printer from your **Printers** folder and choose **File↪Set As Default**

2. Select (click) a network printer and choose **File↪Install** to start the **Add Printer Wizard** (Figure 15.8) that will take you step-by-step through the process of installing the printer on your own Desktop.

3. Follow the instructions given by the Wizard — select **No** for printing from MS-DOS programs, select the appropriate driver, type the name of the printer, and request the printing of a test page. Finally, press the **Finish** button to complete the installation and print a test page to confirm that it was successful.

4. Close the various windows that you have opened in the course of this exercise then tidy-up the Desktop before shutting down Windows 95 (as described in Chapter 2) — the exercises in this chapter are complete!

After you have installed a network printer on your PC it will appear in the **Printers** folder with the other printers that are available to you. This folder can be opened from the **My Computer** window (or your Taskbar's **Settings** menu) to emphasize that its contents are part of your PC — the network serves only to provide a connection.

Sharing other devices across the network

Printers and disk drives are not the only type of devices that can be shared across a network. Depending on the type of network used by your organization and the resources it provides, you might notice some of the following in your **Network Neighborhood** window:

- *scanners* — devices that convert a printed page into a computer file which can be opened within one of your document windows
- *modems* — used to communicate with other computers through the public telephone system
- *tape back-up units* — devices which copy the contents of a disk drive onto a removable cassette tape, to provide a back-up in case of accidental damage to your computer
- *fax services* — folders into which you can copy documents, to send them as fax messages from a computer equipped with a fax-modem.

Note

Networks allow an organization to efficiently use its resources and share information among its staff — the hallmarks of a modern business

Summary

- Connecting your PC to the office network allows you to share folders and printers with other people in your organization.
- Log on to the network by supplying a publicly known user name and a secret password — this combination confirms your right to use the network.
- Use shared folders and printers on your Desktop in the same way as resources located within your own PC — the complexity of network technology is hidden from you.
- The **Network Neighborhood** folder displays the printers and folders that are shared within your workgroup (or domain).
- Permit other people to share one of your folders, by selecting it within a View window then choosing **File↪Properties** and changing the **Sharing** page settings.
- Map a network folder to an unused drive name (i.e. **h:**), so that older programs may open this drive to access the shared files (and folders) it contains.
- After installing a network printer on your Desktop you can use it just like a local printer, but you may have to walk down the corridor to collect the print-out!

Tip

Drag an icon (a printer or a folder, say) from the Entire Network folder into your Network Neighborhood, so you can easily find this shared resource again

Chapter 16

Using your modem to work at home

Objectives

This chapter presents the facilities available to you when a modem is installed on your Desktop:

> ▷ modems and fax machines — how they work and are supported by Windows 95. How to install a modem on your Desktop
>
> ▷ terminal services — use your modem and HyperTerminal to connect with a mainframe computer or obtain advice and assistance from a *bulletin board* service
>
> ▷ working from home — remote access (also called dial-up networking) permits you to link your home PC with the office network (or another PC) so you can share its files and printers
>
> ▷ access to global computer networks — Internet, Microsoft Network and CompuServe give you access to people and services on a world-wide network.

Attaching a modem to your PC enables you to connect your Desktop to the world beyond your organization's local area network (LAN).

Chapter 16

About modems and fax machines

A modem is a device that converts data (bits and bytes) into audible tones that can be transmitted down a telephone line to a corresponding modem. This converts the tones back into data. Connecting a modem between your PC and a telephone socket allows you to communicate with other computers (or networks) that have similar access to the public telephone system — modems communicate with each other according to certain international standards (e.g. CCITT v.32bis).

A fax machine is no more than a modem connected to a scanner and printer:

- a scanner converts the printed page into a series of dots like a newspaper photograph — each dot is represented by a number of data bits
- the modem transfers the data bits, via a telephone line, to another modem inside the recipient's fax machine
- received data bits are converted back into dots on a piece of paper by the fax machine's printer.

Any modem that conforms to the communications standards required for fax machines (i.e. CCITT Group III) can send and receive fax message data. Often modems offer conformance with CCITT Group III fax as well as the standards governing communication between computer equipment (e.g. v32).

A fax-modem allows you to send and receive fax messages (see Chapter 17) as well as communicate with remote computers or networks — the subject of this chapter.

Figure 16.1
Modems convert data into tones

An old style modem – an 'acoustic coupler'

342   Chapter 16   Using your modem to work at home

Beyond fax messages

The ability to send and receive fax messages from your Desktop may not alone justify purchasing a modem, but consider the other services this device is capable of providing:

- terminal services — obtain support for your computer equipment and programs from the dial-up *bulletin board* services that are provided by most manufacturers
- working from home — copy files between your home PC and the computers in your office. Submit a report simply by printing it on your boss's personal printer!
- access to computer networks — send messages, buy goods, and share information with people throughout the world for the cost of a local telephone call.

Note
> Check Communications facilities are installed on your Desktop by inspecting the components listed in the Windows Setup page of the Add/Remove programs property sheet (see page 336)

Modem support provided by Windows 95

The modem installation procedure is very simple (see *Installing a modem*) and, once completed, allows your modem to be shared among all the programs that require communication facilities.

Note
> A single modem can only establish one telephone connection at a time and until your program has finished with this connection other programs cannot use the modem

Programs developed specifically for Windows 95 make using modem communication facilities easier by:

- **Install New Modem Wizard** — a Wizard which guides you through the process of installing a modem on your Desktop
- **Modem Properties** — a property sheet which permits you to adjust the modem's settings in a consistent way
- **Dialing Properties** — a property sheet which ensures the correct access, area and country codes are used when dialing
- the Taskbar's modem icon — which indicates your program is using a modem to transfer information.

Windows 95 makes accessing remote computers and networks like CompuServe, Internet and Microsoft Network as simple as using any of the other services on your Desktop.

How to install a modem on your Desktop

Modems are available in two forms; an adapter card installed inside your PC, or a stand-alone box attached by a cable. You should consult your modem's manual for details of how it should be attached to your PC, but once physically attached it can be installed on your Desktop as follows:

1   *Open the* **Control Panel** *window from your Taskbar (***Start⤷Settings⤷Control Panel***) then double-click the* **Modems** *icon — this starts a Wizard to guide you through the process of installing a new modem. If you have already installed a modem then the* **Modems Properties** *sheet will open instead — press* **Add** *in the* **General** *page to start the Wizard.*

2   *Switch-on your modem, press the* **Next** *button and simply wait for the Wizard to detect your modem — in most instances you can proceed directly to step 5.*

3   *If the Wizard was unable to recognize the exact make and model of your modem, you will be informed that your modem was not*

found — press the **Next** button to open a window from which you can select your modem in the list of supported modems.

> **Note**
>
> If your modem is not directly supported by Windows 95 you may select standard modem types as the Manufacturer then select a matching transmission speed as its Model

4   Select the make of your modem from the list of **Manufacturers** (e.g. **Hayes**) and its model from the list of **Models** (e.g. **Accura 144 + FAX144**) — use the scroll bars to reveal items that are lower down these lists. Press **Next** to open the Wizard's next window.

5   Select the port to which your modem is connected and press **Next** again. After a brief delay a message will inform you that your modem has been set up successfully — press the **Finish** button to close the Wizard and return to the **Modems Properties** sheet. Close this property sheet to complete the exercise!

> **Note**
>
> When you specify the port to which your modem is connected, select the name of the socket at the back of your PC used for its cable (i.e. *COM1*)

Modem properties

The Windows 95 modem installation Wizard usually sets suitable values for the properties of the modems available to your Desktop. However you may need to change some of these values if you have trouble connecting to a particular computer, public network or bulletin board (see Appendix D).

> **Note**
>
> Programs developed for earlier versions of Windows may have different ways of setting their communication parameters and telephone access numbers – refer to appropriate manuals

Chapter 16

1   *Open the* **Control Panel** *window from your Taskbar (***Start↳Settings↳Control Panel***) then double-click the* **Modems** *icon — this opens the* **Modems Properties** *sheet listing the modems that have been installed on your Desktop.*

Figure 16.2
Modems Properties sheet

Add new modems → [Add...]

Change location from which you are dialing → [Dialing Properties...]

2   *Select the modem whose setting you wish to change (click it) and press the* **Properties** *button to display a further properties sheet (see Appendix D). Click on the* **General** *page and set the modem's speaker volume to* **high**.

3   *Press* **OK** *to close your modem's property sheet then close the* **Modems Properties** *sheet — this exercise is complete!*

Note

Listening to the tones made as a connection is being established can often prove helpful; familiarize yourself with the normal dial, ringing and engaged tones of your phone system

Dialing properties

The telephone number you must dial in order to connect with another party depends on your current country and area codes. The popularity of portable computers means that telephone numbers must be stored in a form which makes it easy to adapt them for changes in your location.

Telephone numbers stored in the format:

+country code (area code) number
+44 (171) 2301212

can be dialed correctly by Windows 95 from anywhere in the world simply by changing your **Dialing Properties** so that its area and country codes reflect your current location.

> **Note**
>
> The leading 0 of the area code and the code you need to gain access to international calling (e.g. 00) are omitted from telephone numbers stored in this universal format

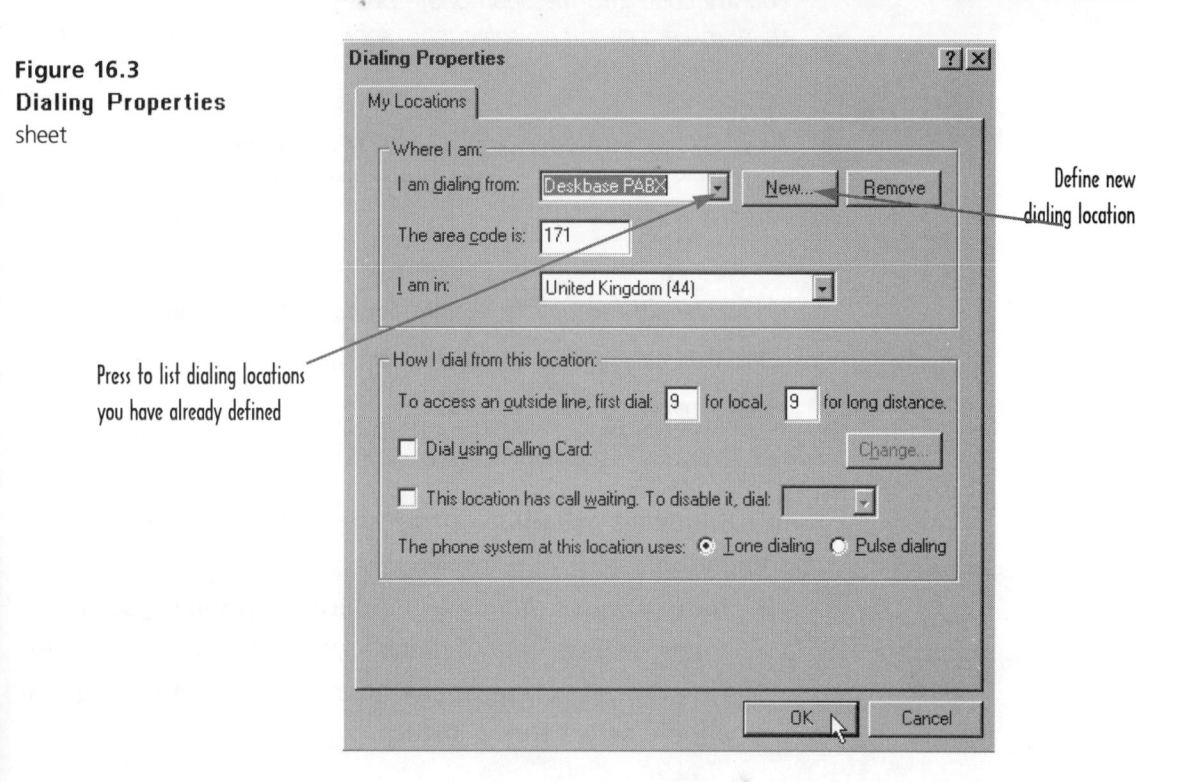

**Figure 16.3
Dialing Properties** sheet

Press to list dialing locations you have already defined

Define new dialing location

Chapter 16 Using your modem to work at home 347

> **Tip:** Create a series of settings for each location from which you will use your PC — activate the appropriate dialing values simply by making a selection from the list as shown in Figure 16.3

1. Open the **Control Panel** window from your Taskbar (**Start**↪**Settings**↪**Control Panel**) then double-click the **Modems** icon — this opens the **Modems Properties** sheet listing the modems that have been installed on your Desktop. Press the button **Dialing Properties** to display the properties sheet shown in Figure 16.3.

2. Press the **New** button to define the dialing properties for a new location. This displays a dialog box prompting you for a name to describe your location — type **My Office** and press **OK**. You must now define the dialing properties for **My Office**.

3. Enter your telephone area code (omitting the leading 0) and country code into the appropriate boxes in the properties sheet, then make any other selections appropriate for your current dialing location (see below).

4. Press **OK** to save your definition of **My Office** and close the property sheet. Close the **Modems Properties** sheet — this exercise is complete!

> **Note:** The *default* location is usually defined when Windows 95 is installed on your PC. It probably contains the correct details for the normal location of your PC

The following dialing properties may also require modification:

> - *tone or pulse dialing* — modern telephone system use tones rather than 'clicks' when dialing a number. However, if you normally hear clicks when dialing you should select **Pulse dialing**

- *access to outside line (local)* — offices often have a telephone system that requires you to dial a number (usually *9*) in order to connect with the public telephone system. If your modem is plugged into this type of socket you must type the access number in the box labelled **first dial _ for local**
- *access to outside line (long distance)* — a variety of telephone companies offer cheap rates for long distance calls. Type the number needed to access their network in the box labelled **for long distance**, so that it will be dialed before any number which is outside your local area code
- *call waiting* — some telephone companies offer a facility which causes you to hear a tone if someone attempts to call while you are using your phone. However, this tone can disrupt the operation of your modem and therefore you should dial a special code (say, *43*) to disable **call waiting**
- *dial using calling card* — charge your calls to your credit card by inserting a tick in the box **Dial using Calling Card** (by clicking it) then entering your card details in the resulting dialog box.

Tip

> Test your modem's telephone socket with a normal telephone handset to determine its access numbers, dialing methods and so forth

Terminal services — HyperTerminal

HyperTerminal is a program that allows your PC to dial-up a remote computer then act like a VDU or *terminal* — its window emulates the terminal screen while your keyboard is made to work like a terminal keyboard.

Note: HyperTerminal can emulate a number of standard terminals, such as *TTY* and *VT100*, which are used to access bulletin board services (BBS) as well as mainframe computers

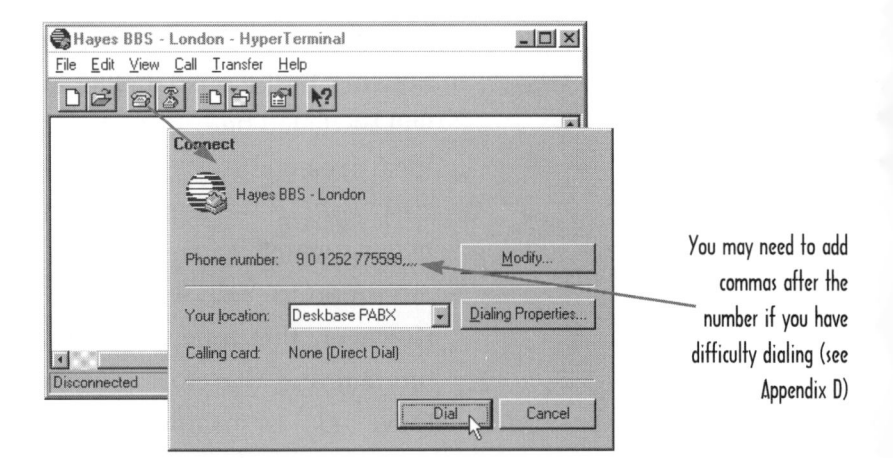

Figure 16.4
HyperTerminal connects your PC to a BBS

You may need to add commas after the number if you have difficulty dialing (see Appendix D)

A bulletin board is the electronic equivalent of a notice board. It provides a convenient way to distribute files as well as share ideas with other people who have a common interest. There are thousands of bulletin board services dedicated to a vast range of subjects and products — they are operated by both commercial organizations and private individuals. Listings of BBS telephone numbers and protocols are often published in magazines or under the heading 'product support' in your computer manuals.

You can use HyperTerminal to dial-up the computer that provides access to a specific BBS, allowing you to read messages that have been left by other people as well as contribute your own. You can also use HyperTerminal to post your own files (upload) to a BBS, as well as copy (download) the files that have been made available to you. Many bulletin boards are operated by commands and menus, much like a traditional DOS program (see *Introduction*) — you type the command from your keyboard then receive a response in the HyperTerminal window.

The following exercise describes how you can download a file from the BBS operated by Hayes Microcomputer Products in the United Kingdom — a similar approach may be used to access data held on your organization's mainframe computer.

1   *Start HyperTerminal (***Start**↪**Programs**↪**Accessories**↪ **HyperTerminal**) *to open a* **View** *window containing* **Hypertrm** *and any other terminals that have been previously defined for your PC.*

Tip

> Type `Help` or `?` at the BBS command prompt to obtain assistance with the operations you can perform — type `quit`, `bye` or `exit` to disconnect or leave a particular menu level

2   *Double-click* **Hypertrm** *to open a* **New Connection** *window (Figure 16.5) for a new terminal. Type* `Hayes BBS - London` *into the* **Name** *box then select an icon from the list at the bottom of the dialog box.*

3   *Select country code* **+44** *and type* `1252` *and* `775599` *into the area code and number boxes of the* **Phone Number** *dialog box. Select one of the modems attached to your PC from the box* **Connect using** *then press* **OK** *to close the dialog box.*

Caution

> Check your organization's policy on obtaining files from an external source before connecting to a BBS (or other network) — you may need to examine such files for viruses!

4   *Press* **Cancel** *(rather than* **Dial***) to close the* **Connect** *dialog box then close the* **Hayes BBS - London - HyperTerminal** *window, saving its settings when prompted.*

Chapter 16   Using your modem to work at home   351

**Figure 16.5
New Connection** window

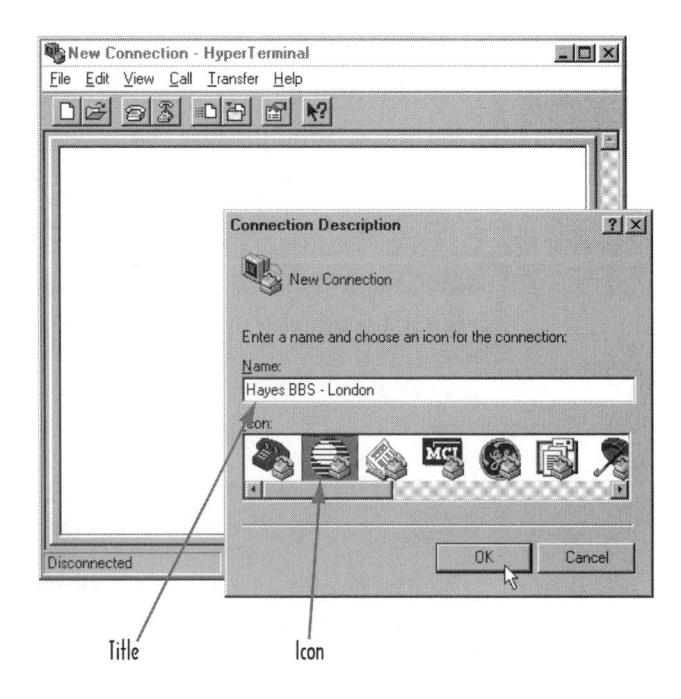

An icon appears in the HyperTerminal View window after you have defined the properties of your terminal — establish a connection with the Hayes BBS simply by double-clicking this icon.

> **Note**
>
> You can change the settings that apply to a terminal by selecting its icon in the HyperTerminal View window, then choosing File↪Properties from the menu bar

5   Double-click the icon labelled **Hayes BBS - London** in the HyperTerminal View window to open the terminal window you have just defined (Figure 16.6) — the **Connect** dialog box appears automatically. Press the **Dial** button to open the **Connect** message box and initiate a connection with the Hayes BBS in London.

While HyperTerminal attempts to establish a connection with a remote computer you might hear a ringing tone after your modem has dialed the number, then a few high pitched tones as the two modems establish a connection. Once the connection has been made your terminal window will display a message requesting your name — in case of problems see Appendix D.

> **Tip**
>
> Press Enter or ⏎ a few times to nudge the BBS into action if the terminal window does not display a message

6   *Type your first name, your second name, then the name of your city (pressing Enter after each name) — press Y when you receive a message asking you to confirm these details. Type* 80 *as the number of characters per line.*

7   *Type* C *to identify your terminal type as TTY — press* N *when asked if you wish to modify the terminal or pause between pages. Type your password and press* Enter *before re-typing the password to verify its spelling. Press* Enter *again to display further messages which form a disclaimer.*

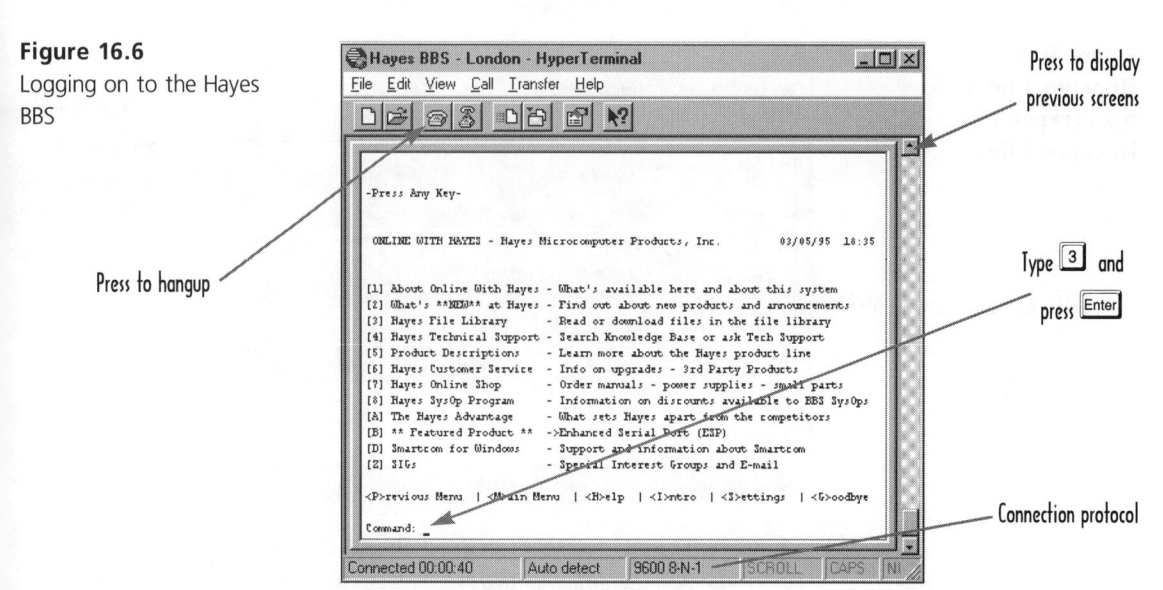

Figure 16.6
Logging on to the Hayes BBS

Press to hangup

Press to display previous screens

Type 3 and press Enter

Connection protocol

> **Note**
>
> The scroll bar attached to the right edge of the window can be used to review information that is no longer visible in the terminal's screen area

Chapter 16   Using your modem to work at home   353

8   Press [Y] to accept these BBS terms and conditions before supplying your name, address and telephone number (pressing the [Enter] key after each entry). Press [Y] when asked to confirm these details then press another key to reach a menu listing the various services available on the BBS — the main menu.

9   Type [3] (Hayes File Library) from the main BBS menu to display a list of file areas. Type [1] and press [Enter] to display a list of files in the general information area and write down the name of the one you wish to download (e.g. **approval.lst**). Press [Enter] until the BBS menu is displayed again.

10 Type [P] and press [Enter] to display a list of the communication protocols available for file transfer. Type [K] to specify Kermit — the menu is re-displayed. Type [D] and press [Enter] to obtain a prompt for the name of the file you wish to download — type the name of the file (approval.lst) and press [Enter] to request the transfer.

Figure 16.7
Receive File dialog box (**Transfer↪Receive File**)

Folder that will receive the file

Press to open a browse window, so you can change the folder that will receive the file

Protocols must match

11 Choose **Transfer↪Receive File** to display a dialog box that permits you to set the protocol used for the transfer — select Kermit from the list box then press **Receive** to start the transfer.

12 While the file is being downloaded a further window is displayed to show the progress of the file transfer — when complete this window closes and the BBS download menu is re-printed. Press

354   Chapter 16   Using your modem to work at home

⌨ *to return to the main BBS menu then press* Ⓖ *to display the Goodbye menu before pressing* Ⓖ *again to disconnect from the Hayes BBS.*

13. Start WordPad (**Start➔Programs➔Accessories➔WordPad**) *and open* **approval.lst**, *the file you have just downloaded. Finally, close the terminal window, the HyperTerminal View window, and also WordPad — this exercise is complete!*

Tip

> You can force a disconnect from the BBS at any time by choosing **Call➔Disconnect** from the Terminal window. However it is always better to use the BBS's own disconnect command

Working from home — remote access

Remote access, also called *dial-up networking*, helps keep you in contact with the office from home by using your PC's modem to dial-up a computer that is attached to the office network (LAN). Once the connection has been established your home PC becomes a member of the network and can share files, printers and other resources, just as if it was located within the same building (see Chapter 15).

The computer whose modem answers your telephone call becomes a server — it must have been set-up to operate as a remote access server, see below.

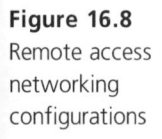

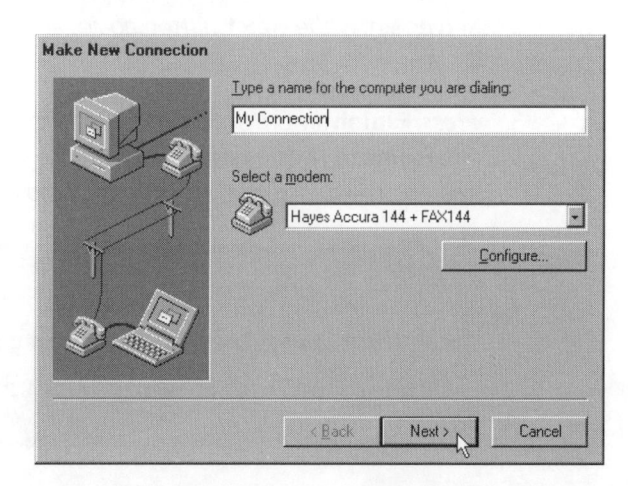

Figure 16.8
Remote access networking configurations

> **Note**
> Remote access can form a network between two computers that are not otherwise connected — the remote access server can be just a simple PC running Windows 95

Setting-up a PC to make a remote access connection

The first time you start remote access networking (**Start↪Programs↪Accessories↪Remote Access**) a Wizard will take you through the following steps in order to set-up your PC for this facility:

- create a name for the computer you are dialing — this allows you subsequently to identify the icon in your **Remote Access** window
- select the modem that will be used by your Desktop to establish the connection
- enter the phone number of the computer you wish to call.

1. Start the **Remote Access** Wizard from your Taskbar (**Start↪Programs↪Accessories↪Remote Access**). Press the **Next** button to proceed to the next window where you can type the name of your remote access connection and select the modem used for this service.

2. Press **Next** to proceed to the next window and enter the country code, area code and telephone number of your remote access server. Press the **Next** button again, and wait for a few moments as Windows 95 sets-up your PC.

3. Press **Finish** in order to close the Wizard and create an icon in the **Remote Access** window for the connection you have just specified — close this window to complete the exercise.

> **Tip**
> You can subsequently define other remote access connections with remote computers by double-clicking the icon **Make New Connection** in the **Remote Access** folder

Setting-up a PC to receive remote access requests

A computer must be configured to act as a remote access server before it can receive remote access requests and establish the appropriate connections with your (home) PC.

Note

> The procedure needed to set-up a computer as a remote access server depends on its operating system — consult your network administrator for specific details

The following steps are required to configure a PC as a remote access server when Windows 95 is its operating system:

- install the **Remote Access Server** program using the **Add/Remove Programs** window accessible from the **Control Panel**
- choose **Connections↪Remote Access Server** from the menu bar of your **Remote Access** window to open a property sheet that permits you to enable caller access for each of the modems used to answer calls from a remote computer
- use this **Remote Access Server** property sheet to define the password that must be supplied by a computer calling the remote access server, prior to the establishment of a connection.

Caution

> Obtain permission from your network administrator before making your PC a remote access server as this may have implications for the security of your office network

Once correctly set-up, the remote access server provides a gateway to the computers in your office network — alternatively, it may just allow resources to be shared between the PCs connected by the remote access link.

Chapter 16   Using your modem to work at home   357

Establishing a remote access network connection

The **Remote Access** window contains icons that represent each of the specific remote connections which have been defined for your PC. Establishing a remote connection is simply a matter of opening this window, double-clicking the appropriate icon, then pressing a **Connect** button.

Figure 16.9
Connect to dialog box

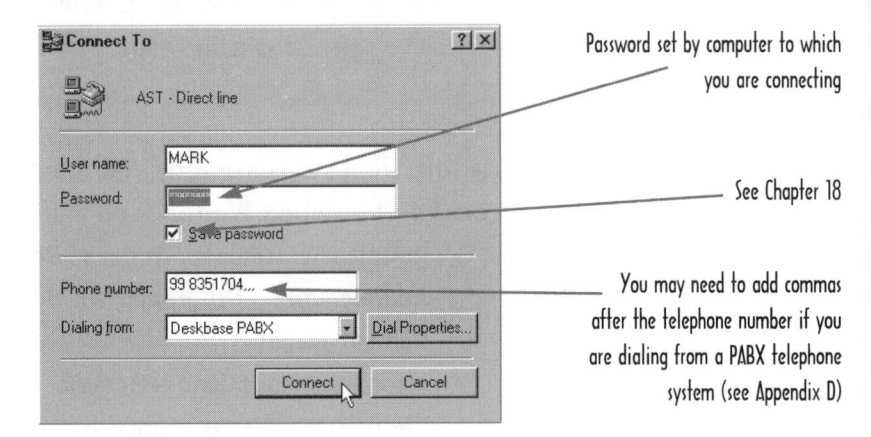

Password set by computer to which you are connecting

See Chapter 18

You may need to add commas after the telephone number if you are dialing from a PABX telephone system (see Appendix D)

1   Open the **Remote Access** folder (**Start→Programs→Accessories→Remote Access**) then double-click the icon which corresponds to the connection you wish to establish — this opens the **Connect To** dialog box. Enter your user name and password before pressing the **Connect** button to initiate the remote access link.

2   Wait for your PC to call the remote access server, establish the connection, then log on to its network — a small window appears on your Desktop to display the progress of this operation.

3   When informed that you are connected to the remote access server you may open the **Network Neighbourhood** window and use the shared resources of any computer whose icon appears in this window (see Chapter 15).

4   Disconnect from the remote access server by pressing the **Disconnect** button in the connection box that appeared on your Desktop during the previous step. Close any windows that you have opened during the course of the exercise — it is now complete.

Remote access allows computers to join an office network through a remote access link. Once connected to the remote access server, you can share files, folders and printers between the computers, in just the same way as a PC connected directly to the network by cable (see Chapter 15).

Access to global computer networks

Fax messages are a crucial component of today's business environment, but increasingly they are being replaced by computer networks which permit you to do much more than just convey a paper-based message:

- Internet — exchange messages or files (email) with anyone who is connected to the network and share information by joining a newsgroup dedicated to a particular topic
- CompuServe — provides access to Internet as well as its own services. Its monthly billing system permits you to order goods and access fee-charging services, such as the *Airline On-line Guide* (AOG)
- Microsoft Network — aims to provide a similar service to CompuServe, but is more tightly integrated with the Windows 95 Desktop.

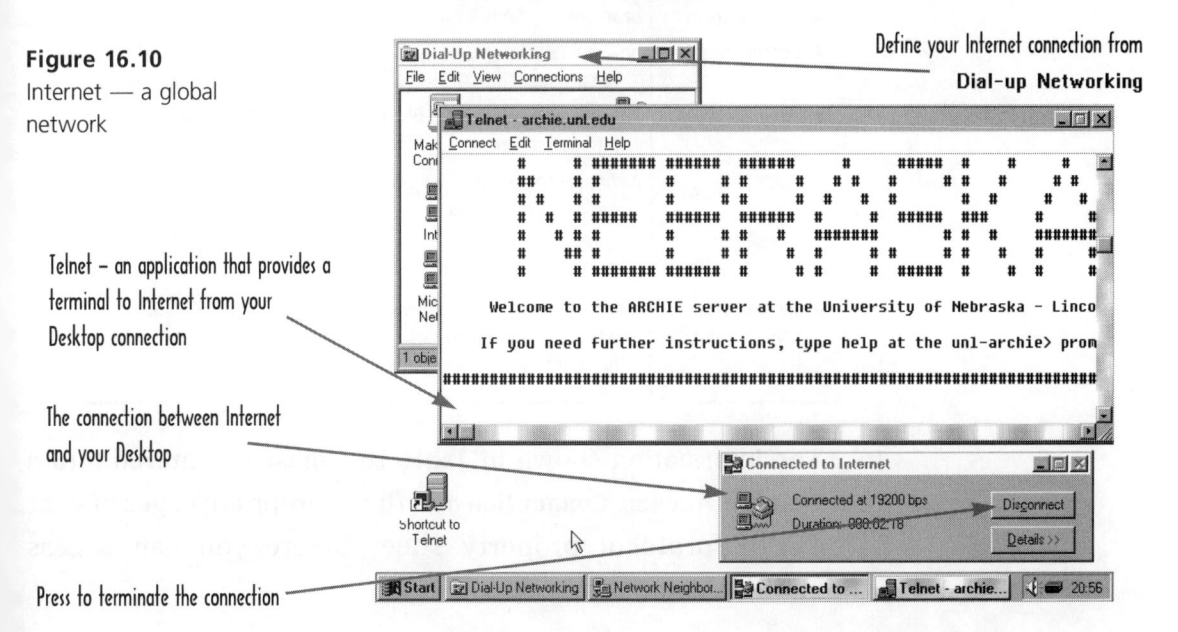

Figure 16.10
Internet — a global network

Define your Internet connection from **Dial-up Networking**

Telnet – an application that provides a terminal to Internet from your Desktop connection

The connection between Internet and your Desktop

Press to terminate the connection

Chapter 16 Using your modem to work at home 359

Chapter 16

> ⚠ **Caution**
>
> Seek permission from your network administrator before connecting your PC to a network, as this may violate your organization's security policy

Using Internet from Windows 95

The appeal of the Internet is its global nature as well as the vast number of computers that belong to the network. You can join the Internet simply by arranging remote access access to a computer in your area that acts as a domain. There's a number of commercial organizations which grant this type of access in return for a small subscription fee — the Internet service provider.

Table 16.1
Information provided by Internet service provider

Information	Description	Sample values
Telephone number	call this number to access the service provider's computer	0181 343 4848
Host name	name used to log on to the service provider's computer	deskbase
Password	assert your right of access	MyPassword
Access protocol	protocol for the link	PPP
Access mechanism	how are host, password and protocol details supplied?	open terminal window after dialing
Internet programs	location of programs needed for Internet services	FTP is supplied with Windows 95
Domain	name use to identify your service provider's computer	demon.co.uk
IP address	a number that uniquely identifies the host	158.152.55.174
IP address of DNS server	a number that identifies the computer which converts your host and domain name into an IP address (and vice versa)	158.152.1.65

The information shown in Table 16.1 must be entered into a **Remote Access Connection** and the appropriate pages of your TCP/IP protocol property sheet before you can access Internet from your Desktop.

> **Note**
>
> My email address is
> **bills@deskbase.demon.co.uk**
> The last three parts of the name indicate that *demon* is a *commercial organization* within the *United Kingdom*

1. Open the Control Panel (**Start↪Settings↪Control Panel**) and double-click the **Network** icon to open its property sheet. Press the **Add** button in the **Configuration** page to open a dialog box. Select **Protocol** and press **Add** to close this dialog box and open the **Select Network Protocol** dialog box.

2. Select **Microsoft** from the list of manufacturers then select **TCP/IP** from the list of **Network Protocols** before pressing **OK** to close the dialog box and return to the property sheet.

3. Select **TCP/IP - Dial-Up Adapter** from the list of network components in the **Configuration** page of the **Network** property sheet and press the **Properties** button. This opens a further property sheet into which you may add the information supplied by your Internet service provider (Table 16.1).

Figure 16.11
TCP/IP protocol property sheet

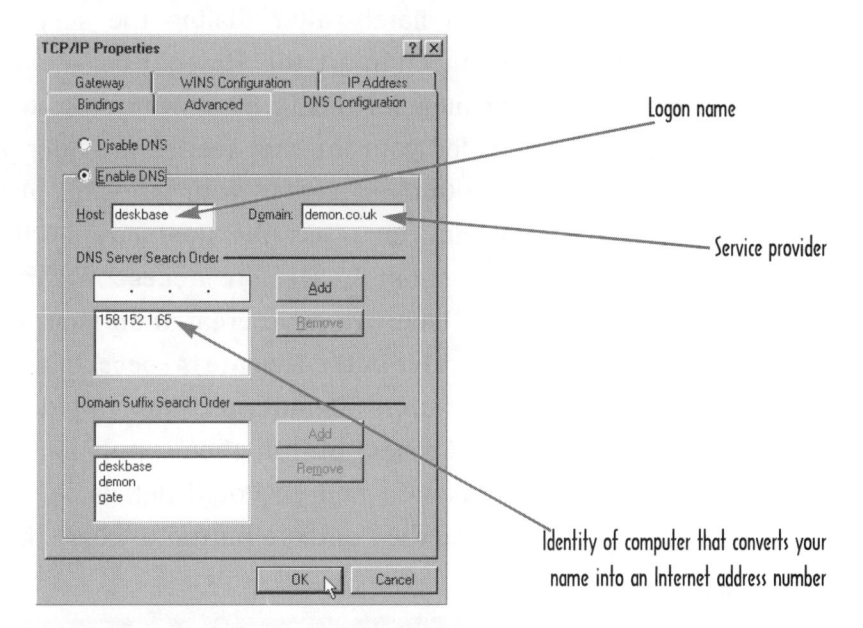

4. Click the **IP Address** tab to bring this page to the forefront and click **Specify an IP Address** so that you can type your IP address into the appropriate box — add zeros in front of any group that does have three digits so you have four groups of numbers.

5   Click the **DNS Configuration** tab to bring this page to the forefront and click **Enable DNS** so you can enter your host, domain and DNS server details into the appropriate boxes. Press **Add** to move the IP address for your DNS server into the list that defines the search order.

6   Finally, press **OK** to close this property sheet then press **OK** again to close the **Network** property sheet — this exercise is complete!

You can now arrange dial-up access to your Internet service provider by following the same procedure that you used to connect your home PC to the office server (see page 362) — double-click the **Make New Connection** icon in the **Remote Access** folder. However, rather than using the **Password** and **User name** boxes in the **Connect To** dialog box (Figure 16.9), you will probably need to enter your *host name*, *password* and *remote access protocol* into a terminal window immediately after dialing the service provider (similar to connection to the Hayes BBS — see page 353). You can arrange for this terminal window to be opened after you have dialed your Internet service provider by changing a setting in the **Options** page of your modem's property sheet — opened when you press the **Configure** button after selecting your modem in the **Remote Access** Wizard.

Once you have created an icon for your Internet service provider in the **Remote Access** folder you may connect your Desktop to the Internet simply by double-clicking it, pressing the **Connect** button, then supplying the necessary *host name*, *password* and *protocol* details in the terminal window — press the **Continue** button to close the window and complete

> TIP: Terminate the Internet connection to your Desktop by pressing the Disconnect button in the small connection window (see Figure 16-10)

your connection. When your Desktop is connected to the Internet a small window indicates status of your connection (see Figure 16.10) and you may access information at an Internet site simply by starting the appropriate program. The following programs may be installed on your Desktop — ask your service provider for further details:

- FTP — a file transfer program that has a command prompt interface like MS-DOS; type ? for a list of its commands
- Telnet — connect to Internet sites and gain access to its facilities using Telnet as a terminal — just like HyperTerminal was used to access the Hayes BBS
- Mosaic — a *World Wide Web* browser that lets you view *hypertext* documents containing text, images and sounds.

Joining Microsoft Network — MSN

Microsoft Network is designed specifically for people who use Windows 95 and provides a high degree of integration with your Desktop. You can obtain a MSN account by double-clicking its icon on your Desktop to start the registration Wizard.

Tip

> Check MSN is installed on your Desktop by checking the components listed in the Windows Setup page of the Add/Remove Programs property sheet (see page 366)

The Registration Wizard takes you through the process of registering your application for a MSN account by taking your Member ID, password and billing method. Once you have successfully registered, you can access the Microsoft Network simply by double-clicking its icon on your Desktop then entering your Member ID and password in the **Sign In** window before pressing its **Connect** button.

Chapter 16

> **Tip**
>
> Think of a Member ID that can be easily remembered and will uniquely identify you – avoid names such as *FlatFoot* unless you want *FlatFoot@msn.com* as your email address

1 *Start the Microsoft Network from your Taskbar (***Start**⤷ **Programs**⤷ **Microsoft Network***) to open its* **Sign In** *window on your Desktop. Type your Member ID and password into the appropriate boxes then press the* **Connect** *button to log on to the network.*

2 *The window displayed after you have successfully accessed Microsoft Network works like a View or Explorer (see Chapter 14). It displays the contents of the network in terms of a hierarchy of folders accessed from the* **Home Base** *folder.*

3 *Open the various folders and files that are stored in MSN in order to investigate particular topics then return to this window to use the other services that are available to you.*

Figure 16.12
The Microsoft Network **Home Base** window

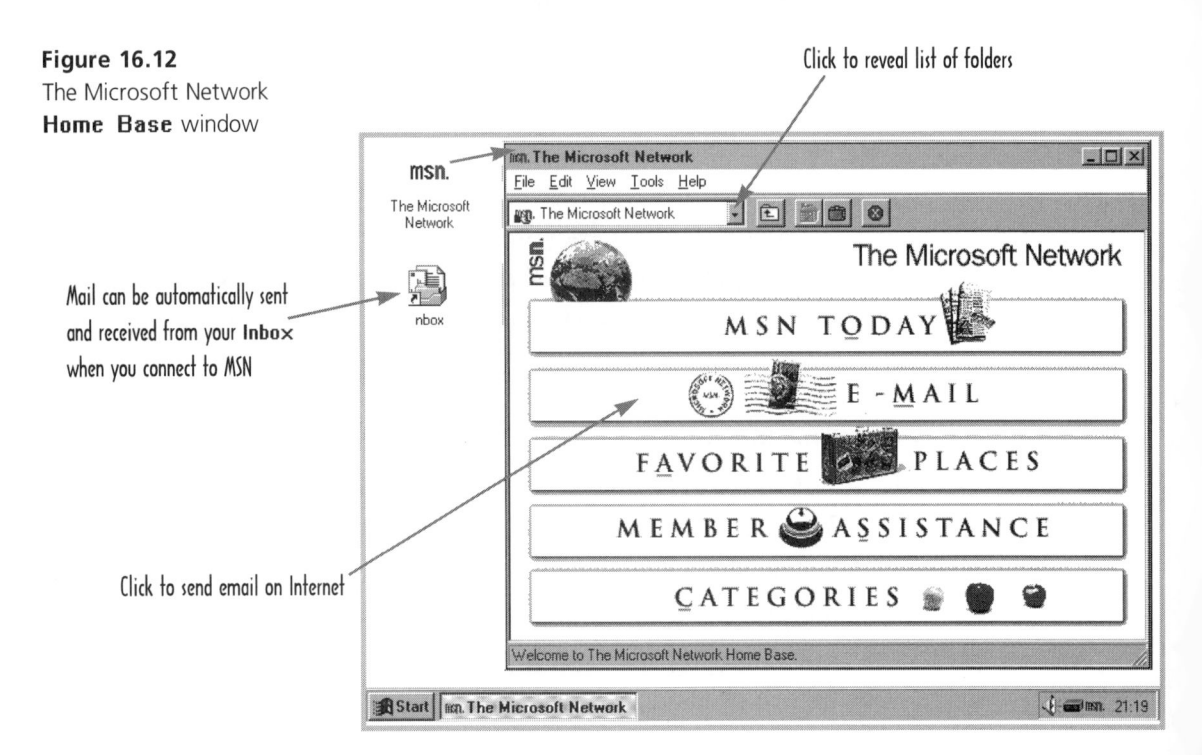

Click to reveal list of folders

Mail can be automatically sent and received from your **Inbox** when you connect to MSN

Click to send email on Internet

364   Chapter 16   Using your modem to work at home

4   When you wish to leave the Microsoft Network choose **File→Sign Out** *from the menu bar of any window that belongs to MSN — the* OH *light on your modem will extinguish as the call is disconnected. Close the* **Microsoft Network** *window to complete this exercise.*

> **Note:** The Microsoft Network window behaves just like the other windows on your Desktop — its response is slower because the information is obtained from your modem, rather than a hard disk

The contents of the network are displayed within a hierarchy of folders within which you may find the following:

- *bulletin board* — a window in which a collection of messages are displayed about a common subject. You may contribute to a topic by opening a message and composing your reply
- *on-line chats* — you can join an interactive discussion group with other members who are also *on-line* (connected) by opening a **chat** window within a folder
- *information* — news, stock market prices, sport results and libraries of programs are available within their own View windows (see Chapter 14)
- *email* — messages can be sent and received over MSN so that you can communicate with other members and anyone who has an Internet email address (see Chapter 17).

> **Note:** New services are frequently added to MSN — open the Categories window for the latest additions

Joining CompuServe

CompuServe is one of the world's leading on-line information services and has over 2,000 services covering a wide range of subjects. You can gain access to CompuServe by installing a special program on your Desktop — the CompuServe Information Manager.

Figure 16.13
WinCim — the CompuServe Information Manager

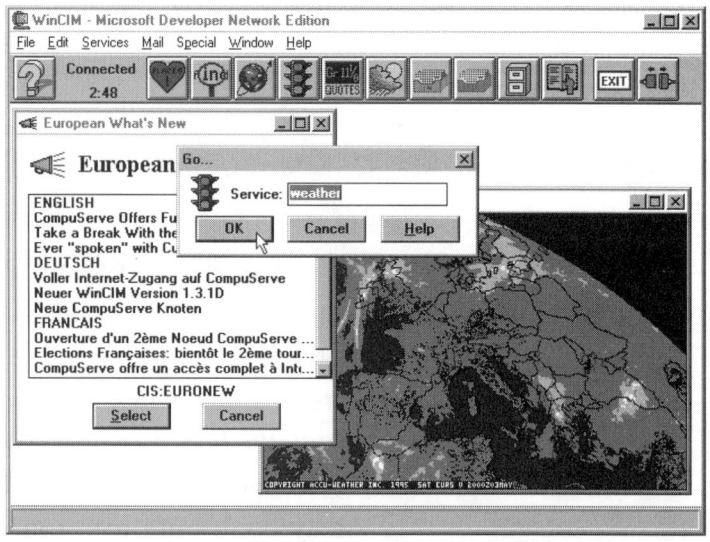

> **Note**
>
> WinCim is used in the same way as any other program on your Desktop – choose **File↪Connect** to access CompuServe and **File↪Disconnect** when you have finished your session

1   Open the Control Panel (**Start↪Settings↪Control Panel**) then double-click the **Add/Remove Programs** icon to open its property sheet. Click the **Install/Uninstall** tab to bring this page to the forefront then press the **Install** button — this starts the Installation Wizard.

2   Insert the CompuServe installation disk in your floppy disk drive. Press **Next** to cause the Wizard to search for the installation program then press **Finish** to start the CompuServe installation program.

3   Follow the instructions given by the installation program in order to register yourself, install the various files and programs needed to access CompuServe, and also create a CompuServe menu within your Taskbar's **Program** menu.

4   Close the various windows you have opened during the course of this exercise as it is now complete — you may subsequently use your Taskbar to start CompuServe Information Manager (**Start↪Programs↪CompuServe**) whenever you want to access CompuServe.

Tip

> You can obtain the CompuServe Information Manager free of charge from your local CompuServe sales office

Computer viruses

The threat of computer viruses has taken some of the fun out of trawling the networks for new downloads. There is always a chance that connecting with a computer network will result in your machine becoming infected — no network is completely safe in this respect. However you can reduce the risk of infection by practising safe on-line procedure:

- familiarize yourself with the security policies adopted by your organization and the steps you should take if your PC becomes infected
- keep a diary of your downloads so you can trace the source of infection
- take recommendations from authoritative sources before downloading files — only download files you know
- obtain a virus scanner program and give your PC a regular check-up — even if it doesn't find the virus, there may be some helpful advice in its manual for dealing with an infected machine.

Note

> The chance of infecting your PC with a virus is very small when compared to the number of people who use a computer network each day — take care and have fun!

The dangers of computer viruses are often overstated in the media and you should not be discouraged from connecting to a network simply by the threat that they pose. The growing importance of computer communication in our everyday lives means the viruses and computer fraud will become just another part of life in the big city!

Chapter 16

Summary

- Start the modem installation Wizard from the **Modems** window — opened from your **Control Panel** folder.
- Change the properties of your modem, by selecting its icon in the **Modems** window then choosing **File↪Properties**.
- Telephone numbers are stored in a format that makes them independent of the location from which they are dialed, e.g. +44 (171) 230 1212.
- HyperTerminal allows you to dial-up a bulletin board service, so that you can download a file or access its messages.
- Double-click an icon in the **Remote Access** folder to connect your home PC to the office network (or Internet).
- Register with networks such as CompuServe, MSN, or Internet in order to gain access to people and services throughout world.

Note

> Appendix D contains information that will improve your understanding of computer communication and troubleshooting procedures

Chapter 17

Microsoft Exchange — fax and mail

This chapter explains how Microsoft Exchange integrates the communication facilities available to your PC, so that you can send, receive, and manage, all your messages in a uniform way. We consider:

Objectives

- message services — add a message service to Exchange so you can send and receive mail from MS Mail, Internet, CompuServe, and fax

- keeping an Exchange address book — different types of addresses can be stored in common format

- sending messages — address, compose and send a fax message with an attached Word document

- your Personal Information Store — locate and arrange your messages within an Explorer window

- reading your mail — read and answer a message

- desktop fax facilities — send a fax and use the Fax Viewer to read incoming faxes

- using Exchange with Office 95 — send documents attached to messages.

Exchange handles all your electronic correspondence, allowing you to share ideas, information and documents with other people from a single window on your Desktop.

Installing message services

Depending on how Microsoft Exchange **Inbox** has been set-up, you may be able to access the following message services:

- MS Mail — messages transferred among people in your organization using a Postoffice located on the office network (LAN)
- CompuServe — messages are transferred among subscribers by its mail facility (links are also provided to cc:Mail and Internet email)
- MSN — messages transferred amongst its members and other people who have an Internet email address
- fax — messages sent and received from any office fax machine (or fax-modem).

Note

> Additional message services such as Internet or *voice mail* may also be integrated with Microsoft Exchange in your organization

Messages are sent and received from your Desktop on a standard form (Figure 17.5). Microsoft Exchange takes care of converting the information on this form into the appropriate format for the type message you are sending. It also converts the different formats of received messages so that they can also be displayed on this same form. Therefore, your messages all look the same irrespective of the underlying delivery mechanism; MS Mail, CompuServe, Internet, or whatever.

Note

> When your PC is connected to a network that provides a full Exchange server you gain access to a central store for all your organization's messages and information

Creating your own Exchange profile — fax service

An *Exchange profile* specifies your own personal connection with the various message services that are available to your PC. An Exchange profile is created by a special Wizard that takes you step-by-step through the process.

> **Tip**
>
> **Check Microsoft Exchange and Microsoft Fax are installed on your Desktop by checking the components listed in the Windows Setup page of the Add/Remove Programs property sheet (see page 366)**

1. *Open the Control Panel from your Taskbar (***Start**➜**Settings**➜**Control Panel***) then double-click the* **Mail and Fax** *icon to open your existing Exchange profile property sheet (go directly to step 2 if the Setup Wizard starts instead). Press the* **Show Profiles** *button (***Services** *page) to open a further property sheet listing the profiles that have been already defined — press the* **Add** *button to start the Setup Wizard and define a new profile.*

The **Microsoft Exchange Profiles** property sheet lists the profiles that have been previously defined on your PC. In addition to defining a new profile you may also use this property sheet to remove or change profiles and specify the one that will be used whenever you open Exchange from your Desktop.

Figure 17.1
Microsoft Exchange
Inbox Setup Wizard

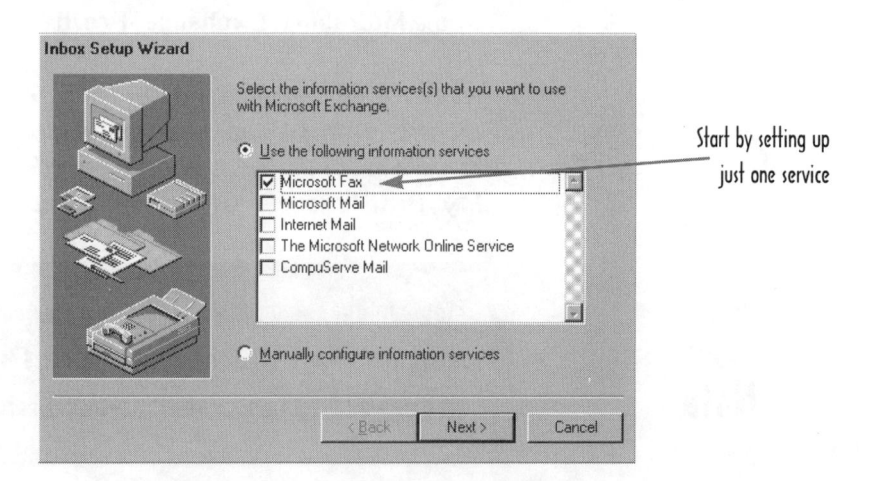

Start by setting up just one service

2   Tick **Microsoft Fax** then press **Next** — *you may wish to add further services once you have completed this exercise. Type* My Profile, *to define the name of the profile you are creating, then press* **Next** *again.*

3   *Select your fax-modem from the list of modems that have been installed on your Desktop (or press* **Add** *if one has not already been installed). Press* **Next** *to reach the window where you define the modem's automatic answering settings — take the option that reflects how you wish to receive incoming fax messages then press* **Next**.

> **Note**
> Press the Add button to install a fax-modem in step 3 (see *page 344*) or press the Properties button to change the settings of the modem you have selected

4   *Enter your name and fax number as you wish it to appear on the cover sheet of your out-going messages. Press* **Next** *to define the location of your Personal Address Book — used to store other people's fax numbers.*

5   *Press* **Next** *once more to define the location of your Personal Information Store which will be used to store incoming fax messages. Press* **Next** *to complete the definition of your Exchange profile — press* **Finish** *to close the Wizard and return to the* **Microsoft Exchange Profiles** *window.*

6   *Press the button attached to the box at the bottom of the property sheet (***When starting Microsoft Exchange...***) to reveal a list of profiles that have been defined for your PC. Select* **My Profile** *then press* **Close** *to complete this exercise.*

> **Note**
> You can change an Exchange profile by selecting it from the list shown in Figure 17.2 then pressing the Properties button, so you can add, remove or alter individual services

Figure 17.2
Microsoft Exchange profiles

Selected profile

Create a new profile

Delete selected profile

Change settings for selected profile

You can only add services to your Exchange profile that are available to your PC — for example, you must join CompuServe and install the program WinCim (see Chapter 16) before adding its mail service to your profile.

Table 17.1
Installation details for Exchange message services

Service	Installation procedure	Information needed
Microsoft fax	❏ install fax-modem	❏ fax telephone number ❏ type of fax-modem
CompuServe mail	❏ join CompuServe ❏ install WinCim program	❏ location of CIS.INI file ❏ user ID, password ❏ CompuServe access telephone number ❏ service type ❏ type of modem
MS Mail	❏ install a Postoffice on your office network ❏ obtain share access to Postoffice and create own mailbox	❏ location of Postoffice ❏ name and password for your mailbox
MSN	❏ join Microsoft Network	❏ member ID and password

Note

Table 17.1 lists the information you need to know before a particular service can be added to your profile — ask your service provider for these details

Chapter 17 Microsoft Exchange — fax and mail

Keeping an Exchange address book

The address format for a message depends on the message service used for its delivery — a number of standard address formats are shown in Table 17.2.

Table 17.2
Address formats

Service	Details	Sample format
MS Mail	user name	BILLS
CompuServe	user ID	100020,1736
Internet	name@host.domain	bills@deskbase.demon.co.uk
MSN	memberID@msn.co	BillStott@msn.co
fax	fax telephone number	+44 (171) 835 1704

Tip

> Many people now include email addresses on their business cards and at the top of letterheads – simply copy this information into your Personal Address Book (see below)

While it is not difficult to type the address directly into the message form you may find it more convenient to keep an Exchange address book — whenever you need to send a message you just look-up the name, then let Exchange take care of filling-in the appropriate address details.

An individual address book is created for each different Exchange profile — this is your Personal Address Book. However, depending on the services available in your Exchange profile there are a number of other address books that might be available to you:

- Postoffice address list — lists all the people who have mailboxes in your MS Mail Postoffice. You may also find (or create) distribution lists for groups of people within your organization who are also connected to the office network

▷ CompuServe address list — the people whose addresses you have stored in the WinCim address book

▷ custom address lists — address books provided by other services that have been added to Microsoft Exchange.

Figure 17.3
Address book —
Tools⇨Address Book

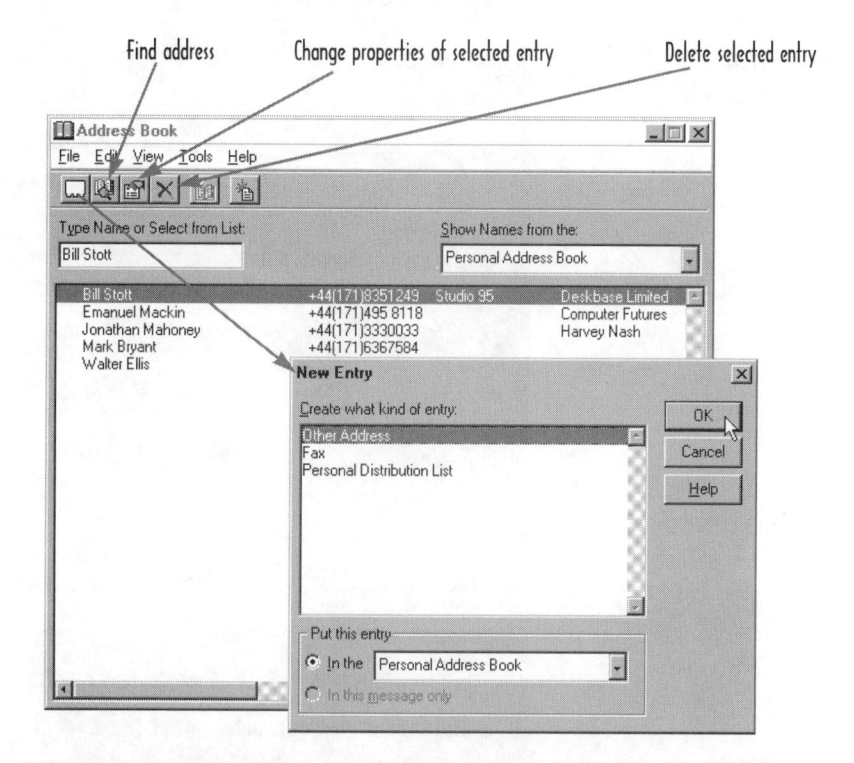

Find address   Change properties of selected entry   Delete selected entry

Note

> The Address Book window shows the contents of the address book which is specified within the Show Names from box (top right)

1 *Double-click the* **Inbox** *icon on your Desktop to open the Exchange window. Choose* **Tools⇨Address Book** *from its menu bar in order to open the* **Personal Address Book** *window.*

2 *Choose* **File⇨New Entry** *to open a dialog box containing a list of the types of addresses whose format is directly supported by the address book. Select* **Fax** *then press* **OK** *to open the* **New Fax Properties** *sheet (Figure 17.4).*

Chapter 17   Microsoft Exchange — fax and mail   375

3   Click the **FAX•Address** tab to bring this page to the forefront. Enter the name of the person together with his/her fax number in the appropriate boxes (use the fax mailbox for people who share fax services).

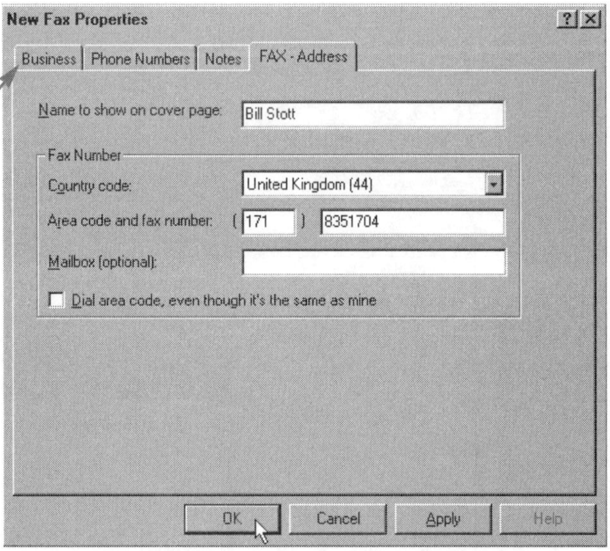

Figure 17.4
Properties for New fax

Address and other details

Tip

> When selecting the type of address entry in the New Entry dialog box you can also select the address book into which it will be added – change the setting Put this entry

4   Click the **Business** tab to bring this page to the forefront then enter the person's name and address details — information that appears on the fax cover sheet. Press **OK** to close the property sheet and add an entry into the specified address book. Close the **Address Book** and **Exchange** windows — this exercise is complete!

The type of address book entry (Figure 17.6) depends on the Exchange service you are using to send your message — the above exercise relates to the fax service. However, once you have obtained the relevant information (see Table 17.2) it is just as easy to enter other types of addresses into your Personal Address Book.

Sending messages

While all types of message are composed on the same form and are posted using the same procedure, the service used to transmit them depends on the recipient's address — the contents of the **To** box in the message form.

1   *Double-click the* **Inbox** *icon on your Desktop to open the Exchange window. Choose* **Compose→New Message** *from its menu bar to open a standard message form (Figure 17.5).*

2   *Press the* **To** *button (top of the message form) in order to open the* **Address Book** *window. This window contains all the names in the address book and these are presented at the top right hand side of its window.*

Figure 17.5
Standard message form

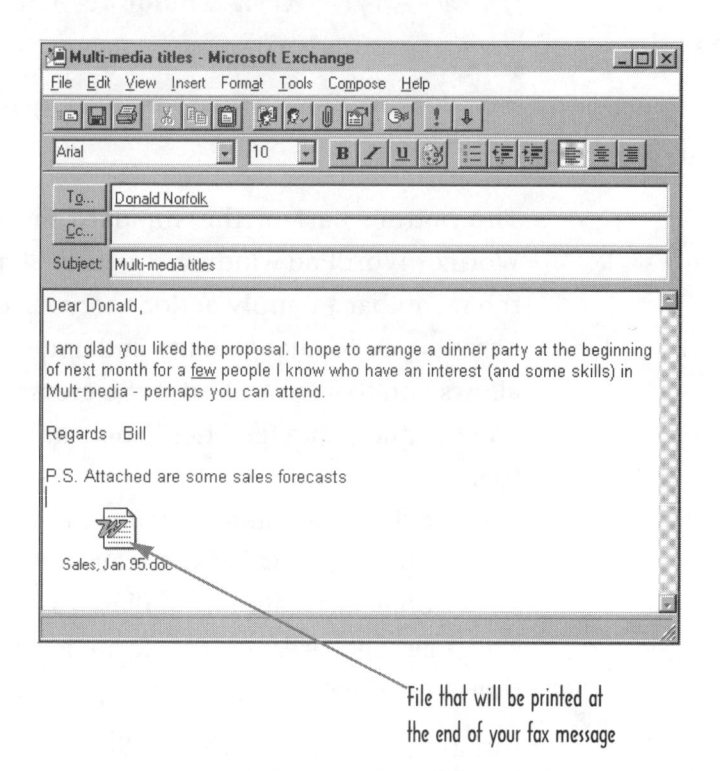

Note

> You may setup Office 95 so that Word is used to edit and display your Exchange message forms – install the WordMail component

3   Select a name from the list in the left side of the window then press the **To** button (middle), in order to add the name to your list of message recipients (right) — you may add several recipients to this list, if required. Press **OK** to close the window and return back to the message form, where the name appears in the **To** box.

4   Type the subject of your fax (it will appear on the cover sheet) into the **Subject** box of the message form. Type your message into the area below — see Composing a message.

> **Note**
>
> You can also create a fax using a Wizard to guide you through each steps – apply Compose↪New Fax from the Exchange window menu bar

Composing a message

The bottom part of the standard message form acts like a Word or WordPad window — you can type a message then use the menu bar to apply actions to your text. The **Format** menu permits you to change fonts and underline text; the **File** menu allows you to save and print the message; the **Edit** menu gives you cut and paste facilities. You can also use the **Insert** menu to add:

- a file containing a document
- other messages from your Personal Message Store
- objects created from files— see Chapter 7.

The message area of the form is OLE activated and can therefore receive objects dropped from other programs — pictures, documents, even sound! The recipients of your message can also drag these inserts from the message area on to the Desktop in order to copy the file into their PC's hard disk.

5   Type some text into the message area, select it, then choose **Format↪Font** from the menu bar in order to open a dialog box

that permits you to change its typeface. Press **OK** *to close the dialog and apply its settings.*

6 *Move your cursor (insertion point) to the beginning of the text and apply* **Insert→File** *from the menu bar to open the* **Insert File** *dialog box — it operates just like the* **Open** *dialog box (see Chapter 6). Select a document file from this dialog box then press the* **OK** *button to add it into your message. Return to the message window by pressing the* **Close** *button.*

> **Note**
> When sending a message by fax, any inserted documents are expanded to form a number of printed pages – other services permit the recipient to copy the inserted document into a file

Message delivery options

A number of settings can be accessed from the message window's **File** menu that determine how your message is delivered. The following properties apply to most message types:

- *importance* — grade your message so that more important messages will be flagged in the recipient's in tray
- *sensitivity* — mark messages as confidential, personal and so forth
- *read receipt* — when your message is read by the recipient, a receipt message is then posted back to you
- *delivery receipt* — when your message is delivered a receipt message is then posted back to you.

7 *Choose* **File→Properties** *from the message window's menu bar to open a property sheet containing settings for the message. Insert a tick in the box labelled* **Delivery Receipt** *then press* **OK** *to close the property sheet.*

> **Note**
> Change the properties of your fax service so that more than one attempt is made to send the message if the recipient's fax number is engaged – press Send Options then press the Dialing button in the Fax page

Chapter 17   Microsoft Exchange — fax and mail   379

Sending the message

Messages awaiting transmission are stored in the **Outbox** folder of your Personal Information Store.

8   Choose **File→Send** *from the Exchange menu bar to post your message with the options you have defined, using the service appropriate for your addressee. Close the* **Exchange Explorer** *window — this exercise is complete!*

Exchange automatically arranges transmission of your messages once they have been put in the **Outbox** — a message appears in your **Inbox** if a particular item cannot be sent. However, depending on the type of service that is required to deliver the message, there may be some delay before the contents of the **Outbox** are finally dispatched.

> **Note**
>
> MS Mail is normally connected to your Desktop so mail is dispatched (and collected) almost immediately – other services may need to wait for the next time you connect to their network

After the message has been dispatched, it is moved from the **OutBox** folder into the **Sent items** folder of your Personal Information Store.

Accessing you Personal Information Store

Your Personal Information Store is displayed in the **Explorer** window (see Chapter 14), opened whenever you start Microsoft Exchange. It usually contains the following folders:

- **Deleted Items** — messages which have been removed from other folders are placed here so that they may be recovered — like pulling files from the **Recycle Bin**
- **Inbox** — messages addressed to you are put into this folder when received by Windows 95

▷ **Outbox** — messages are placed into this folder prior to their dispatch

▷ **Sent Items** — a copy of each message sent from Microsoft Exchange is normally held in this folder.

> **Note**
>
> An Exchange server provides further folders in addition to your Personal Information Store, so that a common set of messages can be shared among a particular group of people

Opening a folder on the left hand side of the window reveals its message contents on the right hand side. This list of messages can be sorted by any column heading simply by clicking its label.

Figure 17.6
Exchange window — **Inbox**

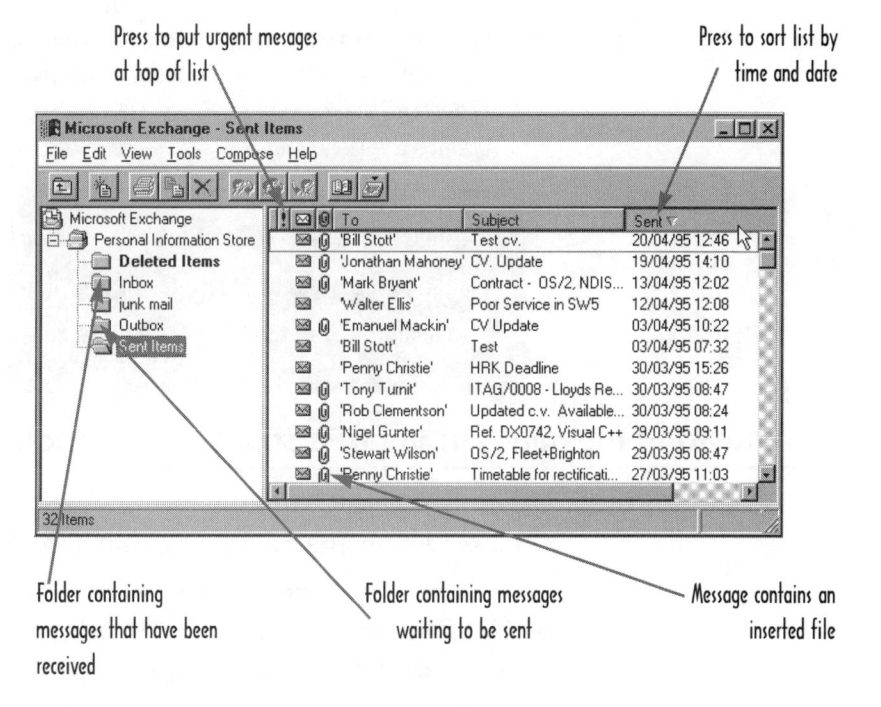

Press to put urgent mesages at top of list

Press to sort list by time and date

Folder containing messages that have been received

Folder containing messages waiting to be sent

Message contains an inserted file

1 Double-click the **Inbox** icon on your Desktop to open the **Microsoft Exchange** window together with your Personal Information Store. Choose **View→Folders** from the menu bar then open the **Sent Items** folder on the left side of the Exchange window to reveal (right side) a list of the messages you have sent.

2 Click the **Subject** column heading in the **Microsoft Exchange** window (right side) to sort the list of messages alphabetically by subject. Click on the **To** column heading to resort the list by the name of the recipient.

The **Columns** dialog box (**Views↪Columns**) allows you to alter the type and order of the columns in your message list. For example, you may specify that **Sent** (that is, the date your message was sent) and **Subject** information should be displayed as the first two columns in the list.

3 Choose **Views↪Columns** from Exchange's menu bar to open the **Columns** dialog box. Select a column heading in the left hand box (**Available columns**) then press **Add** to include it in the list at the right side of the dialog box.

4 Press the **Move Up** or **Move Down** buttons to change the order of the entries in the right hand list — corresponds to the order of the columns. Press **OK** to close the dialog box and update the way your messages are listed in the Exchange window.

Tip

> Choose **Views↪Sort** to open a dialog box that permits you to change the order of messages in your list according to the values (ascending or descending) in a given column

Manipulating messages in your Personal Information Store

The **Exchange** window can be used to manipulate your messages in the same way that the **Windows Explorer** (see Chapter 14) allows you to manipulate files and folders. Use the **Exchange** window to delete, print, move, and copy your messages by dragging them across your Desktop into other windows, and so forth.

5 Open the **Sent Items** folder in the **Exchange** window (left side), then select the message it contains (created in a previous exercise) from the right side of this window. Choose **File↪Print** from the menu bar in order to send the contents of the message to your printer.

6. *Drag a message from the* **Exchange** *window (right side) into the* **Deleted Items** *folder (left side) — the message is moved between the folders.*

> **Note:** Hold-down `Ctrl` while clicking messages with your mouse to select more than one message (this is known as *multiple-selection*)

Receiving messages

Each message service defined in your Exchange profile will periodically deliver any waiting messages to your **Inbox** once an appropriate connection has been established. You can review all the messages in your **Inbox** using the **Exchange** window.

7. *Click the* **Inbox** *folder on the left side of the* **Exchange** *window to reveal a list of received messages in the right side of the window.*

8. *Click the* **From** *column heading (right side) to sort your received messages alphabetically by sender. Click on the* **!** *column heading to resort the list by the importance of each message (see* Message Delivery options*).*

9. *Double-click a message in the* **Exchange** *window to display its contents in a standard message window (Figure 17.8).*

> **Note:** Some message services may establish a remote access connection only when Microsoft Exchange is first started – it disconnects once any waiting mail has been sent to your PC

The bottom of the message window is like a WordPad window and may contain text as well as graphics. It is also OLE activated (see Chapter 7) and therefore can contain objects such as pictures and documents that have been dropped into your message by the sender (see page 378).

Figure 17.8
Exchange's **Inbox** and a received message window

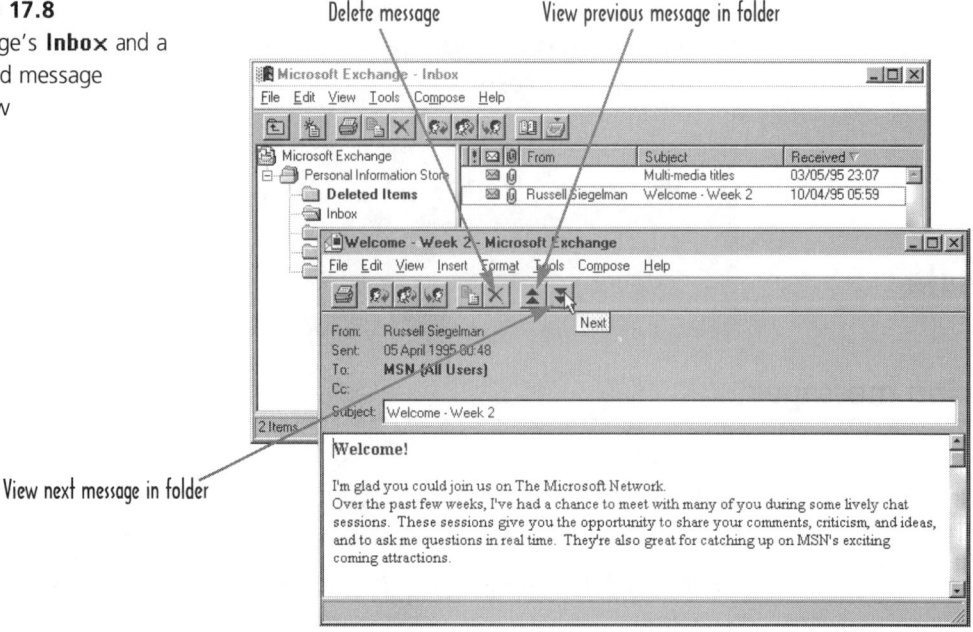

Delete message — View previous message in folder

View next message in folder

> **Note**
>
> Any message marked read receipt will automatically dispatch a message back to the sender when you close its message window

Most messages permit you to cut or copy material from this message area into the Windows 95 Clipboard. You can also retrieve objects that have been attached to a message so they can be saved as individual files on your Desktop — this provides a convenient way to receive files from other people.

10. *Documents or files attached to messages are represented as icons within the message area. Point to any icons in your message and press the right mouse button to reveal a pop-up menu containing the actions that can be applied to the object.*

11. *Select* **Save As** *from the pop-up menu to open the standard* **Save As** *dialog box so you can specify the name and location of the file. Press* **Save** *to close the dialog box and store the object on your PC.*

> **Note:** You can drag an object from the message area then drop it on the Desktop to copy it as a file onto your PC

Replying to a message

You can reply to a message simply by pressing the **Reply** button on the toolbar, in either the **Exchange** or **Message** window — this creates a new message addressed to the sender.

12. Choose **Compose↪Reply to sender** from the **Message** window's menu bar to open a new message window — it is addressed to the sender of the original message. Type your response into the message area of this new message window then dispatch the message by choosing **File↪Send**.

> **Note:** The toolbars in the Exchange and Message windows also contain a Forward button – this permits you to send a message to someone else for their reply or comment

You can read (and answer) all the messages in a folder directly from the message window. This avoids the need to select each message in turn from the **Exchange** window.

13. Close any message windows that are open then close the **Microsoft Exchange** window to complete this exercise!

> **Note:** You will receive a special message from the system administrator if an error is encountered when sending a message from your Outbox – this message contains a Send Again button

Desktop fax facilities

The Microsoft Fax software supplied with Windows 95 provides the following scanning and printing facilities so that you can send and receive fax messages:

- it converts (renders) a document into a series of fax pages, just as if you had printed it on paper then fed the pages through a fax machine
- it converts a series of received fax pages into a document that can be sent to your PC's printer or viewed with programs like Fax Viewer.

Therefore Microsoft Fax, in conjunction with a fax-modem, gives you a full featured fax machine directly on your Desktop.

Note

> When fax messages are dispatched from the Exchange Outbox they are sent to the fax print queue which is operated like a printer queue (see page 315)

Sending fax messages

You may create a fax as a consequence of sending a message to someone whose address requires the fax message service. Alternatively, fax messages can be sent from your PC in the following ways:

- choose **File→Print** from a program's menu bar and select Microsoft Fax instead of the printer attached to your PC (see page 82)
- drag a document across your Desktop and drop it on the Microsoft Fax icon
- use Microsoft Exchange to create a fax message by applying **Compose→New Fax** from its menu bar.

In each case the Fax Wizard guides you through the procedure of sending a fax.

Note

> A fax message is entered into your Personal Information Store like other messages managed by Microsoft Exchange

Figure 17.9
The Fax Wizard

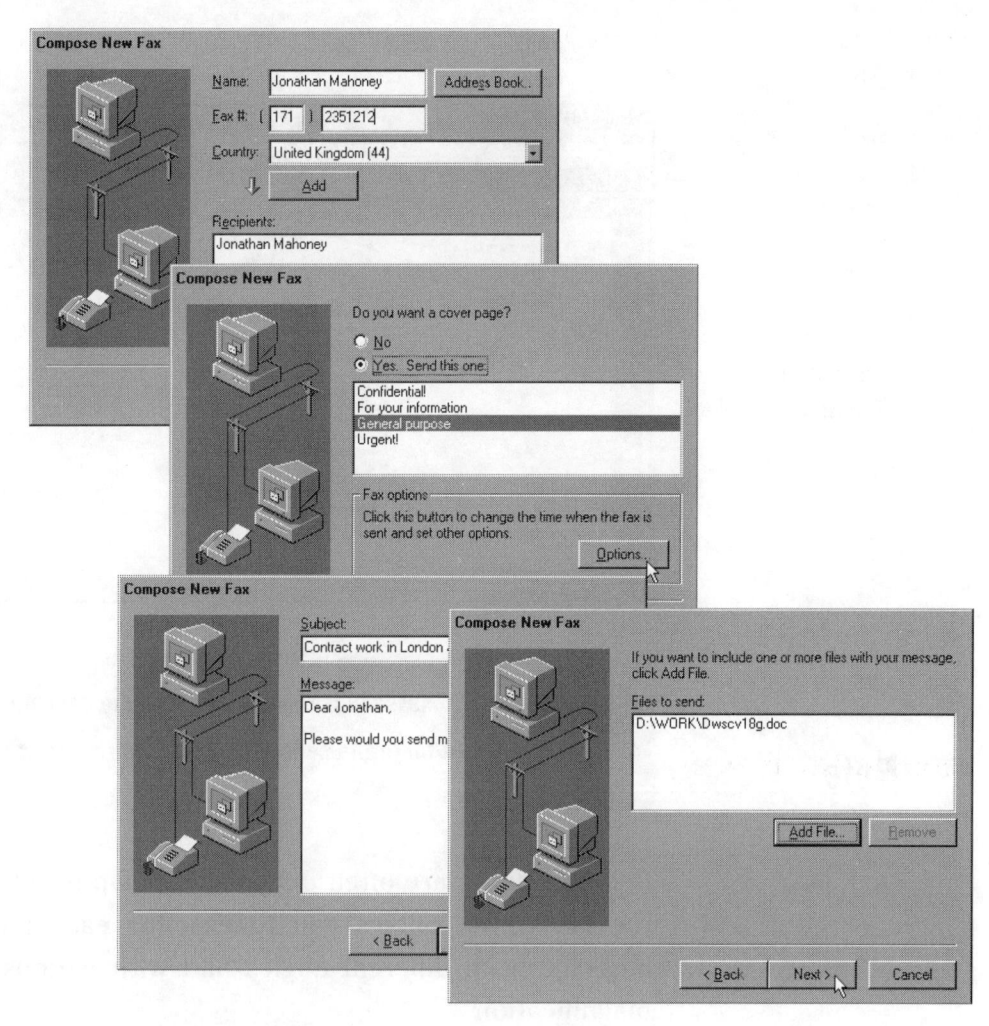

Receiving fax messages

You can receive fax messages whenever your fax-modem is switched-on and connected to your Desktop's Exchange. The receipt of a fax message is signalled on your Taskbar while the message itself is put into your Personal Information Store's **Inbox**.

> **Note**
> You can view the contents of a fax message using the Fax Viewer program – it is started automatically when you open a fax message from the Exchange window

Figure 17.10
The Fax Viewer

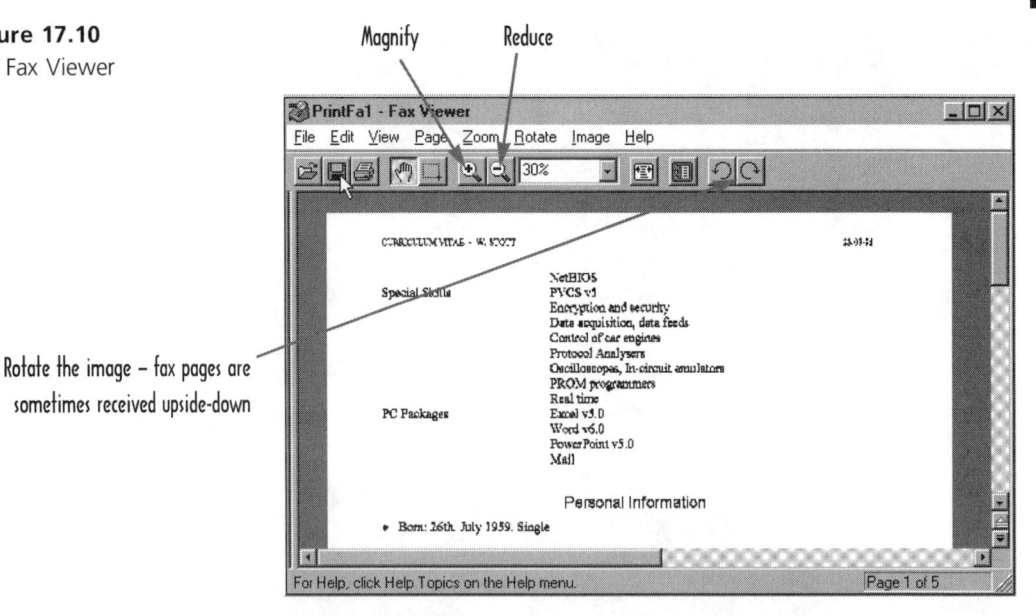

Magnify — Reduce

Rotate the image — fax pages are sometimes received upside-down

> **Note:** A received fax message is rendered as a single document (akin to a graphic) and therefore cannot contain separate OLE objects

Because pages are often put upside down into fax machines the fax viewer allows you to examine each page of a fax message from different angles and with various degrees of magnification.

1   *Select the **Inbox** folder from your Personal Information Store. Double-click any fax message that has been received by your PC in order to start the Fax Viewer.*

2   *Choose **Page↪Next** from the Viewer's menu bar to display the different pages of your message. Choose **Rotate↪Left** to move the page through 90 degrees until it is correctly orientated in the window. Finally adjust the page magnification using **Zoom↪Fit Both** so that the page fits the window.*

3   *Print the fax message on your printer by choosing **File↪Print** from the Viewer's menu bar then close the Fax Viewer and Exchange window — the exercises in this chapter are now complete!*

Using Exchange with Office 95

Word, Excel and PowerPoint provide **File** menu options which allow you to send your documents to people as attachments to Exchange messages — an alternative to sending them to a printer. In this way you can distribute a document without the need to explicitly start Exchange, compose a message, then add its file as an attachment. Options are:

- **File↪Add Routing Slip** — select a list of people from your address book who will receive a message containing the document. You can arrange for the messages to be sent *at once* so that each reviewer receives an identical copy of the document or you can send the messages *one after another* so that each reviewer receives a copy of the document only after it has been annotated by the previous reviewers in your routing list
- **File↪Send** — opens a dialog box so you can decide whether to generate the messages specified by the *routing slip* or open an Exchange message form (Figure 17.5) to create your own messages for distributing the document
- **File↪Post to Exchange Folder** — permits you to put the message containing your document in a folder within your Personal Information Store (perhaps so you can batch-up a number of messages for the next time you connect with MSN). Alternatively, you might wish to place your message in a folder created for a specific topic, so that all the people in your organization can share a common collection of information (*group working*).

> **Tip**
> Design your own message form by choosing Compose↪ WordMail Options from Exchange's menu bar to change the template document which is used to create your messages

Summary

- Microsoft Exchange allows you to process all your messages in a uniform way irrespective of the actual delivery service; MS Mail, Internet, CompuServe, fax.
- The same form is used for reading and writing all your messages — you can insert files and other objects into these message.
- Keep a personal address book, so you can send a message to someone without having to remember their address format.
- Your Personal Information Store automatically receives your messages (**Inbox** folder) and keeps a copy of the messages you have sent (**Sent Items** folder).
- Messages and folders in your Personal Information Store are displayed in a type of **Explorer** window, which makes it easy to review and arrange your mail.
- The Microsoft Fax program convert documents into fax pages (and vice versa) to provide a full featured fax machine on your Desktop.

Note

> Optical character recognition (OCR) programs convert typescript and hand-written text in a fax message into a form that can be stored as characters in a Word document

Chapter 18

Taskbar settings — Control Panel

Objectives

This chapter explains how to change the basic features and functions of your Desktop in Windows 95:

▷ change your **Start** menu — how to alter the contents of the **Start** button's menus

▷ **Control Panel** — adjust your system settings, load fonts, install modems and so forth

▷ **Fonts** folder — add or remove typefaces which are available to documents

▷ date/time — adjust your computer's time and date settings

▷ keyboard, mouse — fine tune the response of your keyboard and mouse

▷ passwords — save user settings and allow other people to manage your PC from a remote computer

▷ display — change the properties of your Desktop to alter its background and activate a screen saver.

Chapter 18

Change your Start menu

The contents of your Start button's menu can be altered so that the items you use most frequently are more accessible.

1 *Drag the* **My Computer** *icon across your Desktop and drop it on the* **Start** *button. Click the* **Start** *button to reveal its menu which now includes* **My Computer** — *selecting this choice opens the* **My Computer** *window.*

Figure 18.1
Properties for Taskbar

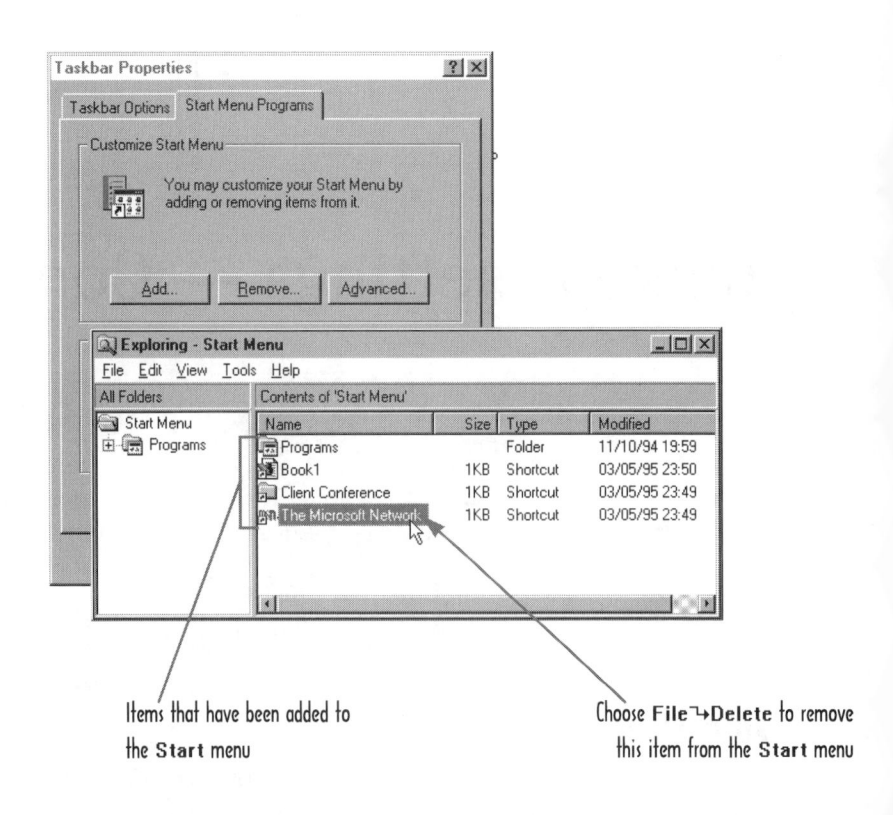

Items that have been added to the Start menu

Choose File→Delete to remove this item from the Start menu

Tip

You can drop any icon onto your Start button into order to add the item to its menu

Items can be removed from your Start button by changing settings within its property sheet.

392　Chapter 18　Taskbar settings — Control Panel

2 *Choose* **Start↪Settings↪Taskbar** *to open your Taskbar's property sheet (Figure 18.1). Click the* **Start Menu Programs** *tab to bring this page to the forefront.*

3 *Press the* **Advanced** *button to open an Explorer-type window that displays the items you have added to the* **Start** *menu. Select one of the these items in the right side of the window then choose* **File↪Delete** *from the menu bar to remove it from your* **Start** *menu.*

4 *Close the* **Explorer** *window then press* **OK** *to close the property sheet — this exercise is complete!*

> **Note**
>
> The Start menu contains shortcuts to your folders and therefore when you delete an item from the menu it is the shortcut which is deleted and not the actual file or folder

Control Panel folder

The **Control Panel** folder contains a collection of icons that can be used to change the content and properties of your computer, as well as the behaviour of its Desktop. Open your **Control Panel** from:

▷ **My Computer** window — the **Control Panel** icon is displayed in this window

▷ **Windows Explorer** — the **Control Panel** folder is contained within the **My Computer** folder

▷ Start button — Start↪Settings↪Control Panel.

Choose **Start↪Settings↪Control Panel** *from your Taskbar to open the* **Control Panel** *window (Figure 18.2) — you will close this window at the end of the chapter.*

> **Note**
>
> The icons that appear in Control Panel depend on the set-up and features of your computer – you may find additional icons to adjust settings of multimedia adapters and so forth

Chapter
18

Figure 18.2
Control Panel

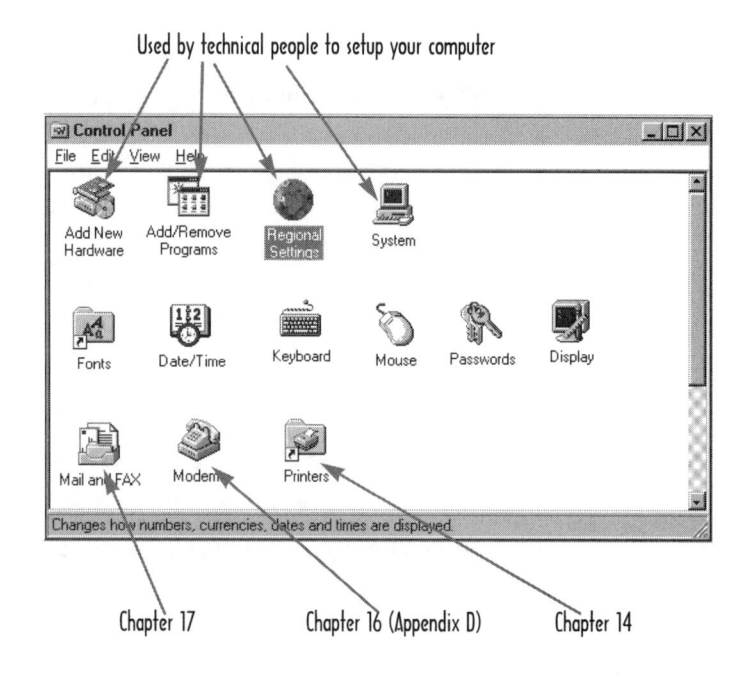

Used by technical people to setup your computer

[Control Panel window showing icons: Add New Hardware, Add/Remove Programs, Regional Settings, System, Fonts, Date/Time, Keyboard, Mouse, Passwords, Display, Mail and FAX, Modems, Printers. Status bar: "Changes how numbers, currencies, dates and times are displayed."]

Chapter 17   Chapter 16 (Appendix D)   Chapter 14

Fonts folder

The **Fonts** folder contains all the typefaces that are available to your programs through the standard **Font** dialog box (see Figure 9.10). These typefaces are displayed in the folder's View window which may be used to add or remove fonts, as well as inspect their properties.

1   *Double-click the* **Fonts** *folder in your* **Control Panel** *to open its View window (see page 190). Choose* **View⇝List Fonts By Similarity** *to display the font files in order of their similarity to the appearance of the font named in the box beneath the menu bar. Click the button attached to this box to reveal a list of the other fonts which may be used in its place — select* **Times New Roman**.

2   *Select* **Times New Roman** *from the list of fonts that now appears in the window area then choose* **File⇝Open** *to open a dialog box that displays a sample of the typeface. Examine the typeface then close this dialog box before closing the* **Fonts** *window — this exercise is complete!*

Figure 18.3
Fonts window and
Times New Roman
font

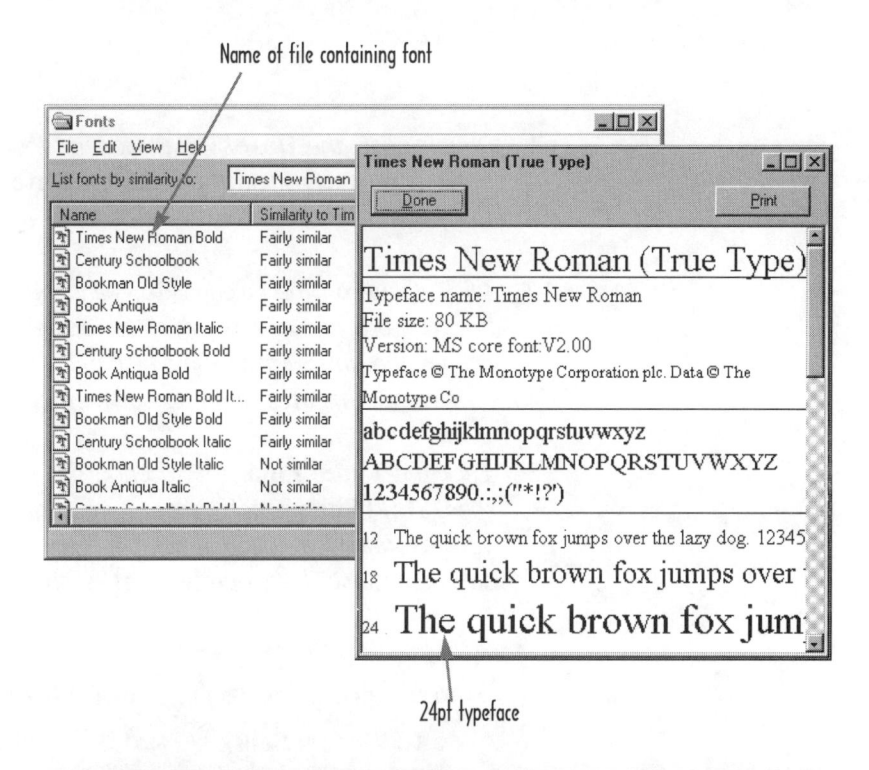

Name of file containing font

24pt typeface

Note

Choose File→Install New Font to open a dialog box that allows you to select a file containing a font (*.TTF,*.FON) then load it into Windows 95

Changing time and date

Your computer keeps track of the time and date in an internal clock with its own battery — the settings are saved when you switch-off your PC. This clock can be adjusted from the **Time\Date** property sheet that is opened when you double-click its icon in the **Control Panel** window.

Note

It is important to keep your computer's internal clock on time so that your files' time and date information is accurate — this can make it easier to locate them

Chapter 18   Taskbar settings — Control Panel   395

1 *Double-click the **Date/Time** icon in your **Control Panel** to open its property sheet then click the **Date & Time** tab to bring this page to the forefront — it contains a calendar and clock.*

2 *Click a date on the calendar to change your PC's date. Click the hours figure in the box which is located beneath the clock to change the time with the small (spin) buttons attached to the box — click the minutes figure to set the clock's minute hand.*

3 *Click the **Time Zone** tab to bring this page to the forefront of the **Date/Time** property sheet — it contains a world map. Click your geographical location on this map to change the time zone settings. Close the property sheet — this exercise is complete.*

> **Note**
>
> Insert a tick in the small box at the bottom left of the Time Zone page then click the next time zone on the map to adjust your PC's time setting for daylight saving (i.e. BST)

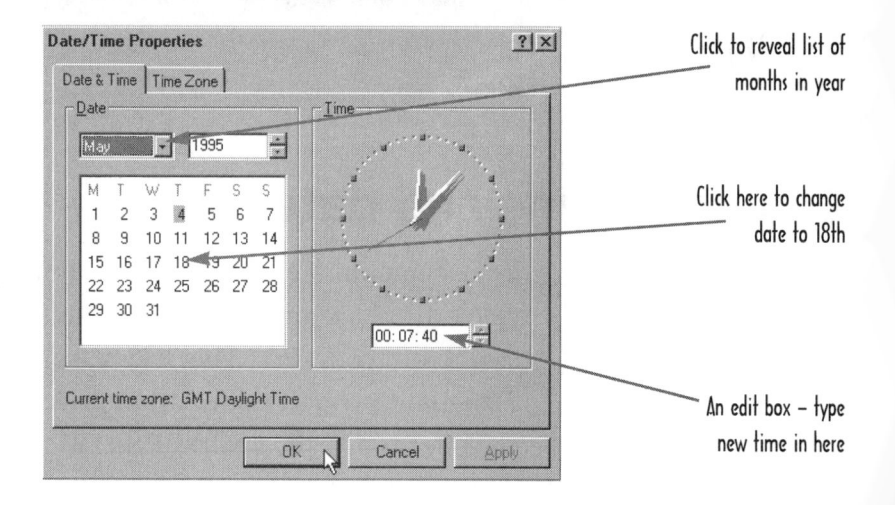

Figure 18.4
Change your computer's time and date

- Click to reveal list of months in year
- Click here to change date to 18th
- An edit box – type new time in here

> **Tip**
>
> The computer's time is displayed in the status area of your Taskbar (far right). Double-click this clock to open the Date/Time properties sheet

Tuning your keyboard and mouse

Keyboard

When editing a document, if you press a key on the keyboard and hold it down, after a short-delay, the character appears in your window then repeats until you release the key. Some manuals call this *type-a-matic* action — it avoids the need to repetitively hammer a key in order to type a string of identical characters.

Note

> You can adjust the settings that control your keyboard's type-a-matic action from the window that is opened when you double-click the Keyboard icon in the Control Panel

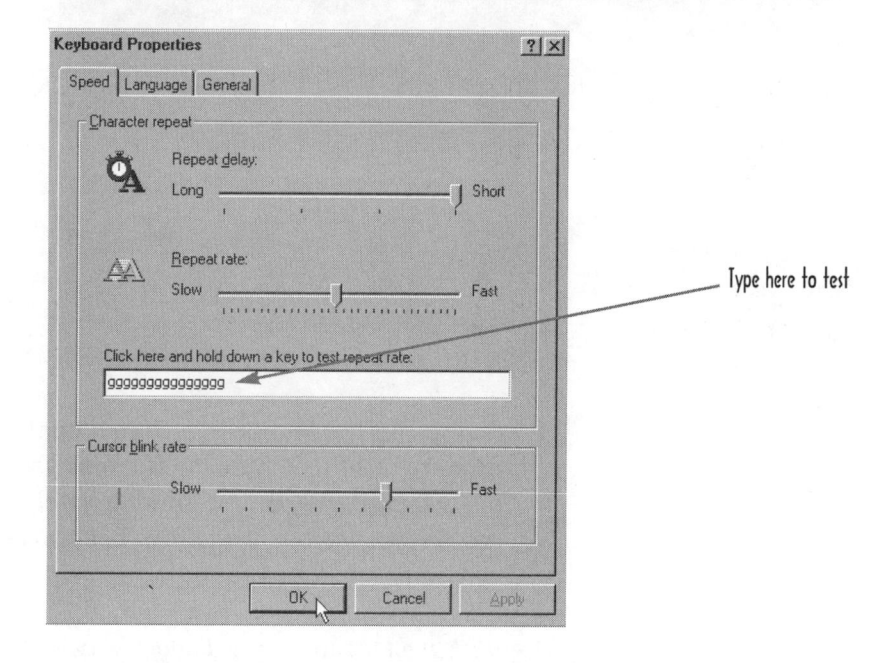

Figure 18.5
Changing the keyboard's type-a-matic action

Type here to test

The behaviour of the mouse can be adjusted to suit individual users in terms of:

Mouse

- click button — left or right handed operation
- double-click speed — adjust delay of the second click to differentiate a double-click from two single clicks
- pointer — alter the responsiveness of the pointer to the movement of your mouse.

Chapter 18

> **Tip**
>
> Increase the responsiveness of the mouse pointer — and reduce the delay between a double-click — as your dexterity with the mouse improves

Figure 18.6
Mouse adjustments

You may wish to change these settings if you have a laptop computer

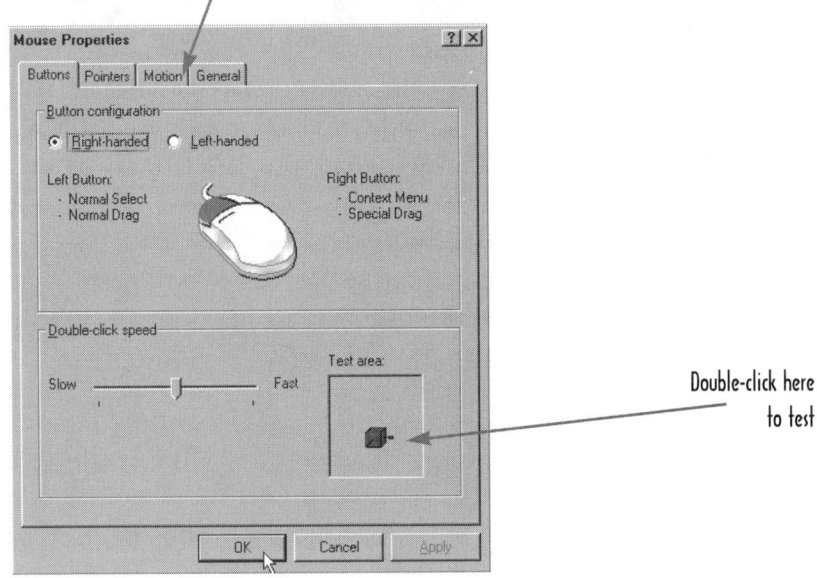

(Mouse Properties dialog box showing Buttons tab with Button configuration (Right-handed/Left-handed) and Double-click speed slider with Test area)

Double-click here to test

1   Double-click the **Mouse** icon in your **Control Panel** to open its property sheet then click the **Buttons** tab to bring this page to the forefront. Adjust the **Double-click speed** control then double-click the box within the **Test area** in order to try this new setting.

2   Click the **Motion** tab to bring this page to the forefront of the property sheet then adjust the **Pointer speed** control. Try these new settings by moving your mouse then close the property sheet — this exercise is complete!

> **Tip**
>
> When using a laptop PC insert a tick in the Show pointer trails box, so that a series of ghost images follow your pointer as it moves on your screen — this makes it easier to find

Storing passwords and user profiles

Passwords

You often need a different password for each network or remote system that is accessed from your Desktop. However, so that you don't need to remember a whole collection of passwords Windows 95 allows you to store passwords on your system.

Tip

> When logging on to Microsoft Network click the box remember password to store your password for future logons

The single (or unified) log on facility means that, once you have correctly entered the password needed to gain access to your Desktop, all other passwords will be automatically supplied to each network as required. These additional passwords are encrypted by your Windows password and stored with your personal user settings (as a user profile), so they are only available while you are personally using the PC.

Note

> Use the Change Passwords page of the Password property sheet to change your Window password (see page 324)

User profiles

Information that is specific to a particular user, including passwords, are stored in a user profile — it is automatically applied whenever the person successfully logs on to the Desktop. In this way, a single computer may be shared by several people while retaining their individual settings and preferences.

1 *Double-click the **Passwords** icon in your **Control Panel** to open its property sheet then click the **User Profiles** tab to bring this page to the forefront. Click on the bottom three options on this page to allow each user to retain their personal settings whenever they log on to the Desktop.*

> **Caution:** Forgetting your Windows password means that you will have to re-register your user name (or supply a new one) and therefore may lose your user profile.

Remote administration

Your PC may be remotely managed from another computer if you enable the **Remote Administration** settings. This allows other people to create shared folders on your PC and can help in the administration of a network.

2. *Click on the **Remote Administration** tab to bring this page to the forefront. Next, click on the box **Enable Remote Administration** and supply the access password. Finally, press **OK** to close the property sheet and complete the exercise.*

> **Caution:** Ask your network administrator before changing the Remote Administration settings, as this may breach your organization's security policy

Altering your Desktop appearance

Display

The way your Desktop behaves and appears is controlled by settings in the different pages of its property sheet:

- *background* — the Desktop can be covered by either patterns or a graphic image
- *appearance* — the colours used for the components of your windows can be changed to give your Desktop a customized colour scheme.
- *screen savers* — protect the screen while you are not using your computer (the Desktop is restored when you touch the keyboard or mouse)
- *settings* — adjust the resolution of your screen and the number of colours it can display.

**Figure 18.1
Display Properties**
— screen saver

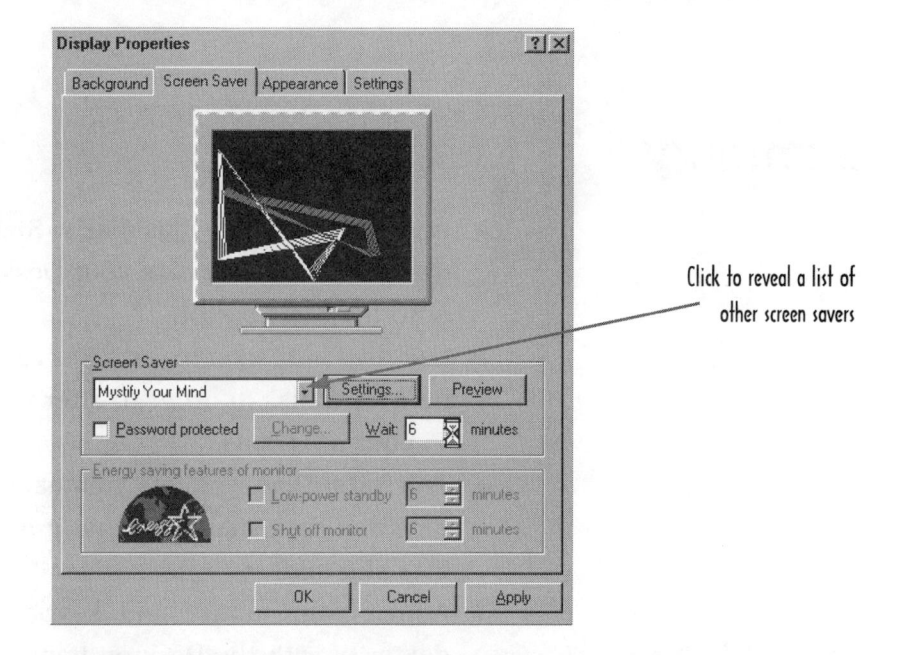

Click to reveal a list of other screen savers

> **Note**
>
> You can open the Display property sheet by selecting Properties from the Desktop's pop-up menu

1 Double-click the **Display** icon in **Control Panel** to open its property sheet then click the **Background** tab to bring this page to the forefront. Select **None** from the list in the **Pattern** box then select **Windows Logo** from the **Wallpaper** list — use the scroll bars to display items at the bottom of the list.

2 Click the **Screen Saver** tab to bring this page to the forefront of the property sheet. Press the button attached to the **Screen Saver** box then select **Flying Through Space** from its list — a sample screen appears in the property sheet.

3 Adjust the value in the **Wait** box to adjust the period of inactivity required to trigger the screen saver then close the property sheet by pressing **OK**. Finally, close the **Control Panel** window and tidy-up your Desktop, before using the Taskbar to shut down your PC — the last exercise is complete!

Screen-savers can conserve power and protect the coating of your monitor's screen. They are activated whenever Windows 95 fails to detect any mouse or keyboard movement for a pre-set period.

Summary

- Add items to the Taskbar's **Start** menu simply by dragging an icon across your Desktop then dropping it onto the **Start** button.
- Use the **Fonts** icon to install or remove fonts from your PC's hard disk in order to alter the typefaces available to your programs.
- The **Date/Time** icon lets you maintain your computer's time and date values, so that it is easier to locate your files and folders.
- Adjust your mouse and keyboard settings as your dexterity with the Desktop improves, using the **Mouse** and **Keyboard** icons.
- Use the **Password** icon to change your Windows password and securely store other passwords on your PC so that, once you have logged on, they can be automatically supplied when needed.
- Customize the appearance of your Desktop to match your environment from the **Display** icon. Install a screen saver to save energy and keep your Desktop secure while you are away from your desk.

Note

The Control Panel is a special folder containing icons which are used to adjust the settings of your PC, as well as allowing you to install new programs, adapter cards and devices

Appendix A

Help

Objectives

This appendix explains how to obtain assistance in several ways while you are performing tasks from your Desktop or application programs, including:

▷ how to obtain help — press [F1] to open the **Help Topic** window, select a topic, then display it in a Help window

▷ using the **Help Topic** window — find a particular topic from the lists (contents, index, find and Answer Wizard) contained in this window

▷ how to use a Help window — use the information and controls in a Help window to complete your task.

The Windows 95 Help facilities provide a consistent way for programs to implement user assistance from their dialog boxes and **Help** menu (see page 69).

Appendix A

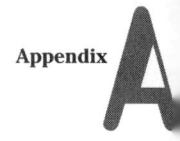

How to obtain help

The ways in which you can gain access to particular components of the Windows 95 Help system are listed in Table A.1.

How to use the Help Topics window

The **Help Topics** window provides a uniform way for you to locate an individual help topic from the set of help topics provided by your program — it is arranged like a book:

- **Contents** — provides a list of categories (or chapters) for the individual help topics
- **Index** — contains an alphabetical list of the help topic titles
- **Find** — lists every word used within the individual help topics so you can search for particular words or phrases

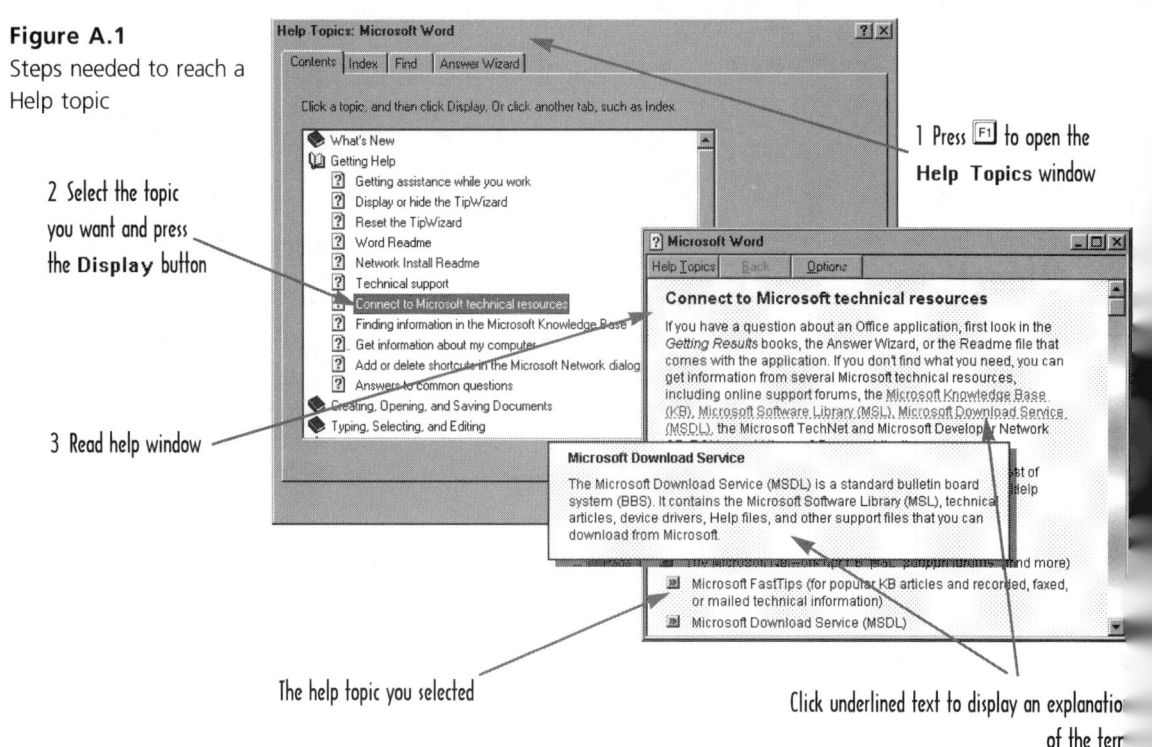

Figure A.1
Steps needed to reach a Help topic

1 Press F1 to open the **Help Topics** window

2 Select the topic you want and press the **Display** button

3 Read help window

The help topic you selected

Click underlined text to display an explanation of the term

404   Appendix A   Help

Table A.1
Ways to access the various types of Windows 95 Help

Type	From your Desktop	From a program
Help Topics window	❑ press F1 ❑ choose **Start**↦**Help**	❑ press F1 ❑ choose **Help**↦**Contents** or **Help**↦**Help Topics** from the menu bar
Help window	❑ make a selection from the **Help Topics** window	❑ make a selection from the **Help Topics** window ❑ press F1 in a dialog box
Pop-up windows	❑ point at a button in your Taskbar	❑ point at an object in the toolbar ❑ click an object with your Help pointer ❑ right-click a setting in a dialog box
Wizards	❑ double-click certain icons on your Desktop	❑ choose certain actions from the menu bar or toolbar
Tutorials	❑ press **Windows Tour** button in the **Welcome** window — this appears at start-up.	❑ choose **Help**↦**Tutorial** from the menu bar
Status bar text	❑ select an icon in a View window	❑ open a menu and highlight a choice ❑ point at a toolbar button
Answer Wizard	❑ Office toolbar button	❑ choose **Help**↦**Answer Wizard**

▷ Answer Wizard — finds a help topic from the description you have given of the problem.

Figure A.1 shows the general procedure, while Figure A.2 shows the **Help Topics** window in detail.

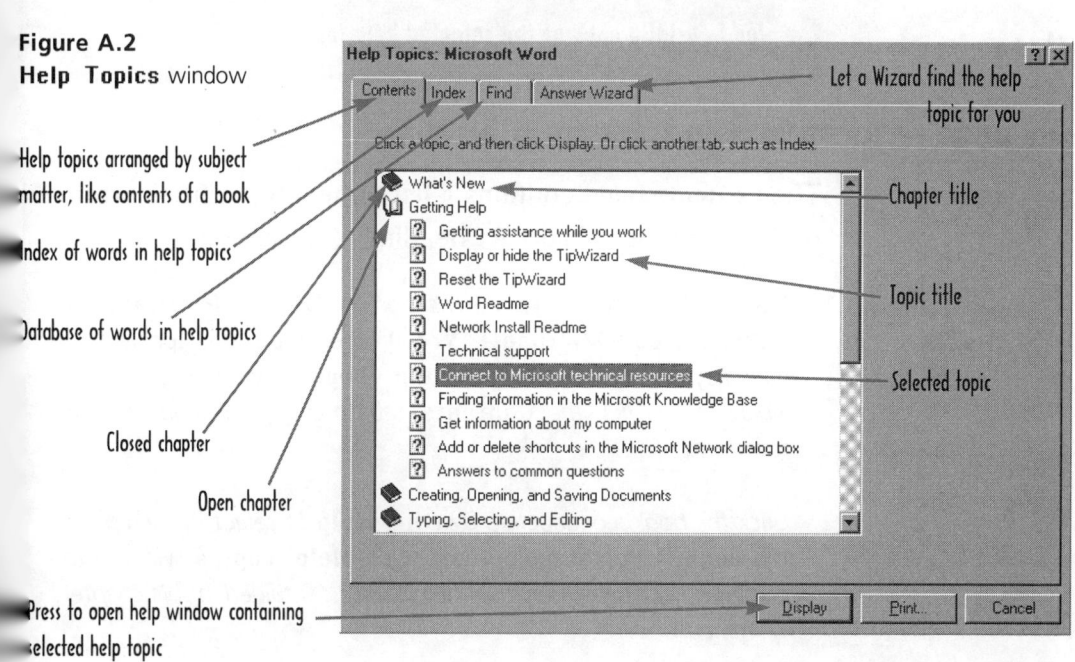

Figure A.2
Help Topics window

Help topics arranged by subject matter, like contents of a book

Index of words in help topics

Database of words in help topics

Closed chapter

Open chapter

Press to open help window containing selected help topic

Let a Wizard find the help topic for you

Chapter title

Topic title

Selected topic

Appendix A Help 405

> **Note:** When you first use the Find page, an index is created that contains every word in the set of individual help topics — just press one button and it's done!

The **Help Topics** window has a push-button (labelled **Display** in Figure A.2) whose function changes according to the item selected in the window:

- **Open** — press this button when you have selected a closed book in order to open a list of its contents; the button's label changes to **Close**
- **Close** — press this button when you have selected an open book in order to close its list of contents; the button's label changes to **Open**
- **Display** — press this button after a page (individual help topic) has been selected, to open a Help window containing the help text.

> **Note:** Press the Print push-button to open a dialog box that permits you to print a copy of the selected help topic

Contents page — locate a help topic by subject

The **Contents** page contains a list of help topic titles arranged under a number of subject headings (or chapters):

1. *Start Word from your Taskbar* (**Start↪Programs↪Accessories↪Microsoft Word**) *then press* [F1] *(top left of your keyboard) to open the* **Help Topics** *window shown in Figure A.2. Click the* **Contents** *tab to bring this page to the forefront.*

2. *Click the book icon labelled* **Getting Help** *to select it, then press the* **Open** *button at the bottom of the* **Help Topics** *window to display a list of the individual help topics contained in this chapter — its icon opens.*

3   Click the page icon labelled **Connect to Microsoft technical resources** then press the **Display** button at the bottom of the **Help Topics** window, to open a Help window containing information about using Microsoft's own technical resources — the **Help Topics** window automatically closes. Close the Help window to return to Word.

> **Tip**
>
> A scroll bar appears on the right-hand edge of the list when it becomes too long — use the scroll bar's arrow buttons to change the part of the list that is displayed in the window

Index page — locate a help topic by name

The **Index** page contains an alphabetical list of the help topic titles — just like the index of a book. A scroll bar is attached to this list because it is usually much longer than the window in which it is displayed.

5   Press [F1] to open the **Help Topics** window (Figure A.2) then click the **Index** tab to bring this page to the forefront.

6   Type `conn` in the box at the top of the Index page and watch the list scroll to **Connect statement** — the first help topic starting with the letters **conn**. Select the next topic (**Connecting to Microsoft technical forums**) then press the **Display** button to open a dialog box listing the individual help topics that contain a reference to this subject.

7   Select the help topic (page icon) labelled **Connect to Microsoft technical resources** then press the dialog box's **Display** button to open a Help window containing the same information displayed in step 3 — the dialog box and the **Help Topics** window will automatically close. Close the Help window to return to Word.

Find page — locate a help topic by searching for a word

The **Find** page contains an alphabetical list of all the words used in your program's set of individual help topics.

8   Press [F1] to open the **Help Topics** window (Figure A.2) then click the **Find** tab to bring this page to the forefront.

> **Note**
>
> The Find page's Wizard takes you through the process of creating Word's database – simply select the Express option, press the Next button, then press the Finish button

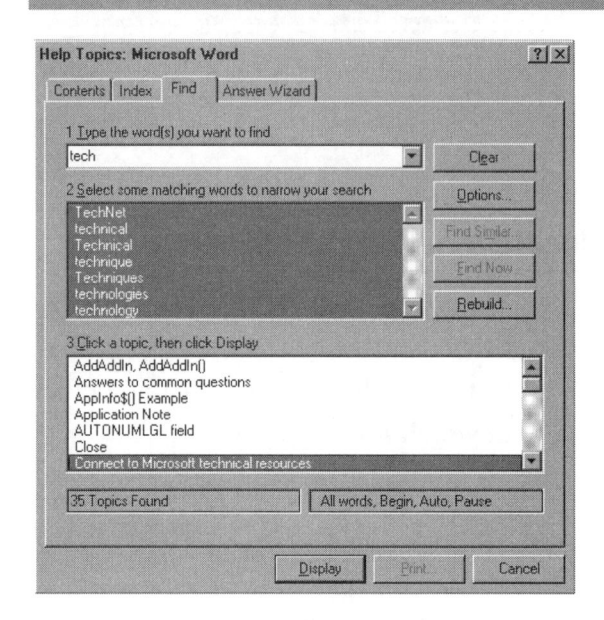

Figure A.3
Help Topics window
— **Find** page

9   *Once Word's database has been created you can list the individual help topics that contain the word* technical *by typing* `tech` *in the box (1) at the top of the page. This causes the word list (2) to scroll, showing (and selecting) the words that match these characters. The help topics containing these selected words are automatically listed (3) at the bottom of the page.*

10 *Click on the item* **Connect to Microsoft technical resources** *within the topics list then press the* **Display** *button at the bottom of the* **Help Topics** *window. This opens a Help window containing the same information displayed in step 3 — the* **Help Topics** *window automatically closes.*

> **Tip**
>
> Use the options button in the Find page to search for topics that contain particular combinations and permutations of the words and phrases for which you require an explanation

Answer Wizard page — ask a question to locate the topic

The **Answer Wizard** page prompts you to ask a question in normal English that the Help program will attempt to answer by displaying a list of help topics containing information it thinks might help you.

11 *Press* [F1] *to open the* **Help Topics** *window (Figure A.2) then click the* **Answer Wizard** *tab to bring this page to the forefront.*

12 *Type* how can I ask Microsoft a question? *in the box (1) at the top of the page then press the* **Search** *button to display a list of suitable help topics in the box (2) at the bottom of the page. Select the topic* **Connect to Microsoft technical resources** *then press the* **Display** *button to open a* **Help** *window containing the same information displayed in step 3 — the* **Help Topics** *window will automatically close. Close the* **Help** *window to return to Word.*

Figure A.4
Answer Wizard

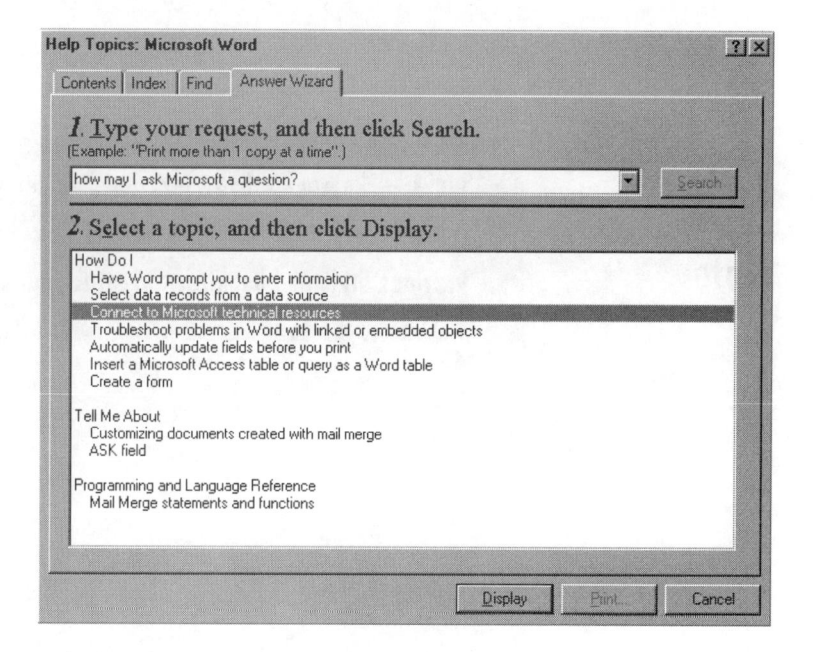

How to use a Help window

The information within the **Help** window describes how to complete a given task or explains something about your program or Desktop. Use is illustrated in Figure A.5.

Appendix A Help 409

Appendix A

Figure A.5
A Help window

Press to return to **Help Topics** windows

Press to return to previous help topic

Always keep Help window visible

Click underlined text to display an explanation of the term

Press to display a related help topic

Options menu

Note

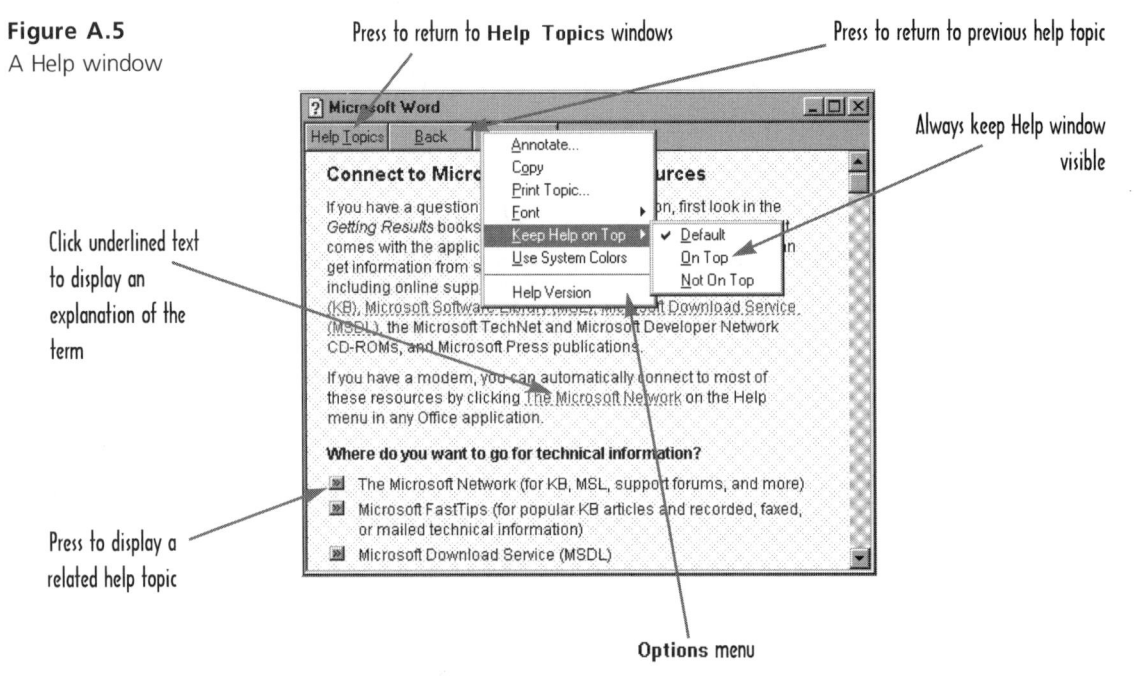

Links — known as hypertext links — let you navigate through related help topics. Press the Back button to display the previous topic and backtrack towards your starting point

410   Appendix A   Help

Appendix B

Windows 95 controls

Objectives

Windows 95 supplies a number of components like push-buttons and check-boxes that provide a consistent way of doing things with windows, dialog boxes and property sheets. These components are called *controls*.

This appendix forms a reference for all the standard Windows 95 controls.

Appendix B

Standard controls

Most of the controls supplied with Windows 95 are shown in the dialog box, Figure B.1.

Figure B.1
Windows 95 controls

[Figure B.1: Dialog box illustrating Windows 95 controls, with labels pointing to: Edit control, Scroll bar, Check box, Spin buttons, Radio button, Combo box, Push button, List box, and Drop-down list box.]

Each control can be operated by your keyboard as well as your mouse:

- operating a control with your mouse is simple, just point and click — it automatically becomes the focus for your actions
- operating a control with your keyboard is more difficult as, before it will respond to your keystrokes, you must make it the focus for your actions.

Note

> Controls are sometimes disabled (greyed) to reflect your program's context – the Find Next button in the Find dialog box, for example, is disabled until you type some text for it to find

When a control has received the input focus for your Desktop it is displayed in a slightly different way. This shows that it will respond to certain keystrokes as described below.

Push-buttons

Pressing a push-button causes something to happen — usually the action described by the label on its face.

Press a push-button by moving the mouse pointer over it then clicking your left mouse button — the push-button moves as you press and release the mouse button. You can also press `Enter` to operate a push-button if it has obtained the focus of your Desktop — indicated by a small dotted rectangle on the button's face.

Note

> **The default push-button has a thicker border and is pressed by your keyboard's `Enter` key if no other push-button has the focus**

Radio buttons

Radio buttons are just like channel selectors on an old radio or television — within a group of radio buttons only one can be depressed and this button indicates the current value of a particular program setting.

Click your left mouse button while the pointer is over a radio button to select the choice indicated by the button's label — any previous selection in the group is then removed. When a group of radio buttons have the input focus, a dotted line is drawn around the label of the button currently selected — you can change this selection by pressing the cursor keys (↑↓→←).

Note

> **A box normally surrounds a group of radio buttons — its label describes the program setting altered by the radio button selection**

Check boxes

Check boxes, unlike radio buttons, are operated independently of each other. A check box indicates whether a particular program setting is on or off — the label describes the setting.

Click your left mouse button while the pointer is over a check box to change the selection state of the box. This is indicated by a

Appendix B   Windows 95 controls   413

Appendix B

> **Note:** Check boxes may appear greyed when the selection state cannot be determined – a bold check box would be grey if some of the selected text was bold while some was not

cross or tick — the check mark. When a check box has the input focus a dotted line is drawn around its label to indicate that the selection state can be changed by pressing the space bar on your keyboard.

Edit boxes

Edit boxes are used to hold text typed from your keyboard — they share many of the editing facilities of a Word document window (see Chapter 4) within the context of a single line.

Click your left mouse button while the pointer is over an edit box to display a flashing cursor within the box — this indicates that the edit box has the input focus and will receive text typed from your keyboard. You can use your cursor keys (or mouse) to move the cursor within any text contained in an edit box. You can also use [Delete] *or* [←] *to remove the character immediately before or after the cursor.*

> **Caution:** Moving the input focus to an edit box often selects any text it contains – deselect this text (move the cursor) to avoid it being replaced by the first character typed at your keyboard

Edit boxes may exhibit some of the following features:

- an edit box can contain more characters than are displayed — use the cursor keys to move to the end or beginning of the your text
- you can cut and paste selected text using the Windows 95 Clipboard (cut — [Ctrl]+[X]; paste — [Ctrl]+[V] or [Shift]+[Insert])
- an edit box may have more than a single edit line so it can be used like a simple WordPad window.

Tip

> Press `Ctrl` + `Enter` to insert a new line in an edit box – pressing `Enter` alone activates any default push-button within the dialog box

Scroll bars

A scroll bar is used when something cannot be completely displayed within a window (or control). The ends of the scroll bar represent the extremities of the document (list or whatever) while the scroll bar's 'thumb' position and size indicates the part currently displayed. For example, a thumb that fills the top 75% of a scroll bar indicates the first three quarters of the document is displayed in the window.

Drag the scroll bar's thumb to change the part of the object that is displayed on your screen. You can also move the scroll bar's thumb by pressing the buttons at either end of the scroll bar or by clicking within the bar itself (above or below the thumb).

When the window (or control) to which the scroll bar is attached receives the input focus, you can then use your keyboard to operate the scroll bar by pressing the cursor keys on your keyboard.

Note

> Chapter 3 describes how scroll bars are used to change the part of a document displayed within a window

List boxes

List boxes contain a number of lines each describing a different item. Some list boxes allow you to select only a single item while others permit multiple selection — the selected items are highlighted.

Click a line within a list box to make a selection — the line is highlighted. When a list box has the input focus a dotted box is drawn around the selected item. You can then use the ↑ or ↓ cursor keys to move this dotted box up or down the list, automatically changing your selection as you go.

To select more than one item from a list box hold `Ctrl` *while clicking on subsequent lines. Alternatively, hold* `Ctrl` *while moving the dotted box (not highlighted) up or down the list — press the space bar to select further items. Once you release* `Ctrl` *the list box returns to its normal single selection mode.*

Tip

> You can select an entire range of items by selecting your first item then pressing `Shift` while selecting the last item in your range – all items between the first and last are selected

A scroll bar is attached to a list control when it contains more lines than can be displayed in the box — press the 'down' button at the bottom of the scroll bar to display lines lower down in the list.

Note

> List boxes provide a convenient way of displaying collections of similar information and often fill an entire window – see *Column controls*

Drop-down list boxes

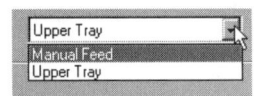

A drop-down list box is like a standard list box except that it normally occupies only the space required to display the currently selected item — a single line. A full list box is displayed when you press the button attached to this type of control and once you have made a selection, it closes up again.

When a drop-down list box has the Desktop's input focus the selected item has a dotted line drawn around it — you can then reveal its full list by pressing ↓. A selection is made from the list by pressing ↑ or ↓ to move the highlighted line to the appropriate item then pressing `Enter`.

Note

> Drop-down lists are operated like standard list boxes apart from the way they display their list

Combo boxes

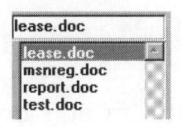

A combo box is a combination of an edit box and a list box. It provides a quick way to create a line of text by filling an edit box with a selection made from a list.

The **Font** dialog box contains a combo box to help you select **Font size** — you may click a font size within the list part of the combo box in order to copy the text into its edit part.

The two parts of a combo box indicate that they have the input focus in the same way as a normal edit and list box. They are also operated in the same way as separate edit and list boxes with two exceptions:

> - when a selection made in the list part, the text is automatically copied into the edit part
> - when text is typed into the edit part, the list part of the combo box attempts to select the nearest matching item — scrolling if necessary. You can also type a filter (e.g. *.doc) into the edit box so that the list will display only those items that match the filter (see Chapter 6).

Note

> Drop-down combo boxes (like drop-down list boxes) are operated in the same way as standard combo boxes apart from the way they display their list – see *Drop-down list boxes*

Column controls

A column control is yet another adaptation of a standard list box. This type of control is characterized by its capability to display separate columns of information within a list — the top line contains the column heading.

Drag the line that divides each column heading to adjust the width of the column in the list below.

Tip

> Press the column heading to sort the list by the items in that column – i.e. press the Date heading to re-arrange the list in order of each item's dates value

Appendix B   Windows 95 controls   417

Appendix B

Spin boxes

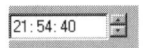

Spin boxes combine two small buttons with an edit box to facilitate the entry of numeric values — click the arrow buttons to change this value.

When a spin box has the input focus a flashing cursor appears in its edit area — you can then type values into the control from your keyboard, or press ⬆ or ⬇ to increase or decrease the value.

Note

> A button will be disabled (greyed) when the value in the edit area of a spin box reaches the limit of its permitted range

Slider controls

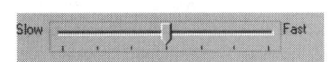

A slider controls looks like the volume control on a radio and serves to adjust values that do not have meaningful numeric settings.

The current value of the slider control is indicated by the position of it knob. You can adjust the setting by dragging this knob with your mouse or by using the keyboard's cursor keys — when the control has your input focus a dotted box is drawn around it.

Split handles

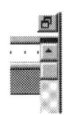

A split handle appears as a black bar at the top (or left hand side) of a scroll bar and allows you to divide the window into two parts — they each form a separate window that can be scrolled to display different areas of the same document.

Drag the split handle down the scroll bar to divide the window into two halves — each capable of showing a different area of the same document. Reunite the two halves of the window by dragging the split bar so that the size of one half is reduced to nothing.

418 Appendix B Windows 95 controls

Appendix C

Common keyboard shortcuts

Objectives

Discover the common keyboard shortcuts that make it easier for you to use Windows 95.

Note

Throughout this book, keyboard shortcuts are shown with key symbols. For example:

`Ctrl` + `Esc` means hold down the `Ctrl` key then press `Esc` – release both keys when done!

Manipulating windows

`F1`	opens Windows 95 **Help Topics** window
`Ctrl`+`Esc`	opens **Start** menu from Taskbar
`Alt`+`Tab`	switch between windows by repeatedly pressing `Tab` while holding down `Alt`

Dialog boxes and property sheets

`F1`	opens a help topic related to the task you are performing
`Tab`	moves input focus to next control
`Shift`+`Tab`	move input focus to previous control
space	inserts or removes a tick from a check box
`↑``↓`	changes your selection from a list
`Alt`+letter	moves the input focus to the control whose label contains the underlined letter (e.g. **Dri_v_es:** `Alt`+`V`)
`Esc`	equivalent to pressing **Cancel**
`Enter`	equivalent to pressing the default push-button (usually **OK**)

Qualifying mouse operations

`Ctrl`+click	after clicking the first item you may select others by holding down `Ctrl` while you click
`Shift`+click	after clicking the first item in a list you may select all the items in a range by holding down `Shift` while clicking the last item

Text manipulation

`Ctrl`+`X`	cut the selected text into the Clipboard — removes the selected text
`Ctrl`+`C`	copy the selected text into the Clipboard — leaves selected text in place
`Ctrl`+`V`	paste the contents of the Clipboard into the document (or edit box) at the cursor position
`Shift`+cursor	selects text from cursor position for each press of the cursor key
`F9`	updates the selected fields in a document

> **Tip:** You can often cut and paste text between edit box controls using these keyboard shortcuts

Menu operations

`Alt`	activates the menu bar — use the right (and left) cursor keys to highlight menu headings and the down cursor key to open them
`Alt`+letter	opens the menu whose heading contains the underlined letter (i.e. **File:** `Alt`+`F`)
`Alt`+space	opens the **Windows** menu belonging to the active main window
`Alt`+`-`	opens the **Windows** menu belonging to the active document window
`Esc`	de-activates the menu bar
`Ctrl`+letter	performs the action whose label contains the underlined letter (i.e. **Print:** `Ctrl`+`P`)

Appendix

Miscellaneous

[Print Screen] copies an image of the Desktop onto the Clipboard so you can paste it into a Paint window (or other graphics program)

[Alt]+[Print Screen] copies an image of the active window onto the Clipboard

Appendix D

Modem troubleshooting

Most modem problems are not difficult to resolve once you are able to identify the cause of the problem. This appendix will help you in this respect by explaining:

- steps required to establish a connection
- how protocols allow programs to communicate
- modem properties — fixing problems with your modem.

Most modems provide a speaker and a set of indicators in order to provide audible and visual confirmation of its operation. For example, when your modem is switched-on it performs a self-test and illuminates its **MR** or *modem ready* light — this indicates it is operational.

Objectives

Tip

Familiarize yourself with the abbreviations or special symbols used to identify the standard indicators provided by your modem — they help diagnose problems!

Appendix D

Steps required to establish a connection

After installing a modem on your Desktop you initiate a connection with a remote computer simply by starting the appropriate program, supplying a telephone number then pressing the **Dial** or **Connect** button. A typical connection is established as follows:

> *Your program seeks access, through Windows 95, to the modem you have specified in its dialing options or set-up (i.e. a Hayes Accura 144 modem) — this proceeds only if the modem has been correctly installed.*
>
> *Windows 95 attempts to communicate with the modem through a specific port (i.e. COM1), which corresponds to a socket at the back of your PC. The modem's terminal ready light illuminates if it is physically connected to the port on your PC that Windows 95 is testing — indicates the port settings are correct and the cable is good.*
>
> *Windows 95 sends a series of commands to your modem to initialize a new connection. The receive data and send data lights on your modem flash — indicates your modem and PC are communicating correctly.*
>
> *Your modem sends a message back to Windows 95 in order to identify itself — confirms the correct type of modem is connected to the port.*
>
> *Windows 95 informs your program that its request for the modem has been successful. Your program sends the telephone number to Windows 95 which is then passed to the modem as a dial command — adding area or country codes to the number as required (see page 347).*

TR

SD   RD

Figure D.1
Establishing the connection between modem and PC

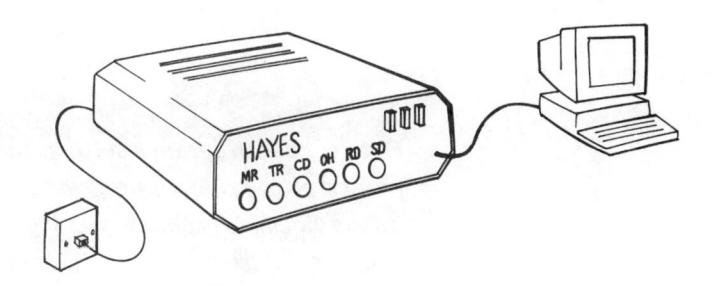

OH

The modem's off-hook *light illuminates and you will hear your telephone system's dialing tone (briefly) from a speaker within the modem* — this indicates the connection to the telephone system is correct.

Following the clicks or tones of a number being dialed you will hear a ringing tone — this confirms the telephone number you supplied is valid.

AA

After a few rings, the modem at the other end of the telephone line will answer your call (its *auto-answer light will illuminate*) and you will hear the two modems attempting to communicate — you have correctly dialed another modem.

CD

When the modems agree a common transmission speed the carrier detect *light on your modem will illuminate and the modem's speaker is switched-off* — the speed setting in your modem's **General** properties page is compatible with the remote modem (see Modem properties).

A special carrier detect *wire in the modem cable is used to inform Windows 95 that the line connection has been established at a particular speed* — both modems are compatible with each other.

Windows 95 tells your program that it can start communicating with the program running on the remote computer. The programs confirm that they share the same communication protocols — the modem's **Connection** page settings are correct.

Appendix D

Finally, your program's settings for user name and password are passed to the remote program so that you might gain access to its services. A greeting message is received from the remote program informing you of the services you may use — your user name and password have been recognized.

Figure D.2
Establishing a connection with a remote program

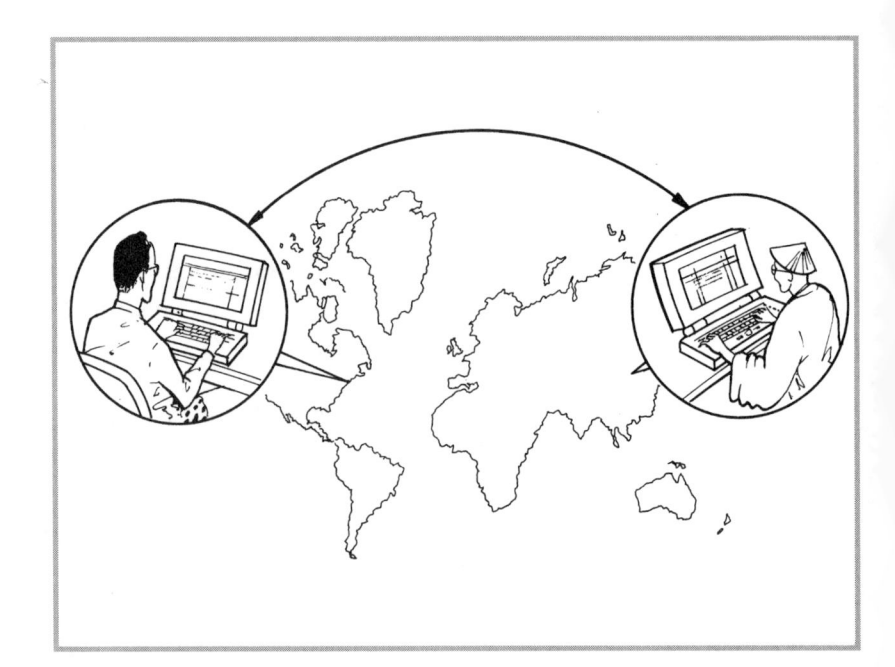

A connection establishes a secure path across which data can flow. The way that this data is used depends on the programs at either end of the connection; some programs transfer fax and email messages across the connection, other programs might transfer files or permit some form of on-line conferencing.

Protocols

Protocol defines the rules for conducting a particular transaction. The rules for communicating with your computer exists at many levels — just like an onion beneath each level there lies another layer.

Netiquette

At the top level there are protocols for language and acceptable behaviour between the people who are communicating. This protocol is formally defined on some networks (Internet's Netiquette) but otherwise may be loosely expressed in such terms as speaking English and being courteous. Failure to conform to behaviour protocols may result in you being *barred* from the network — failure to speak the correct language will simply mean that no one will understand you!

Kermit and TTY

Protocols are needed to control the commands and messages transferred between the program running on your PC and the program used by the remote computer. For example, when you want to *download* a file your program must enter a special mode that allows the data it receives to be stored in a file rather than displayed on your screen — file transfer protocols such as X-modem, Kermit, and so forth define how this will happen. Programs must also agree on the codes used to represent characters (character set) and the way text is handled. ASCII and TTY are common protocols for the *terminal emulation* required to communicate with *bulletin board services* (see Chapter 16).

Note
> Use your program's menu bar to set its *file transfer* and terminal *emulation* protocols — see appropriate help topic or the program manual

9600 Baud, 8 data bits, no parity, one stop bit

Beyond the format of commands and messages, the bits and bytes transferred between two computers must conform to a particular protocol. The serial port on your PC (i.e. COM1) is designed for *asynchronous* communication, such that each character is transmitted at certain rate and contained within a sequence of a *start* bit, a number of *data* bits, an optional *parity* bit and then a number of *stop* bits.

Any computer that is communicating with your PC must understand this simple protocol in order for it to build these characters back into your commands and messages — see *Modem properties*.

The rate at which characters are transferred is often stated in terms of *Baud* rate — in most instances it is the number of bits transmitted per seconds (BPS).

> **Note**
>
> You may buy special adapters for your PC that permit *synchronous* communication which is commonly used by mainframe and other larger computers

Modem standards — v.22, v.32, v.34

Modems have protocols that govern the way bits of data from your PC's serial port are converted into tones and vice versa, for transmission down a telephone line. These protocols are defined by international standards such as CCITT v.22, v32, and so forth — look for a label on your modem box that lists the standards to which it conforms. Table D.1 lists the common modem standards, together with baud rates — an indication of how fast modems transmit and receive data.

Standard	Rate
v.22	1200 baud
v.22 bis	2400 baud
v.32	4800, 9600 baud
v.32 bis	12000, 14400 baud
v.34	28,800 baud

> **Note**
>
> You are unlikely to encounter a modem whose transmission speed (BPS or baud rate) does not signify its support of the corresponding CCITT standard, listed above

Modem properties — fixing problems with your modem

Depending on the type of problem you are experiencing you may need to change your modem's properties.

Figure D.3
Accura 144 + FAX144 modem properties

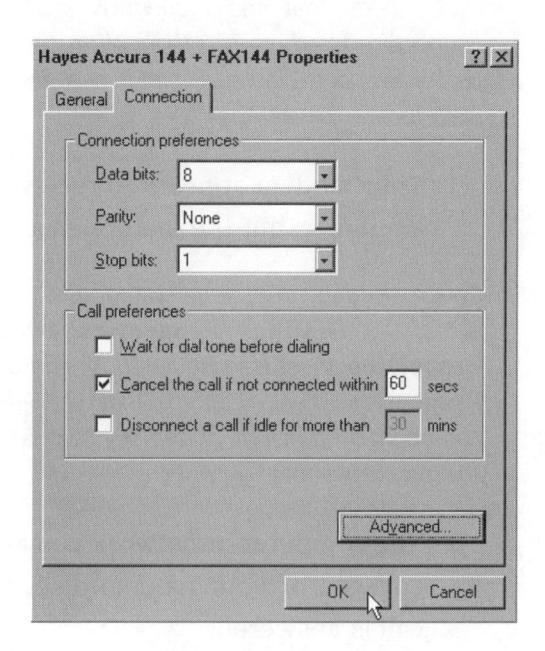

1. Use your Taskbar to open the **Control Panel** folder (**Start**➔ **Settings**➔**Control Panel**) then double-click the **Modems** icon in order to open its property sheet (see page 346). Select the modem whose properties you wish to alter then press the **Properties** push-button to open a further property sheet for this modem (Figure D.3).

2. Adjust the modem's settings with the pages of the property sheet (see below) then press **OK** to close the sheet. Finally, press the **OK** push-button in the **Modems Properties** sheet to close it — this exercise is complete!

Appendix D

Fixing problems with your modem

Here are some changes you might make to the settings in your modem property sheets in order to overcome a number of specific problems:

❑ A message box appears stating that your modem is not available.

*First, check that the modem is switched-on and physically connected to your PC, then click the tab for the **General** properties page (Figure D.4) and check that the value for the **Port** is correct — try another port.*

❑ Your modem appears to receive the instruction to dial a number, but the dial tone cannot be heard.

*Check whether your phone system uses pulse or tone dialing then press the **Dialing Properties** button in the **Modems Properties** sheet (see Figure 16.2), in order to open the **Dialing Properties** sheet. Confirm that your dialing settings are set appropriately (bottom of the **My Locations** page) then close this property sheet.*

❑ The computer or network you are dialing appears to be engaged or your modem disconnects immediately the call is answered.

Dial the telephone number with a normal telephone (connected to the same socket as your modem) in order to confirm that the number is correct and a modem is answering the call (listen for the high pitched tones). Try adding a comma after the telephone number used by your program (see page 432 for reasoning).

❑ A connection with a specific computer or network cannot be established, though the call seems to be correctly dialed and answered.

*Click the **General** tab in the property sheet belonging to the specific modem (Figure D.4) then alter the setting for **Maximum speed,** so that it corresponds to the transmission speed (e.g.*

9600) of the modem you are dialing — also try clicking the box **Only connect at this speed**. Click the **Connect** tab to bring this page to the forefront of the property sheet, then alter the settings for **Data bits**, **Parity** and **Stop bits**, so that they correspond to the connection details of the computer you are attempting to access — normally given as 96, 8, N, 1 (9600 baud, 8 data bits, no parity one stop bit).

❏ The connection often fails while you are transferring data.

Check whether your phone system uses call waiting (beeps if someone attempts to telephone you while you are using your phone) and discover the code that must be dialed to disable this feature (i.e. *43*).

Press the **Dialing Properties** button in the **Modems Properties** sheet (see Figure 16.2) in order to open the **Dialing Properties** sheet. Insert a tick into the box labelled **This location has call waiting** then type the code needed to disable the feature into the adjacent edit box, before pressing **OK** to close the property sheet.

Tip

> Reduce the Maximum speed settings (see above) to make your modem negotiate a slower transmission speed and so provide better resiliance for poor telephone line quality

Special problems when dialing through a switchboard

There's a number of special problems that can arise when your modem is connected to a switchboard (PABX) that requires you to dial 9 before dialing a number (see *Dialing properties*).

❏ Your modem appears to receive the instruction to dial a number but the dial tone cannot be heard.

Click the **Connection** tab in the property sheet belonging to the specific modem (Figure D-4), then remove the tick from the box **Wait for dial tone before dialing** (click it).

Appendix

❏ Your modem appears to successfully dial the number, but disconnects before a connection can be established with the other computer or network.

Add one, two, three or four commas after the final digit of the telephone number used by your program to dial the remote modem. Each comma causes your modem to pause for a few seconds, giving time for the remote modem to prepare itself for answering your call.

Note

> You will probably not encounter any further problems once you have determined the settings that work for your particular modem and telephone system.

Further troubleshooting

Windows 95 provides extensive assistance with modem problems from its help system (see Appendix A). Use your Taskbar's **Start** button to open the Help window then find the following topics from its **Index** page:

- ▷ Dialing telephone calls - troubleshooting
- ▷ Dialing another computer - troubleshooting.

You may also find that your modem manual contains a useful troubleshooting guide.

Appendix E

Microsoft Binder and Briefcase

While small documents are easily managed, it's not so with large one. Documents of more than just a handful of pages become unwieldy. Likewise, when you work on two or more computers you need help to manage the documents you carry between PCs. Windows 95 has in-built help:

- Microsoft Binder — understand how to add a collection of files as sections to a Binder document so that you can manage a large document. Create a Binder template so that you can generate the set of documents needed to start a new project

- Briefcase — why it is important to control versions of your documents. How to use Briefcase to synchronize copies of files located on different computers.

Microsoft Binder

Appendix E

You will seldom create a single Word file that contains more than twenty or thirty pages because large documents are difficult to handle. This book, for example, is divided into chapters which are stored as a collection of separate Word document files. Dividing a large document into separate files makes it easier for you to manipulate the individual parts (sections) but has the drawback of making it more difficult to manage the document as a whole — this is a problem solved by Microsoft Binder.

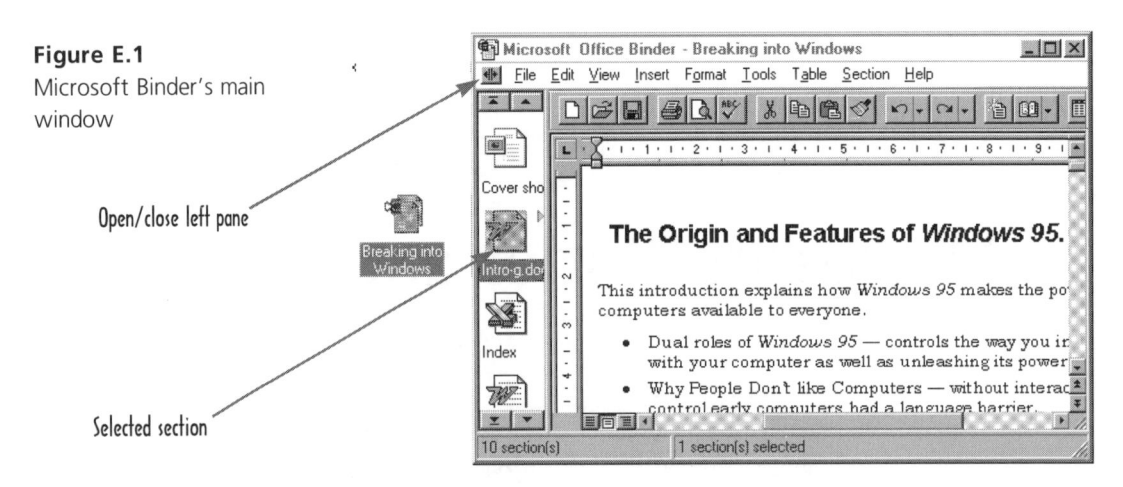

Figure E.1
Microsoft Binder's main window

Open/close left pane

Selected section

Microsoft Binder is a program supplied with Office 95 which allows you to create a single Binder document from a collection of document files which have been dropped into its main window. In this way you retain the capability of manipulating the contents of individual files (sections) while also being able to manage the document as a whole.

It may help you to think of a Binder as a program which displays the sections of a document in a special folder called

Note

> You can only add into a Microsoft Binder those documents which have been created by Microsoft Office programs – it does not currently accept other types of files

434   Appendix E   Microsoft Binder and Briefcase

a Binder document. Its window is arranged so that the contents of the Binder document are listed in the left hand pane and the currently selected section is displayed in the right hand pane.

The right hand pane of the Binder window assumes the character of the document window belonging to the program (Word, Excel, PowerPoint) which created the section it is displaying. The Binder's menu bar also changes to reflect the menus provided by the program which created the section it is displaying. Indeed, you can edit a section of the Binder document in the same way as you can from its original document window (this is part of the OLE technology described in Chapter 7).

There are two menu headings which contain items specifically belonging to Microsoft Binder:

- **File** — actions that apply to the whole Binder document; open, save, print, send and so forth. These menu options operate on Binder documents in the same way as **File** menu options operate on documents in other Office 95 programs
- **Section** — actions that apply to the selected sections of the Binder document; add, delete, print, save as and so forth. These menu options operate on selected sections of a Binder document just as if it was a separate document.

Tip

> Convert a Binder document into a collection of separate files within a standard folder by right-clicking its icon on your Desktop then applying the Unbind option

Creating a set of documents for a new project

You can create a new Binder document simply by starting the program and choosing **File→New Binder** from its menu bar — just like any of the other Office documents you have previously created.

Appendix E

Figure E.2
File→New — creating a new Binder document

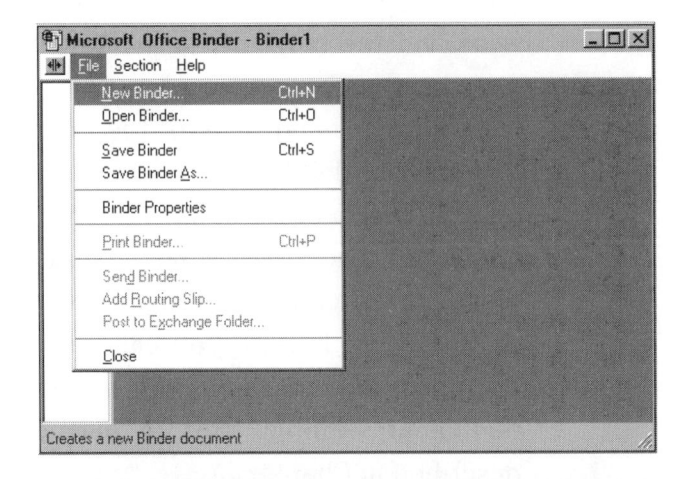

> **Tip**
>
> Create a new Binder document by pressing the Office Toolbar button Start a new document (see page 164) then select a suitable template from the Binder page of the New property sheet

Binder templates serve the same purpose as other types of Office templates — they provide a standard content and style for the document you are creating. You might, for example, decide to create a Binder template for generating all the standard documents needed for a new project. In this way whenever you need to start a new project you simply use this template to create a new binder document and all your standard project documents would be automatically created.

1   *Use your Office 95 programs to create the collection of documents needed to start a new project — leave gaps in these documents for information that is specific to a particular project. Store these documents on your Desktop then close any of the windows you have opened.*

2   *Start Binder from your Taskbar (*Start→Programs→Microsoft Office→Microsoft Binder*) and choose* File→New Binder *from its menu bar to create a new Binder document — select* Blank *binder and press* OK*.*

3. Open the left hand side of the Binder window by pressing the button on the far left of its menu bar. Drag the collection of documents created in step one then drop them into the left hand area of the Binder window to create the sections of your template.

4. Choose **File↪Save Binder As** from your Binder window's menu bar then select **Binder templates** from the control **Save as type** before saving the Binder template file in the **Binder** folder of the Office **Templates** folder (see page 165). Close the Binder window — this exercise is complete!

> **Note**
> When you create a new Binder document, the New Binder property sheet lists all the Binder templates that are stored in the Office Templates folder as well as any Binder templates you have created and stored in its Binder folder

Briefcase

Each time you make a copy of a file you also give yourself the opportunity to create a new version of the document it contains. Problems can arise when there are several versions of the same document stored in different folders:

- ▷ you might forget which file and folder contains the latest version of the document
- ▷ you can easily overwrite the latest version of your document with an older version from a different folder — particularly if they share the same file name.

The Windows 95 Briefcase has been developed to address these problems to manage your document's versions. It is particularly useful if you often copy files between different computers because you work at home as well as the office.

> **Note**
> Check Briefcase is installed on your Desktop by inspecting the components listed in the Windows Set-up page of the Add/Remove programs property sheet (see page 366)

Appendix E

1 *Open the **Briefcase** folder by double-clicking its icon on your Desktop. Drag some of your documents into the **Briefcase** window — this makes a copy of the documents and puts them in your Briefcase. Close the window.*

2 *Insert a floppy disk into your (office) PC then double-click the **My Computer** icon to open its View window so you can see the icon for this floppy disk drive. Drag the **Briefcase** icon from your Desktop onto the floppy disk icon in the **My Computer** window — this moves the Briefcase from your Desktop to the floppy disk.*

Figure E.3
Briefcase Update window

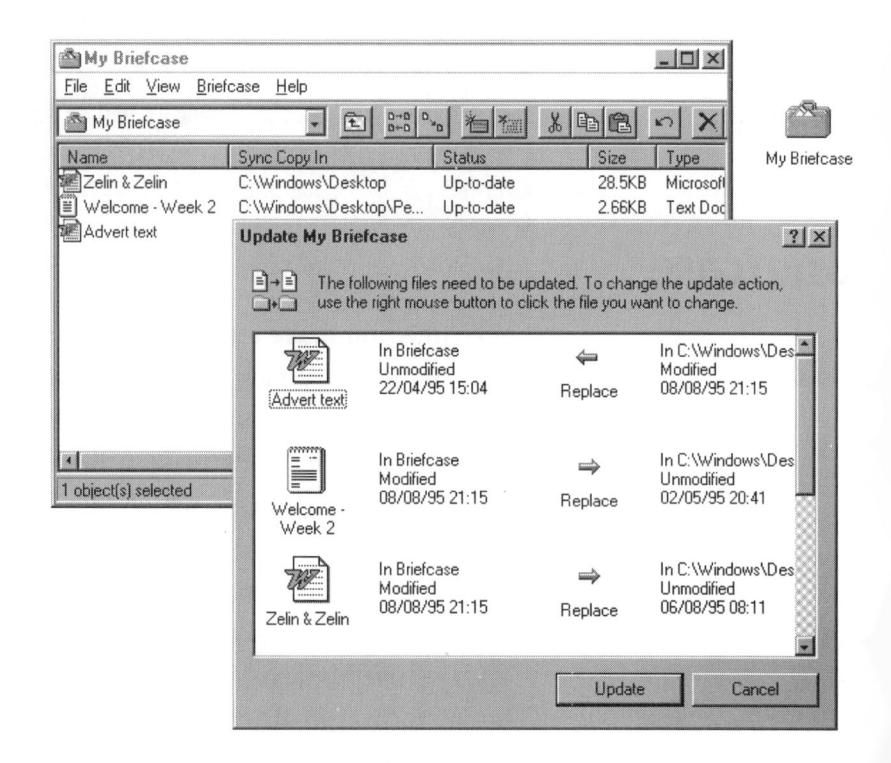

Note

Your Briefcase is *moved* not copied when dragged between locations on your PC — it is much easier to manage just one Briefcase so avoid creating other briefcase folders unless absolutely necessary

4   Eject the floppy disk and insert it into your home PC. Double-click the **My Computer** icon on this computer's Desktop to open its View window then open a further View window for its floppy disk drive (double-click the appropriate icon). Drag your **Briefcase** icon from the floppy disk's window onto the Desktop just like you would any other file or folder that you want to move into your home PC.

5   Open the Briefcase folder on your home PC's Desktop so you can work on the documents you have brought home (just double-click the document icon to start its program and open a document window). When you have finished with a document choose **File↪Save** from the menu bar and close its window — the changes are saved in the file located in your Desktop's Briefcase.

6   At the end of the evening update the contents of the Briefcase folder in your home PC's floppy disk by choosing **Briefcase↪Update All** from the menu bar of your Desktop Briefcase window. You will be prompted to confirm the update action (Figure E.3) — press **Update**. After the files have been copied across remove the floppy disk from your home PC.

7. Next morning insert the floppy disk into your Office PC and update the contents of the Briefcase folder on your office PC by choosing **Briefcase↪Update All** from the menu bar of its window — only the files that you changed while working at home are updated.

> **Tip**
>
> Display the contents of your Briefcase as a list (**View↪Details**) so you see the updated status of each file — orphan files (**Briefcase↪Split**) will never be updated because you have decided that they are not versions of the same document

Files and folders can be shared so they can be accessed from other computers on the network (see page 330) rather than being physically transported between PCs on floppy disk. This would permit the following:

Appendix E   Microsoft Binder and Briefcase   439

▷ You create a number of documents on your Desktop then put a copy of them into your Briefcase before moving them to the folder which you share with your boss

▷ Your boss connects to your PC and copies the contents of your shared folder into his Briefcase. He then alters some of your documents and updates the shared folder simply by choosing **Briefcase↪Update All**

▷ Next day you open your Briefcase folder and choose **Briefcase↪Update All** from its menu bar. All the files altered by your boss are identified and you are given the opportunity to update the original documents on your Desktop.

> **Note**
>
> When changes are made to both copies of the same file the alterations in each file must be *merged* together – Briefcase warns you of this conflict and ask which file should be updated so you can manually add the changes from the other document

Glossaries

Objectives

There are two glossaries:
- a glossary of common Windows 95 terms
- a glossary of common Windows 95 icons.

While neither is exhaustive, they both cover the Windows 95 interface to a degree most readers will find more than adequate.

Text glossary

access rights	rights are associated with your user name, so you can access resources (files, printers and so on) located on other computers, after logging on to a network.
active cell	the cell within an Excel worksheet that receives text typed from your keyboard; its insertion point.
annotation	a comment added to a document by a reviewer.
archive	to store files and folders away from your PC in case they are needed again (see *back-up*).
archive attribute	a value associated with a file that is *set* when the file is altered and *reset* by a program that makes *backup* copies of the files in your PC (see *file attributes*).
aspect ratio	the height of a display in relation to its width.
backup	copies of a file (or folder) made in case the original is lost or accidentally erased from your hard disk.
BBS	bulletin board service; used for distributing information among people who share a common interest.
box	see *dialog box, message box, check box*.
branch	the part of a pathname needed to locate a file from a specific folder.
briefcase	a special Windows 95 folder that can be used to coordinate updates to the documents it contains.
bulleted lists	a list whose items are marked by bullet points (small dots).
call waiting	a facility provided by your telephone system that causes a tone to be made when someone attempts to call you while you are already using your telephone.
carriage return	inserted at the end of a line of text in order to start a new line (see *enter key, hard return, soft return*).

check box	a box that contains a check mark (tick). Specify an option by clicking the box to remove or insert the check mark.
child window	a window that belongs to another window (i.e. document windows are child windows of the program's main window).
client area	the working area of a window in which documents and so forth are displayed (see Figure 2.2).
client PC	a computer that uses the facilities provided by a *server* PC (files, folders, database, and so forth).
client-server network	a LAN composed of many *client* PCs and much fewer *server* computers (contrast with *peer-to-peer network*).
ClipArt	a collection of drawings that can be inserted into your documents.
close button	the small button at the top right of a window that closes the window when pressed (clicked) with your mouse.
context-sensitive help	Windows 95 Help invoked in such a way that it displays a help topic related to the task you are performing.
continuation menu	a menu that pops-up when you point at the arrowhead in another menu.
Control Panel	a folder that provides access to the windows needed for maintaining your computer (i.e. install new devices, programs, change system settings and so forth).
cue cards	a window containing a sequence of instructions for performing tasks.
database	a structured collection of data.
dialog box	a small window that appears on your Desktop so that you can apply values or change settings used by your program (or Windows 95).
dial-up networking	see *remote access*.
dial-up server	see *remote access server*.

directory	an alternative term for folders, often used by Windows 3.1 and MS-DOS programs.
DNS Server	the computer at an Internet site that converts your IP address into a host and domain name, and vice versa.
document window	serves to display a particular document and is contained within a program's main window.
domain name	1) the name of a group of computers within an office network. 2) the name of an Internet site (see *host name*).
download	to transfer a file from a remote computer on to a PC (contrast with *upload*).
drag-and-drop	mouse action, in which you drag an object to another position.
drag-select	selecting an object by dragging the mouse pointer around it.
email	a message transmitted through a computer network to a specific person or group of people (see *message services*).
email address	an address (such as BillStott@msn.com) used to send a message to someone who has a connection to a particular message service (see *Personal Address Book*).
embed	insert a separate copy of an object into a document (see *OLE*).
endnote	a reference that appears at the end of a document (see *footnote*).
enter key [Enter]	(1) inserts a carriage return into text, or (2) performs some action.
Exchange profile	a collection of settings that determine the properties of the message services made available.
Exchange Server	a program located on the office network's server that accesses a central store for messages and documents.
Explorer	a special window divided into two that displays a collection of items within a hierarchy.

extended selection	selecting more than one object by pressing Ctrl while clicking.
fax-modem	a modem that can send and receive fax messages as well as transfer data with other computers.
field	the values in a particular column within a list; a value that belongs to an item (see *record*, *table*).
file attribute	a setting that changes the properties of a file (see *read-only*, *hidden*, *system*, *archive*).
file transfer protocol	the syntax and message format required to transfer files between computers using a modem (e.g. Kermit).
filter	(1) a special program that converts the format of one file into that of another; (2) removing all the items in a list that do not match a special *filter value* (see *wildcards*).
Find window	a window that displays a list of files, folders and so forth that match specified criteria.
floppy disk	a magnetic disk that can be removed from your PC on which you store a collection of files and folders.
font	a collection of characters belonging to the same typeface. Typefaces are defined in terms of design, size, and style (e.g. Times Roman, 10 point, italic).
footer	the area at the bottom of a page that contains information such as page number.
footnote	a reference that appears at the bottom of a page (see *endnote*).
format	the structure and organization of the data within a file depends on the program that created it — its format.
Formula bar	an edit box located in Excel's main window that permits you to change the contents of the *active* cell.
frame	a container for pictures, tables and so forth in a Word document.
FTP	a program used to transfer files across the Internet.

greyed	an item that is not available due to the context of the program (or window).
gridlines	lines that mark rows and columns in a document; they are displayed in your window but are not printed in the final document.
GUI	graphical user interface; a Windows 95 style Desktop.
hard disk	a magnetic disk internal to your PC that can store a large collection of files and folders.
hard return	press [Enter] to insert a hard return at the end of a paragraph (see *carriage return*, *soft return*).
hardware	the physical components of your PC such as the disk drive, processor and memory chips (contrast with *software*).
header	the area at the top of a page that contains information such as the document's title (see *footer*).
help topic	information about a particular subject displayed in a help window.
Help Topics window	the window that permits you to select an individual help topic.
help window	a window that contains a help topic.
hidden attribute	a setting that normally prevents a file or folder from being displayed in a window; hidden files usually belong to a program or Windows 95.
hierarchy	a collection arranged like an family tree from an apex or *root* folder; an item's position indicates its relationship to the collection.
highlighted	items that are displayed differently to signal that they have the Desktop focus or are selected.
host name	the name used to log on to the Internet; the name of a computer that is connected to an Internet domain.
hotspot	the part of a mouse pointer than must cover an object in order that an action can be applied (click, drag, etc.).

hourglass	the mouse pointer assumes the shape of an hourglass when your system is busy and cannot accept further input.
hypertext	(1) an item of text in a Help window that contains a link to another help topic; (2) the link within a document that connects it to other documents.
in-place editing	double-click on an object inserted into your documents in order to open the window required to edit it.
insert mode	characters typed from the keyboard are inserted into the text, existing characters are moved along to make room (see *over-write mode*).
insertion point	the position in a document where something is entered, usually marked by the cursor (see *cursor*).
Internet site	a computer that forms part of the Internet, with resources you can access.
IP address	a series of codes that uniquely identify a computer location on the Internet.
Kermit	a communications protocol used for transferring files between computers.
LAN	local area network; (see *office network*).
link	to insert an object into your document that maintains a reference to its source file, rather than forming a separate copy (see *OLE*).
list box	a special control that permits you to make a selection from a list of items.
local devices	devices that are physically located in your PC (contrast with *network devices*).
log off	disconnect from a network.
log on	supply a user name and password to connect with a network, so that you can share files and resources with other people.

macro sheets	a special form of program that can be added to an Excel's workbook in order to perform a particular task.
mail	a message received from an email service.
mailbox	a store for messages; often located on a server computer in case your PC is not switched on.
main window	the window opened on your Desktop when you start a program (see Figure 2.2).
mainframe	a large computer system that usually contains an organization's central database.
mapping devices	assigning a drive name (i.e. *h:*) to a folder accessed across a network so that it behaves like a local disk drive.
maximize window	a window in a form that occupies the largest area of your Desktop permitted by its program, often the entire screen.
member ID	user name on the Microsoft Network.
menu bar	a list of menu headings immediately below the window's title bar. Click one of these heading to reveal its menu.
message box	a small window that appears on your Desktop for informational purposes (see *dialog box*).
message services	message delivery systems such as MS Mail, CompuServe mail, Internet email and so forth.
messages	a collection of text, graphics or embedded files that have been sent to you through a message service (see *email*).
minimize window	a window that has been hidden from your Desktop and is represented as a button on your Taskbar (or within the client area of its main window).
modal	a dialog box or window that must be closed before you can continue working with other windows.
mouse	the device attached to your PC that allows you to point, click, drag and double-click things on your Desktop.
MS-DOS mode	an operating mode of Windows 95 that provides complete compatibility with previous versions of MS-DOS.

multiple selection	selecting more than one object by pressing `Ctrl` while clicking further objects (see *extended selection*).
network	a collection of computers that can communicate with each other (see *WAN, LAN*).
network adapter card	a card that connects your computer to a particular type of network cable (i.e. an Ethernet or Token ring card).
network administrator	the person who administers a network and controls the access rights of its users.
network devices	devices that are physically located in other computers and must be accessed through the network (contrast with *local devices*).
object	a general term for pictures, graphics, figures, text and so forth.
OLE	object linking and embedding — the Windows 95 technology that permits pictures and other objects to be inserted into *container* documents.
object packaging	putting an object into a package that is represented by an icon.
OCR	optical character reader; a program or device that converts a printed page into a computer readable form (see *scanner*).
office network	a computer network formed by connecting together PCs within a single building or area (LAN).
on-line	interaction between programs (or people) using remote communications.
operating system	a collection of programs and modules that work beneath the surface of your Desktop to make the power of the computer's hardware available to you.
outline	a document displayed in terms of its section headings, so that you can view (and alter) its structure.
overwrite mode	characters typed from the keyboard overwrite existing characters, right of the cursor (see *insert mode*).

parent window	a window that contains, or owns, other *child* windows (i.e. Word's main window is the parent of its various child document windows).
password	a secret word used to control access to a file or other resource.
pathname	the absolute location of a file in terms of the various folders in which it is contained (see *hierarchy*).
PC	a computer that can operate Windows 95. It is defined as an IBM-compatible personal computer based on Intel processor architecture.
peer-to-peer network	a LAN composed of PCs that share resources among each other without the need for a *server PC* (see *client-server network*).
Personal Address Book	a collection of addresses that are used to send messages to people through a particular message service (see *email address*).
Personal Information Store	a folder within Microsoft Exchange that contains your messages.
Photo-CD	a compact disk that contains photographs taken with a conventional camera.
plug and play	a technology that permits devices to be added to your PC without complex installation procedures. Plug and play devices are often made immediately available to your Desktop.
point size	the size of a font is measured in points (pt); one point is approximately 1/72 inch.
pop-up menu	a menu belonging to an object that is revealed when you use your right mouse button to click the object.
pop-up window	a small rectangular area that provides a description of an object on your Desktop or (underlined) word within a help topic.

port	an external connection to your PC (LPT1, COM1, etc.) used by a printer, modem and so forth.
Postoffice	a collection of mailboxes used by MS Mail to deliver messages (see *message services*).
printer driver	a program supplied by a printer manufacturer that makes specific facilities of the printer available to the Desktop.
Printer folder	a folder that contains an icon for each of the printers that have been installed on your Desktop.
program	a set of instructions to a computer (see *software*).
properties	the settings that control the behaviour of an object.
protocol	the convention required to complete a transaction or pass a message between two computers.
push-button	a control that has the appearance of a rectangular button — press it to initiate the action indicated by its label.
Quick View window	a window opened from an icon's pop-up menu that displays the contents of its document file.
radio button	a control that belongs to a group of similar buttons and which permits the selection a particular option.
read-only attribute	a setting that prevents a file or folder from being altered, i.e. it can be viewed (read), but not changed.
record	the values in a particular row within a list; an item that has a number of associated values (see *field*, *table*)
relational database	a collection of tables that share common columns of information.
remote access	attaching a computer to your office network in a dial-up link through a modem and telephone network (also known as *dial-up networking*).
remote access server	the computer that answers calls from other computers in order to establish a dial-up link (also known as *dial-up server*).

resizeable window	the normal form of a window on your Desktop (see Figure 2.2) that can be moved and resized.
restore button	press a window's restore button to change it into a resizeable window.
review marks	the marks that appear in the margin next to lines in a document that have changed.
right-click	point to an object and then press your right mouse button.
rounding errors	errors in a calculation caused by *rounding* a number to a particular precision (i.e. 9.127 rounds to 9.13).
scanner	devices that convert a printed page into a document that can be stored as a file on your PC (see *OCR*).
screen saver	a moving image that covers the Desktop when you have not used your mouse or keyboard for a pre-set period (move your mouse to restore the Desktop).
scroll bar	a horizontal or vertical bar attached to the edge of a window (or list); used to view other parts of a document or list.
series	a sequence of information that can be described by a mathematical formula (i.e. 2,4,16…).
server PC	a computer that provides the facilities required by *client* PCs — access to shared resources and so forth.
shortcut	an icon that knows the location of a specific file; double-click it to start a program or open a particular document.
soft return	programs automatically insert a soft return when a line of text exceeds a certain length (see *hard return, word-wrap, carriage return*).
software	the programs and modules needed to operate your computer.
sorting	re-arranging the order of rows within a list according to the values in a particular column.

sound card	an adapter card installed inside your PC that gives it stereo sound facilities.
split handle	a control located at the end of a scroll bar; used to divide a window into two parts.
spreadsheet	a document formed from a collection of cells arranged into rows and columns — used to manage information as well as performing calculations.
Start button	a special button on your Taskbar that provides access to a large hierarchy of menus.
status bar	the bar at the bottom of a window that displays information about the program or the selected menu choice.
styles	a set of formatting information that applies to a particular component of your document.
system administrator	the person who administers your computer system (see *network administrator*).
system attribute	a setting that normally prevents a file or folder from being displayed in a View window or elsewhere; system files usually belong to Windows 95.
tab	(1) a hidden character inserted into a document by pressing the [Tab] key; it serves to align columns of figures by representing a specific distance from your margin or previous tab; (2) the flap at top of a page in a property sheet that contains its title — click the tab to bring the page into view.
table	a list of information formed by columns (fields) and rows (records).
tape backup	a device that stores files and folders on its magnetic tape in order to backup the hard disks in your computer.
Taskbar	the grey bar attached to an edge of your screen that contains the **Start** button and message area, as well as a button for each window that is open on your Desktop.

terminal emulation	a program (or setting within a program) that makes your PC behave like a VDU or terminal for the purposes of communicating with another computer.
title bar	the bar immediately below a window's top border containing its name — use the title bar as a handle to drag the window across your Desktop.
trends	the analysis of data to reveal an underlying mathematical *series* that can be used to extrapolate the information.
tutorial	a program that provides an interactive learning tool about a particular subject (computer based training).
upload	to transfer a file from a PC to a remote computer (contrast with *download*).
user interface	the part of a program that is operated by you the *user*.
user name	the name used to identify someone on a computer network.
user profiles	the settings that apply when a particular user logs on to the network (see *access rights*).
VDU	visual display unit; a traditional terminal.
view	a specific collection of information that is formed by combining a number of different tables sharing common columns (see *relational database*).
View window	a special window that displays the contents of a folder.
virus	a rogue computer program that hides itself within your PC and then disrupts its operation.
WAN	wide area network; a network, such as Internet or CompuServe, that connects computers over long distances using data communication equipment.
what if scenarios	a means of modelling data in an Excel worksheet .i.e. *what if my profit figure was 10% higher... what sales data would be need to support this scenario?*
wildcards	the characters '?' and '*' serve to match any individual letter or sequence of letters when searching a list of text.

window menu	menu at the top left of a window that permits you to control its appearance on your Desktop.
Windows 3.1	the previous version of the Windows operating system for your PC, now replaced by Windows 95.
Windows 95	the latest Windows operating system for your PC.
Wizard	a special program that takes you step by step through a complex task by asking you to select options from a series of windows.
word-processor	a type of program like Word that is used for producing reports, correspondence and so forth.
workbook	an Excel document that is stored in its own file and contains a number of worksheets.
workgroups	a group of computers that form a *peer-to-peer* network, sharing resources and information without need of a *server* PC.
worksheet	the part of a workbook that contains the rows and columns of cells forming a spreadsheet.
wrap-around	when a line of text exceeds a certain length it automatically starts a new line; a soft return is inserted so that you do not need to press [Enter] (see *carriage return*, *enter key*).

Icon glossary

Note

> An icon is a small picture that represents an object in the Windows 95 environment

Desktop

My Computer	My Computer
Network Neighborhood	Network Neighbourhood
Recycle Bin	Recycle Bin
Inbox	Inbox
Shortcut to Telnet	Shortcut to a program

Devices

HP DeskJet 1200C	Printer
Modems	Modem
3½ Floppy (A:)	Floppy disk drive
Win95 (C:)	Hard disk drive

CD-ROM

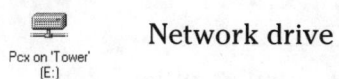

Network drive

Network printer

File types

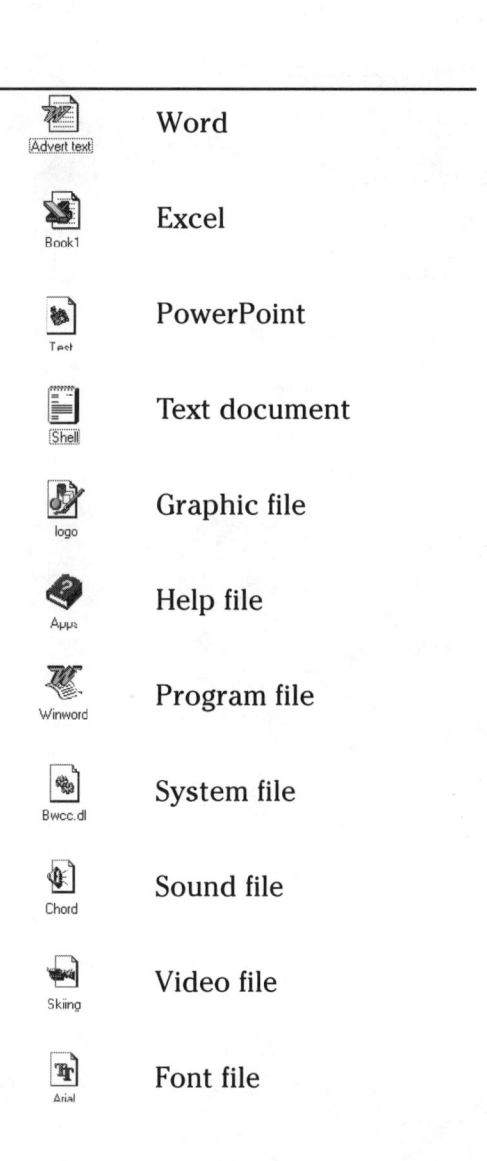

Word

Excel

PowerPoint

Text document

Graphic file

Help file

Program file

System file

Sound file

Video file

Font file

Containers

⊞-📁 bill		Closed folder (containing other folders)
⊟-📂 hill		Open folder (part of a path)
📕 Introducing Windows		Closed help chapter
📖 Introducing Windows		Open help chapter
📁 Fax Folder		Shared folder

Index

A

action 61
    applying (table) 93
    undoing 94
Address book 375
    create entry 375-376
    email address 361
Answer Wizard 409
application 25

B

backspace 104
backup, see *files and folders*
baud rate, see *data transfer rate*
Binder 434
branch, see *filing system*
Briefcase 10, 437
browse, see *dialog box*
bulletin board services 349-355

C

caps lock key, see *keyboard*
carriage return, see *document, enter key*
CD-ROM 119
cell 184
character 56

characters per second, CPS, see *data transfer rate*
check box, control 413
check mark 65
click 20, see also *mouse*
client-server 328
clipboard 141, 143
column 202
COM1, communications port 345
combo box, control 417
communication 424-426
    standards 342
    support for 10
CompuServe 359, 366, see also *WimCim*
    address 374
    mail 370, 373
computer
    access to remote, see *HyperTerminal, dial-up*
    adding fax facilities 371-373
    busy 23, 100
    changing date and time 395-396
    changing settings 393-394
    connecting to a modem 345, 424
    connecting to a network (LAN), see *network*
    connecting to a printer 337-338
    connecting to Internet 361-363

    contents of your 300
    Dial-up access 357
    list of drives in 118
    name on network 334, 288
    remote administration of 400
    security 357
    server PC 329
    setting dialing location of 347
    sharing with other people 325, 399
    stored passwords 399
    switching-on,off 14, 27, 278, 276, 290
    using Desktop 5
    using GUI 5
    using MS-DOS 2
    using Windows 95 2
container 148, see also *OLE*
continuation menu 23
control 75
    operating with keyboard 102
    list of 412-418
control panel 285, 393-394
copy, cut 142, see also *clipboard, file, folder*
correction 94, 104, see also *undo, delete, backspace*
crop 183, see also *Word document*
cursor 54
    moving with keys, mouse 55, 109

D

data bits, modems 428
data transfer rate, modems 428
database 239
date, changing, see *computer*
default 65
delete 104, see also *Exchange message, file, folder*
Desktop 5
   benefits of 8
   changing background 400
   contents of 15, 277, 400
   copying image to Clipboard 421
   folder hierarchy 310
   how to use 93, 96, 290-295
   list of installed printers 82
   obtaining assistance 404-410
   pop-up menu 291
   printing from 318
   properties of 400
   relationship to window 34
   restoring settings 325, 399
   security 401
   shutdown 14, 27, 276, 278, 290
   tidy-up 48-50, 291, 295
   using icons 296
   using several programs 279-280
   devices 338-339
   dial-up 355-358, see also *network*
     access to Internet 360
     server 357

dialog box
   types 33, 75, see also *property sheet*
   use 65-66, 74-76, 77, 420
dialog box, general types
   about 70, 81
   browse 149, 320
   font 395
   insert picture 153
   link 152
   Microsoft ClipArt gallery 264
   object 149
   open 132
   print 66, 74
   print (adjusting settings) 77
   print (select printer) 82
   replace text 199
   save As 128-129, 130
   spelling 195
   toolbars 67
dialog box, specific
   Address book, new entry 375
   Desktop, changing password 325
   Desktop, changing Windows password 325
   Desktop, enter network password 16, 322-323
   Desktop, map network drive 334
   Desktop, run 289
   Desktop, shut down 25, 326
   Dial-up, connect to 358
   Excel, AutoFormat 229
   Excel, define name 221
   Excel, protect sheet 251
   Excel, series 216

   Excel, sort 244
   HyperTerminal, connect 350
   HyperTerminal, connection description 352
   HyperTerminal, receive file 354
   PowerPoint, apply design template 267
   PowerPoint, print 272
   PowerPoint, slide setup 271
   PowerPoint, slide show 269
   Word, Break 188
   Word, Header and Footer 173
   Word, modify location 127
   Word, paragraph 191
   Word, printing 70
   Word, Style 192
distribution lists, see *Exchange*
DNS server, see *Internet*
document 33
   adding to Start menu 392-393
   attaching to messages 379
   classification, see *file*
   clearing document menu 393
   combining together 434
   create from Desktop 292
   creating from Office Bar 164
   creating set for new project 436
   default folder for 127
   downloading 354
   electronic distribution, see *Exchange*

faxing, see *Exchange message*
filing, see *folder*
finding lost 68, 286-287
for formulas, see *Excel*
for graphics, see *PowerPoint*
for lists, see *Excel*
for presentations, see *PowerPoint*
for text, see *Word*
group-working 389
importing, see *file conversion*
inserting lines, paragraphs (return) 55-56
inserting pictures, see *Word, inserting pictures*
inserting sound, see *Word, adding sound*
linking to 148-152
looking-up information, see *Excel*
managing versions of 437
moving information between 141-142
opening from Desktop 292
opening from Office Bar 164
opening from Taskbar 284
preview as printed 88
print preview 87-88
print settings 80
print, copies 77
print, selection of pages 78
printing, see *print job, dialog box*
printing binder 435
printing from Desktop 292, 318
printing, abort 316
properties of, see *file*
protection and security,
see *Excel-cell, file, folder*
quick view 293
read-only 331, see also *protection*
restoring from file 132
save as different file type 147
saving changes 130
scrolling 109
setting tabs 103
setting typeface 190
sharing with other people
storing in file 115, 128-130
types of 162
transferring information 140-158
document icon
  dropping on Desktop 96
  pop-up menu 292, 294-295
document properties
  custom page 206
  statistics page 257
  summary page 169
domain 322, 328-330
DOS prompt 3, see also *MS-DOS*
double-click, see *mouse*
drag 21
drag-drop, see *mouse*
drag-select, see *mouse*
dragging, see *mouse*
drive 118
  creating free space 119, 314, 305
  display contents of 120, 300
  mapping network drives 313
  names, labels 122, 305
  types and properties 119
drive icon 118
drop-down list, control 416

E

email, see *Exchange*
email address, see *Address book*
edit box, control 414
editing text
  aligning columns (tabs) 103
  backspace, delete 60, 104
  cutting and pasting 141-142
  edit box 414, 417
  insert, overwrite mode 60
  starting new paragraph 104
enter key 55, 76
Entire network folder 329
esc key, see *cancel*
Excel
  #errors 251, 252
  accuracy, rounding errors 248
  data entry forms 241
  function Wizard 238
  entering formula 213, 246
  main window 162, 209
  names box 222
  workbook, worksheet 203
Excel document
  capacity of 234
  creating a workbook 204
  creating a worksheet 207
  finding data 235-239, 242
  formatting worksheet 228-229
  hidden rows, columns, worksheets 228
  hiding formulas 250
  importing data into 240
  improving presentation of 225
  invoice 237
  list, creating 210-211

Index   461

lists, designing 234-235, 252
lists, filtering 243-245
lists, sorting 242-244
looking-up information 235-239
moving worksheets 207
removing gridlines and headings 227
setting margins 226
setting print area 226
totalising a column of figures 213-214
Excel template 205
Excel, cell
  format, shading 229
  moving 218, 220
  capacity 209
  clearing and deleting 218
  cut and pasting 217-218
  filling with a series 214-216
  format, codes 231
  format, currency values 211
  inserting rows 219
  naming 220-223
  operating on 210-218
  operators and values 247
  protection 249-251
  reference 223
  selecting 217
Exchange
  accessing your PostOffice 373-374
  address book 374-376
  address formats 374
  addressing messages 377-378
  changing message service 371
  designing message forms 389
  distributing documents 389
  distribution lists 374
  email 381-384
  Fax Wizard 386-387
  fax, support for 385-388
  installation information 373
  installing message service, fax 371-373
  main window 377
  managing your mail 381-384
  message form 374
  message services 370-390
  MS-mail 370-373
  MSN mail (Internet) 370, 373
  personal address book 372
  personal information store 372
  personal information store 380-383
  profile 371, 373
Exchange folder
  delete items 380
  inbox 380-384
  outbox 381
  sent items 381
Exchange message
  attaching files to 378-379, 383
  deleting 383
  delivery options 379
  managing 381-384
  printing 382
  receiving 383-384
  receiving, fax 387-388
  replying to 385-386
  sending messages 377-380
  sending, fax 386-387
  sorting 382
  standard form 377
Explorer window, see also *Windows Explorer*
  Exchange 381-384
  MSN 364

F

F1 key, see *Help*
Favorites folder 130
Fax 342, see also *Exchange*
Fax Viewer 388
field 180
file 115
  archiving, backup 307
  attaching to messages 379, 384
  backup 307
  changing properties 305
  classification 114
  combining together 434
  conversion 146-147
  copying 292
  delete 291, 296, 303
  down-loading 351-355
  embedding, linking 148-152
  finding lost 286-287
  listing information about 309
  moving 307, 311
  naming rules 123
  opening different types of files 146-147
  properties 206, 216, 257, 169
  protection, password 135
  protection, read-only 134
  recovering from delete 293,

462 Index

314
   recovery after power-cut, see *Word, options*
   referencing and naming 123-125
   renaming 304
   sending to fax 294
   sharing with other people 330-335
   short-cut 293
   transfer protocol 427
   updating versions of (Briefcase) 437
filing system
   creating your own 125-127, 302
   hierarchical 114, 302
   pathname, referencing files 120, 124-125, 335
filtering a list, wildcard 132
find
   files, folders, computers 286-287
   finding text, see *Word document*
floppy disk, see also *drives*
   backup 307
   formatting 118
   running a program from 289
focus 45
   applying to a control 412
   applying to a window
   changing in dialog box 420
folder 117
   arranging into hierarchy 302
   backup 307
   Briefcase 437
   controlling access to 331
   copying 294, 296, 307

   create from Desktop 291
   create your own 125, 130, 301
   create from Save as dialog box
   create from View window 301
   delete 303
   display contents of 120, 300
   filing documents 125-127
   finding lost 286-287
   fonts 395
   listing from toolbar 313
   moving 307, 311
   naming rules 123
   personal information store 380-381
   properties of 117
   protection 305, 336
   sharing with other people 330-335
   short-cut to 293
   rename 292
   root 300
font, see *typefaces*
formatting, see *floppy disk*

G

games, support for 9

H

handle 41
hard disk, see *drives*
help
   answering your questions 409
   F1 404
   how to obtain 69, 108, 288, 404-405
   topics window, locating topics 405-408
   window, assistance with task 410
hierarchy, see *file system*
hints, how to display 98, 404
host name, access to Internet 360
HyperTerminal 353
   access to BBS 349-355
   making a connection 351-353

I

icon 38
   Control Panel 394
   Desktop 42
   dropping documents to printer 318
   Inbox, see *Exchange*
   Mail and Fax 371, see *Exchange*
   menus 97
   Microsoft Network 277, 363
   My Briefcase 277, 438
   Network Neighborhood 277, 326-327
   pop-up menu 291-292
   pop-up menu 292
   Recycle bin 277, 296
   window menu 42
installing
   dial-up networking 355-356
   Exchange 371-373
   modems 344-345
   MSN 364
   printers 337-338
   programs 366
   TCP/IP 361-362

Internet
  terminal (TTY, VT100) 351-352
Internet
  connecting and disconnecting 359-363
  DNS Server 360
  email address 361
  programs available with 363
  service provider 360
Internet mail, see *Exchange*
invoice, see *Excel template*
IP address 360

J

justified 191

K

kermit, file transfer protocol 427
keyboard
  advantages of 110
  changing focus 412
  editing text 103-104
  lock keys 107
  operating menu bar 106-107
  settings for 397
  standard short-cuts 107, 420-422
  switching between programs 110

L

landscape, page orientation 188
letter heading, see *Word template*
list 234
list box, control 415
log on, log off, see *network*
LPT1, port name 83

M

member ID 363
menu 22
  making a selection 22
  menu bar 62-66
  operating with keyboard 105-106, 421
message box 34, 86
  print manager 86
  save changes 27, 87
messages, see *Exchange*
Microsoft Backup 308
Microsoft Binder, see *Binder*
Microsoft Exchange, see *Exchange*
Microsoft Mail, see *Exchange*
Microsoft Network, see *MSN*
modem 10
  changing settings 346
  connection to computer 424
  dial-up access to office network 355-359
  dialing 424
  how it works 342-343
  indicator lights 424-426
  installing on your desktop 344-345
  pulse or tone dialing 348
  ringing tone 425
  standards 428
  steps in making connection 424-426
  support for 10
  troubleshooting 429-432
  using from office telephone system 348, 349
monitor 31
mouse
  help pointer 76, 101
  operations 17-18, 94-101
  settings for 397-398
  types of pointers 98-101
mouse, click
  applying focus 46, 412
  left button 20
  right button 97, 98, 291
  selecting 20, 92
mouse, double-click 95
mouse, drag-and-drop 96, 97
  cannot drop symbol 100
  copying files into folders 292
  message forms, files 378, 384
  moving objects 21
mouse, drag-select 217
  objects on Desktop 292
mouse, dragging 95
  how to move 21
  text between windows 140
mouse, pointing 19, 397-398
MS-DOS mode 290
MS-DOS prompt, see *DOS prompt*

464 Index

MSN 359, 363-365
  finding services 288
  mail (Internet), see
    Exchange
multimedia 9
  adding sound to
    documents 156-157
  support for 10
My Computer 300, 393

N

names, see *computer, file, folder, drive*
netiquette 427
network
  access rights 329
  accessing drives, mapping drive 333-335
  administered by 324
  computer name 334
  connecting to 16, 322
  dial-up access 355-359
  disconnecting from 26, 290, 326
  domains 328-329
  LAN (local area) 322
  mail addressees 374
  peer-to-peer 327
  sharing a printer 82, 335-336
  sharing files 330, 332-335
  sharing other devices 338-339
  support for 10
network administrator 323
Network Neighborhood 327, 329
new, see property sheet

O

object packaging 156
object, handling in documents 148-152
Office 95
  Binder 434
  programs packaged with 163
Office Bar 163-166
Office toolbar 163
OLE
  Binder 434
  Exchange message form 378, 383
  141, 144-146
operating system, what is 2

P

Paint 162
password 323
  access to Internet 360
  access to MSN 363
  access to office network (LAN) 16, 322
  access to remote computer 426
  how to change 324-325
  sharing a folder 331
  storing on your computer 399-400
paste 143, see also *Clipboard*
pathname, see *file system*
Personal Address Book, see *Exchange*
Personal Information Store, see *Exchange*
Phone dialer 162

picture, see *Word document*
plug and play 10
point 18
point size, typeface 190
pop-up menus 97, 291
port, communications 83, 345
portrait, page orientation 188
PostOffice, see *Exchange*
PowerPoint
  giving slide show 269-270
  main window 258
  matching slides to paper size 271
  toolbars 261, 265
PowerPoint document
  arranging slides 263
  copying styles from others 266
  creating 256
  creating speaker's notes 262
  for presentations, graphics 260
  improving presentation of 266-268
  inserting a new slide 261
  inserting ClipArt 264
  master slides 268
  preparing an outline 260
  views: slide, outline, slide sorter 259
PowerPoint template
  creating your own 257
  standard presentations 256
precision 248
print, see *dialog box, document*
print job 85
  managing 292

managing from printer window 314-317
properties of 316
running out of paper 86

Print Screen key 144, 422

printer
check before printing 83-84
features 83
installation on your Desktop 337-338
pop-up menu 315
setting its properties 318
sharing on network 335-336
sharing with other people (dial-up) 355
specify paper tray 318
status of 82
printer driver 81

Printer folder
adding new printer 337-338
changing properties 285
managing printers 315

printer queue
managing 314-317
opening from printer icon 292

printer, your own
changing its behaviour 80
managing its print queue 315
selecting 82

program
access to modem 424
adding, removing from Start menu 392-393
different types of 160
help menu 69
how they are consistent 162

installing 366
learning how to use 162
MS-DOS style 160
obtaining assistance 404-410
running from floppy disk 289
sending fax messages from 386-387
starting from Taskbar 23, 284
switching between 109-110
program menu, see *Start button*
properties, see *files, folders, drives*
property sheet 53, see also *dialog box*
adding page to 165
dialing properties 347-348
display properties 401
drive 305
font 190
keyboard, properties 397
modem properties 346, 429
mouse, properties 99, 398
new 52

property sheet, specific
Address book, new fax 376
Binder, new, 435
Excel, format cells 212, 230
Excel, Page setup 226
Excel, new 205-206
Exchange, profile 373
Office Bar, new 165
PowerPoint, new 256
Word, new 168
Word, options 79
Taskbar, properties 392

TCP/IP, properties 361
Time/date properties 396
Word, bullets and numbering 179
Word, options (save) 135-136
protocol, communications 425, 426-427
push-button, control 76, 86, 413

R

radio-button, control 413
read 134, see also *file-protection*
read-only, see *document*
Recycle Bin, recovering files 314
remote access, see *dial-up connections*
remote administration 400
refresh, see *View window*
rename, see *file, folder*
replacing text, see *dialog box*
resources, finding 324, 326
root 120, see also *folder*
row 202, see also *Excel*

S

save 27, see also *file*
Schedule+ 162
scrap, text 140

screen, changing resolution 400
screensavers 400-401
scroll 57
scroll bar 58, 415, 109
security policy 351, 357, 360, 400
security, Desktop 401
select, from list 415, 416
selection
   effects and indications of 92
   options 413
   several items (extended) 108-109, 412
send to, adding items to menu 307
serial port, communication 427-428
server 148, see also *computer sharing, controlling access to* 330-336
short-cuts
   creating 293
   favorites folder 130
   keyboard 420-422
   reference to file or folder 165
shut down
   disconnecting from network 326
   options 26, 289-290
slider, control 418
sorting lists, column control 417
sound, see *Word, adding sound*
spin box, control 418
split handles 418

spreadsheet, see *Excel*
Start button
   contents of 278, 283
   customizing its menu 392-393
   document menu 284
   finding files, folders, computers 286
   opening Control Panel 393
   opening Printers folder 393
   program menu 284
   running a program 23, 289
   settings menu 285
   help 288
status bar, see *window*
stretching, see *Word document*

T

tab key, see *controls, editing text*
Taskbar 278
   hiding 281
   make visible 278
   moving 280
   pop-up menu 281
   properties of 281
   Start button 278
   status area, document being printed 85
   status area, time and date 396
   tiling and cascading windows 281
   window buttons 38, 47, 279
   starting a program 23
TCP/IP, installing 361-362
telephone codes, format of 347

telephone, settings for 346-349
template 52, see also *Word, Excel, PowerPoint, Binder*
   creating your own folder for 165
   normal 52
terminal, see HyperTerminal
terminate 49
text, see *editing text*
time, changing, see *computer*
toolbar 64
toolbar 66-67
typefaces (viewing, selecting) 190, 394-395

U

undo 94
user interface, what is 2
user name 16, 322-324, 426
user profile 325, 399
   v.32bis, standard for modems 342

V

View window 300
   arranging and displaying contents 308-309
   browsing for network resources 326
   displaying contents of a folder 120-121
   displaying folder's pathname 121
   displaying toolbar 310, 313
   file menu 303
   moving files and folders 306

MSN 364
Network Neighborhood 327
refresh 308
selecting objects 306
virus, how to avoid 367

W

Welcome window 277
wide area network 322
wildcard, filtering a list 132-133
WinCim, installing 366
window 24
   adjusting size 40
   advantages of 30
   arranging document windows 44
   arranging with Taskbar 281
   changing form of 39
   child 32
   client area 33
   copying image to Clipboard 421
   dividing with split handles 418
   document 33
   finding lost 47
   forms of 32, 33, 36-40
   Help 404
   Help topics 404
   how to move 41
   main windows 162
   making active 46
   managing on your Desktop 43-50
   maximized behaviour 37
   minimized behaviour 38, 279
   moving focus with keyboard 102-103
   opening its menu 43
   opening, closing 35
   relationships to each other 34
   resizing 39
   splitting into two 59
   status bar 32
   types of 33
window buttons 279
window menu 68
Windows 3.1
   evolution to Windows 95 6
   file names 123
   upgrading from 9
Windows 95 8-11
   changing settings (Control Panel) 393-394
   connecting to Internet 361-363
   controls 412-417
   evolution from Windows 3.1 7
   file names 123
   Help 404-410
   installing a printer 337-338
   installing dial-up networking 355-356
   installing fax service 371-373
   MS-DOS mode 290
   multi-tasking capabilities 280
   printing facilities 83
   programs packaged with 160
   registering 278
   starting, shutting down 14, 25, 276, 289
   support for fax 385-388
   support for modems 343-344
   support for programs 9
   Tour 278
   typefaces 394-395
Windows Explorer 310-313
   displaying contents of folders 310
   displaying folder hierarchy 312, 313
Windows folder 301
Wizard
   answer 409
   dial-up, make a new connection 355
   Exchange, fax 386-387
   Exchange, setup 371
   function 238
   help setup 405
   modem installation 344-345
   MSN installation 363-365
   program installation 366
Word
   AutoCorrect 195
   creating new document 52-53
   dictionaries 195
   displaying toolbars 67
   document window 54
   fields 180
   help pointer 101
   main window 171
   menu bar 61
   page setup 188
   print dialog box 77
   print progress (status bar) 85
   printing options 79

restoring your work from a file, see *dialog box, Save As*
saving your work in a file, see *dialog box, Open*
starting 52
view menu: normal, page layout 65

Word document
   creating templates 168-169
   cropping and stretching pictures 183
   displaying hidden characters 191
   editing Excel data 154-155
   embedding, linking 148-152
   entering text 54-61
   finding and replacing text 198-199
   for text 169
   improving presentation of 186
   indenting paragraphs 191
   inserting annotations 174, 196
   inserting boxed text and shading 189
   inserting bulleted/numbered lists 178
   inserting change marks 197
   inserting copyright symbol 179
   inserting footnotes 173, 177
   inserting header/footer to pages 172-173
   inserting page and section breaks 187-188
   inserting page numbers 173
   inserting pictures and frames 152-154, 181-182
   inserting sound 156-157
   inserting tables 183-185
   inserting time, date fields 180
   line spacing 191
   margin settings 188, 191
   moving text (drag-drop) 176
   paper size and orientation 188
   paper tray setting 188
   paragraph styles 192-193
   positioning objects on the page 181-183
   replacing text 175-6
   reviewing and annotating 196-197
   selecting information in a table 184
   selecting text, objects 175
   setting position of tabs 103
   spell-check 194-195
   starting new paragraph 191
   typeface, changing 190
   views: outline, normal, page layout 170-172

Word template
   creating 168
   standard — normal.dot 168
   styles 193

Word, options
   file locations 127
   file recovery 135-136
   revision settings 198
   spelling, AutoCorrect 196
   update document links 151

WordPad, starting, stopping 23-24
workbook, see *Excel document*
working at home
   Briefcase 437
   dial-up networking 355-359
working folder 128
worksheet, see *Excel document*
write 134
write protection, see *files, protection*

X

X-modem, file transfer protocol 427